NO
STAINED-
GLASS-
WINDOW
SAINTS

DAVID G. SHARP

NO STAINED-GLASS-WINDOW SAINTS

*The Church
in the New Testament
and Today*

London EPWORTH PRESS

7162 0268 9

Enquiries should be addressed to
The Methodist Publishing House
Wellington Road
Wimbledon
London SW19 8EU
Printed in Great Britain by
The Garden City Press Limited
Letchworth, Hertfordshire SG6 1JS

Contents

Introduction

LIKE all schoolboys, we liked to 'take the mickey' out of our teachers, not least out of the form-master who took us for R.E. and used to say, 'Paul was no stained-glass-window saint'. I must confess with shame, however, that it has taken some twenty years for the truth of that statement to sink in and then to emerge again as the thoughts expressed in the following pages. For the New Testament is not about super-saints, but about ordinary people like ourselves, and what was true of the apostle is also true about the church as a whole.

There are people today who feel that the church has lost its way and that, if it is ever going to find it again, a new point of departure will be necessary. This feeling is not confined to any one group within the church. It occurs in every denomination and among people of a variety of theological viewpoints. The common factor is a sense of frustration with the church as an institution. These people feel that the machinery of church administration and tradition is preventing them from being what God wants them to be as members of the church in the last part of the twentieth century.

The frustration expresses itself in different reactions by different people. For example, up and down the country one can find groups of young Christians, deeply committed to Jesus Christ, but very suspicious of the institutional church. They are reluctant to become members or accept responsibilities in the church. They do not see how they can express their commitment to Christ through their local church, with its traditional patterns of worship, its old buildings and its largely ageing membership. Some of these groups do keep their links with a local, denominational church, albeit remaining on the fringes of that church's life. Others, however, eventually become independent house churches or fellowships, and largely cut themselves off from the traditional church.

The radicals, similarly, have reacted against the individualism of traditional western Christianity by establishing communities of Christians on the fringes of the institutional church. They also feel that the institutional church is remote from the realities of urban life in the twentieth century. So, from their para-church groups, members have gone out into the community at large to become involved in its problems. Jesus was the man for others; therefore the church must be the servant church, the church for the world. If the institutional church is too inward-looking to care for the needs of the world, then those who are concerned must do the work, if necessary from outside the church.

The evangelical is frustrated by the institutional church in yet another way. He compares the church as he sees it today, divided into denominations, set about with administration and tradition, with the New Testament church. There he sees spontaneity, freedom, power, purity of doctrine, Biblical standards of morality and a world-shaking missionary activity. He longs for his own local church and denomination to return to this Biblical standard. He has little time for church 'politics', because these divert him from the primary task of preaching the gospel. He views those in the church, especially those in authority, who do not share his outlook, with suspicion. And in the end, if the church will not reform itself, he will be forced to leave and find in an independent evangelical fellowship a more scriptural pattern of life and worship.

The problem that faces the denominations today, therefore, is that of keeping within them those who are ready, perhaps all too ready, to seek their Christian fellowship elsewhere. Clearly there will have to be changes, in administrative structure, in patterns of worship, in forms of ministry, in order that the denominations may meet the needs of the twentieth century. The patterns of the sixteenth, eighteenth or nineteenth centuries will not do. But on the other hand it will not do either just to jump on the bandwagons of radicalism or evangelicalism or the Jesus movement or anything else. It is first and foremost necessary to ask the question, 'What is the church?' Only when this has been answered can we begin to tackle the frustrations and tensions that exist for the members of the church.

It is not the intention of this book to minimize these tensions. I have felt them myself and have seen the devastating effect that they can have on the lives of individual Christians and of churches. Something is obviously radically wrong when churches are split and when able ministers feel compelled to leave the denomination in which they have been brought up and trained, and in which they have served, in order to seek a more satisfying ministry elsewhere. It was concern over facts like these which first led to the thoughts contained in this book being formulated. Must these tensions lead inevitably to breaking point? Is the church any less the church because in it we feel frustrated? If working within the church leads to tensions, do we have to go outside to continue our work? The answers to questions like these may help us to put our frustrations in perspective. They depend, however, on the answer to our basic question, 'what is the church?'

This is not the only reason, however, why we should be looking at this issue. The doctrine of the church is likely to be central in the next round of debate about unity between the denominations in Great Britain. Previous debates centred on aspects of the church like ministry and ordination. These, however, are only subsidiary questions. This book, therefore, is offered also as a contribution to the discussion on church unity.

There are many things which could be said about the church which this book will not say. Readers who would like a total picture of the church, either from the point of view of the Biblical doctrine or of historical development, should consult some of the books suggested at the end of this Introduction. If the present approach seems one-sided, it is because other books tend to ignore the issue which is central for us: the fact that tension, similar to the tensions we feel in the church today, has been built into it from the start. There were fundamental tensions within the New Testament church. Yet it is possible to read the New Testament and miss this important truth. One can concentrate on what the New Testament teaches about the church and not give full weight to what it says about the actual state of the church in New Testament times. In this study, therefore, we shall attempt to highlight this tension.

To do so, we shall take some representative passages and look at them in turn from two points of view. Part 1 will examine some of the New Testament teaching about the church. Then in Part 2 we will discuss the New Testament's description of the church in the first century. Finally, Part 3 will look at some of the counterparts of these tensions in the church today. Material for further study and discussion will be offered, not necessarily with the aim of resolving them all, but at least of attempting to explain them and to enable us to live with them in our local situations.

Suggested Reading on the Church

History
A. M. Renwick, *The Story of the Church* (I.V.P.)
O. Chadwick (Ed.), *The Pelican History of the Church* (5 vols.) (Penguin Books)

J. W. C. Wand, *History of the Early Church* (Methuen)

M. Deanesly, *A History of the Medieval Church* (Methuen)

J. W. C. Wand, *A History of the Modern Church* (Methuen)

Doctrine

A. M. Stibbs, *God's Church* (I.V.P.)

R. N. Flew, *Jesus and His Church* (Epworth)

R. Schnackenburg, *The Church in the New Testament* (Burns and Oates)

E. Schweizer, *The Church as the Body of Christ* (S.P.C.K.)

Part 1

The Pattern

The New Testament Teaching About the Church

The Word Itself

THE word used in the New Testament and translated 'church' in our versions is the Greek work *ekklēsia*. It was not a word by any means confined to religious language. It had two main everyday uses. First, it stood for an assembly, particularly for a regularly summoned assembly, a political or administrative body. An example of this use of the word in the New Testament itself occurs in Acts 19:39, where it is rendered 'the meeting of citizens'. It is important to note the element of calling or summoning in this basic meaning. *Ekklēsia* is, in fact, the noun formed from the verb meaning 'I call, summon out'.

The second everyday use of the word was more general. It stood for an assembly or gathering of people, without any idea of calling. Acts 19 also provides an example of this use, in verses 32 and 41, where it is translated 'meeting'.

Finally, there is a religious use of the word outside the New Testament. This is to be found in the Greek translation of the Old Testament, the Septuagint. Here *ekklēsia* was used chiefly to translate the Hebrew word *qāhāl*, the congregation of Israel. This term was applied to the people of Israel especially when they were summoned and gathered for religious purposes, for example, to hear the Law (Deuteronomy 4:10; 9:10; 18:16). An example of this use of *ekklēsia* from the New Testament is Acts 7:38, 'the people of Israel assembled'.

There are, then, two things to bear in mind if we want to use the word 'church' in its New Testament sense. First, it refers to people rather than to any building or organization. Secondly, these people have not just come together by chance. The word contains the idea of a call or summons to the people concerned which brings them together.

The *ekklēsia* in the New Testament

Having considered the meaning of the word itself, we can turn to look at some of the ways the New Testament writers speak about the church. There are several ways we could tackle this, but there is a certain logic in taking our examples in the order in which they were written, as far as that is possible. This, of course, is not the order in which the books appear in our New Testament, where they have been arranged according to other criteria. So we begin with the letters and, in particular, with the first letter of Paul to the church in Corinth. For here Paul devotes more space than in any other letter to matters concerning the church.

The Background to 1 Corinthians

The story of Paul's first dealings with Corinth and of the founding of the church there is found in Acts

18:1–18. We are told that Paul stayed there for eighteen months and that, after he left, Apollos went across from Ephesus (Acts 18:24–19:1). Later, Paul continued to keep in touch with the church by correspondence. He wrote the letter which we know as 1 Corinthians about AD 55, that is, some twenty to twenty-five years after the death of Jesus, and about five years after the founding of the Corinthian church.

The Church as the People of God

Some of the most significant of Paul's remarks about the church in 1 Corinthians are contained in the opening greeting (1:1–3). Here, especially in verse 2, Paul expounds to his readers the meaning of the word 'church'.

The church is first of all the church of God. It is not merely a human institution, like a social club, which comes into being because of the common interests of the members. On the contrary, the church is able to hold together people of the most diverse interests and backgrounds (Galatians 3:28). The church is a divine institution. God has called it into being. In the Greek, translated literally, Paul goes on to address the Christians in Corinth as the 'called saints'. *Today's English Version* (T.E.V.) translates this phrase by 'all who are called to be God's people'. Here is the element of summons which we noticed in the basic meaning of *ekklēsia*. The church is God's because he called it. It is not a chance coming together, but a summoned gathering.

Secondly, the church is God's because it belongs to

15

him through Jesus Christ. Paul also addresses the Christians as those 'who belong to him in union with Christ Jesus' or, as it has been more traditionally translated, 'those sanctified in Christ Jesus'. This is really only another way of expressing the ideas contained in the other phrase, 'called saints'. But whereas there the emphasis was on calling, here it is on possession. For the sanctified person, the saint, is one who is set apart for God. R. H. Strachan, in his article 'Saint' (in the *Dictionary of the Apostolic Church*), wrote, 'The saint is one on whose whole life God has an irresistible claim. . . . The saint is "called" by God in the sense of receiving not an invitation, but rather a royal summons, expressed in the free gift of an overwhelming love'. Like the Old Testament *ekklēsia*, the congregation of Israel, therefore, the New Testament *ekklēsia* is 'God's own people' (1 Peter 2:9, compare Deuteronomy 10:15; Isaiah 43:20–21).

Thirdly, the church comes into being and continues to grow as individuals respond to the love of God in Jesus Christ. Strachan writes, 'Saintliness is an impossibility unless it contains as its essence an experience of God's love'. Therefore the church is made up of 'all people everywhere who call on the name of our Lord Jesus Christ'. The New Testament missionaries did not preach the church or invite people to join the church. Their good news was 'the message about Christ's death on the cross', even though it was 'offensive to the Jews and nonsense to the Gentiles' (1 Corinthians 1:18, 23). This is how the call of God came to the Corinthian Christians (1

16

Corinthians 1 : 26). Paul had preached no message 'except Jesus Christ, and especially his death on the cross' (1 Corinthians 2 : 2).

Fourthly, it is a particular kind of response to the love of God in Jesus Christ that is required: the response of faith. This is implied in 1 Corinthians 1 : 2 by the use of the phrase 'call on the name of our Lord Jesus Christ'. The Greek verb is used particularly in the context of calling on someone for aid, which in itself suggests confidence in the person called on. It is frequently used of calling on a god, again suggesting trust and dependence. But if the idea of faith is only implied here, it is clearly stated elsewhere in the letter. The Corinthians' response to Paul's preaching of Jesus Christ, for example, was faith (1 Corinthians 2 : 5). Moreover, in the opening greetings of other New Testament letters, the idea of faith is explicitly linked with the term 'saints, God's people' (Ephesians 1 : 2; Colossians 1 : 2).

Finally, while individuals respond to the love of God in Jesus Christ by faith one by one, they become automatically a community. The saints in the New Testament are always viewed in this way. Their belonging to God means that they belong also to one another. There was no need for the missionaries to encourage new converts to Christianity to join the church. Their experience of the love of God not only bound them to him but also to one another. 'See how these Christians love one another' was the comment of the pagan world. 'Saintliness', writes Strachan, 'is an impossibility unless it contains as its essence an

17

experience of God's love common to all which finds expression in common worship, and certain corresponding mutual obligations of loving thought and ministry towards others.' It is this aspect of the church's life that Paul expounds through the metaphor of the church as the body of Christ.

The Church as the Body of Christ

This metaphor occurs in various parts of the New Testament but is nowhere so fully developed as in 1 Corinthians, chapters 12–14. We are also introduced here to the factor which distinguishes the church as a divine institution from human institutions: the activity of the Holy Spirit.

Paul began with the response of faith to the love of God in Jesus Christ. That response is expressed in the words which were probably the first Christian creed, 'Jesus is Lord' (1 Corinthians 12:3). The apostle states quite categorically that faith and its expression depend on the working of the Holy Spirit. He has previously argued this point in detail in chapters 1:18–2:16. There can be no effective preaching of the message about Jesus Christ, no understanding of the message and no positive response to it except as the Holy Spirit opens the minds of both preacher and hearer. This is the theological principle of which the events of the day of Pentecost (Acts 2) are an illustration. There is no church apart from the activity of the Holy Spirit. So the Acts of the Apostles has been subtitled by different writers, 'The young church in action' and 'the acts of the Holy Spirit'. These are two ways of looking at the same thing. The church cannot act effectively unless the Holy Spirit is also active. Similarly, the coming of the Holy Spirit to the apostles at Pentecost has been described as 'the birthday of the church'. If the church is the body of Christ, it is the Holy Spirit who gives life to that body (compare Ezekiel's version of the dry bones, Ezekiel 37:1–14).

The apostle Paul, however, was a practical man, and so, having established the basic principle, he goes on to explain how that principle works out in practice. He describes what forms the activity of the Holy Spirit takes within the life of the church, beginning with the variety of the Spirit's operations (12:4–11). Notice the repeated contrast in verses 4–6 of 'different' and 'same', and then, in verse 7, the important principle that 'each one is given some proof of the Spirit's presence for the good of all'. As the church is people, so the Spirit works in people as individuals, rather than in 'the church' as an anonymous mass. And as people are all different, so the Spirit works in a variety of ways. Some of these Paul lists to illustrate his point (verses 8–10), concluding with the reminder that as the church belongs to God, it is he who determines how the Spirit will work in any individual.

The next thing Paul stresses is the unity of the church (verses 12–13). The body is one. Christ is one. In union with Christ Jesus, God's people are one. To deny the essential unity of the church is to divide Christ, which is a nonsense (1 Corinthians 1:13).

Equally, however, to attempt to impose uniformity

on the church and its life is a nonsense (verses 14–21). But notice that Paul is not speaking here about different forms of church government. He is talking about the functions of different members within the body, the variety of forms the Spirit's activity takes in the church. What God has called into being in the church is like the body: an organism in which the different members have different functions which bring more or less honour to those who exercise them. But whether they bring honour or not, all the functions are necessary, all are equally important to the life of the body. In verses 22–26 Paul elaborates this principle of interdependence. To use a more modern metaphor, the church is a team. And a team cannot carry passengers, members who do not pull their weight, without its overall effectiveness being reduced. Every one of God's people has a vital part to play in the life of the church; the Holy Spirit has something for each one to do.

So Paul comes to specific functions (verses 27–31). Here we are to a certain extent on controversial ground, as the debate about neo-pentecostalism and the charismatic movement continues in the denominations. The controversy is in part caused by the fact that our information about some of these functions is scanty. The New Testament writers knew what they meant by such terms as prophecy, helping, directing, speaking in strange sounds or tongues (*glossolalia*), and so did their readers, so they did not explain them. We can only surmise. But it is not necessary for us to discuss their problems in detail here. Readers who wish to dig deeper should consult the suggestions for further reading. Our aim is to examine the types of gift listed and to discover what this examination has to say about the purposes for which God has called his church into being.

1. *Apostles.* When we use this word we normally think of the Twelve whom Jesus chose from among the larger body of disciples, and to whom he gave the task of preaching and performing miracles (see Mark 3:13–19). But the term is not restricted to them. Paul was an apostle (Romans 1:1, etc.). So were James, the Lord's brother (Galatians 1:19) and Barnabas (Acts 14:4, 14). The word means 'sent one', and the essential qualification of an apostle was to have seen the risen Jesus Christ, and his main function was to go and bear witness to what he had seen (Acts 1:21–22; 9:3–6, 15; 1 Corinthians 15:3–11). The apostles' first responsibility, therefore, was towards those who did not know the good news about Jesus and his resurrection. They were a gift to the church for mission.

2. *Prophets.* 'What turned a man into a prophet was not eloquence but vision, not getting the message across but getting the message. Prophecy is essentially an act of recognition by which one sees the significance of an event as *a revelation which must be passed on*' (John V. Taylor, *The Go-between God*, S.C.M. Press, p. 69, my italics). This includes seeing the relevance of Scripture to a new situation (for example, Stephen's speech, Acts 7, and preaching today). So prophecy is another gift, the relevance of

21

which is not confined to those in the church. The prophet's message is for all who have not seen God's revelation. It too can be a gift for mission.

3. *Teachers.* This function is more familiar. But we should note the kind of context in which reference to teaching occurs in the New Testament. Teaching is what one might call the follow-up to mission (Matthew 28:20). Notice how the task given to the church is not to make converts but disciples, learners, who will always need teaching. The Christian should never be without his L-plates. This appetite for learning was one of the things which characterized the first Christians (Acts 2:42). In several passages in the letters to Timothy teaching is linked with the explaining of the scriptures to those who are committed to Jesus Christ. The gift of teaching presupposes the maintenance of the mission of the church.

4. *Miracles.* There are two words for miracle in New Testament Greek: *dynamis* = deed of power, wonder, and *sēmeion* = sign. The first highlights the nature of the miracle, the second its purpose as a pointer to the activity of God through the one performing it. Miracles cannot compel belief (the Jews did not believe Jesus) but they can corroborate the missionary message (Acts 14:3–4). They point again to the missionary purpose of the church.

5. *Healing.* From the first, this particular form of miracle characterized the mission of the church (for example, Acts 3:1–10; 5:15–16), as it had the mission of Jesus. Both Old and New Testaments view man as

a whole. The church, therefore, is concerned to meet the needs of the whole man.

6. *Help.* This practical gift can, of course, be exercised both inside and outside the church (Acts 6:1; 9:36). Notice how the Holy Spirit is not limited to conferring purely supernatural abilities, but also heightens what are basically natural ones. The church is the place where the helpless find the support they need.

7. *Direction.* As Paul points out later (1 Corinthians 14:33), God is a God of order. Even practical help must be properly administered, so that no one is overlooked and the resources of the church are not squandered. It was to meet such a situation that the seven so-called 'deacons' or helpers were appointed (Acts 6:1–6). It was the Holy Spirit who gave them their qualities of administration and leadership. And, while these were exercised within the fellowship of the church, their purpose was to free others for the missionary task (Acts 6:2–4). Moreover, at least two of the seven were not prevented from being effective evangelists into the bargain (Acts 6:8–10; 8:4–8).

8. *Speaking in strange sounds (speaking in tongues, glossolalia).* The exact nature of this phenomenon must not detain us now. What is important is its purpose. On the surface it is an inward-looking gift (1 Corinthians 14:13–17). Unless there is an interpreter, only the speaker himself is helped. With an interpreter, the whole congregation can be helped. But even this gift is not without its usefulness in the church's wider task. Tongues can be the evidence of the supernatural,

23

of the presence of God, to the unbeliever coming into a meeting where Christians are speaking in tongues (1 Corinthians 14:22). But as on the day of Pentecost, when something akin to speaking in tongues occurred (Acts 2), the supernatural phenomenon needs to be followed up by the intelligible proclamation of God's message (1 Corinthians 14:23–25).

We can conclude, therefore, from the nature of these gifts, that the church is intended to be a missionary body. Its task is to make plain to men the message about Jesus Christ that God has revealed. At the same time the church is to bring to these men, by natural and supernatural means, the practical help they need. By the exercise of these gifts the church grows, both as new members are added and present members grow towards maturity. But Paul adds two warnings.

As the illustration of the body made clear, each member has a different function. Just as there is no point in the ear wanting to be an eye, there is no point in wanting someone else's gift or function (1 Corinthians 12:29–31). The lesson that Jesus had to teach Peter is very pertinent here (John 21:20–22). We cannot tamper with the functioning of our own body without impairing our health. An imbalanced diet, however fashionable, does no one any good in the long run. Similarly, the Holy Spirit's infinite variety and balance cannot be reduced to any man-made pattern without impairing the health of the church.

The second warning is that none of these gifts or functions is of any use unless it is exercised in love

(1 Corinthians 12:31–14:1). The church is God's people. We call God Father. It is the aim of Jesus to reproduce in the children of God the family likeness (Matthew 5:48), and God is love (1 John 4:8). As Jesus is, in Bonhoeffer's phrase, 'the man for others', the church, as it is in union with him, is the people for others. This means the exercise of the Spirit's gifts in a selfless and self-effacing manner. The mission of the church stems, to recall Strachan's phrase, from the overflowing love of those who have been touched by the love of God (Romans 5:5). 'The love of Christ leaves us no choice' (2 Corinthians 5:14 *New English Bible*).

Finally Paul picks out for emphasis two aspects of the work of the Spirit. They were particularly relevant to the church in Cornish, because of the disorderly state of worship there. But they are not temporary things. They are permanent features of the life of the Spirit in the church. In the first place the Holy Spirit is one who makes plain God's revelation (1 Corinthians 14:1–25). Where he is there is intelligible communication of the message about Jesus Christ. John Taylor (*The Go-Between God*, pp. 58 ff.) points out the close relationship between the Spirit and the word in the Old Testament, and lists passages, such as Psalm 36:6; 147:18; 2 Samuel 23:2; Isaiah 59:21, in which the two Hebrew words mean virtually the same thing. A comparison of the opening verses of Genesis 1 with those of John 1, or a study of the calling of the prophets, bring out the same point. As Taylor puts it, Spirit and word 'are as closely related as breath and voice'. Paul's concern in 1 Corinthians 14 is that the Spirit of God shall not be divorced from his word.

The other aspect of the Spirit's work which Paul underlines is his creating of order (1 Corinthians 14:26–40). Orderliness, as we have seen, does not mean uniformity. Nor does it mean inflexibility or limited scope. Creation is described as a bringing of order out of chaos, with the Spirit of God acting as agent (Genesis 1:2), and creation is infinitely varied in its forms. Paul seems to imply (1 Corinthians 14:33) that order is yet another characteristic of God himself that is to be reproduced in his people. (On this section see also the two books by A. Bittlinger: *Gifts and Graces* and *Gifts and Ministries*, both published by Hodder & Stoughton.)

The Letter to the Ephesians

If the body is the first great metaphor used of the church in the New Testament, the temple is the second. It is most fully developed in the letter to the church in Ephesus, chapters 2 and 4. (The background to this letter is extremely complex, particularly the questions of authorship, destination and date.)

After the opening greeting to the people of God we have a great thanksgiving for blessings received in Christ and a prayer for the Ephesian Christians (chapter 1). Chapter 2 commences with a description of the work of God's grace in salvation and then continues by explaining the results of that salvation in terms of the church.

The Church as the Temple of God

Salvation means reconciliation: the reconciliation of men to God and to one another. In Christ, those who were divided (like Jews and Gentiles in the Jerusalem Temple) by race and religion have become one people, God's people, the church. The means by which this peace has been established is the death of Christ, and it is the Spirit through whom those who have been reconciled are united to one another and to the Father. This one people is now God's family, 'a sacred temple', 'a house where God lives through his Spirit' (Ephesians 2:19–22). This house is 'built on the foundation laid by the apostles and prophets' (verse 20). This T.E.V. translation is only one possible interpretation of the Greek. The apostles and prophets could themselves be the foundation. But does it make a great deal of difference? As we have seen, the apostles and prophets were those through whom God's message about Jesus Christ was proclaimed. The church came into being in response to that message. So whether it is the act of preaching or the preachers themselves that is the foundation, the church rests on God's message, the key to which is Jesus Christ, 'the cornerstone . . . who holds the whole building together' (verses 20, 21).

The picture of the building is combined with that of the body in chapter 4:1–16. In a condensed development of the body metaphor we find the same emphases as in 1 Corinthians: the unity of the body, the variety of gifts, with each member having some gift which is his contribution towards the building up

27

of the whole. There is the same insistence on mutual interdependence and love. The goal of the church is also the same, although here expressed in different terms: the family likeness will be reproduced as the church becomes a mature man, 'reaching to the very height of Christ's full stature' (verse 13). One new note is struck and that is an emphasis on the lordship of Christ over the church as head (verses 15–16). We see here, perhaps, a counter-thrust to a developing self-confidence on the part of the church, a fresh reminder that it is not an autonomous human institution but belongs to God as the instrument of his purposes, and is therefore under his control.

The Church as the Bride of Christ

God's sovereignty over his people, however, must be set in context, and its context is always love. Ephesians 5:21–33 adds a further metaphor to our list, one taken over from the Old Testament teaching about the people of God (Hosea 2). Our God is a God of covenants, of binding agreements. By his covenants, both old and new, he has committed himself to his people. However wayward they are, he cannot permanently abandon them, for he cannot go back on his word once given. So in Christ he has already given himself in anticipation to and for the church. The New Testament looks forward to the fulfilment of the engagement, of all the promises that God has made to his people. Thus Revelation 21 pictures the church, the people of God, made perfect, as the bride ready to be married. All that is said about the church in the

New Testament needs to be put in the context of this most intimate, caring, loving relationship of God to his people. The metaphor of the bride gives us some measure of the love of God to which he calls us to respond. It also gives us some idea of the nature of the love which we, in turn, are to show to others.

The New Testament Church as Organization

The relatively early writings, at which we have been looking so far, have concentrated on the church as a spiritual entity, emphasizing its distinctiveness as a divine institution. The early writers, however, were not unconcerned about organization, for they were practical as well as spiritual men. But if the organization of the earliest church is not commented on much in the documents, it seems to be because the Christians adopted the kind of organization already existing in Jewish and Gentile communities. For example, Acts 14:23 records the appointment of elders in all the churches Barnabas and Paul had founded on their first missionary journey. There is no comment, because everyone knew what the functions of an elder (Greek: *presbyteros*) were. The word could refer, among the Jews, to the officers of a synagogue and the members of city council, among the Greeks to senior citizens or civic officials. The elders were the responsible people in any community, religious or civic, Jewish, Greek or Christian. If, as seems probable, Acts 14:23 records the pattern for the whole early church, the first elders were appointed by the apostles. Certainly the apostles at first personally supervised the churches (Acts 8:14; 9:32, etc.; compare the letter-writing activity of the apostles). But the supervision of the apostles was limited to their lifetime. How was the organization of the church to be supervised after their deaths? For the answer to this question we turn to the later letters.

The Letters to Timothy

Scholarly debate surrounds the question of the authorship of these letters, which are different in style and content from the earlier letters of Paul. We do not need to pursue the issue here, because in any event they could not have been written before AD 63–65 at the earliest. (At the other end of the scale, the period AD 100–125 has been suggested, and even dates after AD 140.) By any reckoning, therefore, they are later than the documents we have looked at so far.

The letters to Timothy and Titus have long been called, by a convenient shorthand, the Pastoral Letters, because they contain, among other things, instructions to pastors on how to look after their congregations. In these instructions we see the development of the pattern of elders and helpers (or deacons) which we have glimpsed already. The key passages are 1 Timothy 3:1–13; 5:17–25.

We must first note that in chapter 3 there is no reference to elders by name, but to leaders or overseers (Greek: *episkopos*, from which we derive our word 'bishop'). It is acknowledged by most scholars today, however, that the terminology of the New Testament is ambiguous (compare Titus 1:5, Acts

20:17, 28). It seems most probable that elders and overseers were the same people called by two different names and indeed, in chapter 5, there is no mention of overseers, but only of elders.

When we look at the actual qualities required of the church leaders and helpers (1 Timothy 3:1–13), they seem remarkably common-sense, down to earth and even 'unspiritual'. Indeed, it has been argued that they reflect a state of affairs in the church so institutionalized and so far removed from the manifestations of the Spirit described in 1 Corinthians (for example), that they could only have been written long after the time of the apostle Paul. We noted, however, that even the gifts of the Spirit listed in 1 Corinthians 12 were, to some degree, supernatural heightenings of natural capicities. And, while we are told that Barnabas and Paul appointed elders (Acts 14:23), we are not told on what criteria they based their choice. A careful reading of the new Testament documents concerning Paul suggests that he exercised a mixture of supernatural spiritual insight and natural common-sense in weighing up the situations with which he had to deal. So here natural and spiritual qualifications were required. But it is interesting to note that the latter were emphasized more in the case of the helpers than the leaders. This was no doubt because it might appear at first sight that the helpers' job was largely practical and administrative. But it was they who would most have come into contact with people in need and therefore had, in one sense, the greater opportunity to serve the whole man, bringing practical help and the comfort of the Christian message. It is equally significant that prospective elders must be 'respected by the people outside the church'. Even in this 'ecclesiastical' passage the church is an outward-looking, missionary organization.

1 Timothy 5:17–25 adds to the qualities required of church officers those demanded of the church in its relations with its officers. Here is the principle of mutual interdependence applied to a practical issue. There is advice about payment and discipline (where necessary) and appointment. Notice how emphasis is laid on preaching and teaching as particularly worthy of reward. As in the earlier passages we have studied, the message about Christ is vital to the life of the church.

The Church and the Churches
The passages we have been examining so far were all addressed to particular local churches. In them general truths about the church as a whole were applied to local situations. The New Testament does not have a great deal to say about the relationship between the local *ekklēsia* and the universal. But it is vital that we look at this question, on the one hand because of questions of denominationalism and church unity, on the other because of the mushrooming of independent house churches in recent years. One of the justifications for this latter development is that the New Testament pattern is of independent, autonomous local congregations, with no kind of 'denominational' structure. But is this the whole truth?

The fact that the same word, *ekklēsia*, is used for

• •

both local and universal church suggests that the same principles apply to both. Passages like 1 Corinthians 1 : 1–3, where Paul refers to local and universal church alternately, point in the same direction. We have noted a repeated emphasis in the New Testament teaching about the church not on *in*dependence but on *inter*dependence. There are several factors which illuminate this principle or provide concrete illustrations of it in operation. Space forbids more than a bare reference to them.

First there is the whole background of Jewish consciousness of being the one people of God, with the result that the Jewish communities scattered throughout the Roman world kept in close contact with one another (Acts 2 : 5–11; 14 : 19). Acts bears witness to the ease of travel in the first century and to the fact that both Christians and Jews travelled widely, Christians being commended from one congregation to another (Acts 18 : 24–27; Romans 16 : 1–2, compare Paul's travels). The Gentile churches of Europe and Asia gave financial support to the impoverished Judaean church (Acts 11 : 27–30; 1 Corinthians 16 : 1–4). Churches exchanged letters from the apostles (Colossians 4 : 15–16) and the apostles often wrote circular letters (Galatians; Acts 15; James; 1 Peter).

This leads to the further important fact that local churches did not exist without any overall supervision from above. We have noted the apostolic supervision already (above, p. 28–29). But with the passing of the apostles and the formation of the new Testament canon the new people of God became, like the old, the

33

people of a book. They continued to live under the apostolic witness to Christ, but now in written form. This gave them a consciousness of unity as the new people of God in the face of both the Jewish and pagan worlds.

It would seem, therefore, that the principles which govern the individual Christian's relationship to the local *ekklēsia* also govern that church's relationship to the universal *ekklēsia*. Independency, as it is often understood and advocated today, seems only to approximate to the New Testament pattern. This is not to say, of course, that denominationalism is any closer to it, but that is a question we shall examine later.

The Church and the Teaching of Jesus

So far we have made no reference to the gospels and their record of the teaching of Jesus. There are several reasons for this. First, although in time the ministry of Jesus went before that of the apostles, as far as the documents are concerned, the letters were written before the gospels. It was only as the generation which had actually witnessed the ministry of Jesus began to die that it was felt necessary to write down their testimony. The first gospel to be written is usually reckoned to be Mark, and the earliest date which is suggested for its writing is about AD 55. Other scholars suggest dates up to AD 70 or a little later. The other gospels followed, Luke and Matthew probably fairly closely on Mark, John towards the end of the century, probably about AD 90. We set out

to take the documents as far as possible in chronological order, and so the gospels fit in towards the end
of our survey.

This fact, however, raises the question of the reliability of the gospels as evidence for the teaching of
Jesus. If they were written so long after the event, can
we be sure that what they record is accurate? Would
not the writers have been influenced by conditions in
their own time? The gospels must surely reflect the
life of the church, perhaps even more than they reflect
the life of Jesus. Now there is some truth in this conclusion. The material that the gospel writers selected
from the mass of teaching about Jesus that was available was what was relevant to their own particular
purpose. That purpose was determined by conditions
at the time of writing. Then each writer also had his
own special interests. This is what makes each gospel
different from the others. The arrangement of the
material, too, is largely the responsibility of the writer,
within a broad common framework: all the gospels
lead up to the story of the crucifixion, but they get
there by different routes. In this sense it is true to say
that the gospels reflect the life of the church in the
second half of the first century, rather than the life of
Jesus in the first half. But it is also true to say that,
allowing for the individual writer's purpose and interests, selection and arrangement, the gospels do give a
reliable picture of the life and ministry of Jesus. The
most dramatic example is that of John's gospel, by
common consent written last, a long time after Jesus'
death. Because it is so different from the other three,

35

synoptic gospels (which all present a similar view of Jesus' ministry), it was once considered that John's gospel presented a historically unreliable picture of the ministry of Jesus. A better understanding of the process of handing down material from one generation to another (tradition), coupled with archeological discovery and other research, has, however, resulted in a change of opinion since the second world war. A. M. Hunter, in *According to John* (S.C.M. Press, 1968), explains this change and can say (p. 16), 'The result is to give us a confidence in the gospel as a historical source quite inconceivable fifty years ago'. We can, in fact, test this reliability for ourselves, to some extent. Had the gospel records of Jesus' teaching about the church been seriously influenced by thinking in the church at the time the gospels were written, we should expect to find terminology and ideas like those we have been examining so far. We shall find them notable for their absence, or for their appearance in an undeveloped state.

There is one more preliminary question to mention before we actually turn to the gospels, and that is whether Jesus ever intended to found the church at all. It may seem a strange question, but it is one that has to be taken seriously. Some New Testament scholars have suggested that Jesus expected the end of the world and the establishment of the kingdom of God very soon after his own death. He therefore made no provision for any interim period. It was only when the apostles found that the end did not come that they began to consider the need for the church

36

as a continuing entity. This issue really falls within the sphere of eschatology, the study of the last things, and is discussed fully in G. E. Ladd's book, *Jesus and the Kingdom* (S.P.C.K., 1966). But we must bear it in mind as we turn to look at the gospel material.

Ekklēsia in the Gospels

In view of what we have just said about the influence of the church on the writers of the gospels, it is interesting to note that the word *ekklēsia* occurs in only two passages: Matthew 16:18 and 18:17. The uniqueness of these passages has led some commentators to conclude that this is an example of the church putting words into the mouth of Jesus. Others agree with F. V. Filson (*Black's New Testament Commentary*) that, allowing for rearrangement and selection by the writer, 'Jesus could have said essentially what Matthew contains'. The basis for saying this is that these verses are not out of keeping with other sayings of Jesus in the gospels, and we shall therefore include them in our survey.

Matthew 16:18 occurs in the context of Peter's confession of faith at Caesarea Philippi, 'You are the Messiah, the Son of the living God.' Jesus' reply, 'I tell you, you are a rock, Peter, and on this rock I will build my church', has been interpreted in three main ways. Jesus will build his church on Peter's confession, on Peter as chief apostle and first in a line of apostolic succession, or on Peter as the first believer. In fact, there is an element of truth in all three. In Matthew 10:32 Jesus says, 'Whoever declares publicly that he belongs to me, I will do the same for him before my Father in heaven.' The letters also record public declaration of faith in Christ as essential (Romans 10:9; 1 Corinthians 12:3). But then, if it is the confession that Jesus is primarily referring to, the point of the word-play in verse 18 is lost. For Peter and rock have the same root in both Aramaic, the language Jesus spoke, and in Greek, the language of the written gospel. The emphasis must be on Peter rather than his confession. And in the gospels, Acts and letters we find that Peter has a special place among the apostles. In Luke 22:31–32 Jesus gives Peter a special ministry to his fellow apostles. John 21:15–19 records a similar commission. In Acts 1 and 2, Peter is the spokesman for all the apostles (as he is in Matthew 16). But on the other hand, he never had the pre-eminent place accorded to him in some interpretations of this verse. As leader of the Jerusalem church, his place was taken by James, the Lord's brother. Paul resisted Peter at Antioch. There is no mention of Peter passing on his authority to any successors: as we have seen, apostle-ship was necessarily limited to those who had been eye witnesses of the risen Jesus. In Ephesians 2:20 it is the 'apostles' (plural) who are just part of the foundation of the church. Peter has a special place, but not the pre-eminence, among the apostles. On the other hand, to say that it is only as first believer that Peter is the rock is not to do justice to that special place. We may therefore sum up Jesus' teaching in this passage as follows: the church is founded on the authoritative apostolic confession of faith in Christ as expressed on behalf of the Twelve by Peter.

When we turn to Matthew 18:17 we find two main lines of interpretation. On the one hand there are those who say that *ekklēsia* should be translated here, congregation, synagogue'. For them, this saying of Jesus does nothing more than repeat current Jewish moral instruction. On the other hand, the saying is sandwiched between remarkably un-Jewish passages. The idea of the God who seeks the lost, expressed in the parable of the lost sheep (verses 10–14), was new (see G. E. Ladd, *Jesus and the Kingdom*, p. 168 ff.). And in verses 18–20 we find Jesus using one of the phrases which so angered his Jewish opponents, 'my Father in heaven', and claiming a special authority ('in my name', verse 20). If verses 15–17 were only Jewish ethics, they have been misunderstood by the writer of the gospel and placed in a foreign context. This is possible. But if other teaching of Jesus suggests that he did intend to found the church, then it is most probable that the church was being referred to here in Matthew 18. So to the other teaching we must now turn. For although the word *ekklēsia* itself is rare in the gospels, the essential idea it conveys, a called people, is not.

The Call of the Twelve

This incident was first recorded in Mark 3:13–19 (see also Matthew 10:1–4; Luke 6:12–16). The verb used here is not *ekkaleō* but *proskaleō*: 'he called to himself'. But the passage also contains the idea of selection out of a larger number: 'he called to himself the men he wanted.' The initiative of Jesus is very clearly brought out: in the space of three verses Jesus is described as calling, wanting, choosing (twice), naming, sending and giving authority to the Twelve. Their only action is one of response, 'they came to him' (verse 13). The Twelve was no voluntary association of like-minded people. These men were Jesus' men by his calling and for no other reason. Normally they would not all have been found together. Matthew the tax-collector and Simon the patriot represented the opposite ends of the political spectrum. Matthew was a collaborator with the occupying Roman government, a Quisling to his fellow-Jews. Simon was the Romans' bitter opponent, a member of the first century equivalent of the Front for the Liberation of Palestine. These diverse outlooks and personalities were held together by Jesus' call.

This togetherness is emphasized in the first of the purposes for which the Twelve was called. Jesus wanted them 'to stay with' him. They were brought into fellowship with one another through him. Political opponents were reconciled because they had both entered a relationship with Jesus. We remember this every time we share in a communion service. 'Because there is the one bread, all of us, though many, are one body; for we all share the same loaf' (1 Corinthians 10:17). The New Testament word for fellowship or communion is *koinōnia*, which does not occur in the gospels. But the seed of the idea is to be found here in Jesus' calling of the Twelve. The development occurs in Paul's metaphor of the body and in other passages in the letters. A full and very helpful study of the church as *koinōnia* is contained in John Stott's book, *One People* (Falcon Books, 1969), which repays careful reading.

Jesus also, however, called the Twelve in order to send them out. Fellowship is balanced by service, coming by going. And as the calling was for a dual purpose, so was the sending. Christ told the Twelve that he wanted them to serve the whole man: to preach good news to him but also to deliver him from bondage. Our present passage refers only to exorcism, the casting out of demons. The parallel passage in Matthew and further accounts of the mission of the Twelve (Mark 6:7–13 and parallels) also mention healing. Implied in this twofold call, to proclamation and practical service, is the love that Jesus demonstrated in his own mission. David Sheppard, now Bishop of Liverpool but then Warden of the Mayflower Family Centre, Canning Town, wrote, 'It is just worth asking how on the one hand I can truly evangelize without loving people and therefore being ready to meet their whole need; and on the other hand how I can truly love people without sometime, however far down the line it may be, wanting to share what is the best thing I know' (*Mission in the Modern World*, Patmos Press, 1968, p. 45). The same truth was expressed more picturesquely by the Revs. Dick Jones and Don English at the President's teach-in on evangelism at Leeds in 1972. They concluded that the social gospel and the evangelical gospel go together like the two legs of a man when he is walking. But some of us limp!

We have seen how, in the calling of the Twelve, there are some of the features we noted in the teaching on the church contained in the letters. The Twelve belonged to Jesus by his calling, which united different individuals for fellowship and mission. But by themselves these similarities do not necessarily mean that Jesus intended to found the church. It could be that the apostles, when they found that they needed a continuing organization, just took up those features of Jesus' teaching that were relevant and built them up into their own doctrine of the church. We must ask, therefore, whether there is anything in these verses which points to Jesus' intention.

The significant feature of the passage, in this respect, is the number of men chosen by Jesus: twelve. This figure was not selected at random. Other New Testament passages make it clear that Jesus chose the Twelve to be the nucleus of a new people of God, a new Israel, corresponding to the old twelve tribes (cf. Luke 22:28–30). The giving of a missionary task to the Twelve suggests that Jesus' intention was the growth of this nucleus over a period of time (cf. Matthew 10). And the whole course of Jesus' ministry, marked as it is by increasing opposition from the upholders of the religious establishment, points to the new Israel as really new. This was never made clearer than in the parables of the patched coat and the new wine (Mark 2:21–22) and that of the tenants in the vineyard (Mark 12:1–12). The general picture of

Jesus' ministry that emerges from the gospels is not of a reform movement within existing Judaism. There is continuity with what went before (particularly with the Old Testament prophets), but the novelty of Jesus' mission and message demanded a new people of God on a new basis, that of personal allegiance to Jesus as Lord. This began with the call of the Twelve.

The Call of the Seventy-Two

As if to confirm that the Twelve were to be merely the nucleus of a greater company, Luke records (chapter 10:1–12) the calling and sending of the seventy-two (or seventy: the evidence of the manuscripts varies). They have the same twofold commission, to proclaim the good news of the kingdom and to heal, and the same authority as Jesus' representatives. Jesus also indicates (verse 2) that the mission will not be completed even by them. It will require a still greater force of workers. The mission to which the Twelve were called was only a beginning. It was not peculiar to them or to the seventy-two. It belongs to all who are followers of Jesus (see Luke 10:16).

These passages by no means exhaust the synoptic material, but they indicate its main lines. For a full treatment readers are referred to R. Newton Flew's book, *Jesus and His Church* (Epworth Press, 1938).

Jesus' Last Words to His Disciples

We turn last of all to John's gospel. It alone records Jesus' last words to his disciples as an almost continuous discourse stretching over chapters 13 to 17. Here the evangelist unfolded his understanding of Jesus' teaching. Three factors, in particular, indicate that it was teaching about the church with which the evangelist was largely concerned in these chapters.

First, Jesus was addressing the Twelve, the nucleus of the church. Secondly, he draws on Old Testament imagery in 15:1-11, where he speaks of himself as the real vine. In the Old Testament the vine stood for the people of God (cf. Isaiah 5; Psalm 80). Finally, in chapter 17, Jesus prays for the disciples, 'Make them your own, by means of the truth' (verse 17). The Greek word used here has more traditionally been translated 'sanctify' or 'consecrate'. It is the verb from the same root as the noun 'saint'. Jesus, therefore, was praying for, and talking about, the church.

In this study we shall concentrate on aspects of chapters 14 to 16 and notice in particular Jesus' teaching on the role of the Holy Spirit in the life of the people of God.

The opening verses of chapter 14 show that the important relationship for man is with God the Father (verses 1-7). This relationship is established through faith in Jesus Christ (verses 8-14). The word 'believe', from the same root in Greek as 'faith', occurs four times in verses 10-12, to underline this foundation truth about the church which we have also noted in other passages. Equally clear in verses 1-14 are Jesus' claims to a special relationship to the Father and to special authority. The church is God's people through faith in Jesus Christ as Lord and Messiah.

The church is also God's people through the Holy

Spirit. It is through him that God the Father and Jesus Christ the Son live with the church (verses 15–31). This is what makes the church a supernatural body and not just a human organization (verse 17). The church comes into being through the commandments and message of Jesus and the whole relationship of God to the church and of the church to God is characterized by love. The Holy Spirit as the Spirit of truth has the special task in the church of making God's message plain (verse 26). Here are some of the ideas developed by Paul in his exposition of the work of the Spirit in the church (1 Corinthians 12–14).

The image of the vine (15:1–17), as we have seen, links us with the Old Testament teaching on the people of God. But now Jesus takes a central position as the only real vine. There is an emphasis in this passage on God's initiative in calling his people into being, on fellowship and on the mission of the church (the emphases we found in Mark 3). Here the Old Testament background is instructive for the light it sheds on the nature of the church and its mission. The fruit of the vine in Isaiah 5 is social righteousness, not personal piety or 'soul-winning'. It is all summed up in one word, love (verse 17).

This leads us to the distinctiveness of the people of God (15:18–16:4). The church is to be different as Jesus was different, like light in darkness showing up what the world would prefer to keep hidden (cf. John 3:19–21). The life of Jesus called for decision, for or against him. The church as the body of Christ is called to live the life of Christ on earth and by that

45

life to demand the same decision, for or against him. The consequences may be the same as faced Jesus: hatred and persecution. But this is part of the church's witness to the nature and character of God. It is reproducing the family likeness. Note, however, that this witness is not to be merely what one might call the Christian presence in the world. There is also a spoken witness (15:26–16:4). Presence and word go together, for God is not only present in the world but has communicated verbally with men. And here the Holy Spirit, as the revealer of God, has his vital part to play.

The final section at which we shall look (16:5–15) expands this work of the Spirit towards the world in the mission of the church. As we saw when we looked at 1 Corinthians (see above, page 18), there can be no effective preaching of the message about Jesus Christ, no understanding of the message and no believing response to it unless the Holy Spirit works in the minds of both preacher and hearer. Jesus promised this to the apostles (John 16), the early church saw the Holy Spirit doing the work (Acts 2, etc.) and Paul developed the theology of it (1 Corinthians 1:18–2:6).

Conclusion

It is now time to draw together the threads of this survey of key New Testament passages and see what pattern of teaching about the church emerges.

The church is the people of God. They are called together out of the world by his love, expressed in the ministry of Jesus and the message about him. They respond to that love by faith in Jesus Christ as Lord and Messiah. It is the Holy Spirit who makes the message clear to both preachers and hearers, so that the church is a supernatural body, not a human society. It can hold together, therefore, people of diverse backgrounds, interests, outlooks, race and age in a living fellowship characterized by mutual love and interdependence.

The church is not an inward-looking body, however; God's purpose is that it should be a growing organism, sharing his love by word and action with all who need it. To this end the Holy Spirit equips the church with a variety of abilities, giving every member some gift that can be used in the common task. No one is unimportant. Leaders and 'ordinary' members all have responsibilities towards one another and all are called to serve the world.

For the church is the instrument of God in the world. He is to be seen in his people, experienced loving and working through them and his word is to be heard through them also. They are to reproduce the family likeness, to live the life of Christ, corporately and individually, among those who do not acknowledge him, in such a way as to demand decision. This is true whether we are thinking of the whole church world-wide, our own denomination, our local branch of it, or two or three Christians in the same school, factory, office or home. The church, to put it simply, is the people who belong to God through Jesus Christ and, in the power of the Holy Spirit, are doing his work wherever they are in the world.

Part 2

First-century Reflections
The New Testament Picture of the Church

A Rose-Tinted Ideal?
THE impression one gains from some preaching and teaching about the church in New Testament times, particularly among evangelicals, is that it always lived up to the pattern we have attempted to set out in Part 1. It is assumed that the New Testament gives us a blueprint for the church which is without flaws and which is valid for all times. But, if one may be permitted colourfully to mix metaphors, that perfect blueprint can only be obtained by looking through rose-tinted spectacles.

Those who attempt to follow a New Testament pattern for church organization place a heavy reliance on the Pauline writings. But they should pause to consider the origins of these and many of the other New Testament documents. They were not written in a vacuum, nor as calm academic exercises to set out patterns of doctrine or of church government. Inferences about these matters may certainly be drawn, but they must not be taken out of context, for many of the documents were written in times of crisis, and a large proportion of them was specifically intended to put right things that were wrong with the church. So, while it is perfectly possible to do what we have attempted to do in Part I and trace the pattern of New Testament teaching about the church, we must not forget that this is set against a New Testament picture of the state of the church which often differs greatly from the pattern. To sketch this picture, drawing where possible on the materials we have already used, will be the aim of Part 2.

A Divided World

The Christian message was, according to Paul, the message of reconciliation (2 Corinthians 5:9). It was certainly an appropriate message for the world of the first century AD, for it was a divided world. Roman society was a rigidly stratified pyramid, with the ruling aristocracy at the top and slaves at the bottom. Then the Romans looked in contempt on the Jews within the Empire and the barbarians without. The Jews, in turn, held aloof from the Gentile Romans and, indeed, from all non-Jewish peoples.

Even within Judaism, however, there were divisions. There were the opposing theological and political groupings, the Sadducees and the Pharisees. These, in turn, despised the ordinary people, the people of the land (those who flocked to Jesus). Then Judaism was also divided between the Jews of Palestine and the Jews of the Dispersion, scattered to almost every corner of the then-known world (cf. Acts 2:9-11). This division was related to, but did not necessarily coincide with, a division between Aramaic-speaking Jews (Hebrews) and Greek-speaking Jews (Hellenists;

cf. Acts 6:1). The latter admired the Greek way of life and adopted it to a greater or lesser degree—and were consequently accused by the stricter Hebrews of having betrayed Judaism.

Space will not permit us in this brief survey to do more than outline these social, cultural and religious divisions which characterized the world in which the church grew up. For further information the reader is referred to the bibliography. But this background of deep-rooted divisions must be borne in mind if the true state of the church in the New Testament is to be understood. For it was from this divided society that the first Christians came, and the divisions were in many cases reflected in the life of the church.

Hebrew versus Hellenists

We have spoken (see Part 1, page 33) of the consciousness of belonging to the one people of God which united Jews throughout the ancient world, however widely they were scattered (cf. Acts 2:9–11). But, as in our own day, within this broad Jewish harmony there were discordant notes. One of these was a clash of language and culture between Palestinian, Aramaic-speaking Jews, and Jews coming originally from the Dispersion, from outside Palestine, whose language and cultural background were Greek. Many of these Hellenists were strongly attracted to the Greek way of life: some of them, wishing to participate in Greek sports, in which athletes competed naked, went so far as to try to remove the marks of their circumcision.

This attempt to obliterate the distinctive sign of their Jewishness was, in the eyes of the more conservative Hebrews (the Aramaic speakers) nothing short of a betrayal of Judaism. This was an extreme example of cultural clash. But there were suspicion and misunderstanding at lower levels too. The Greek speakers had their own synagogues and used the Septuagint Greek translation of the Old Testament. Communication with the Hebrews was therefore limited.

What happened, then, when both Hebrews and Hellenists became Christians? Theologically and ideally there was reconciliation. But, in practice, suspicion was carried over. Conversion meant a change of relationship to God, but the corresponding change of social relationships did not always follow, at least, not immediately. And so 'there was a quarrel between the Greek-speaking Jews and the native Jews' (Acts 6:1). This is the reality, and the realism, of the New Testament picture of the church: old animosities breaking out afresh between those who have now become one in Christ. So, among the first decisions the church had to make, was how to resolve a cultural tension between members. The argument over the distribution of funds was no doubt coincidental: the tension would have shown itself in some other way if not in this. What is important is the fact that cultural tensions seem to have existed among the first Christians in Jerusalem within a decade of the founding of the church.

The decision to appoint the seven helpers (Acts 6:5)

did not mean the end of this particular tension. The Hebrews and the Hellenists represented two lines of thought in the church, the one conservative and the other progressive. The Seven, to judge by their Greek names, were probably all Hellenists. Certainly it was one of their number, Stephen, who, in his famous speech (Acts 7), pointed the way towards the eventual breach between Judaism and Christianity. His argument, very briefly summarized, was that, because the Jews had repeatedly rejected God and his messengers, God would turn outside Judaism (as he had often done in the past) to work out his purposes.

This progressive attitude, characterized by its openness towards non-Jews, also appeared in Philip, another of the Seven. He went and preached to the hated Samaritans (Acts 8:4 ff.). It was he, moreover, who baptized one who was expressly excluded by the Jewish law from the people of God: the Ethiopian eunuch (Acts 8:38; Deuteronomy 23:1). It was Hellenists who first preached the gospel to Gentiles without the prompting of any special vision, such as that needed by the Hebrew Peter (Acts 11:20; cp. 10:9 ff.). These progressive attitudes were a source of potential friction throughout the early period of the church's growth. Even Peter, the leader of the apostles, had to justify to his fellow Hebrews in Jerusalem his action in going to the house of the Roman centurion Cornelius (Acts 11:2). It was this friction which gave rise, in the late AD 40s, to the crisis which threatened to divide the church. As we turn to it now we must

53

remember that what lies behind it is a tension going back to the pre-Christian origins of the people involved.

Jews and Gentiles

Among the earliest of the New Testament documents is Paul's letter to the Galatians, dated by different scholars between AD 48 and AD 55. There are problems concerning both the dating and the destination of this letter, but we do not need to discuss them here. What is clear is that the letter dates from the period of the Council of Jerusalem, which met in about the year AD 49. Both the letter and the council dealt with the situation which had arisen as the result of the tension between conservatives and progressives on the question of the admission of Gentiles to the church. For, of course, the church had, up to this time, been predominantly Jewish. Here one of the great racial tensions of the ancient world coincided with a cultural tension which had originated in Judaism and been carried over into Christianity.

The Jews were very conscious of their special position in God's plan of salvation. They were the chosen people. The logical corollary of this was that other nations were not chosen. At some periods of their history the Jews remembered that their election gave them a mission to the other nations, for whom also God had a purpose. At other times they withdrew into an exclusiveness from which, for example, the message of the book of Jonah tried to recall them. This exclusiveness was easily interpreted as arrogance by the other nations, with the result that in the ancient world, as indeed today, there was an underlying current of anti-Jewish feeling, which came to the surface from time to time. This latent anti-Semitism can be traced in the attitudes of some of the Roman officials we meet in the pages of the New Testament, and in incidents like the riot in Ephesus (Acts 19 : 34), where Christians and Jews alike aroused the opposition of the mob. Thus a great gulf came to be fixed.

It was not an easy gulf to cross. Some Gentiles did find Judaism attractive, because its simple monotheism and high ethical principles contrasted so starkly with their own all too human gods and the widespread immorality of the pagan world. Three things, however, were required of the Gentile who wished to become a convert to Judaism, a proselyte. He must be baptized, offer sacrifice in the Temple, and be circumcised. The first two steps presented no difficulties, but the vital third step was a stumbling block. To many Gentiles circumcision, the distinctive mark of being a Jew, was a barbaric ritual, and one before which they stopped short. So relatively few became full proselytes. The rest remained content with the status of God-fearer, what we might call today an adherent of the church, who had not committed himself to full membership. It was into this situation that the church came, with the Hellenists in particular preaching the good news about Jesus to Jew and Gentile alike.

The trouble arose over the terms upon which Gentiles could become Christians. The Hellenists, following the theological insights of Stephen and the experience of Peter, maintained that the only condition was faith in Jesus Christ as Lord. The conservatives, known as Judaisers, many of whom had been Pharisees before their conversion, insisted that circumsion was necessary also. There was the real danger of a split between the conservative and progressive elements, which would have been in effect between the Aramaic speaking Jewish Christians and the rest of the church, including the Gentiles. The matter was calmly debated in the Council of Jerusalem (see Acts 15) and heatedly argued in Paul's letter to the Galatians.

The strength of feeling on both sides can be judged by the tone of Paul's letter, and by the fact that Peter and Barnabas were persuaded to retreat from the more progressive stance they had adopted back to the conservative position of their upbringing (Galatians 2:12 ff.). Old attitudes reasserted themselves and the church faced a crisis.

Its outcome, and how it was achieved, are not our concern in this study, at least not at this point (see Part 3, p. 93). What concerns us now are the complex social, religious and human factors which lay behind the crisis. Many of those who demanded the circumcision of the Gentiles *had been Pharisees*. Peter and Barnabas reverted to attitudes *in which they had been brought up* and which, in Peter's case at least, they had only reluctantly abandoned. The deep-seated mistrust between Hebrews and Hellenists, Jews and

Gentiles, *had existed long before the church came into being.* There was probably also an element of personal fear in the attitude of the Judaisers. Rationalized as fear that uncircumcised Gentile Christians would not keep the law of Moses (Acts 15:5), it was the fear that the nucleus of Palestinian Jewish Christians, including the apostles, would lose its position of leadership if there were a large influx of Gentiles into the church. Insisting on circumcision would be a means of excluding many of them. *Personal, human* motives became inextricably entangled with theological arguments.

This is the New Testament church as it really was: a socially, racially and culturally mixed body of very ordinary human beings. When it was threatened with division, it was along the lines of the old divisions brought into it by the members from their previous backgrounds. These divisions were often given theological justification after the event by appeals to different parts or different interpretations of the Old Testament scriptures.

Troubles in Corinth

If it could be demonstrated that the tensions we have been describing were confined to the Jerusalem church and its immediate offshoots in the Palestinian region, we might be led to conclude that it was the Jewish background of these first Christians which caused all the trouble. Such a conclusion, however, would not be borne out by the rest of the New Testament evidence. We turned to Paul's first letter to Corinth for much of our light on the ideal for the church. The same letter demonstrates just how far short the early Christians could fall, and the complexity of the strains and stresses with which they had to deal. And this was a church, of course, which included a large proportion, probably a majority, of Gentiles among its membership (cf. Acts 18:5–8).

Party Spirit

The Corinthian church was a church divided into factions (1 Corinthians 1:11–13). The essence of the divisions seems to have been that the Corinthian Christians emphasized the means by which they had come to Christ rather than Christ himself. (The exception is the 'Christ party', perhaps best interpreted as the ultra-spiritual, who set themselves above the party squabblings of the others). So there was a 'Paul party' an 'Apollos party' and a 'Peter party', according to which evangelist had first brought the good news to that particular group of Christians. One could almost say that there were four denominations in the Corinthian church, vying with one another for the position of true representatives of the gospel in the city. What had happened? The means had been made an end, the way of entry into the church which was appropriate and effective for one group had suppressed the object for which the church exists. 'If you don't worship God our way, if you do not come to him our way. . . .' The Corinthians were behaving like children, and Paul rebuked them for their childishness in chapter 3. There was room, he said, for a variety of ways, a variety of means, but all serve a common end.

> 'Love, like death, hath all destroyed,
> Rendered all distinctions void;
> Names, and sects, and parties fall:
> Thou, O Christ, art all in all.'
>
> CHARLES WESLEY
> *Methodist Hymn Book* 720

But this was only true in theory in Corinth. Into the common life of the church they brought the names of the first preachers of the gospel in Corinth, turned them into party labels, and the result was division.

Immorality

The Corinthians, however, brought into their Christian lives traits from much farther back, from before their conversion. Corinth was a cosmopolitan city, a trading centre and a seaport. Like many such cities in our own time, it was notorious in the ancient world for its immorality. That in itself was remarkable, for standards of morality in the ancient world in general fell short even of those of our 'permissive society' (see William Barclay, *Ethics in a Permissive Society*: Fontana, 1971). 'Corinthianizing' was a polite way of describing a life of gay abandon.

It was out of such an environment that some at least of the first Christians in Corinth came: not the Jews and God-fearers, of course, but those who were drawn into the church as it expanded beyond the first, synagogue-based nucleus (Acts 18:6–8). 1 Corinthians 5

59

reveals something of the difficulty the Corinthians experienced as they sought to break free from their old environment. A few continued to indulge in old practices (1 Corinthians 5:1). But the rest were not shocked. In fact, they appeared to Paul to be condoning the action of the offender. They could scarcely be expected to be shocked, one might say, seeing that this sort of thing went on all around them every day. But Paul argues that, since they have been made new in Christ, they must live like new people (5:6–8). So the old way of life came into conflict with the new. There was tension, and its roots lay not in the church as such but in the environment in which the church was set. The Corinthians were not aware of what was wrong because their thinking was conditioned by the society in which they lived. It needed the voice, or in this case the letter, of someone from outside to awaken them to the true state of affairs.

Paul's directions on, and comments about, marriage in chapter 7 must also be seen against this background. The concern of the Corinthians about sexual purity was influenced perhaps partly by Greek philosophy, with its view that the material, including the body, was evil, but certainly also by the purely practical problems of living as a Christian in a place like Corinth. Before we begin to make general rules out of what Paul says, or to draw conclusions about his attitudes to women, we must see the statements of this chapter in their social context. For, as we are beginning to see, this is an important factor in determining the shape of the church, and the shape of the church helped to determine what the apostle wrote to it.

Immaturity and Maturity

We have already noted (p.58) one area of the church's life where immaturity manifested itself. Coupled with another aspect of life in a pagan world, immaturity gave rise to a further tension in the Corinthian church. Again, we must look at the background first, against which the discussion of chapters 8:1–13 and 10:14–33 is set.

In the ancient pagan world the modern distinction between sacred and secular was unknown. The whole of life was seen as an expression of the relegous life. Thus most meals contained an element of worship and involved some kind of sacrifice to a god. Similarly, most of the animals which were slaughtered were killed in connection with the worship of one or other of the temples which were to be found in every town and city. Hence the Jewish insistence on their own slaughtering by their own methods. For the meat which was sold in the butchers' shops consisted of what was left over from the temple sacrifices.

This led to tensions in the church, especially in the matter of relations between Jewish and Gentile Christians. The Jew had been brought up in an atmosphere which shunned everything to do with idols. Idols were part of the Gentile's world, however. Now he had discovered that the true God was the living God, the Father of our Lord Jesus Christ, it did not appear to him to matter whether or not the meat he ate had first been sacrificed in front of a lifeless lump of wood. This was part of the Jew-Gentile issue which came out into the open at the Council of Jerusalem. On this occasion it was dealt with by an accommodation: Gentile Christians were asked to respect the long-standing scruples of their Jewish brothers and to refrain from eating meat which they knew had been offered previously as a sacrifice in a pagan temple.

But the question recurred as each new Christian community which contained a mixture of Jews and Gentiles faced the problem of living in a pagan world. When Paul wrote to Corinth it had given rise to tension there. Some Corinthian Christians, who prided themselves on their strength (10:22), maintained that it did not matter whether they ate meat which came originally from pagan temples. Others had scruples, and were confused by the stance of their stronger brothers (8:7). Paul had to remind the strong of their responsibility to the weak (8:9–13). As in the human family, the mature have a responsibility towards the immature, in order to help the latter to grow to maturity themselves. This principle, of course, applies in every aspect of the church's life. But in the instance we have been discussing, the immaturity and the tension stemmed from attitudes originating before the Corinthians became Christians.

Sacramentalism

We have been seeing through this study that old attitudes die hard. There was a lowest common denominator in both the paganism and the Judaism from which the first converts to Christianity came, an attitude which they found it hard to shake off. As far as Judaism is concerned, it is the attitude of the legalists, whether those of Old Testament times, or those we meet in the New Testament accounts of Jesus' ministry. It may be summed up as, 'The most important thing is to keep the letter of the Law'. The prophets attacked the legalists (for example, Isaiah 1:10–17; Micah 6:6–8) and Jesus followed their example (Matthew 23). External ritual without a change of inner attitude could not please God. Whilst the best elements in Judaism agreed with Jesus and the prophets, there were sufficient numbers who took the legalistic line to justify the attacks made on them.

The same kind of attitude was encouraged by pagan religion. As long as you paid your annual lip-service to the cult of the Emperor by offering a sacrifice, you could follow any other religion you pleased or none at all. The Christians and Jews, of course, would not even go as far as one sacrifice, and brought persecution upon themselves as a result. But for many people, to go through the external ritual did not imply any further commitment at all. They had fulfilled their obligation.

When people from this background became Christians, they discovered that Christianity too had its rituals, two of them to be precise: baptism and the Lord's supper. They too readily assumed that the obligations required of the Christian were the same as those required of the devotees of other religions: the fulfilment of the ritual and nothing more. And so in

Corinth there was a group of Christians who had been baptized and who participated in the Lord's supper and who thought that, having done so, they had done all that was required to put them right with God. They were 'Sacramentalists', in the bad sense of that word. They believed that the sacraments had a magical quality which worked irrespective of the attitude of the worshipper. These are the people against whom Paul directed the arguments of 1 Corinthians 10:1–11. But note how the attitude of these Christians came with them into the church from their background.

Women's Lib

The Preacher reminds us that there is nothing new under the sun (Ecclesiastes 1:9), and one can see certain parallels between the behaviour of the women in the church in Corinth and the advocates of Women's Lib today. There are differences, of course. In many cases today, the women are campaigning to gain their rights. In Corinth, the women described in chapter 11:12–16 had obtained their rights, but were enjoying them in such a way as to turn liberty into licence.

There is a difference, too, between this trouble of the church in Corinth and the others we have looked at so far. In this case, the women's attitude was not brought into the church from their pre-Christian background, but it was a reaction against the situation in which they had lived before becoming Christians.

This was also an area in which Jewish and pagan backgrounds were similar. In both societies, women occupied a subsidiary role. They were second-class citizens with no rights. A Jewish man could divorce his wife, but a woman could not divorce her husband. When it came to statistics, women (and children) did not count (see Matthew 14:21). The existence of the Women's Lib movement today serves to indicate just how deeply the anti-feminist feeling is rooted in most human societies. (In Jewish and Christian circles justification for it is often sought in Genesis 2:18–25, where woman is described as 'taken out of man'. But in this passage the emphasis is not on the subordinate position of woman, but on the fact that she is of the same kind as man, as verse 20 makes clear.)

Christianity, however, changed the status of woman. The gospels record Jesus' concern for them, especially Luke's which mentions thirteen women who do not appear in the other gospels (for example: 7:11–17, 36 ff.; 8:2–3). Women played a significant part in the growth of the church (for example: Acts 12:12; 16:14–15; Romans 16:1–5) and in its worship (1 Corinthians 11:5). And so, when the good news of 'Women's Lib' reached the women of Corinth, some reacted by abusing their new freedom. They did so by shocking the whole of society, inside and outside the church, by flaunting social conventions and appearing bare-headed in public like prostitutes. They also set out to prove their equality in spiritual matters by interrupting speakers at public worship (14:34–35). Their behaviour was a reaction against the restrictions they had previously suffered in the society in which they lived. So we cannot understand this situation

65

without an appreciation of the background, for the church in Corinth did not exist in a social vacuum.

Rich and Poor

Different social backgrounds produced the next tension that we discover in the Corinthian church: that between rich and poor. It was one that had existed for many centuries in Judaism, as the writings of the prophets bear witness (for example: Amos 2:6–7). It was present throughout the New Testament period (cf. James 2:1–6. Jesus himself is recorded as remarking that 'you will always have poor people with you' (John 12:8). In Corinth it seems that many of the Christians were poor (1:26–28). But all the same, there were those who were well off, and so a situation developed of tension between those who were of different means and different social status.

In Corinth this tension manifested itself, of all places, in the fellowship meal, in the context of which the Lord's supper was celebrated (1 Corinthians 11:17–34). The tragic irony of this situation is conveyed by the tone of Paul's words in the opening sentences of this section, which comes across even when translated into English. 'In the following instructions, however, I do not praise you: for your church meetings actually do more harm than good. . . . What do you expect me to say to you about this? Should I praise you? Of course I do not praise you!' The fellowship meal was intended to express the love of the Christians for one another—hence the name, agape, the Greek word for Christian love, which came to be used for it. The Lord's supper was meant to express, among other things, the unity of all participants in Christ (cf. 1 Corinthians 10:16–17). How, then, could the rich stuff themselves like gluttons, and even get drunk, while the poor went hungry? There was an inconsistency between the profession of faith and its practice, and the result was division. And all this had its origin in the attitudes and situations of the people concerned before they became Christians. Now they were members of the church. They had been awakened to Christ, but they had not been awakened to themselves and to one another. They were not aware of their own real attitudes and others' real needs.

One aspect of the tension between rich and poor which we have not mentioned is the relationship between masters and slaves. But while there are several references in the New Testament to this relationship (for example: Ephesians 6:5–9; Colossians 3:22–4:1; Philemon; 1 Peter 2:18–25), it seems to have remained a potential, rather than an actual, source of serious friction. Perhaps, just because it was so obvious an area in which the church might find itself divided into two groups, a conscious effort was made to avoid division. The other divisive aspects of wealth and poverty which we have been considering, however, operated on a more subtle, less conscious, level. The church was caught off guard by them, therefore, with the results that we have seen.

Truth and Error

It is strange how naïvely some of us accept a picture of the New Testament church as pure both in its teaching and its practice. Yet the evidence of the New Testament letters is almost exactly the opposite. For some of them were written specifically to combat false doctrine within the church (for example: Galatians; 1 John). Most of those that were not actually occasioned by false teaching contain some reference to it (for example: Philippians 3; 1 Timothy 4). And almost all spend their final paragraphs dealing with the true pattern for Christians' conduct in a pagan world. In the last passage at which we shall look in 1 Corinthians, chapter 15, we find evidence for the tension, or rather the head-on collision, between truth and error in this church too.

The remarkable thing about the error at Corinth is that it concerned so fundamental a doctrine as the resurrection. But perhaps it was not so remarkable when one turns to consider the climate of thought in the first century AD. (For a full discussion of this, see Michael Green, *Evangelism in the Early Church*: Hodder & Stoughton, 1970, chapter 2.) Briefly one can say that no one was predisposed in favour of the idea of resurrection as it was presented by the apostles in the preaching of the early church.

First, let us look at the attitude of the Jews. From the evidence which we possess today, both in the Old Testament and outside it, we can trace the development of a belief in personal resurrection at the end of time. It arose particularly through the pressures of times of persecution, when the problem of God's justice presented itself in an acute form. It was helped by the earlier use of the idea of restoration from death as a metaphor for the renewal of the nation or for deliverance from disease (for example; Hosea 6; Ezekiel 37:1–10; Daniel 12:2; Psalm 16:9–11). This belief was not, however, universally accepted and we have evidence from the New Testament and elsewhere of division of opinion, specially between the Pharisees and the Sadducees (for example: Mark 12:18–28; Acts 23:6–10). At the level of the priestly, official religion of the Jews, belief in the resurrection was not accepted. The Pharisees exercised a wider popular influence, and so there was no doubt considerable general belief in a *future* resurrection to right the injustices of this life. But a *present* resurrection was a different matter (cf. John 11:24). And there seems to have been no connection made between the resurrection and the hoped-for Messiah. It was a Christian development to interpret Psalm 16:9–11 first literally and, secondly, as relating to the Messiah (Acts 2:25–32). The greater difficulty, however, for the Jew was the *death* of the Messiah, if he was Son of God, not his resurrection. 'The Messiah cannot die', says Nicodemus in Stuart Jackman's fictionalized investigation of the resurrection of Jesus, *The Davidson Affair* (Faber, 1966). So the Jew was not prejudiced in favour of the Christian's insistence that the Messiah must die and rise from the dead (cf. Luke 24:26; 1 Corinthians 15:3–4).

Resurrection did not fare any better among the Gentiles. The Greek poet, Aeschylus, said bluntly,

'There is no resurrection' (Eumenides, 647 f., cited in F. F. Bruce, *The Book of the Acts*, pp. 363–4). So the central plank in the Christian message was folly to the pagan world, as it was a stumbling block to Jews (cf. 1 Corinthians 1:18–25). The background to such a categorical denial was the widespread dualism in nearly all religions and cultures outside the Judaeo-Christian orbit. In its bare essentials this dualism stated that matter, including the body, was inherently evil, and only the spirit was good. If God is good, then he can have nothing to do with bodily resurrection. (There is evidence in the letter of Paul to Colossae and in 1 John that dualistic teaching of this kind was beginning to penetrate the church.)

With this background, therefore, it is perhaps no wonder that some of the early Christians, whether formerly Jews or Gentiles, had difficulties over the resurrection. And yet, in the face of all the difficulties, the early preachers continued to insist that it was 'of the greatest importance that Christ died for our sins and was raised to life on the third day' (1 Corinthians 15:3–4: see A. Skevington Wood, *The Evangelical Understanding of the Gospel*, C.E.I.M., 1974). But even so original and essential a doctrine was under question in Corinth, because of the pre-Christian background and the environment of the believers there.

Isolated Case or Endemic Disease?
So far we have looked at a fairly limited area of the New Testament evidence. The reasons for this are

two-fold: first, the wealth of material in the Corinthian correspondence and, secondly, the need to see the reverse side of the pattern for the church which we drew in Part 1. We have noted some parallels in other New Testament letters. We have looked at Acts. Can we, however, confirm the picture of a far from perfect church? Was this just because they were removed from the personal presence of Jesus? Did the personalities of the apostles get in the way of a proper development of relationships within the church? Although the gospels were written later than many of the letters, and although their shape has been influenced by the situations in and for which they were written, they contain the only record we have of the state of things in the lifetime of Jesus. How does this compare with the apostolic age?

Jesus and His Disciples
We noted (Part 1, p. 40) how diverse outlooks and personalities were held together in the band of Jesus' disciples by his call to them to follow him. But that holding together was not without its strains. In the picture which Mark paints of the ministry of Jesus, we find above all repeated misunderstanding on the part of the disciples of who Jesus was and of what following him involved for them. Sometimes this led to rebuke from him, sometimes to squabbles among themselves. Because they had not grasped the mind of Christ, we find the disciples frequently pulling against him, rather than with him, in much the same way as

71

the church later seemed to be frustrating rather than forwarding his purposes.

First, the disciples failed to understand Jesus' priorities (Mark 1:35–38). All had a right to his ministry, and so he had to keep moving from place to place. They failed also to understand the significance of his parables (4:10–12), so that he had to explain them. Then they failed to appreciate the meaning of his presence and person (4:35–41) when, in a moment of crisis, fear overtook them. More than once Jesus had to rebuke them for their lack of faith and understanding (for example: 8:14–21). The sternest rebuke was delivered to Peter, when he failed to realize the necessity of suffering for the fulfilment of Jesus' mission (8:31–33). This failure to understand the climax of Jesus' ministry is high-lighted three times in the final chapters of the gospel (cf. also 9:30–32; 10:32–34). It seems, indeed, as if Mark deliberately emphasizes the human frailty of the disciples as the gospel draws to its climax. In 9:33–37 he records their arguments about which of them is the greatest. In 9:38–41 the disciples try to limit the number of those who are for Jesus. In 10:13–16 they try to prevent the children from coming to him, and in 10:35–45 an open rift occurs among the disciples when James and John request the places of authority in the Kingdom. All this has been leading up to the passion narrative, which occupies the closing chapters of the gospel. The narrative includes the accounts of the betrayal of Jesus by Judas, one of the Twelve (14:10–11, 43–50), of the failure of the disciples, even of the closest friends, to sustain Jesus as he faces the greatest crisis of his ministry (14:32–42), of the desertion of Jesus (14:50) and of Peter's denial (14:66–72).

The picture which Mark gives us of the disciples, then, is very like the one the letters have given us of the early Christians. For all that the disciples were specially called, chosen and taught by Jesus himself, they were ordinary and fallible. Their misunderstanding of Jesus' teaching can be understood against their Jewish background, for what Jesus taught was in many ways radically new (although foreshadowed in the Old Testament). Their quarrels were typical human reactions, hardly surprising in the light of the very mixed nature of the group. Once again, the New Testament has not given us a rose-tinted ideal but frank realism.

The End of the Century

So far we have been looking at the church in the period from the time of Jesus to about AD 60. There is one more strand among the New Testament documents at which we can look, which will take our survey down to the closing decades of the first century. We turn, therefore, to the book of the Revelation, and in particular to the letters to the seven churches of Asia, contained in chapters 2 and 3.

First of all, we must put these chapters in their context. After a brief introduction (1:1–3) to the whole Revelation, the remainder of chapter 1 is a kind of covering letter to the seven churches, explaining the circumstances under which the seven letters came to be written (1:4–20). The letters themselves then follow. Before we examine their content, we must ask whether there is more to them than appears on the surface. There must be a reason for the choice of these seven churches. They were not the only churches in Asia at the time (cf. Acts 22:5 ff.; Colossians 1:2; 4:13, R. H. Charles, *Revelation*, vol. 1, p. 8). They lie in a rough circle and are named in the order in which a messenger would reach them. They are key points in the areas in which they lie. But the fact that the writer of Revelation frequently uses the number seven (for a list, see Charles, p. 9) suggests that it is not the geographical factor that is important here. The number seven has a significance of its own. It 'is a figure of completeness' (L. Morris, *Revelation*, p. 47), 'its use here indicates that the church as a whole is in mind' (W. Hendriksen, *More Than Conquerors*, p. 10). While it is true that we have here seven individual letters to seven clearly characterized and individual churches, which actually existed (cf. W. M. Ramsay, *The Letters to the Seven Churches*, chapter 4), these seven are representative. At a lower level of meaning they represent, first, all the churches of their own areas and, secondly, the cities in which they are located. But, thirdly and most important, they stand for the whole church (cf. 2:7, 11, 17, 29; 3:6, 13, 22). The Seer takes the state of these churches as typical of all the churches that he knows and speaks to the whole church through his message to these seven representatives of it.

What sort of a church, then, does he see? First of

all, it is remarkable how some of the phrases he uses to describe it are those which we, in our worse moments, use of the church today. It is unloving (2:4), poor (2:9), containing and tolerating false teachers (2:14, 20), dabbling in evil (the occult or pornography, 2:24), dead (3:1), weak (3:8), lukewarm (3:16). The other remarkable thing is the extent to which these seven churches have absorbed characteristics of the communities in which they are set. The Seer deliberately highlights these common factors as he unfolds his message. For example, a number of the Christians in Pergamum (2:12–17) had compromised by failing to show exclusive loyalty to the Christian faith. Pergamum was a centre for the cult of the Emperor, as well as containing temples to many of the chief gods and goddesses of the Greek pantheon. The social pressures on Christians in such an environment to conform and worship like everyone else were considerable. In Thyatira (2:18–29) the chief problem was immorality, encouraged by those who found a theological justification for it. Those who followed such false teaching were promised a fate no different from that of the pagans whose standards they had adopted. Sardis (3:1–6) was a city noted for its unpreparedness. Twice, in 549 and 218 BC it had been captured because no guard had been set. This slackness seems to have infected the church, of which the Seer writes, 'I know that you have the reputation of being alive, even though you are dead! So wake up, and strengthen what you still have, before it is too late' (3:1–2). Laodicea (3:14–22) was a self-reliant city, which had been rebuilt after an earthquake in AD 60 without outside help, for it was one of the richest commercial centres in the ancient world. This self-reliant spirit had penetrated the church. ' "I am rich and well off," you say, "I have all I need." But you do not know how miserable and pitiful you are!' (v. 17). As in the earlier period we have already examined, the church at the end of the century was subject to the influence of the age and place in which it was set. This influence gave rise to problems, which were the occasion of the writing of the seven letters, just as the problems in churches like Corinth had occasioned the earlier letters.

Conclusion

When, therefore, we draw together the strands which go to make up the New Testament picture of the church, we find that the result reflects, in many areas, the world of the first century AD. The great divisions of that world reappear in the church in the form of tensions and quarrels. Racial divisions reappear in the form of mistrust of Gentile Christians by Jewish. Cultural divisions within Judaism manifest themselves in the early quarrels in Jerusalem between Hebrews and Hellenists. The great economic gulf between rich and poor was not easily bridged, despite the communism of the first church in Jerusalem. As the church moved out into the great Gentile cities, converts found it difficult to break old attitudes and habits, or else they over-reacted to their new-found freedom. Even in matters of essential Christian doctrine, the beliefs

(Jewish or pagan) which first constituted obstacles to the gospel, reappeared after the conversion of those who held them as heresies and deviations from the faith. Human factors, personality clashes, the things that divide social groups today, all appeared in the New Testament church. To ignore these things because we have an idealized picture of that church in our minds is to fail to do justice to the Biblical evidence. Like Cromwell's portrait, the New Testament church is painted warts and all.

At the end of Part 1 we defined the church as 'the people who belong to God through Jesus Christ and, in the power of the Holy Spirit, are doing his work wherever they are in the world'. That definition we attempted to draw out from the New Testament. But now it seems we have drawn out from the New Testament a very different face of the church. Just as today we feel a tension between what the institutional church professes to be, and what we see it is, the New Testament has presented us with the same tension right from the beginning of the church! The last part of our study will set out to look at the manifestations of the tension in the church today and, if it is not too daring a task, attempt to suggest ways in which the tension may be resolved.

Part 3

'Mirror, Mirror, on the Wall'

The Church of Today in the Light of the New Testament

Are we really like that?

AT ONE of the London teaching hospitals the medical students every year present a play in which the characters are mainly caricatures of the hospital consultants. One of these was overheard asking his wife, after the performance, 'Am I really like that?' When we ask such a question about ourselves, our tone of voice usually betrays disbelief. That cannot possibly be a picture of us! Perhaps this has been the reaction that we have had on reading Part 2. We have advanced beyond the stage of the New Testament church and we do not let the world around us squeeze us into its own mould (Romans 12:2, J. B. Phillips), as the first Christians seem to have done.

In some respects, it is true, the church is far from reflecting the spirit of the age. One of the reasons for which so many people reject the church and its message is that both seem irrelevant and out-of-date. One has only to look at the language, dress, music and architecture of some sections of the church to realize that there is substance in the accusation. But in other ways, are we really very different from the New Testament church? Perhaps you have already begun to answer that question as you have been reading Part 2. In this third and last section of our study we shall be trying to discover what we are really like. To do so, we shall look at the parallels between our own situation and that of the New Testament church, and see whether the solutions suggested then have any relevance today.

It is here that this study is offered primarily as a basis for further research and discussion. There are no pat answers to the tensions and problems facing the church in the twentieth century, just as there was none in the first. It may be that we shall conclude that there are some tensions which we must learn to live with. But we shall get nowhere until we, the people of God, have discovered what we are really like, and what help God has provided for us to cope with that situation. Each section in Part III, therefore, ends with suggestions for study or questions for discussion, aimed at leading us toward these two vital discoveries. We are following this method, rather than that of propounding general solutions, because each local group of Christians and each local situation is different. Each one, therefore, must make these discoveries for itself.

A Divided World

As with our study of a passage of scripture, our study of ourselves must begin by examining the context in which we are set. Our world of the twentieth century is no less divided than that of the first. There are the obvious divisions of nationality and race, of wealth, of religion, of denomination. There are also subtler divisions of class and culture, resulting in differences of attitude of which we are scarcely aware. There are differences of political outlook, of moral standards, of churchmanship, for which, very often, we would be hard put to it to give a reason. Many of these divisions match up. Being 'chapel' rather than 'church' may go with being employee rather than boss and voting Labour or Liberal rather than Conservative, for example.

The problem is not so much the fact of these divisions as our attitude towards them. Take, for example, differences of nationality. People of different nations have their own customs and their own languages. Do we accept these as having value in themselves or do we feel, however unconsciously, that only the British way of doing things is normal, and that all the rest are odd or quaint? Must they all learn English, or are we humble enough to make the effort to learn French or Spanish or whatever? One so often hears even Christian people saying, in a patronizing tone of voice, 'Oh, we must make allowances for them; they're Americans.' Such attitudes serve only to accentuate the divisions and make them more divisive.

So the first thing we must do, if we are to understand ourselves, is to acknowledge the fact that we are part of a divided world, and to discover just how and why that world is divided the way it is. For there is no way in which we can opt out of these divisions. We have been born members of a particular nation, speak its language, follow its customs. We belong to a particular cultural and economic group within the

society of that nation and, quite probably, to a particular geographical sub-group too (Yorkshiremen do
not behave like Londoners!). We attend a particular
church of a particular denomination, we vote for a
particular party. All this makes us different from other
people—but not necessarily better or worse.

Discussion and Study

What divisions and differences can we identify in our
local community and church?

How and why did we become what we are today?

R. Bottomore, *Classes in Modern Society* (Allen &
Unwin)

J. Blondel, *Voters, Parties and Leaders* (Penguin
Books)

D. Martin, *A Sociology of English Religion*
(Heinemann)

D. Edgington, *Christians and Colour in Britain*
(Scripture Union)

Class and Culture

The first division which we examined in the case of
the New Testament church was the cultural division
between Hebrews and Hellenists. The word 'culture'
has a variety of meanings, but the sense in which we
are using it in this study could perhaps best be para-
phrased as 'the life-style and way of thinking of a
particular social grouping'. So we could talk about
the Hebrew culture as opposed to the Hellenistic.
Now, as we turn to today's church, we shall be able

to talk about working-class or middle-class culture as convenient shorthands.

Before we become too involved with the subject it may be helpful to set down a few facts and incidents. The facts are recorded by David Martin in *A Sociology of English Religion* (pp. 18–47), but can be found in many surveys. They are that the church is, and has been for more than 100 years, a predominantly middle-class institution. Martin concludes (p. 47), 'The upper middle class is more practising than the lower middle class, and a large gap yawns between the lower middle class and the working class'. Such a conclusion is based on surveys of church attendance, from the 1851 Census onwards, and a variety of statistics published by churches themselves. Most of us would be able to confirm this conclusion from our own experience. The possible reasons for it we must look at a little later.

Three incidents may also help illustrate the way in which the church is hampered in its missionary task by being identified with a particular culture. A few years ago a consultation was held at Cliff College with the title 'Mission in a Pop Culture'. The panel of speakers were all involved in some way in the popular arts. The approach they advocated was based first of all on knowledge of oneself and on being real and genuine. It was also necessary to listen to and know those to whom our mission is directed, so that we may communicate the good news about Jesus in personal face to face contact, rather than from a pulpit twelve feet above contradiction. The reactions of the College students to this approach were very interesting. There was a sharp polarization, such as one might have expected across a generation gap. Some found the weekend stimulating and helpful, but the others were left completely cold: the ideas and attitudes expressed belonged to a different world from theirs. In a striking way it was brought home to us that even within one age-group inside the church there are clear cultural divisions, reflecting different backgrounds and up-bringings. What appeals to and is effective for one group may not be for another.

The second incident is superficially more trivial but reveals an equally fundamental problem. The hymn 'Amazing Grace' by John Newton has, as we all know, twice been top of the charts and therefore has provided a point of contact between Cliff College students on mission and youngsters with no church background. But frequently the College students have found that the hymn is incomprehensible to the young people, because they assume that 'grace' is a girl's name. We are accustomed to using theological language: it is part of the culture we enter by belonging to the church. But it is a foreign language to many outside the church, not only because it is a technical jargon but also because, so often, we talk in abstract terms (like 'grace') to people whose vocabulary and ideas are largely concentrated on concrete realities.

The third incident follows on from the second. At the Morecambe conference, 'Strategy for Evangelism' in 1972, the Rev. Tom Houston of the British and Foreign Bible Society spoke about the linguistic research behind the new translation of the New Testament *Good News for Modern Man: Today's English Version*. (This is the translation from which most of the New Testament quotations in this Study are taken.) He demonstrated how in most of the English versions with which we are probably familiar the language is either literary, or old-fashioned, or both. In either case, it requires of the average English reader a wider vocabulary than he possesses. Moreover, it uses a more complex sentence structure than he is accustomed to see in his daily newspaper or use himself. T.E.V., therefore, was designed to employ, as far as possible, the vocabulary of the average reader of English. It was impossible, of course, to avoid all technical terms, but these were explained in a glossary. Similarly, the sentence structure was deliberately broken down into shorter units. If the Bible is central to our worship and our message, it must be in the language which we can all understand. It was written in everyday language, which was accessible to people of a variety of cultures. We are not being true to it if we restrict it to one literary culture in our own society.

How has it come about that the church in the twentieth century is so much identified with one class and one culture? J. A. Walter, in an article entitled 'The Class-bound Church' (*Christian Graduate*, June 1973) describes a hypothetical group of Christians and shows how social factors cause it to split up in a variety of ways. First, as John Wesley foresaw (*Thoughts upon Methodism*, 4 August 1786, paras 9–11), he traces how religious motivation produces hard work, and hard work affluence and affluence a move to a 'better area' and a new church in an area occupied by people in a higher social class. Then he traces the rise of denominations, as the spontaneity of the original group becomes subordinated to organization. Differences of opinion lead to new breakaways 'and so the cycle goes on, of sects breaking away from denominations, and then themselves with time slowly forming into denominations, the cycle reflecting sometimes all too accurately the conflicts and transitions in the rest of the world'. The third source of division is differences over worship. These may arise when 'for example, some members have been at hard and repetitive physical labour all week and want not only to sing vigorously but to have the whole service in a vigorous and for them releasing style, with clapping of hands, hallelujahs and spontaneous prayer, while other members, worn out emotionally by the stress of running, say, a modern business, want not just a sermon on the peace of God but want the whole tenor of the service to be one of peace and of comfort being proclaimed, not by the congregation, but by the special authority of the minister'. In these three areas, then, Walter argues, what happens in church is being largely directed by class and cultural considerations. Our income will determine what church we attend, for we will want to go where we feel we fit in. Where it comes to matters of organization the same factors tend to operate. The standards which govern our church affairs are adopted from our environment, from business or industry or government. And our job, education and temperament will contribute to determining the kind of worship we find helpful Sunday by Sunday.

It is not difficult to see how, on such a basis, the church becomes alienated from one class in society. The vicious circle principle operates. In a predominantly middle-class institution, working-class people feel ill at ease, and either adopt middle-class ways themselves (moving away geographically and socially from their home territory) or cease attending the church. The church in turn only attracts middle-class people from outside. And so the cycle goes on. But is the picture painted by Walter a true one? Other evidence, unfortunately, seems to suggest that it is.

First, articles in the correspondence *Christians in Industrial Areas* (founded by the Bishop of Liverpool, the Rt. Rev. David Sheppard, and available three times a year from the Rev. J. A. Stanley, Huyton Vicarage, Huyton, Liverpool L36 7XE) support in general the conclusions reached by Walter. What the working man looks for in his worship, for example, is referred to in very similar terms in Issue No. 30 (June 1974) by the Rev. I. K. W. Saville of Wandsworth: 'The middle-class, especially those over 40, see reverence in terms of silence and order and structured services. The working-class see reverence in terms of reality, fellowship and singing one's head off.' The irrelevance of the church to many working-class people is further explored in other articles in the same issue.

On a much more massive scale is David Sheppard's

consideration of the church's relations to the inner city in his book *Built as a City* (Hodder & Stoughton, 1974). It shows how, by missing opportunities (when, for example, the early Primitive Methodists were becoming involved in the first trade union activities), adopting negative attitudes and approaches (for example, over drink and Sunday observance), and by not moving with the times (for example, in some of the Methodist Central Missions), the church alienated itself from the life of the inner city. That life, too, is characterized, especially the sense of powerlessness felt by the inner city dweller in the face of his circumstances, local government and institutions in general. The church is in the position now of having to win back for itself the right to be heard in the inner city. It has to prove its relevance, not by intellectual argument, but by being seen to be 'for real'.

Massive and searching and impressive as it is, however, *Built as a City* is perhaps not so moving a piece of evidence as John Benington's little book, *Culture, Class and Christian Belief* (Scripture Union, 1973). This arises from the story of a small group of converts from a working-class background. The adjustments which they have to make as they embark on their new-found faith are great. They not only have to learn what it means to be a Christian. They also have to adapt to the middle-class ways of the church into which they are introduced. The result, often recounted in their own words, is, first, a loss of personal identity. They do not feel they belong anywhere. Then comes loss of faith: the strain is too great. They cannot cope with becoming middle-class and Christian. And, of course, the vital question which John Benington throws into such sharp relief is, 'Is there any need to compel them to become middle-class and Christian?'

To those of us brought up in essentially middle-class churches such questions are uncomfortable, to say the least. Have we been wrong, all these years? Is what we have imagined to be Christianity not the real thing after all? Have we got to change? It is essential that we ask these questions, however. We cannot continue fooling ourselves that the church in Great Britain is fulfilling its function and proclaiming good news 'to all peoples everywhere' (Matthew 28:19) when every statistic—church membership, church attendance, numbers of clergy—indicates that the church is declining. On the other hand, the situation is not one of unmitigated gloom. The New Testament church found a way of reconciling its cultural divisions, and the various writers to whom we have just been referring also have pointers to the way ahead.

The cultural tensions in the New Testament church came to a head in Acts 6:1 (see Part 2, pp. 51–53). The tension was reconciled by participation: the aggrieved group in the church, the Hellenists, was given a part in the leadership of the church by the election of the seven helpers. Notice that the apostles did not dictate terms, or nominate those who were to help them. The seven were appointed by the people and the apostles confirmed the appointment. The apostles might have chosen differently, employing different standards of judgment, but they trusted God the Holy Spirit to throw up the right men for the job, and then they let them get on with it.

This principle of participation is one which many modern writers on the relations of the church to the working class see as essential. The last part of John Benington's book tells the story of an experiment in integrating working-class young people into the church on a very different basis from the one which failed. It began with a youth club, in the running of which the youngsters themselves took the major responsibility. When one or two eventually reached the point of making a commitment to Christ, they were again left to work out responsibly for themselves what this commitment was going to mean in terms of their working-class background. The (middle-class) club leaders were always available to give help and encouragement, but they were enablers, not dictators. And so a responsible partnership was able to develop.

For this partnership to come into operation another principle had to be brought into play: that of acceptance. We saw it in the attitude of the apostles, who accepted the people's choice (the seven). They were different; the seven were Hellenists, the apostles Hebrews. But they could accept one another and work together towards their common goal because of their common allegiance to Christ. The same principle of acceptance was involved in the experiment John Benington describes. Lack of it is one of the causes of the situation David Sheppard reveals in the inner city. Acceptance means openness, acknowledging differences between those of different backgrounds but not placing value judgments on them. As Frank Deeks, a correspondent in *Christians in Industrial Areas* put it, 'For me, the situation is full of promise. I see more and more evangelicals who recognise that we do belong to different classes; that are different not inferior or superior. I know more and more working-class Christians who have no intention of leaving their roots but intend staying and making it a bit more of the Kingdom' (No. 29, page 15).

Theologically, the justification of the principles of participation and acceptance is not far to seek. The fundamental Christian doctrines of creation, providence and grace teach us that God is no respecter of persons, but is the one Father of us all. They go on to show how men have been created, are cared for and redeemed for one another, that we are interdependent. Such great doctrines thus become the foundation for a relevant theology, which will speak to the situation in which we find ourselves. We must not be afraid to face, and to work out in practice, the implications of that theology. We may then be able to move out of our mood of despair and share the hope of men and women like Frank Deeks.

Discussion and Study
Are there any ways in which the life of our church is class bound?

How can we enable people of different backgrounds and abilities to participate equally and responsibly in the life of our church?

91

What abilities are there already among our members which we have not previously recognized?

John Benington, *Culture, Class and Christian Belief* (Scripture Union).

David Sheppard, *Built as a City* (Hodder & Stoughton).

'Change and Decay'

Part of our trouble in the church today stems from the fact that we live in a rapidly changing world. It has been said that in the United States there is a 'generation flip' every three years (cited by the Rev. Tom Houston at Morecambe). The statistics with which we are so frequently bombarded in the press or on television tell the same story. It is confirmed by our own experience if we are prepared to stop and remember. How many readers of this book recall ITMA, Children's Hour, riding in trams, rationing?

Although, however, we live in a changing world, we are not obliged to acknowledge the fact. It is all too easy to forget the changes and go on living, as far as possible, as we have always done. It is all too easy to stigmatize change as bad: 'change and *decay*', as the hymnwriter put it, or to express the same sentiment in more popular form, 'Fings ain't wot they use'ter be'. This attitude seems to be one which has for a long time afflicted the church. In David Martin's words (*A Sociology of English Religion*, p. 109) 'for many people the church acts as a still point in a turning world'. Ronald Fletcher in the introduction to the first edition of *The Family and Marriage in Britain*

(Pelican), quotes many church leaders as deploring the decline of the family. But the evidence he cites in the body of the book aims to demonstrate that the position of the family, though greatly changed, has considerably improved. Or, to go back to the early church (see Part 2, pp. 54–57), we found a resistance to change on the part of the Jewish Christians when they were faced with the mass entry of Gentiles into the church.

In our own generation the church has been faced with the possibility of the mass entry of Christians from overseas, especially the West Indies, into our congregations. We have been faced with the move-ment of large numbers of immigrants from many countries into our residential areas. And we are being faced today with the entry into the church of large numbers of young Christians more or less influenced by the Jesus People. In their dress and attitudes they are unlike any youngsters most of us have ever seen in church. The question is, will there be integration or segregation, unity (as advocated by the Council of Jerusalem) or division (as promoted by the Judaisers)?

The history of the recent years suggests that success-ful integration is the exception rather than the rule. Our fears of change and our suspicion of the strangers, the feeling that we may be overwhelmed (the feelings that were stirred up among the conservatives in the 40s of the first century AD) combine to create barriers against integration. It is a similar problem to the one we dealt with in the previous section. We do not recognize these people as different: we class them as

93

inferior. 'They will lower the tone of the neighbour-hood.' 'We don't want that kind of person in our church.' 'They have no sense of dignity or worship.' 'They are too noisy.' How often do we hear remarks like these? The result has been that immigrant groups have kept together, the Christians among them forming their own congregations with their own style of worship. Similarly the young Christians associated with the Jesus movement have tended to come together in house churches on the fringes of the main-line denominations. They have not felt wanted.

The picture, however, is not all gloomy. There are many churches where the 'hippie' type of young Christian has been successfully integrated into the church family. There are some places, too, where there has been a happy marriage between immigrant Christians and the local congregation. The writer was told of one church in which, for a time, there were two services each Sunday morning. The local West Indian Methodist congregation met first for morning prayer, to which they had been accustomed at home but missed in England. The English congregation, unaccustomed to liturgical worship, met later for their 'hymn sandwich'. Eventually the two groups came to realize how ridiculous this situation was, and a compromise was reached: the two congregations would meet for worship together every Sunday, with the two different patterns of worship alternating.

This is the kind of solution the early church found to the problem of integration. The Council of Jerusalem reached a compromise, not on the doctrinal issue under discussion, but upon its practical application. The Council reaffirmed that salvation is by grace through faith, not by law through works. But then it asked Gentile Christians to observe certain articles of the law, for the sake of the scruples of their Jewish Christian brethren. So there was give and take by the two parties to the disagreement, and the result was unanimous. 'The Holy Spirit and we have agreed. . . .' (Acts 15:28) and the decision was met with rejoicing. Changed circumstances later (witnessed by the changes in later versions of the text of the decrees) rendered the compromise unnecessary. But the way to deal with such issues had been established.

The first thing that the apostles and elders did was talk the whole matter out openly. There was a genuine effort made at communication between the opposing sides, an attempt to understand the other's point of view. It is noticeable how the most controversial figure in the whole affair, the apostle Paul, remained in the background, saying very little. How unlike some of us who enjoy controversy! Personalities were kept out of things, so that the issues could be kept clear. Then, at the end, both sides made concessions on matters where no principle was at stake, and the chairman was able to bring the meeting to a conclusion without a vote. No group had 'won'. No group had 'lost'. All had found the will of God in this very delicate area, and integration was achieved. There are obvious lessons for us to learn from this story. If we are to achieve an integrated church, we must first be prepared to come out from our prepared position, from behind the barriers of prejudice, and listen to one another. For some of us, this will mean stopping talking! That is costly. And the whole process is difficult, because the barriers have been there for so long. But it is the first step. It is also part of what we mean by fellowship—an openness and willingness to share with one another. It is another aspect of the participation and acceptance we have considered earlier. It is also obvious that we need to learn the distinction between what is essential and what is peripheral, between principles we cannot compromise and secondary matters where, in love, we can make concessions. And we must be prepared to make the concessions that are necessary—in matters like forms of worship, dress in church, church government. This is the only way that integration can take place. Finally, perhaps, we need to revise our ideas of how decisions ought to be taken in the church. The pressure on our time results, in most church business meetings, in no real discussion, a hint from the chairman and a decision by majority vote, with the minority left feeling, somehow, wronged. In Methodism, at least, we may have the opportunity, now that we are restructured, to be more leisurely in the conduct of our business and to rely less on the vote and more on being led by the Spirit to a common mind on the issues we have to discuss. This in itself is a means of integrating the Christian family.

We began this section talking about change, not integration. But the necessity of integrating new groups into the church causes changes and the fear of change is the greatest obstacle to integration. If we learn how to integrate new groups, we shall find we have nothing to fear from the changes this will entail. We ought, indeed, to expect change, if we are Christians. Although God does not change (James 1:17) he is always doing 'new things' (Revelation 21:5; Isaiah 43:19). Becoming a Christian is being made new (2 Corinthians 5:17) and being a Christian is a process of being changed (2 Corinthians 3:18). Change is not necessarily decay. Things will never again be what they used to be. But if we are ourselves constantly open to being changed and renewed by the changeless God of change, we have nothing to fear.

Study and Discussion

Do you feel that all the groups in your church are fully integrated into its life? If not, what changes may be necessary to bring about integration? How could such changes be introduced so that people's fears of change would be minimized?

What changes have taken place in the last thirty years in the life of the community in which your church is placed, and among its members? Have any changes taken place in the life of the church to meet changed times and circumstances? Should any further changes be made?

Gavin Reid, *The Gagging of God* (Hodder & Stoughton)

Clive Porthouse (ed.), *Ministry in the Seventies* (Falcon Books)

Christian Unity

A better heading might be 'Christian Disunity'. We are all too well aware of the divided state of the church for any statistics to be necessary. If anything the divisions are increasing, rather than decreasing. For every movement to unite churches there are movements to continue one or both of the uniting groups as a separate body. Issues from the Anglican-Methodist Scheme down to the trivia of local church affairs have all been found sufficient reason for some Methodists to go elsewhere, or to form their own group. The sects (Christian and near Christian) and cults flourish. House churches proliferate. The mobility of the population, especially of young people, adds to the confusion. At an institution like Cliff College, where it has always been required of prospective students that they be church members, it has become increasingly difficult, in some cases, to apply a uniform standard to all applicants. Among the people of God there seems to be a general splitting up, a loss of the common ground that once held us together, and a regrouping farther apart.

It is no comfort to note that this phenomenon does not appear to be confined to the church. The general election of February 1974 suggested that a similar centrifugal force is at work in the political sphere. At the time of the October election the two main parties seemed further away from each other than ever, despite calls to unite to face the crisis which confronted the nation. The minority parties gained some support, and the political scene was darkened by clashes between extremists of right and left like that in Red Lion Square. It is but a small step from Red Lion Square to some of the verbal clashes that have appeared in recent months in the Christian press.

It seems that we are finding it increasingly difficult to get along with one another, especially with those who think differently from ourselves. Pluralism is not the great uniting force some have hailed it as—even though we may be forced to live with it. At the moment, however, we are moving slowly but steadily apart. The situation is reminiscent of C. S. Lewis's description of hell (*The Great Divorce*, Fontana). Its inhabitants first settled together round the bus stop at which they had alighted. But differences drove them one by one to move out into the suburbs until everyone was living in complete isolation from everyone else. It may perhaps be that our present situation is demonically rather than divinely inspired. One can well imagine Wormwood and Screwtape rubbing their hands delightedly!

Is there then no remedy? We have already pointed to the direction in which it lies—in a proper discrimination between what is essential and what is peripheral. This is the remedy Paul prescribed for the church in Corinth in a similar situation (Part 2, p. 58). We are saved by belonging to Christ, not to Paul or Apollos or Peter. Christ was crucified for us and it was into Christ that we were baptized. The agent, by whom the news of salvation came and by whom the baptism was carried out, is unimportant. There is a warning here to all of us who think of ourselves first as Methodists or Anglicans or Baptists and only secondarily as Christians. There is a lesson, too, for those of us who are preachers and teachers. The fundamental Christian creed is that Jesus is Lord. This is what does not change. How it is to be worked out in terms of worship, church buildings, church government will vary from place to place and from generation to generation. But how often do we insist on clinging to symbols that are outdated, and thus miss the essential message that they represent? Our buildings and clerical dress are largely empty symbols today, and only confirm to people at large their impression that the church is irrelevant. Our insistence that we cannot preach the gospel (itself a meaningless phrase to many) without using words like 'sin', 'sinner', 'repent', 'faith', ignores the fact that these words in themselves are empty symbols: printing on paper or sounds on our lips. They have no significance or meaning apart from the truth that lies behind them. The essential good news that we want to preach is that truth. It does not matter, therefore, what words we use to represent it. Once people have come to understand the truth we can begin to show them the relevance and meaning of the traditional symbols. But we must not mistake symbols for meaning. So many of our divisions and disagreements turn on the use of words, or other symbols, and are based on the erroneous assumption that there is only one symbol for every aspect of truth. But just as Paul reminded the Corinthians that there were many ways to Christ, but only one Saviour, so we must remember that there are many symbols although only one truth. We must learn to discriminate between the essential and the secondary.

Discussion and Study

What are the essentials of the Christian faith, which distinguish a Christian from a non-Christian? Are there any ways in which we are today in danger of making a belief in secondary matters a condition of belonging to the church? Have we done so in the past?

What is the real meaning conveyed by such traditional Christian words as 'sin', 'repentance', 'faith', 'justification', 'sanctification'? How can these truths be expressed today for people for whom the traditional language is meaningless?

Malcolm Furness, *Vital Doctrines of the Christian Faith* (Lutterworth)

I. Howard Marshall, *Christian Beliefs* (I.V.P.)

Owen Brandon, *Christianity From Within* (Hodder & Stoughton)

Communicating the Essentials

The communicating of the truth of the gospel was a central concern of the New Testament church. The church, indeed, was called into being specifically in order to communicate the good news of the kingdom (Mark 3:14; Part 1, p. 41). The literary form 'gospel' was created as part of the work of conveying that good news. Many of the New Testament letters were written in order to correct false emphases or downright distortions of the good news which the young church was seeking to communicate (cf. Part 2, pp. 68–70). As we saw in Part 2, the whole of 1 Corinthians 15 was taken up by Paul with an explanation of the Christian teaching about the resurrection. The essential truth had failed to come over at Corinth and so further clarification was needed.

We may feel in our highly educated age that it is understandable that scarcely literate slaves, peasants, fishermen and shopkeepers would have difficulties wrestling with the good news as presented to them by such an intellectual giant as Paul. But before we pat ourselves on the back and congratulate ourselves on our understanding of what Christianity is really about, we do well to consider some of the facts presented by the various surveys on religious belief conducted in this country in recent years. David Martin summarizes these (*A Sociology of Religion in Britain*, chapter 3) and draws a picture of ignorance and confusion, even among the regular churchgoers. My own experience with the students entering Cliff College confirms this impression. Not only among those who have no long-standing church background, but even sometimes amongst sons and daughters of the clergy there is surprising ignorance of the Bible and confusion on Christian basics. It is scarcely surprising, therefore, that Christian young people can be so easily induced to break away from 'unsound' denominations to join 'pure' house fellowships (see p. 8) whose purity may consist only in allegiance to the highly individualistic (not to say unorthodox) theology of the forceful personality who happens to be the leader of the group.

That such breakaways frequently take place in the name of the Holy Spirit only serves to bring the charismatic movement into disrepute and to make people in the main-stream churches more suspicious of any serious attempts to work out in practice the doctrine of the church as the body of Christ. Disunity has its origin in ignorance as a result of our failure to communicate the essentials of the truth.

It follows from all this that those of us who are ministers and preachers must take seriously our responsibility to teach the people in our congregations Sunday by Sunday. The traditional pattern of preaching to the 'saints' in the morning and 'sinners' in the evening will not do when so many come only once. Nor will it do for us to say that our congregations cannot take solid Christian teaching. Kenneth Waights, when he was President of the Conference, wrote (*Methodist Recorder*, 28 October 1971), 'I have been received by large audiences and congregations. Nobody has been honest about numbers in Methodism—even the Founder himself made some extraordinary claims for his listening members, so I will avoid statistics. Whatever be the numbers, the people are hungry to hear the reality of the gospel. They are tired of spiritual entertainment. Life is too hard for spiritual hors d'oeuvres. The need is for the true food—the Bread of Life.' Some of us need, perhaps, to ask ourselves searching questions about our sermons.

The Rev. Howard Belben suggests the following 'Ten Tests for a Sermon' (*CEIM Newsletter*, No. 13

p. 3, also available as a cassette from Cliff College, Calver, Sheffield S30 1XG):

1. Is it in every sense a Christian sermon?
2. Will all the congregation understand it?
3. Would everyone be able to say at the end what the message had been?
4. Is it biblical, and is the exegesis sound?
5. Is the text easily remembered, and worth remembering, in itself?
6. Is it earthed in the life situation of the hearers?
7. Does it contain a strong teaching element?
8. Does it avoid overlapping my other sermons too much?
9. Is it the right length?
10. Does it appeal to conscience, mind and will?

In short, will our sermons challenge people and lead them on to new visions of God's possibilities for them? Or will they leave them sitting where they are, confirmed in their present attitudes and content with or, worse still, resigned to their present situations?

As we consider our task as Christian teachers, we could do worse than adopt David Sheppard's Six Aims of Education (*Built As A City*, p. 133): 'I hope that education will offer . . .: equipment with basic tools and techniques to go on learning; a vision of greatness leading to ideals of personal and corporate behaviour; awareness of the whole community and the wider world; confidence in the gifts they possess and ambition to use them for the good of the community; respect for reasoned authority; creative discontent with society as it is and experiences of bringing about changes for good.'

It will not be enough, however, for us to put our preaching under the microscope, essential though that may be. Preaching and teaching are part of a process of communication, which must be two-way. We need, therefore, to look at both ends of the process, for our sermons will not communicate until they are earthed in the daily experience of the members of the congregation. It is here that the lay preacher has the advantage over the minister. The laymen is at his office desk, or his bench, or in the classroom, and has no excuse, therefore, for failing to make his sermons relevant to real life. The minister, by the nature of his job, has to work harder at this question of relevance. He may have to learn that he alone cannot interpret Biblical truth for his congregation. Bruce Kaye, in an article, 'The Hermeneutical Church' (*Christian Weekly Newspapers*, 28 May 1971), argued that what every church needs is group Bible interpretation: the minister and laymen working together to find the meaning of God's word for their situation. 'The meeting together of Christians is vital to the achievement of the hermeneutical task for two basic reasons. First, because the understanding of any situation is improved by working together with other people on the situation or problem in which they are trying to discover and do the will of God ... The second reason is theological and is that the New Testament clearly indicates that gifts are distributed with considerable variety within the congregation. ... On the one hand the group will

need to have an on-going theological education programme, and on the other hand it will need to have a
programme which involves consideration of particular
issues in which individual members of the group have
to act as Christians.' Here, perhaps, is a task for the
new consultation groups which have been set up by
our restructuring. But, if the minister cannot work
without the layman, he has one advantage over his
lay colleague. He has the theological training and the
possibility of giving a Biblical perspective on daily
life, precisely because he stands outside it. Lay
preacher and minister, therefore, need one another.
The one with his experience of life and the other with
his Biblical expertise can together work at preaching
and teaching which will be both relevant and
prophetic. There will be effective communication because the preaching will have worthwhile content and
will be earthed in real life.

The preaching may, of course, only communicate
effectively to those who are used to listening to
preaching. Could it be that the advocates of the aboli-
tion of the sermon are right? Ought we to replace it
with discussion or dialogue or drama in order to gain
the ear of those who will not come to listen to plain
preaching? The answer to these questions depends on
who we want to come. If it is the intellectual minority
whose daily bread and butter is earned by discussion
and dialogue in boardroom battles, fair enough. But
this group is surely not our major problem. More important is the question of how we can communicate

to the unchurched masses of ordinary working people. Here both ministers and lay preachers may find themselves needing the assistance of a third group, the visual artists and designers. For we live in an age when the majority of the population is accustomed to learning facts from pictures and diagrams, rather than from statements. The sales figures of the national daily newspapers should have alerted us to the fact that more people read the highly illustrated tabloids than the large format papers with their long columns of unbroken print. Even in the tabloid, many people turn first to the cartoons, and it has been said that the print is only for the benefit of those who cannot understand the pictures. In the light of all this, if we wish to be a church that communicates effectively, we need to ask ourselves how we can visualize as much as possible of what we want to say. This may involve no more than putting up the headlines of our sermon as we go along, on a blackboard or flannelgraph. It may involve more sophisticated techniques with slides or overhead projectors. But, if we are taking communication seriously, all these things must be considered. Of course, the first objection is, 'I haven't the time', or 'I don't know how to'. One church found a way around this problem by making use of the (uncommitted) parents of Sunday School scholars. From their records of contacts they knew that these parents had the necessary skills, so they were invited to provide the visual aids week by week: the preacher described what was wanted, the church supplied the materials and the professional artists did the work. What is more, they started coming to church to see their handiwork in use, and so came eventually to faith in Christ themselves. Both Old and New Testaments abound in material which lends itself to visual presentation. If we refuse to make the effort, do we not raise questions about the seriousness of our concern to get our message across?

Discussion and Study

Discuss the total Christian education programme of your church in the light of David Sheppard's 'Six Aims for Education'. Are you satisfied with the standard of preaching and teaching in your church? If so, why? If not, suggest ways in which it could be improved.

Are there any people in your church with skills that could be used to make its communication of the gospel more effective? Are those skills being used?

What opportunities are there for preachers, ministers and laymen, to meet for serious Bible study along the lines suggested by Bruce Kaye? Discuss the value of creating such opportunities.

Michael Botting, *Teaching the Families* (Falcon Books)

John Wood, *The Preacher's Workshop* (Tyndale Press)

Colin Morris, *The Word and the Words* (Epworth)

Capon and Webley, *Loud and Clear* (Falcon Books)

P. Liddelow, *Know How to use Audio and Visual Aids* (Scripture Union)

108

Conflict or Contraction

It is at this point, perhaps, that we notice the chief difference between the New Testament church and the church in the twentieth century. The first Christians were passionately concerned to communicate the good news they had received, even when to do so brought them into conflict with the authorities. When they were commanded not to preach, Peter and John replied to the Sanhedrin, 'You yourselves judge which is right in God's sight, to obey you or to obey God. For we cannot stop speaking of what we ourselves have seen and heard' (Acts 4:19–20). Persecution became the spring-board for the wider spread of the good news (Acts 8:1, 4). The motive force for this widespread missionary activity, not just by the apostles but by all the Christians, seems to have come from within. It was the result of Pentecost, repeated in individuals and groups of believers, in accordance with Peter's promise (Acts 2:38–39), rather than the result of obedience to Christ's command. It was a spontaneous explosion resulting from a deep spiritual experience, whether corporate or private, and it led to the remarkable growth of the church, both geographically and numerically.

But it was not growth without growing pains. As we saw in Part 2, almost every extension of the church's frontiers was accompanied by tension and beset with problems. How to keep pace with rapid change? How to integrate pagans into a hitherto Jewish based society? How adequately to supervise the proliferating congregations? We have seen how some of the early churches (e.g. in Asia; see Part 2 pp. 74–76) gave up in face of these problems. Most New Testament Christians, however, rejoiced in the fact that God was alive and active, and set about tackling each fresh crisis as it arose. The church was not a comfortable place of retreat: it was a spiritual battleground, and being a Christian was harder work than not being a Christian.

When we look at the church of today, and honestly examine our own attitudes, we find a marked contrast. For many people, the church is a refuge from change and tension. Some of our hymns encourage this attitude, for example, John Greenleaf Whittier's,

> 'Drop Thy still dews of quietness,
>   Till all our strivings cease;
> Take from our souls the strain and stress,
> And let our ordered lives confess
>   The beauty of Thy peace.'
>   (*Methodist Hymn Book* 669)

One particular brand of evangelical piety has also offered a calm and a peace which do not seem related to the New Testament picture of the Christian life. A representative is Thomas Cook's *New Testament Holiness*: 'Nothing for a moment broke the serenity of Christ's life on earth. Tempest and tumult met Him everywhere, until outwardly His life was one of the most troubled that was ever lived. *But the inner life was a sea of glass. The highest tranquility, serenity, and peace of mind were always there*' (pp. 125–6; my italics). That, according to Cook, is the goal for the

110

Christian. It is of course true that the good news offers us peace, but it also promises us persecution and battle. It is also true, however, that, when we hear the language of a Whittier or a Cook, we hear more than they intended, and extend their overemphasized description of inner peace with God to the whole of life. We would like to lead peaceful, untroubled lives. There is enough trouble and strife in our work, our families, the world in which we live. So we shut our ears to the challenge of the gospel and withdraw into the Christian ghetto, to enjoy the peace and comfort offered by patterns of worship that have not changed for decades (or even longer) and sermons which encourage our other-worldly piety. We have opted, in other words, not for the New Testament pattern of conflict with expansion, but for comfort with contraction.

That the church in this country is contracting it is difficult to deny. Statistics have been telling us this for many years. Much more serious is the fact that, despite various calls to mission and evangelism, little or nothing has been done to stop the decline. We remain in a situation of contraction. We may perhaps be able to pinpoint two reasons. The first is structural. *The Times* of 4 November 1974 carried a report on a study conducted for the General Synod of the Church of England by the Urban Church Project. While the conclusions apply primarily to the Church of England, they cannot be ignored by the other denominations. The author, the Rev. D. Wasdell, finds that the present form of church organization is self-limiting. 'Statistically, there is an upper limit of congregational size, beyond which a congregation is unlikely to grow, except spasmodically as a result of short-term enthusiasm, after which it will revert to its previous size and perhaps even contract as a result of disillusionment.' The congregational limit is calculated at about 175 for a parish of 2,000 or more with only one clergyman. If you increase the number of clergy, you get some increase in congregation and, of course, large parishes with large staffs can hold large congregations. The overall impression of this report is that too much emphasis is placed in the churches on the role of the clergy in missionary activity. This, of course, is not new. What is new is the searching analysis of the church's structures and the conclusion that something far more radical than has hitherto been attempted will be needed before churches are structured for mission. In particular, the nature and size of the basic unit of the local church (the Anglican parish or the Methodist society), a pattern with which all Christians in this country have been familiar for generations, is called in question. Moreover, 'it is clear that the only way to break out of the self-limiting church structure is to increase lay mobilization in mission and to minimize the lapse rate. In other words, we need structures of high motivation, maturation, education, training and pastoral care, together with a deep sense of belonging.'

This conclusion leads us to the second reason for our acceptance of the contraction situation. It is the poverty of our own spiritual experience. It is significant that the mission of the New Testament church did not grow out of a response to a call, or by the application of new techniques. It sprang directly from the experience of the Christians involved, whether they were apostles like Peter and John, or unnamed believers who preached the good news wherever they happened to be. Whoever they were, they could not stop speaking about what they had seen and heard. How different it is with most of us, who are reluctant in conversation even to admit to going to church, let alone to talk about deeper spiritual realities! But is it not just here that the ineffectiveness of calls to mission or evangelism lies? Our Christian experience plays so insignificant a role in our life as a whole, that the call to share it does not strike any chord of response. The Denver Call for a year of world-wide evangelism in Methodism was launched by the then President of the Conference, Harry Morton, in a challenging message which put the emphasis at this point of personal commitment to and experience of God. But this is an aspect of mission which, sadly, has been much overlooked since. The Denver Call has resulted, for example, in Cliff College students being in demand to conduct campaigns and missions in different parts of the country. But the teams sometimes find that what was intended as a mission to those outside the church—evangelism in the proper sense of the word —has in fact to be a mission to the members. Their own spiritual experience is such that they would have little to offer any new Christians who might seek to join them as a result of a campaign. The life of the church needs to be renewed before the church can offer new life to others.

Once again, the responsibility for this state of affairs must be laid largely at the door of those of us who lead congregations as ministers and preachers. Like the false prophets of old, we have cried 'Peace! Peace!' where there is no peace (cf. Jeremiah 6:14). By our failure to teach we have encouraged a false complacency and acceptance of the present contracting situation. We have produced shallow disciples, untrained for mission and without the essential spiritual motivation. We have allowed a superficial idea of Christian fellowship to develop, instead of the sense of belonging which provides real peace and security, on the basis of which it is possible to go out into the world and take the good news to all people everywhere. And instead of tackling these issues at the local level, when our conscience has been pricked about the need to evangelize, we have called in the 'experts' and had a campaign in the hopes that the evangelist or the students would do for us what we should have been doing ourselves.

The picture is not all one sided, however. Most congregations have gratefully accepted the shortcomings of their leaders, because this has meant that fewer demands have been made of them. The member in the pew, therefore, also has some hard questions to face. Are we prepared for the cost and the responsibility of church membership? Are we willing to apply our Christian principles and live out our Christian experience in the totality of our daily routine? The

New Testament is unanimous that the life of the Christian disciple has to be lived in contact with the real world, and that no area of life is outside the scope of the gospel. In many spheres, therefore, there will be conflict. The experience of the church in Corinth, for example (see Part 2), makes it plain that to live as a Christian in the world is to invite tension. When your standards are different from those of people around you, what are you to do? When you believe in values opposed to those of the majority in society, are you to retreat into a 'holy huddle' or stand up to be counted? The New Testament Christians chose the way of discomfort and conflict—and the New Testament church was an expanding church. To use the word 'choose', perhaps, is to suggest it was deliberate policy. In fact they felt they had no option. Their experience of the love of God in Christ compelled them (see 2 Corinthians 5:14, *New English Bible*, 'The love of Christ leaves us no choice'). For whatever reasons, we have chosen the way of comfort and 'peace', and must now face realistically that this is the way of contraction and decline.

Ultimately we have to face, therefore, the question posed at the very beginning of this study: What is the church? If it is to be a place of refuge from tension and conflict, very well. We must reconcile ourselves to the fact that it is doomed to extinction. This was the fate awaiting the churches in Asia (Revelation, chapters 2 and 3) who chose the easy way of conformity to this world, of lukewarmness and complacency. The visitor to modern Turkey will find no trace of those seven congregations. But if we are to be true to the Biblical picture of the church, we have to give a more ambiguous answer. The church is certainly a place of refuge. But it is refuge in God, and God is engaged in a conflict with all the powers of evil in the world. If we take refuge in God we commit ourselves to his conflict also. If we are his church, his people, we are front line fighters, mobilized for mission in the world.

Discussion and Study
What can we do within the structures of our local church to produce among lay people:

> high motivation
> maturity
> training for mission
> a deep sense of belonging?

How can we improve the pastoral care of our members and adherents?

What steps could we take to produce an increasingly deep spiritual experience among our members?

Michael Green, *Evangelism in the Early Church* (Hodder & Stoughton)

Paul Little, *How to Give Away Your Faith* (I.V.P.)

Keith Miller, *The Taste of New Wine* (Word Books)

Keith Miller, *A Second Touch* (Word Books)

This Age and the Age to Come
It seems, then, that we are reaching the point at

which we can give some explanation of the apparent
contradiction between the New Testament teaching
about the church and the New Testament picture of
the church. We have seen that the two are in tension.
This tension is, however, only part of a more deep-
rooted tension which underlies the whole of the New
Testament world view. It manifests itself not only in
the different aspects of the church we have been
considering, but also in Jesus' teaching about the
Kingdom and in the New Testament view of what a
Christian is and will be. It is perhaps most easily
understood when looked at from the standpoint of
time.

The New Testament speaks of two ages, this age,
and the age to come. In the older English versions
these are often called this world and the world to
come, but this is misleading. The use of 'world' in
English suggests a spatial concept and has led to
'worldliness' being thought of as certain kinds of
attitudes or acts associated with certain places or
things; for example, gambling, drinking, dancing or
acting. If you avoid going to Bingo halls, pubs, dance
halls or theatres you will avoid worldliness and lead a
spiritual life. There is a New Testament word for
world in the sense of the material, tangible universe
in which we live. That word is *kosmos*. It is the word
used for world, mankind, in John 3:16, 'God loved
the world so much. . . .' It frequently has a good or a
neutral meaning.

The word we are considering, however, is *aiōn*. It
is the word used by Paul in, for example, Romans

117

12:1–2, 'Don't let the world around you squeeze you into its own mould' (J. B. Phillips). Despite the use of 'world', however, by the translators of almost all the English versions, *aiōn* is not primarily a spatial concept. It is a word for a period of time, an age. It occurs, for example, in Matthew 28:20 and is there translated 'age' in *Today's English Version*. This age is the age in which the first Christians were called to live. They could not escape its influence merely by changing location, any more than we can. The only way to escape from this world, this age (*aiōn*), is to leave this world (*kosmos*), that is, to die! Paul has to remind his Corinthian friends of this (1 Corinthians 5:10). This age is characterized by evil and by opposition to God, God's standards and God's people (hence the warning of Romans 12:1–2). It has its own god, who prevents people receiving the good news about Jesus Christ (2 Corinthians 4:4), and who is usually identified with the devil (cf. Ephesians 2:2). However, this age, so the New Testament implies, is coming to an end (cf. Matthew 12:32; 13:39, 40, 49, etc.) and is contrasted with the age to come. The contrast is explicit in Mark 10:30 and Ephesians 1:21, but implicit in many of the other passages which refer to *this* age.

We should not think, however, of the two ages as running consecutively: this age stopping at some date in the future and the age to come taking over. The New Testament suggests, in several ways, that the two ages overlap. First, there is a reference in 1 Corinthians 10:11 to 'the end(s) of the ages'. This is frequently interpreted as meaning that Christians live at the time when the end is about to come (cf. T.E.V. translation). But J. Héring (*Commentary on 1 Corinthians*, Epworth Press), following Weiss, suggests the translation, 'who are at the meeting point of the (two) ages'. C. S. C. Williams (*Peake's Commentary*) takes the idea a stage further and writes, 'the present age and the coming age may be visualised as two separate "lengths" overlapping now for Christians'.

We find this idea of the overlapping of two ages when we look at the New Testament account of Jesus' teaching on the Kingdom. He taught us to pray for the future coming of the Kingdom (Matthew 6:10), but also suggested to his hearers that it had already come (Luke 17:21). A tension exists between these two aspects of the Kingdom, a tension which has been reflected in the different interpretations of the meaning of the Kingdom which scholars have given: sometimes this-worldly (the Kingdom has come), sometimes other-worldly (the Kingdom has yet to come). G. E. Ladd, in his book *Jesus and the Kingdom* (S.P.C.K., 1966), gives us a full discussion of the New Testament material and of the different interpretations, and concludes that the tension is one that we have to accept as an integral part of Jesus' teaching.

Similarly, if we turn to another concept frequently used by the New Testament writers in connection with Jesus' ministry, that of life, we find a tension between present and future. In John's gospel, but also in the synoptics (e.g. Mark 10:17) and regularly in the letters, Jesus is described as the bringer of life or eternal life. The adjective, eternal, is derived from the noun *aion*, and so conveys not only the idea of quantity (everlasting duration), but also of quality (the life of the age to come). But eternal life is not just for the future ('pie in the sky'). It is for the present, e.g. John 6:47, 'He who believes has eternal life'.

Finally, we find support for the idea of the overlapping of the two ages when we consider the use made of the title 'The Coming One' with reference to Jesus. It was used particularly by John the Baptist in the context of his expectation of the age of messianic salvation (Luke 3:15–17). Later, following his imprisonment, he sent disciples to Jesus asking, 'Are you the one John said was going to come, or should we expect someone else?' Jesus' reply was to let John's messengers see what he was doing: carrying out a ministry along the lines indicated in the prophecies of Isaiah, especially Isaiah 61:1–3 (cf. Luke 7:18–23), prophecies refering to 'the visitation of God to bring his people the messianic salvation' (Ladd, p. 161, cf. T. W. Manson, *The Sayings of Jesus*, pp. 66–70). When the messengers had left, Jesus went on to talk about the relative roles of himself and John the Baptist (Luke 7:24–35). The implication of his remarks was that the Coming One had already come, thus initiating the age to come, the area of messianic salvation. And yet in his parables and in his eschatological teaching (e.g. Matthew 24 and 25) Jesus speaks of a coming that is future, that has not yet taken place.

When we represent this diagramatically, following C. S. C. Williams' suggestion, we get something like this:

Christ's second coming: The end of this age.

This age, the kingdom of Satan, life in the flesh ↓

```
              ┌─────────────────────────────────────────┐
              │   The period between the ages,          │
              │   the period of the church.             │
              │                                         │
              └─────────────────────────────────────────┘
        ↑
```

Christ's first coming: Dawn of the age to come.

The age to come, the Kingdom, eternal life, the age of the Spirit, the messianic age.

And when we see it like this, we see the reason for the tensions which we experience as we live between the ages. For we live in a period of conflict. Christ has entered the territory of Satan (the god of this age) and inaugurated a rival kingdom with a rival worship (the Kingdom of God). What is more, he has inflicted a decisive defeat on all the powers of evil by his death and resurrection. In his own language, he has defeated the strong man and looted his property (Luke 11: 14–22). But, although the decisive victory has been won, although the new age has been inaugurated, the final victory lies in the future and this age still runs parallel to the age to come. Satan is defeated but still active, the more desperately, perhaps, because he knows he is defeated but will not admit it. There is nothing more dangerous than a cornered and wounded beast; cf. 1 Peter 5:8. On the other hand, we can see signs of God's Kingdom coming, but know very well that it has not yet fully come.

So we can look at all our experience in this period between the ages either from the side of this age or from that of the age to come. From the side of the age to come we see the church as God intends it to be, as we defined it at the end of Part 1: 'the people who belong to God through Jesus Christ and, in the power of the Holy Spirit, are doing his work wherever they are in the world'. From the side of this age we see the same church, but very much as a human institution, marked by all the cultural and racial divisions, and with all the personality clashes and weaknesses which characterize any other institution in this age.

Given, then, that the church is this kind of body— caught in the conflict between Christ and Satan, between the age to come and this age—is it surprising that we feel tensions? We see what we ought to be, indeed, what we feel we could be. But we are frustrated in our attempts to achieve it. Sometimes we seem to succeed, but the success is at best only temporary and we are soon back where we were before. In this situation we look for a scapegoat and find it more often than not in the institution, the church organization to which we belong. 'So', we argue, 'we must change (or leave) this organization in order to set up another in which we will not feel frustrated or disillusioned.' But what we do not realize is that, while we are living between the ages, wherever we are, there will be the pulls in the two directions. Had we read our New Testaments with our eyes open we should have realized this! What we have to learn is to live with the tensions, not escape them.

The situation is the same as that which faces us in our individual Christian life. We all know the story of the Salvation Army lass and the bishop. They met on a train, and he was in 'plain clothes'. Full of evangelical zeal she asked him, 'Are you saved?' He replied gravely, 'Do you mean, "Have I been saved?" "Am I being saved?" or "Will I be saved"?' In our traditional theological language, we say that we have been justified, are being sanctified and will be glorified. Christ's death on the cross has secured for us the forgiveness of our sins, we have been made God's friends, have been adopted into his family. But we know that the process is not yet complete. We reproduce the family likeness only imperfectly or intermittently. But we shall be like him. And yet, looking at it from the side of the age to come, from what Christ has achieved for us, the New Testament writers can say that we have already been raised with Christ to the heavenly places (e.g. Ephesians 2:6). Often, therefore, the New Testament encourages us to become what we already are in Christ, acknowledging that there is a tension within us between the actual and the potential. All this is part of living between the ages.

123

The question which faces us, therefore, is whether we are prepared to accept this situation. It is in part a theological question, a question about our understanding of the Kingdom and of God's purposes in history. It is a question about eschatology, about the end, the consummation of the Kingdom. For some this has become an area to be avoided, because of the weird speculations of the cults and cranks. For others, it is merely part of the first-century world view of the New Testament writers which does not seem to fit in with the scientific world view of twentieth-century man. But it is an area that must at least be examined afresh if we are taking seriously any discussion about the church.

More fundamentally, however, the question is psychological or emotional. The concept of living between the ages not only demands that we accept the idea of tensions within the church, but that we also accept the idea of tensions within ourselves. We have to learn to live without guilt with the fact that while, on the one hand, we belong to God in union with Christ Jesus (1 Corinthians 1:2), on the other we are men of the world, children in the Christian faith (1 Corinthians 3:1–5). We are not to be satisfied with this state of affairs—that was part of the trouble in Corinth. Our aim is always to become what we have been made in union with Christ. But we must learn to accept the reality of what we are now, not hiding it either from ourselves, or from one another, or from God. Discovering this reality may be a painful process: living with reality, once discovered, may not be comfortable either. But though we may readily accept, theologically, that we have to live between the ages, it is not enough to stop there. We must accept life between the ages emotionally too.

Discussion and Study

Examine afresh the teaching of the gospels on the Kingdom and of the letters on being a Christian. Set against this your own experience of tension or frustration in the church and in your personal Christian life. Put side by side like this, do the doctrine and the experience begin to make sense?

Form a group in which, in a spirit of acceptance of one another, you can share your feelings and experience honestly and openly.

How far is the church, in its preaching and fellowship, guilty of dishonesty and unreality by ignoring real tensions that lie below the surface? How can we bring them out into the open, so that we can support one another in them?

Stephen Travis, *The Jesus Hope* (Word Books)

Paul Tournier, *The Meaning of Persons* (S.C.M. Press)

Michael Wilcock, *I Saw Heaven Opened* (I.V.P.)

Conclusion

A New Perspective

WE STARTED with the frustrations and tensions which so many of us feel in the church today, and we have ended with them. But we have come to see them, I hope, from a new angle, in a new perspective, which comes with looking at the life of the church in the light of the future—not the future of the prophets of doom, but the Christian future.

In the *Church Missionary Society Newsletter* (February 1972) Canon John Taylor (now Bishop of Winchester) wrote: 'To look back is to invite death, whether for Lot's wife or for Orpheus. There is a profound difference between those who felt that the present is always being given to them by the past, stained and twisted by the past's mistakes, and those who feel that the present is flowing towards them, now, out of the future. The first is the more natural point of view, the second the more Christian. For it is the Resurrection of Jesus which made it possible for us to reverse, as it were, the flow of time. That event owed nothing to the past but came, new and unprecedented, out of the future. It broke the old entail of cause and effect and turned "events" into "advents".

'Anyone whose eyes have been opened by Christ should be able to live with this new look, knowing

127

that "now" is not an end product but a new start. It was at the height of the Mau Mau revolution in Kenya that a young African, whose father had been murdered, said: "The real difference in being a Christian is simply this—we know we have a future." '

Theology of late has been turning more and more towards the future, to consider our Christian hope, the goal towards which God's purposes are moving (e.g. J. Moltmann, *The Theology of Hope*). That purpose is not yet to take us out of this world and out of the conflict with this age and all that it stands for. By all that God has done for us in the past he claims us for his Kingdom in the present. But we shall only be the people of the Kingdom, the church, the people who belong to God through Jesus Christ and, in the power of the Holy Spirit, are doing his work wherever they are, as we live in the light of God's future. It is only in the future, at the consummation, that present problems, frustrations and tensions will finally be swept away. But in the light of that future they can here and now be lived with, transcended and overcome.

'To him who is able to do so much more than we can ever ask for, or even think of, by means of the power working in us: to God be the glory in the church and in Christ Jesus, for all time, for ever and ever! Amen.'

Ephesians 3:20–21

THE 'WAR ON TERROR' AND AMERICAN FILM

Traditions in American Cinema
Series Editors Linda Badley and R. Barton Palmer

Titles in the series include:

The 'War on Terror' and American Film: 9/11 Frames Per Second
by Terence McSweeney

American Postfeminist Cinema: Women, Romance and Contemporary Culture
by Michele Schreiber

Forthcoming:
Film Noir
by Homer B. Pettey and R. Barton Palmer (eds)

www.euppublishing.com/series/tiac

THE 'WAR ON TERROR' AND AMERICAN FILM

9/11 Frames Per Second

Terence McSweeney

EDINBURGH
University Press

Dedicated to Olga

© Terence McSweeney, 2014

Edinburgh University Press Ltd
The Tun – Holyrood Road
12 (2f) Jackson's Entry
Edinburgh EH8 8PJ
www.euppublishing.com

Typeset in 10/12.5pt Sabon by
Servis Filmsetting Ltd, Stockport, Cheshire,
and printed and bound in Great Britain by
CPI Group (UK) Ltd, Croydon CR0 4YY

A CIP record for this book is available from the British Library

ISBN 978 0 7486 9309 2 (hardback)
ISBN 978 0 7486 9310 8 (webready PDF)

CONTENTS

ILLUSTRATIONS

ACKNOWLEDGEMENTS

A book of this size and scope would not have been possible without the help and support of a large number of people. I would like to thank the staff and students at Southampton Solent University for their support and encouragement, in particular Donna Peberdy, who has always been there for me, not just in this project, but throughout my career. I would also like to give credit to the staff at the British Film Institute Reuben Library and the often uncelebrated role they play in the formation of manuscripts like this one. I consider myself fortunate to have been a part of the team at Edinburgh University Press that includes Gillian Leslie, Jenny Peebles and many others. Many thanks also to the wonderful Dean Semler (ASC, ACS) who invited me to watch him work at Pinewood Studios in the autumn of 2012.

I would also like to thank several members of my family: my mother, who has always been a constant source of support; my father, who introduced me to film; and my two beloved sons, Harrison and Wyatt, who continue to help me rediscover it. Thank you also to my nephew, Lewis McSweeney-Terry, for his insights into a generation now very far removed from my own. Above all, my loving and always patient wife and proofreader, Olga McSweeney, who is the inspiration for so much that I do and who knows her way around commas better than anyone else I know.

INTRODUCTION

The films of a nation reflect its mentality in a more direct way than other artistic media ... What films reflect are not so much explicit credos as psychological dispositions – those deep layers of collective mentality which extend more or less below the dimension of consciousness.
Siegfried Kracauer, *From Caligari to Hitler: A Psychological History of the German Film*

While the precise definition of post-traumatic stress disorder [PTSD] is contested, most descriptions generally agree that there is a response, sometimes delayed, to an overwhelming event or events, which takes the form of repeated, intrusive hallucinations, dreams, thoughts, or behaviours stemming from the event, along with numbing that may have begun during or after the experience, and possibly also increased arousal to (and avoidance of) stimuli recalling the events.
Cathy Caruth, *Trauma: Explorations in Memory*

Every history really is two histories. There is the history of what actually happened, and there is the history of the perception of what happened. The first kind of history focuses on the facts and figures; the second concentrates on the images and words that define the framework within which those facts and figures make sense.
W. L. T. Mitchell, *Cloning Terror. The War of Images, 9/11 to the Present*

Just forty-eight hours after two hijacked jet airliners struck the World Trade Center (WTC) on 11 September 2001, the trailer for Sam Raimi's upcoming *Spider-Man* (2002) was hurriedly withdrawn from cinemas all across America. The short teaser, shot exclusively for marketing purposes and not consisting of scenes meant for inclusion in the final film, had shown the perpetrators of a smoothly orchestrated bank robbery fleeing in a helicopter through the skies of New York. Their celebrations, however, are abruptly brought to a halt, as somehow they become suspended precariously in mid-air, high above the city streets below. As the camera slowly pulls back, it reveals that they are actually caught in a giant spider's web, trapped between the imposing Twin Towers still dominating the Manhattan skyline. Not only was the trailer removed, but all of the film's posters in which the World Trade Center could be seen reflected in Spider-Man's eyes were also recalled. The distributor, Sony Pictures Entertainment, released a press statement, asserting,

> Due to the devastating events that took place yesterday [11 September 2001] and out of respect for those involved, Sony Pictures Entertainment is requesting that all *Spider-Man* teaser posters and trailers be taken down and returned to the studio. Our profound sympathy goes out to the friends and families of those who have lost loved ones in this tragedy. (Sony Pictures Entertainment cited in Grossberg 2001)

The removal of the trailer for *Spider-Man* proved to be the opening shot in a protracted cultural battleground that continued throughout the post-9/11 decade and beyond. In the years that followed, American cinema had a distinctly problematic relationship with the traumatic events of September 11th 2001. As we will see, 9/11 was paradoxically both erased from the cinema screens and returned to in film after film. Some commentators expressed the view that the gratuitously violent spectacles that had characterised American cinema in the preceding decades, films that revelled in outrageous displays of wanton destruction and flagrant loss of human life, would lose their audiences after 9/11. In November 2001 Peter Matthews, in an article entitled 'Aftermath', predicted that such films would become forgotten relics of a bygone era.

> For a long time to come, there will be little appetite for the entertainment staples of bombs, plane crashes and burning buildings, since to enjoy such kinetic excitement affectlessly seems a violation of the dead. Temporarily, the whole idea of entertainment becomes obscene – or at least those versions that offer clean, airbrushed carnage for fun and profit. Escapism in all its cultural forms might be said to rest finally on a denial of the fact of death. Now it cannot be denied, and that circumstance threatened to shake popular cinema to its roots. (Matthews 2001: 20)

Even studio executives articulated similar concerns. Amy Pascal of Columbia Pictures remarked: 'The world changed profoundly on Tuesday [11 September 2001] and clearly some of what we thought was entertaining yesterday isn't today' (cited in Eller 2001: A36). Mark Slouka in the article 'A year later: Notes of America's intimations of mortality' worried that art and, in particular, popular film, might become irrelevant after 9/11, echoing Theodore Adorno's widely quoted contention in his 'Cultural criticism and society' that 'after Auschwitz, to write a poem is barbaric' (1967: 34). How could American cinema possibly continue to function *semper idem* after America at large had been subjected to such a 'monstrous dose of reality' (Sontag 2001)?

As a direct result of these uncertainties a whole succession of films were re-shot, re-edited or had their release dates delayed by worried film studios, eager not to offend the public in the national outbreak of grief and mourning following 9/11. Barry Sonnenfeld's *Big Trouble* (2002), for example, had been set for release just a few weeks after 9/11 but was pushed back due to its portrayal of a nuclear device being smuggled onto a hijacked plane, a plot point that went from being a potentially humorous episode to a cultural taboo overnight. *The Sum of All Fears* (2002) had its Islamic jihadist terrorists changed to the less contentious neo-Nazis. *Bad Company* (2002) was delayed because of a key scene featuring a bomb primed and ready to explode in Grand Central Terminal, and *The Time Machine* (2002) suffered the same fate due to its depiction of a meteor attack on New York being seen as bearing too close a resemblance to the disturbing imagery of 9/11. The innocuous Gwyneth Paltrow romantic comedy *View from the Top* (2003) about a small-town woman and her dreams to become a flight attendant had its release date postponed because it was felt inappropriate to joke about air cabin crews in the aftermath of 9/11. *Buffalo Soldiers* (2003), which had been filmed before 9/11, saw itself delayed and then criticised for its satirical depiction of the US Army at a time when America was seen to be at war. The director of the film, Gregor Jordan, stated,

> The film was finished before 9/11 and then got its premiere screening at the Toronto [International] Film Festival on September the 8th 2001. It was received very well and a bidding war amongst distributors ensued. We finally closed a deal with Miramax (Harvey Weinstein) on the night of September the 10th. So the timing for a film about drug fucked American soldiers was probably not so good. The film was delayed in the US and then when it was released it was effectively flushed down the toilet – put out on two screens with no marketing spend. (Jordan 2012)[1]

Images of the Twin Towers, which Terry Smith described as 'key symbols within the later twentieth century society of spectacle, icons with the capacity to stand for crucial values' (2003: 37), became the focus of much heated debate. Should they be shown on-screen or removed for fear of offending the grieving families of the victims of 9/11 and America as a whole? They were airbrushed out of the frivolous *Zoolander* released on 28 September 2001, as they were from *Serendipity* (2001), *Sidewalks of New York* (2001) and *People I Know* (2002).[2] However, Steven Spielberg, Cameron Crowe and Martin Scorsese decided to retain them in *A.I. Artificial Intelligence* (2001), *Vanilla Sky* (2001) and *Gangs of New York* (2002). This discourse reached its zenith in May 2002 when an online appeal entitled 'Rename [*The Lord of the Rings:*] *The Two Towers* [2002] to something less offensive petition' gained some momentum in the media. The creator of that appeal, Kevin Klerck, wrote,

> Those of us who have seen *The Lord of the Rings: The Fellowship of the Ring* [2002] know what an amazing director Peter Jackson is. When I learned that there apparently was to be a sequel, I was overjoyed. However, Peter Jackson has decided to tastelessly name the sequel *The Two Towers*. The title is clearly meant to refer to the attacks on the World Trade Center. In this post-September 11 world, it is unforgiveable that this should be allowed to happen. The idea is both offensive and morally repugnant. Hopefully, when Peter Jackson and, more importantly, New Line Cinema see the number of signatures on this petition, the title will be changed to something a little more sensitive. (Klerck cited in Refrag 2002)

Of course, the novel was published in 1954, and Klerck was well aware of this, yet more than a thousand people signed the document. It was later revealed to be a hoax, although many of the responses to it were genuine. Klerck's act was a satirical one aimed at the hypocrisy of studios altering their films because of 9/11. He noted, 'It's my way of pointing out how ridiculous people have gotten post-9/11' (cited in Refrag 2002).

In the days after the attacks, the media frequently framed its coverage of the tragic events as a series of personal narratives, focusing on tales of loss, heroism and redemption, removing any discussion of why the attacks may have been perpetrated in the first place. George W. Bush's assertion that America was targeted for attack because it is 'the brightest beacon for freedom and opportunity in the world' became echoed in editorials all across the country (Bush 2001). This rhetorical self-aggrandisement set a tone that was continued for the rest of the administration and would be mirrored in many American films produced in the subsequent decade. It was one that identified a stark divide between good and evil, with America uncritically on the side of the former. Anyone who sought to challenge this binary rhetoric or place the attacks in some sort of historical or socio-political context was vociferously criticised by the mainstream media and condemned as unpatriotic. Susan

Sontag was labelled a 'terrorist sympathiser' for suggesting that 'a few threads of historical awareness might help us understand what has just happened, and what may continue to happen' (Sontag 2001). One of the foremost commentators on American foreign policy, Noam Chomsky, was attacked by an army of critics led by Christopher Hitchens who called him one of those liberals who sought 'to "rationalise" the aggression of September 11' (Hitchens 2001). When Bill Maher pondered on air (on *Politically Incorrect* on ABC on 17 September 2001) whether the terrorists should be called cowards or not, his show was discontinued shortly after. Maher dared to suggest, 'We have been the cowards, lobbing cruise missiles from 2,000 miles away. That's cowardly. Staying in the airplane when it hits the building, say what you want about it, it's not cowardly' (cited in Goldberg 2002: 77). Jean Baudrillard found himself denounced for arguing that 9/11 was a manifestation of our collective fantasies, citing Hollywood's perpetual destruction of American iconic landmarks as evidence that bore witness to it. He stated, 'The fact that we have dreamt of this event, that everyone without exception has dreamt of it – because no one can avoid dreaming of the destruction of any power that has become hegemonic to this degree – is unacceptable to the Western moral conscience' (2003: 5).

Russ Feingold, one of only twenty-three US senators to vote against the Iraq War Resolution in 2002 (formally the Authorization for Use of Military Force Against Iraq Resolution of 2002) that gave the go-ahead to President George W. Bush to use military force against Iraq, argued that in the immediate aftermath of 9/11 it became almost impossible for anyone to disagree with the policies of the Bush administration without being labelled unpatriotic.

> If Afghanistan and Iraq were linked in the fight against terrorism, then anyone who questioned the Iraq intervention was somehow questioning the pursuit of Osama Bin Laden, which of course no one was doing. It then followed, of course, that if you did not support every military venture of the Bush administration you did not really support the troops and your patriotism was doubtful. (Feingold 2012: 92)

Given this tempestuous climate, it came as no surprise that the American film industry was initially reluctant to produce films about 9/11 and the war on terror, and it was not until four years later in 2005 that the first theatrically released features about the conflict emerged. Yet no one could deny that there was something resolutely cinematic about the image of the two planes striking the Twin Towers on 11 September 2001. A familiar refrain by those who witnessed the events, whether first-hand or through the television screen, was, 'It's like a movie.' The British journalist David Usborne, in New York at the time of the attacks, insisted that the dust appeared from nowhere, like a huge tidal wave, barrelling down the canyons of the financial district . . . The police went berserk, we went berserk, just running, running for our lives . . . we were in a scene from a Schwarzenegger film . . . thousands of Hollywood extras, mostly in suits for the office, with handbags and briefcases, just tearing through the streets of the city. Every few seconds we would snatch a look behind us. (Usborne cited in Summers and Swann 2012: 70)

Subsequently many concurred that 'no national event has been more cinematic, and more suited to cinematic representation, than the planes flying into the World Trade Center' (Cousins 2007: 63). The reason why these tragic images seemed so cinematic was because such destruction of iconic monuments had been a staple of American popular cinema for decades. Science-fiction and disaster films had regularly perpetrated great crimes on prominent American landmarks in the guise of earthquakes, tidal waves, bombs, meteors and even alien invasions. The World Trade Center had undeniably become a synecdochal image of New York and even America for many cinema-goers around the globe: its construction can be seen in the backgrounds of *The French Connection* (1971) (see Figure 1) and *Klute* (1971); throughout the 1970s it was both immortalised in black and white in Woody Allen's iconic *Manhattan* (1979) and climbed by a giant ape in *King Kong* (1976); in the 1980s it provided a backdrop for narratives about the American experience in *Coming to America* (1988), *Bright Lights, Big City* (1988) and *New York Stories* (1989), and even featured on the poster for all three of these films; and in the 1990s it was memorably destroyed in *Independence Day* (1996), *Deep Impact* (1998) and *Armageddon* (1998) (see Figure 2). When the actual images of the destruction of the Twin Towers on September 11th 2001 were repeated on television day after day as if on a loop, we *knew* that they were real, but they *felt* like some special effect conjured up by the tech wizards at Industrial Light & Magic (ILM) (see Figure 3).

J. Hoberman was certainly not alone when he described how the experience of 9/11 only made sense to him through the medium of film: 'the *déjà vu* of crowds fleeing Godzilla through Lower Manhattan canyons, the wondrously exploding skyscrapers and bellicose rhetoric of *Independence Day*, the romantic pathos of *Titanic* [1997], the wounded innocence of *Pearl Harbor* [2001], the cosmic insanity of *Deep Impact*, the sense of a world directed by Roland Emmerich for the benefit of Rupert Murdoch' (Hoberman 2007).[3] Roland Emmerich, the director of *Independence Day* before 9/11 and *The Day After Tomorrow* (2004) and *2012* (2009) after, one of Hollywood's foremost purveyors of what has become known as 'disaster porn', went even further, expressing concern that Hollywood's obsession with death and destruction might have even inspired the terrorists (see Corliss 2009). Emmerich stated, 'A lot of people mentioned

Figure 1   The construction of the World Trade Center seen in *The French Connection* (1971).

Figure 2   The reason why the tragic images of 9/11 seemed 'just like a movie' was because the destruction of iconic monuments had been a staple of American popular cinema for decades in blockbusters like *Armageddon* (1998).

Independence Day because of the images of destruction, which disturbed me a little. I had this feeling that there is some terrorist watching my movie in some cave and saying he should do it like the aliens' (cited in Epstein n.d.s.). The maverick auteur Robert Altman contentiously concurred, 'Nobody would have thought to commit an atrocity like that unless they'd seen it in a movie. How dare we continue to show this kind of mass destruction in movies? I just believe we created this atmosphere and taught them how to do it' (cited in Hoberman 2007).

Figure 3   When the actual images of the destruction of the Twin Towers on 11
            September 2001 were repeated on television as if on a loop, audiences *knew*
            that they were real, but they *felt* like some special effect conjured up by the
            tech wizards at Industrial Light & Magic (ILM). Permission granted by
            Brian Boyd, Sr ©.

Popular cinema is often derided with the epithet 'it's only a movie', but *The 'War on Terror' and American Film: 9/11 Frames per Second* argues that there is no more potent cultural artefact than popular film. Where should one turn to for a more resonant and compelling cultural barometer than cinema? Which artefacts are able to reveal more to us about the turbulent social and political climate of, for example, 1970s America than visceral cinematic texts like *Dirty Harry* (1971), *Chinatown* (1974), *The Texas Chainsaw Massacre* (1974), *Taxi Driver* (1976), *Invasion of the Body Snatchers* (1978) or *Apocalypse Now* (1979)? Regardless of their political perspective or genre, they *are* the 1970s. We do not take them at face value, nor do we naively view them as simply reflecting the cultures in which they were made; instead, we regard them as dynamic texts, almost living time capsules of the era, rife with the discontinuity and ambiguity that characterised the decade. In them the fears and the anxieties of the times are projected on the screen for all to see. Correspondingly, a study of American cinema in the years that followed 9/11, eight years of which were during the presidency of George W. Bush, similarly reveals its trends: a period that came to be largely defined by the war on terror. Simply put, American film in the first decade of the new millennium became a war of representation and nothing less than 'the locus for America's negotiation of September 11 and its aftermath' (Schopp and Hill 2009: 13).

The central question explored in *The 'War on Terror' and American Film: 9/11 Frames per Second* is in what way was American cinema able to uniquely reflect, interpret and even influence the cultural discourse of the era? This book examines the shifting coordinates of post-9/11 film to reveal a body of work that functions not as a simplistic cinema of escapism, as we are often led to believe, but as a collection of visceral responses to the era, whether consciously designed by the filmmakers to be so or not. In this way a substantial number of the films that emerged from the United States in the decade after 9/11 can be quite clearly seen as a reaction to the 'cultural trauma' of 9/11 and the war on terror. In *Cultural Trauma and Collective Identity* (2005) Jeffrey C. Alexander argues that a 'cultural trauma' occurs 'when members of a collectivity feel they have been subjected to a horrendous event that leaves indelible marks upon their group consciousness, marking their memories forever and changing their identity in fundamental and irrevocable ways' (2004: 1). Alexander asserts, as many writers on trauma have, that the origin of a trauma is not located within the event itself, but in its aftermath: how it is culturally represented and how it comes to be understood by the society that it affected. In this definition, a trauma is never a 'natural' event, even if it appears to be so; traumas emerge as a process that is constructed at both cultural and symbolic levels: 'historically made, not born' (Smelser 2004: 37). Just as in September 1945 the holocaust had not yet become 'the Holocaust', we must ask ourselves how and when did the events of 11 September 2001 become '9/11'? The role of the media is instrumental in this process of enculturation and frames how a society develops an understanding of a traumatic event, not just for the generation that experienced it, but just as significantly, for those generations that follow.

Even if the traumatic event is highly contested, a master narrative soon emerges, which is a collective understanding of the incident. It is one that appears on the surface to be ideologically neutral, but is, in actual fact, highly politicised. This master narrative is an almost sacred one; so central does it become to national identity that denial of it is considered an act of solecism bordering on the heretical. The master narrative of the cultural trauma of 9/11 was quickly formed within a matter of days of the attacks and saw itself perpetuated in a variety of media forms over the ensuing decade. Its understanding of 9/11 is of a heinous and unprovoked attack on a virtuous and blameless nation, an attack that was impossible to anticipate and that brought about a reluctant 'end of innocence' for the United States. Thus, according to this logic, America's responses to 9/11, whatever they may be, were legitimised due to the nature of the crime that had been perpetrated against it by individuals who, rather than being soldiers or criminals, were examples of Immanuel Kant's 'radical evil' (2009: 42).

As the years progressed, American film played a central role in propagating this hegemonic narrative, both in explicit (yet fictionalised) depictions of 9/11 and the war on terror and in allegorical accounts. Indeed, many of the cinematic texts explored in this book offer variations of this template and seek to reify 9/11 as an almost ahistorical moment.

- In Oliver Stone's *World Trade Center* (2006) the unprovoked and monstrous terrorist attacks on September 11th 2001 emerge from nowhere on an unsuspecting population. In the few days portrayed, New York is a vividly realised community, populated by those who put aside their differences to come together in response to a great national tragedy. The film concludes with the rescue of two of those trapped under the rubble of the Twin Towers offering a cathartic sense of closure to a highly traumatic event. One of them, John McLoughlin (Nicolas Cage), suggests that the harrowing experience they have all shared offers a lesson not just to America but to the whole world. He states, '9/11 showed us what human beings are capable of. The evil, yeah, sure. But it also brought out the goodness we forgot could exist. People taking care of each other for no other reason than it was the right thing to do.' (See *War of the Worlds* (2005), *United 93* (2006) and *Act of Valour* (2012) for other films of this pattern.)
- *Extremely Loud and Incredibly Close* (2011), based on the novel of the same name by Jonathan Safran Foer, views 9/11 through the eyes

of a young boy, Oskar Schell, who loses his beloved father Thomas (Tom Hanks) in the destruction of the Twin Towers. Oskar finds a key left behind by his father that he presumes is part of one of their elaborate puzzle games and embarks on a search across New York looking for clues as to what the key fits, during which he meets many people whose lives have been similarly touched by the tragedy. (See *Remember Me* (2010), *Julie & Julia* (2009) and *Reign Over Me* (2007) for other films of this pattern.)

- Even films that portray the broader events of the war on terror adopted a comparable perspective. Kathryn Bigelow's Academy Award-winning combat drama *The Hurt Locker* (2008) (explored in more detail in Chapter 2) is a visceral recreation of the tour of duty of a team of bomb disposal experts stationed in Iraq. The film provides an intimate and moving insight into the traumatic experiences of American soldiers at war. (See *Zero Dark Thirty* (2012), *Lone Survivor* (2013), *Stop-Loss* (2008) and *Body of Lies* (2008) for other films of this pattern.)

These three films and the greater part of post-9/11 American cinema embody the collective understanding of 9/11 and the war on terror as a resounding cultural trauma. Outwardly, they appear to be ideologically neutral dramatisations of historical events, however, whether they portray a family worrying about the fate of their loved ones at Ground Zero, a young boy grieving over the loss of his father or an American soldier just trying to do his job and make a difference to the people of Iraq, they reproduce an uncritical and unreflective narrative of American victimisation, a pronounced disconnection from the complexities of the geopolitical arena, and, in some cases, even an elaborate erasure of political and historical context.

- *World Trade Center* offers up an idealised, almost prelapsarian New York, populated by martyrs in place of human beings in the working-class everymen heroes of John McLoughlin and Will Jimeno (Michael Peña) and their adoring, grieving families anxiously waiting for their return. While the film purports to be apolitical and 'not about the motives of the terrorists, or who the terrorists were, or the politics of 9/11 in any way' (Oliver Stone cited in Abramowitz 2005b: E1), by depoliticising one of the defining events of the new millennium it manages to bind itself to quasi-religious ideas about US exceptionalism and recreate the Bush administration's interpretations of 9/11 as an event without historical context (outside of the attack on Pearl Harbor on 7 December 1941). The defining character of its redemptory narrative is not McLoughlin or Jimeno, but Marine

Sergeant Dave Karnes (Michael Shannon) who is called, as if by God, to the ruins of the World Trade Center. Karnes says, 'God gave me a gift – to be able to help people, to defend our country. I feel him calling on me now for this mission.' The film's postscript reveals that after 9/11 Karnes volunteered for service in Iraq: 'We are going to need some good men out there to avenge this.' The centralisation of this character led B. Ruby Rich to suggest that the film 'seems explicitly to endorse the bloodthirsty revenge that has soiled America's hands ever since, positioning a Marine, an agent of war, as the film's savior' (Rich 2006: 18).[4]

- The same is true for the portentous and manipulative *Extremely Loud and Incredibly Close* that presents Tom Hanks's Thomas Schell as an idealised father who becomes a surrogate for the sense of security lost to the whole of America on 9/11. The character of Oskar is a shrewdly calculated exercise in contrived sentimentality, half Kevin McCallister from *Home Alone* (1990) and half Raymond Babbitt from *Rain Man* (1988). The film was described by Andrea Peyser (2012), writing for the *New York Post*, as '9/11 porn' for its cynical appropriation of cultural trauma and its use of the unidentified 'falling man' re-envisioned as Tom Hanks tumbling from the Twin Towers in slow motion towards the camera and his death (see Figure 4). In doing so the film turns an image that Mark D. Thompson called 'perhaps the most powerful image of despair at the beginning of the twenty-first century' (2008: 62–3) into an aesthetised and opportunistic pop culture moment designed to give a lacklustre tear-jerker emotional resonance.

- Despite its undeniably visceral re-creation of deployment in Iraq, *The Hurt Locker* rewrites the war as an exclusively humanitarian enterprise with the United States cast as the saviour of innocents and its soldiers as victims rather than as the perpetrators of acts of violence (see Figure 5). This highly subjective perspective led Mamoon Alabassi to assert that the film should not be truly considered an Iraq War film at all, as it 'does not really address the Iraq war, the reasons for the presence of the US squad or even the bombs they are supposed to defuse, and most importantly it ignores the feelings of the Iraqis' (2010).

These narratives share a conspicuous detachment from disconcerting questions of politics, history and causality. While it may seem unjustified to single out individual films for failing to provide socio-political context, when they are a part of such an overwhelming pattern such a criticism becomes not only pertinent, but entirely necessary. These films insulate audiences by providing them

Figure 4   Tom Hanks as the 'falling man' in *Extremely Loud and Incredibly Close* (2011), a film that was described by one critic as '9/11 porn' (Peyser 2012).

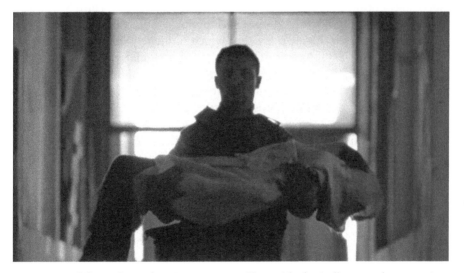

Figure 5   While on the surface it appears to offer an ideologically neutral perspective on the Iraq War, *The Hurt Locker* (2008) envisions the conflict as a distinctly humanitarian enterprise with the United States cast as the saviour of innocents and its soldiers as victims rather than as the perpetrators of acts of violence.

with a cinema of proselytisation, one that is content to perpetuate the master narrative of 9/11 instead of asking troubling questions, as Anthony Summers and Robbyn Swann did in their book *The Eleventh Day*: 'Did the story begin twenty years ago during the Gulf War, when a great American army was installed in Saudi Arabia, a land sacred to Muslims? Did it begin in 1948, when the United States recognised the declaration of a Jewish state to be known as

Israel? Or on the day in 1938 when Americans discovered in Saudi Arabia one of the largest reserves of oil on the planet?' (2012: 11). Or Chalmers Johnson in his *Blowback: The Costs and Consequences of American Empire* (2000), who did not predict the events of 9/11, but did correctly anticipate that '[w]orld politics in the 21st century will in all likelihood be driven primarily by the blowback from the second half of the twentieth century – that is, from the unintended consequences of the Cold War and the crucial American decision to maintain a Cold War posture in a post Cold War world' (229).

This is not to say that 9/11 was not a terrible tragedy, for it most certainly was, yet in the subjective narratives of victimisation and the quasi-mythological approaches to the event that emerged from the American film industry, much is lost. Slavoj Žižek acutely emphasised the moral quandary faced by those in the West about their reactions to 9/11 when he pointed out: 'If we simply, only and unconditionally condemn it, we simply appear to endorse the blatantly ideological position of American innocence under attack by Third World Evil; if we draw attention to the deeper sociopolitical causes of Arab extremism, we simply appear to blame the victim which ultimately got what it deserved' (2012: 62). Post-9/11 American cinema faced a similar predicament and in the overwhelming majority of cases it chose the first option. Yet Žižek went on to offer a third path: 'The only possible solution here is to reject this very opposition and to adopt both positions simultaneously' (2013: 62). However, this 'third-way' was an approach very rarely adopted by American society or film in the ensuing decade. In these cinematic texts we are able to observe a marked hierarchy of identity and subjectivity on display, where Western (most often American) experiences, almost without exception, are prioritised and portrayed as of greater worth than the experiences of non-Westerners, a vivid embodiment of what Judith Butler described as the 'precarious life' of non-Western people in her book *Precarious Life: The Powers of Mourning and Violence* (2004). Therefore, while Dori Laub (2003) quite rightly called 9/11 'an event without a voice', in the decade after 9/11 American cinema provided it with one that played a substantial role in how 9/11 and the war on terror came to be understood by the public at large.

While some have argued that 'popular culture, or at least the part of it transmitted by the mass media, tends to "go in one eye and out the other", and that most individual television programmes, movies, and magazines are ephemeral for most people' (Gans 1999: xiii), writers like Siegfried Kracauer (1947), Robin Wood (1986) and Anton Kaes (2011) as well as many others have persuasively demonstrated how national cinemas are frequently able to function as a materialisation of ideological currents and are particularly revealing of the political and social climate in which the films are made. In his ground-breaking work *From Caligari to Hitler: A Psychological History of the German Film* (1947), Siegfried Kracauer argued that German films from the Weimar period were able to reflect national consciousness in compelling ways, depicting a deep fear of chaos and a passionate desire for order that would see Germany embrace the National Socialist German Workers' Party (NSDAP) and Adolf Hitler's promise of a restoration of national dignity and pride. Kracauer was criticised at the time (and it is contentious even today) for so explicitly linking popular culture with political ideology, but Anton Kaes's remarkable *Shell Shock Cinema: Weimar Culture and the Wounds of War* (2011), despite a different theoretical approach, advocates something similar. Kaes sees films of the same period, not as a foreshadowing of the rise of fascism, but as rather a personification of the traumatic aftermath of Germany's bitter defeat in World War One. Even though their conclusions are different, theirs is a shared contention that films are able to function as a potent embodiment of national discourse and what Kaes calls the 'historical unconscious' (2011: 2). Therefore, just as Kracuaer and Kaes read films of the Weimar era like *The Cabinet of Dr. Caligari* (1920), *Nosferatu* (1922) and *Metropolis* (1927) as literal manifestations of the ideological currents of Weimar era Germany, *The 'War on Terror' and American Film: 9/11 Frames per Second* proposes that new millennial American film is able to articulate the divisive discourse of American identity in the immediate post-9/11 years. The films that emerged in America at this time are far from a homogenous entity: they are rife with the paradoxes and contradictions that characterised the decade. However, they often embodied a powerful fear of an Other that frequently happened to be Muslim or Arabic (e.g. *300* (2006), *Act of Valour* (2012) and *Taken* (2008)), or from elsewhere (Eastern Europe in *Hostel* (2005), *Chernobyl Diaries* (2012) and *Transsiberian* (2008), or Mexico in *Man on Fire* (2004), *How I Spent my Summer Vacation* (2012) and *Conspiracy* (2008)); they expressed anxieties about the effects of the USA Patriot Act and the expanding powers of executive authority (e.g. *Children of Men* (2006) and *Source Code* (2011)); they explored the ramifications of the collusion between corporations and politics (e.g. *The Manchurian Candidate* (2004) and *Michael Clayton* (2007)); they explored fears of an environmental apocalypse (e.g. *The Day after Tomorrow* and *The Road* (2009)); they debated the morality of torture (e.g. *Rendition* (2007), *Mission: Impossible III* (2006) and *The Dark Knight*); and they both embraced U.S. unilateralism (e.g. *The Expendables* (2010) and *The Kingdom* (2007) and criticised it (e.g. *Syriana* (2005) and *Green Zone* (2010)). In doing so, they provide a revealing interrogation of the fears and fantasies of the United States and an agreement with Kracauer's assertion that 'the evolution of the films of a nation are fully understandable only in relation to the actual psychological pattern of this nation' (1947: 5). At the very least, as Mark Lacey suggested, American cinema became 'a space where "commonsense" ideas about global politics and history are (re)-produced and where stories about what is acceptable behaviour from states and individuals are naturalised and legitimated' (2003: 614).

Trauma theorists like Cathy Caruth have long suggested that a certain amount of time is required between when traumatic events occur and when those traumatised by those events can begin to come to terms with their experiences. She suggests that 'a traumatic event cannot be "assimilated" or experienced fully at the time, but only belatedly, in its repeated *possession* of the one who experiences it' (1995: 4). In one of the epigraphs that open this book Caruth argues that this delayed response to trauma 'takes the form of repeated, intrusive hallucinations, dreams, thoughts, or behaviours stemming from the event' (4), a more fitting description of American cinema in the post-9/11 years would be hard to find. In fact, in the first decade of the new millennium, 9/11 and the war on terror became a symbolic touchstone for American film with a sense of repetition bordering on the compulsive, as the injunction to 'Never Forget' seemed wholeheartedly embraced by the American film industry. September 11th 2001 permeates the screen in detailed re-creations of its mise en scène: the dust, debris, panic and falling buildings of films like *Cloverfield* (2008), *2012* or *Man of Steel* (2013) or the crashing planes of *Knowing* (2009), *Vanishing on 7th Street* (2010) and *War of the Worlds* (see Figures 6 and 7).[5] These visual motifs were returned to again and again in films that frequently refused to directly acknowledge 9/11, but self-consciously evoked it almost obsessively, their fictional re-creations becoming almost palimpsetic images, with September 11th lingering, still visible beneath the surface. In this way post-9/11 films become inextricably bound to 9/11 and the war on terror almost regardless of genre.

- When aliens attack New Jersey in Steven Spielberg's *War of the Worlds*, a young girl asks her father, 'Is it the terrorists?' as she has been raised to view terrorism as an omnipresent fear in her life. From its ash and dust-covered victims, to its sustained depiction of destruction and devastation shot with a deliberate eye on 9/11 iconography, *War of the Worlds* uncomfortably 'remakes' 9/11 through the prism of a science-fiction blockbuster. As Spielberg himself stated, 'I think 9/11 reinformed everything I'm putting into [the film] ... We now know what it feels like to be terrorised' (cited in Abramowitz 2005a: E26).
- When her daughter is abducted in *Gone Baby Gone* (2007), Helene McCready (Amy Ryan) cries out in anguish, 'I feel like 9/11,' as the only comparable impactful event of her life were the terrorist attacks in 2001.
- In the interplanetary colonial narrative of *Avatar* (2009) the aggressively militaristic Colonel Miles Quaritch (Stephen Lang) seeks to secure the precious resource known as Unobtanium found on the distant planet of Pandora. He targets the indigenous Na'vi who

refuse to move from their homeland with a war cry of, 'Our only security lies in pre-emptive attack. We will fight terror with terror!' The connections to the war in Iraq are so pronounced that some suggested, 'Ironically, and contrary to official film labelling, for many Iraqis *Avatar* is seen as the most accurate Iraq movie so far' (Alabassi 2010).

- In George Romero's apocalyptic zombie film *Land of the Dead* (2005), a Cheney-esque figure, Gerald Kaufman (Dennis Hopper), presides over the only secure location left, evocatively named Fiddler's Green in one of many references that connected America to the decline of the Roman Empire throughout the decade. Denied entry to the tower, one of Kaufman's erstwhile employees targets the building with a Weapon of Mass Destruction (WMD) and the threat, 'I'm gonna do a jihad on his ass.' In response, Kaufman offers the deadpan retort, 'We don't negotiate with terrorists,' – a line that was echoed in several films throughout the era from *Tropic Thunder* (2008) to *Olympus has Fallen* (2013).
- In *Shortbus* (2006) when the drag artist Justin Bond is asked why so many young people flooded into New York in the 2000s, he answers, '9/11. It's the only thing *real* that's ever happened to them' (emphasis in original) (see Figures 6 and 7).

The 'War on Terror' and American Film: 9/11 Frames per Second postulates that American cinema's obsession with 9/11 and the war on terror evokes the Freudian notion of 'repetition compulsion' in which the traumatised individual is repeatedly compelled to return to the traumatic event in an attempt to come to terms with the trauma. Undoubtedly we saw this as early as the morning of 11 September 2001 itself, with the continuous loop of the planes striking the Twin Towers broadcast on television, which was then repeated for days and days almost without end, as stunned Americans tried to reconcile themselves to the fact that they had been attacked on their own soil for the first time since 1812. Despite the aversion to recreating the events of 9/11 directly on-screen, there was a compulsive re-enactment of 9/11 and the war on terror in various forms in American cinema in film after film. In many of these fictionalisations, which range from explicit dramatisations to allegorical accounts, the events of 9/11 are rewritten in order for the subject to retroactively gain mastery over the trauma: whether the attacks are portrayed as entirely unprovoked, emphasising the wholesome righteousness of the United States (e.g. *World Trade Center, United 93, Taken* and *Cloverfield*), or American soldiers are depicted as the undeserving victims of the war both during their time in combat and after (e.g. *The Hurt Locker* and *Stop-Loss*), or the conflict is rewritten to portray the United States as some sort of plucky underdog fighting and

Figure 6   *Man of Steel* (2013) was one of many films to symbolically re-enact the collapse of the Twin Towers. It was an image that became a recurring visual motif in American cinema after 9/11.

Figure 7   Distraught crowds fleeing the wall of dust after the collapse of the World Trade Center. Permission granted by Denver Casado ©.

winning a war against incredible odds (e.g. *Transformers* (2007), *Act of Valour* and *Zero Dark Thirty*). Even the only two direct accounts of September 11th to be released at the cinema, *United 93* and *World Trade Center*, chose to focus on the heroism and redemption of the day rather than on the great loss of life or the historico-political context of the attacks. The more provocative films that emerged from America in the post-9/11 decade, many of which are also studied in this book, replay the war on terror but in very different ways. Some do provide a striking sense of context, often through a process of reverse focalisation and an attempt to deconstruct the quasi-mythological approach to dramatisations of trauma, revenge and justice that emerged after 9/11, even daring to suggest that the United States may not be such a bastion of moral clarity as President George W. Bush would have had us believe.

It is important to register that this sense of national trauma was not just an abstract one; several studies showed that after 9/11 many Americans suffered from recognisable symptoms of post-traumatic stress disorder. Herscher and Pascual (2008) recorded that as many as 7.5 per cent of New Yorkers and 20 per cent of those who were near the World Trade Center when it collapsed declared themselves to be suffering from psychological conditions typically observed in soldiers returning from combat zones. Of course, one cannot directly equate the experiences of those who witnessed the events through their television screens to those who found themselves directly affected by the attacks. However, there certainly was a sense that many were profoundly moved and shocked by the events of 9/11, and a body of literature strongly supports the assertion that one does not need to experience a harrowing event directly in order to be traumatised by it and that vicarious trauma is a very real phenomenon (see Sontag 1977; Hirsch 2004). The genocide of the Native American Indians, the forced enslavement of Africans and the Holocaust are still profoundly affectual traumas that resonate throughout the generations, impacting on the present even though the event was perpetrated decades or even centuries ago. In the case of 9/11, Robert Jay Lifton asserted, 'As a result of 9/11, all Americans shared a particular psychological experience. They became "survivors". A survivor is one who has encountered, been exposed to, or witnessed death and has remained alive' (2003: 93).

In the overwhelming presence of these rather uncritical adoptions of the hegemonic master narrative of 9/11, audiences were forced to turn to documentaries or allegorical depictions of the war on terror for more compelling and sustained reflections on the issues that arose in the wake of 9/11.[6] Such allegorical films can be found across a varied range of genres, many of which are explored in this book: in science-fiction (e.g. *Cloverfield* and *The Dark Knight* (2009)), in horror (e.g. *Hostel* (2005), *Land of the Dead* (2005) and *The Village* (2004)), even in historical drama (e.g. *There Will Be Blood* (2007), *Kingdom of Heaven* (2005) and *The Eagle* (2011)). All can be read, with varying degrees of success, allegorically, their texts redolent with themes that evoke America's turbulent political and social climate in the years since 2001. Despite the writings of many on the value of the allegorical mode (see Benjamin 1977; de Man 1979; Jameson 1981), a lingering distrust of allegory remains in favour of an uncritical acceptance of the ability of realism to render the world objectively. This book explores the value of allegory while at the same time offers analysis of several films that on the surface purport to offer 'realistic' and apolitical depictions of events (see Chapter 1 on *Zero Dark Thirty* and *United 93*). To disregard allegory is to refute its ability to articulate concerns, which, for a variety of reasons, become impossible to express explicitly in the climate in which they are made. The allegorical form often provided a valuable witness to ideological tension throughout the twentieth century: from Cold War fears of the House Committee on Un-American Activities (HUAC) and Soviet invasion (also fears of the intrusion of HUAC upon civil liberties in the same period) reproduced in the science-fiction films of the 1950s to what Douglas Pye described as the 'Vietnam Western', in films like *The Wild Bunch* (1969), *Little Big Man* (1970), *Soldier Blue* (1970) and *Ulzana's Raid* (1972), which were able to manifest the ideological ruptures of the 1960s and 1970s before they were dealt with explicitly by American cinema in films directly about the Vietnam War (see Pye 1981). Walter Benjamin (1977) suggested that allegory emerges most frequently in periods of crisis and uncertainty; correspondingly, it is no coincidence that some of the most powerful films to emerge from American cinema in the new millennium are allegorical texts. Allegorical interpretations of these films are present to those who wish to seek them out and absent to those who do not care to. Therefore, one can appreciate Christopher Nolan's *The Dark Knight* as a consummate example of the popular superhero genre, Paul Greengrass's *The Bourne Ultimatum* (2007) as a thrilling spy caper and a direct descendant of *Dr. No* (1962) and *Goldfinger* (1964), and Steven Spielberg's adaptation of *War of the Worlds* as a rip-roaring sci-fi adventure, or one can look beyond their spectacularly realised blockbuster patina to see how far the films may offer a discourse on the war on terror era.

One may argue that this displacement into allegory is evidence of the failure of American cinema to adequately confront the war on terror era directly, and this is certainly true. However, in displacement into allegory, American cinema often proves able to function as a site of sustained and interrogative discourse on the era. Furthermore, Claire Sisco King argues that allegory is actually an inherent part of the trauma process: 'Allegory itself might be understood as a post-traumatic form. Characterised by both repetition (a return to a prior tale) and displacement (a refusal to confront that past openly), allegory performs symptoms characteristic of trauma at the same time that it attempts to enact a sense of mastery' (2012: 128–9). Therefore, we can discern that the popular films American audiences embraced in these years, films like *Land of the Dead*, *Cloverfield* and *Taken*, texts that may seem on the surface like escapist fare, on closer inspection often reveal themselves to be vivid encapsulations of the prevailing ideological debates of the decade and able to, as Hillary Chute has argued about Art Spiegelman's remarkable comic book *In the Shadow of No Towers* (2004), 'unmoor the trauma of 9/11 from 2001' (2007: 240).

In his book *Shocking Representations: Historical Trauma, National Cinema and the Modern Horror Film* (2005), Adam Lowenstein traces how periods of historical and political turmoil, what he calls 'allegorical moments', often become manifested in film where one is able to observe 'a shocking collision of film, spectator, and history where registers of bodily space and historical time are disrupted, confronted and intertwined' (2). Therefore, in his chapter on American cinema of the 1970s he is able to consider a film like *The Last House on the Left* (1972), which ostensibly seems to have no explicit connection to the political realities of the 1970s, as a text able to 'confront the divisive historical trauma of the Vietnam era along the axes of political demonology that constitute it' (113). Similarly Robin Wood and Peter Lev perform a remarkable disquisition of 1970s' American cinema in their works *Hollywood from Vietnam to Reagan* (1986) and *American Films of the 1970s: Conflicting Visions* (2000). They are able to see genre films like *Dirty Harry* (1971), *The Poseidon Adventure* (1972), *Sisters* (1973), *Star Wars* (1977) and *Dawn of the Dead* (1978) not just as disposable entertainment, but as 'key moments of a debate on what America is and what America should be' (Lev 2000: 185). Thus Wood, Lowenstein and Lev join writers like Kracauer and Kaes in their desire to challenge preconceived assumptions that popular cinema is an inconsequential medium with little to say about the ideological realities in which it is produced.

Despite many concurring with Gene Seymour who wrote in the *Los Angeles Times* on 21 September 2001 that 'the whole notion of making spectacle out of mass destruction now seems trivial and indulgent at best, insensitive and tasteless at worst' (2001: F10), within a few brief years American cinema had not only begun to make films that evoked 9/11, but unquestionably subsumed one of the greatest traumatic events in the history of the United States into its narratives, re-packaged it and used it in order to sell movie tickets. In this understanding film becomes part of an extensive collection of ways in which 9/11 was constructed as a national trauma and then consumerised, as Dana Heller asserted in *The Selling of 9/11: How a National Tragedy became a Commodity* (2005). Heller charges that Americans 'both participated in, and bore witness to, a rapid transformation of the World Trade Center attacks into commodities aimed at repackaging turbulent and chaotic emotions, reducing them to pious, quasi-religious nationalism' (6). Like the 9/11 memorabilia that flooded the markets in the guise of memorial T-shirts, snow globes, poker chips and postcards, 9/11 was incorporated into American cinema as one of its fundamental narrative and visual tropes in the first decade of the new millennium. As Stephen Prince argues in his book *Firestorm: American Film in the Age of Terrorism* (2009), Hollywood 'seized upon terrorism as a kind of godsend, as a trope capable of animating popular genres for the foreseeable future because the issues posed by terrorism presently show no end coming' (306).

While I have used (and continue to use) the word 'reflect' to describe the relationship between film and society, one must recognise that the term is not entirely sufficient. Films do much more than reflect the cultures in which they are made; they instigate a dialogical relationship with them and even influence the public's perception of the events they portray. John Markert, writing in *Post-9/11 Cinema: Through a Lens Darkly* (2011), recognised the inadequacy of the word 'reflect' for its task, preferring to suggest that films may refract their cultural climate. Markert posits: 'Refraction theory suggests that recurring exposure to a film's message may not just reinforce existing attitudes and beliefs but shape them' (xx). Douglas Kellner chose to use the term 'transcode' with its pertinent contemporary technological associations to 'describe how specific political discourses [are] . . . translated, or encoded, into media texts' (2). This volume concurs with both Kellner and Markert and argues that American film in this decade did much more than just reproduce national fears and fantasies, but rather played a fundamental role in shaping them, restructuring how audiences viewed the war on terror. What is certain is that *every* film is ideological regardless of its genre or subject matter; as Comolli and Narboni memorably argued in 1976 '*every film is political*, inasmuch as it is determined by the ideology which produces it' (24). Thus, many films that on the surface seem to be disconnected from the contemporary political arena are, on close analysis, extremely politically charged texts. Films like *The Eagle, 300, Taken* and *Marvel Avengers Assemble* (US title: *The Avengers*) appear to be generic American films, variations on those that have been made for decades, and in one sense they are, but at the same time they are affective dramatisations of moods and debates inextricably intertwined with new millennial America. Whether they are reifications of the ideological myths underpinning the identity of the United States or deconstructions of them, each, without a doubt, are the bearers of ideology and our political unconscious, what Frederic Jameson called highly 'socially symbolic acts' (1981: 20), whether their writers and directors intended them to be or not.

These complicated relationships are at the centre of *The 'War on Terror' and American Film: 9/11 Frames per Second*, which asks the problematic question: 'What is a post-9/11 film?' Arguably, it is not enough to simply categorise all those films made after 11 September 2001 as post-9/11 films. While in a chronological sense they undoubtedly are, to truly be a post-9/11 film is to resonate with the decade. For every *Dark Knight, Avatar, Bourne Ultimatum,*

Hostel, War of the Worlds and *Cloverfield*, films this book contends positively resound with the tensions of the era, there are dozens of films made in the 2000s worthy of critical study but not included here by virtue of the fact that they are not regarded by the author as post-9/11 texts as the term has been defined. Of course, this selective process requires judgements to be made as to which films are and are not germane to debates about 9/11 and the war on terror. What makes Brian De Palma's *Redacted* (2007) more than just another war film? What makes Christopher Nolan's iteration of Batman (*Batman Begins* (2005)) distinctly post-9/11 in its presentation of a narrative that has existed in various forms since 1939? Or Steven Spielberg's adaptation of H. G. Wells's classic alien invasion novel *The War of the Worlds* (1898) intrinsically connected to the post-9/11 era? In the same way we must be careful not to see apophenic images of 9/11 and the war on terror everywhere, something I am quite sure this book will be accused of in any case. It is possible to get carried away, as Tom Pollard does several times in his otherwise astute *Hollywood 9/11: Superheroes, Supervillains, and Super Disasters* (2011), when he insists there is a 'subtle yet distinct post-9/11 message' (45) in Robert Zemeckis's *Beowulf* (2007), which apparently equates the three monsters Beowulf defeats with Bush's 'Axis of Evil' Iraq, North Korea and Iran. How can we discern what might be, as David Holloway calls them, 'modish' (2008: 75) references to the war on terror and what constitutes a text that has a discernible reciprocal relationship with the era? Is a science-fiction film like *Cloverfield* simply a new millennial reincarnation of a classic monster B movie, a cynical manipulation of traumatic imagery designed to make a quick buck at the box office, or a film that provides us with an opportunity to both vicariously experience and deconstruct the spectacle of 9/11 through the safety of an alien invasion film? Once again we see that the films American audiences escaped to in the post-9/11 era are not at all disconnected from the historical moment they are made in, but, on the contrary, are deeply immersed in it. Thus, it is readily apparent that the classification 'post-9/11' is inherently unstable in a variety of ways, as films like *28 Days Later* (2002), *The Bourne Identity* (2002) and *Minority Report* (2002) reveal. All three of these films were in production before, during and after 9/11, but have come to be regarded as key post-9/11 films. Of course, films are not closed texts and they certainly do not have one all-encompassing meaning. As Anton Kaes observes, 'Films are never organic, unified wholes carrying a single message. Rather, they are fractured entities that must be read, like products of the unconscious, by means of their omissions and silences' (2009: 5). It is this 'fractured' nature of post-9/11 cinema that makes it so compelling, and one of the central aims of this book is to open up these fractures to further debate, by suggesting how these texts might be connected to the era and asking the reader to decide for theirselves.

While American cinema certainly did not experience some sort of monolithic change in the post-9/11 era, it is clear that a sustained set of changes in emphasis can be observed, a foregrounding of tropes that may have been existent in prior decades but that were often presented rather differently after 9/11. We then must ask the question, 'What kind of films have emerged from the United States in the years since 9/11?' Did they endorse the Bush administration or were they critical of its policies? Matthew Alford's *Reel Power: Hollywood Cinema and American Supremacy* (2010) would have us believe that all Hollywood movies made for more than $30 million are inherently conservative and have been so for decades. Whereas Michael Medved in his *Hollywood against America* (1992) has argued the complete opposite – that Hollywood has historically functioned as a left-wing factory producing film after film that undermines core American values and traditions. Alford states, 'The most critical position Hollywood adopts on screen is to say that well-meaning forays into other countries backfire, with Americans – particularly those representatives of powerful institutions – being the significant victims of such innocent lapses' (3). There certainly is something to this, as we will see, as many American movies discussed in these pages wholeheartedly embraced the so-called Bush Doctrine and its values. However, America undeniably produced films across the broad political spectrum, many of which were vociferous in their criticism of the ideological path that the United States took at the beginning of the new millennium. Yet this book attempts to not adopt the style of Douglas Kellner's *Cinema Wars: Hollywood Film and Politics in the Bush-Cheney Era* (2010), which despite its frequent partisanship, is the defining book written on post-9/11 cinema to date. Kellner implicitly categorises American films made in this period as either progressive, and, therefore, worthwhile (i.e. those that criticise the Bush administration) or reactionary, and, therefore, contemptible (those that endorse the Bush administration). This book approaches post-9/11 American cinema in a less reductive fashion, regarding a film's value not exclusively by its political ideology. Thus, conservative films like *Taken, Act of Valour* and *300* are not failures just because of their reactionary perspectives, but are regarded as significant texts for what they are able to reveal to us about a nation at war.

The 'War on Terror' and American Film: 9/11 Frames per Second asks, 'What role does film play in the understanding of cultural and historical events?' One might argue that as memory of the original events fades, the importance of media representations of cultural traumas may even grow in significance when the trauma is transmitted from generation to generation, as in the process 'media and memory transform each other' (van Dijck 2008: 21). Marita Sturken asked,

> What does it mean for a *culture* to remember? The collective remembering of a specific culture can often appear similar to the memory of an individual – it provides cultural identity and gives a sense of the impor-

tance of the past. Yet the process of cultural memory is bound up in complex political stakes and meanings. It both defines a culture and is the means by which its divisions and conflicting agendas are revealed. To define a memory as cultural is, in effect, to enter into a debate about what memory means. (Sturken 1997: 1; emphasis in original)

Whether it is World War Two, the Holocaust, the Vietnam War or 9/11, cultural understandings of a historical event become highly mediated through their representation. Alison Landsberg argues that these media texts, rather than being inconsequential, actually function as powerful 'prosthetic memories' that are able to give us memories of events and experiences we did not gain through first-hand involvement. She states, 'What this suggests is that the experience within the movie theatre and the memories that the cinema affords – despite the fact that the spectator did not live through them – might be as significant in constructing, or deconstructing, the spectator's identity as any experience that s/he actually lived through' (1995: 180). Andrew Hoskins provides an insight into how this process may work in his *Televising War: From Vietnam to Iraq* (2004), describing images or sequences called 'media flash frames' that prove so potent that they can be later misremembered as memories rather than images on a screen. As evidence of this he cites a 1992 *The New York Times* (*NYT*)/CBS survey concerning the assassination of President John F. Kennedy that reveals that many years later a considerable number of people believed they had seen the Zapruder assassination footage live, whereas in truth it was only broadcast on television to the public for the first time in March 1975, some twelve years after the initial event. The same poll revealed that 75 per cent of those asked believed that there had been an official cover-up in the case. Is it a coincidence that Oliver Stone's visceral conspiracy drama *JFK* (1991) had been released the year before? (See D. Esch (1999).) Michael L. Kurtz suggested that 'with the exception of *Uncle Tom's Cabin* . . . *JFK* probably had a greater impact on public opinion than any other work of art in American history' (2000: 174). Films also function as 'media flash frames' and are capable of influencing our understanding of real-life events that are mediated through the screen. In her book, *Tangled Memories: The Vietnam War, the AIDS Epidemic, and the Politics of Remembering* (1997), Marita Sturken quotes a Vietnam veteran by the name of William Adams who stated, 'When *Platoon* [1986] was first released, a number of people asked me, "Was the war really like that?" I never found an answer . . . because what "really" happened is now so thoroughly mixed up in my mind with what has been said about what happened that the pure experience is no longer there' (cited in Sturken 1997: 121). If films can be so influential to those who encountered an event first-hand, what might the effects be on those who only ever experienced it vicariously through the media?

Landsberg's prosthetic memories can be progressive in that they 'enable individuals to have a personal connection to an event they did not live through, to see through another's eyes, they have the capacity to make possible alliances across racial, class and other chasms of difference' (Landsberg 2003: 156). According to this logic, the Deleuzian 'machinic eye' of the camera facilitates the experience of perspectives not of our own and thus offers the possibility of greater understanding and empathy. However, as the vast majority of popular media emerge from capitalist, corporate-owned enterprises, the texts that are produced and disseminated most widely frequently adopt and therefore inculcate dominant ideological perspectives. Thus, the collective memories that are memorialised and culturally transmitted transgenerationally are not the progressive ones that Landsberg describes, but hegemonic narratives that perpetuate the master narrative we have previously identified.

Just as significant as those events and perspectives that are selected for cultural memorialisation are those that are ignored and even erased from the framework of collective memories. This purging process proves not to be as uncomplicated as merely forgetting, which implies a passive experience; events, rather, become 'dis-remembered' in a procedure that requires a conscious effort on behalf of society and plays a fundamental role in the construction of national narratives. As Jeffrey Walsh and Alf Louvre observe in the introduction to *Tell Me Lies about Vietnam* (1988), popular culture representations of these narratives are vital, 'because the suppression of memory, of remembered alternatives, is one means by which dominant views win their power' (3). Witness how unpalatable historical truths are redacted from collective memory and rewritten as part of a larger national narrative: for example, how extirpative wars against Native American Indians have been rewritten to frame narratives of Manifest destiny and American exceptionalism; how the atrocities perpetrated by the Allied powers in World War Two like the fire bombings of Dresden (that killed more than 125,000 innocent civilians) and the atomic bombings of Hiroshima and Nagasaki (that killed more than 100,000 people) are marginalised or represented as both necessary and legitimate, while those analogous acts by the Axis powers are portrayed as monstrous crimes against humanity; how the war crimes committed by the American soldiers who liberated France have been elided in representations of the conflict that prefer to embrace the mythic narrative of 'the Greatest Generation', ignoring claims that about 14,000 rapes were committed from 1942 to 1945; how the issue of slavery has been erased from the Battle of the Alamo, an event that Richard R. Flores regards as one of the fundamental examples of a 'Master Symbol' in American identity (explored in Chapter 7).[7] These events are potent examples of what has been described as cognitive dissonance, moments in which a subject is confronted with destabilising challenges to their firmly held conceptions of identity or beliefs.[8] Franz Fanon in *Black Skin, White Mask* (1967) stated,

> Sometimes people hold a core belief that is very strong. When they are presented with evidence that works against this belief, the new evidence cannot be accepted. It would create a feeling that is extremely uncomfortable, called cognitive dissonance. And because it is so important to protect the core belief, they will rationalize, ignore and even deny anything that doesn't fit in with the core belief. (Fanon 1967: 194)

These events (and many others not mentioned here) do not correspond with the master narrative that the United States has created for itself and thus are purged from the majority of popular culture representations or rewritten to some more amenable form.[9]

So while 9/11 *was* a 'monstrous dose of reality' for America at large, it was a reality that the American public quickly withdrew from and a reality that rarely found its way on to the cinema screen. Perhaps the most 'Real' moment in the history of America was systematically 'de-realised', first by the media that immediately imposed a series of perspectives on it: whether by narrativising the effects (see King 2005) or redacting its horrors from the screens. Žižek wrote 'while the number of victims – 3,000 – is repeated all the time, it is surprising how little of the actual carnage we see – no dismembered bodies, no blood, no desperate faces of dying people . . . in clear contrast to reporting on Third World catastrophes, where the whole point is to produce a scoop of some gruesome detail' (2012: 15).

With this in mind it becomes of paramount importance to ask in what way American cinema of the post-9/11 era may in fact be a cinema of disrememberment and mythologisation? In what way is it a cinema that chooses to construct a particular narrative, one that, for whatever reason, refuses to confront disconcerting questions about 9/11 and the war on terror? By portraying 9/11 as the 'end of innocence', what George Will called 'America's holiday from history', American cinema perpetuates the myth that the United States had excluded itself from international events prior to 9/11 and was forced to enter into the geopolitical world against its will. Yet this narrative only works by disconnecting itself from the history of the twentieth century, by ignoring American interventions in places like Iran (1953), Guatemala (1954), Cuba (1961), the Dominican Republic (1965), Vietnam (1965) and Chile (1973), to name but a few. As Noam Chomsky reminds us, 'The U.S. is the only country that was condemned for international terrorism by the World Court and that rejected a Security Council resolution calling on states to observe international law' (2001: 44). By separating themselves from troubling questions of historical and political cause and effect, films like *World Trade Center, United 93* and *Zero Dark Thirty* perpetuate a hegemonic narrative that ironically *becomes* a reality to those who embrace it. John Shelton Lawrence and Robert Jewett, writing in 1988, labelled this concerted desire for narratives that favour moral binarism and fantasy over reality the 'American Monomyth' (2002). After 9/11 this theoretical paradigm was vocalised by none other than Karl Rove, the architect of Bush's *Top Gun* landing on the deck of the USS *Abraham Lincoln*, who saw an actual distinction between the 'reality-based community' and what the Bush administration was trying to achieve. Rove suggested:

> We're an empire now, and when we act, we create our own reality. And while you're studying that reality – judiciously, as you will – we'll act again, creating other new realities, which you can study too, and that's how things will sort out. We're history's actors ... and you, all of you, will be left to just study what we do. (Rove cited in Suskind 2004)

Yet this monomyth has troubling repercussions in the way that it retreats from reality. Lawrence and Jewett stated, 'It gives Americans a fantasy land without ambiguities to cloud the moral vision, where the evil empire of enemies is readily discernible, and where they can vicariously (through identification with the superhero) smite evil before it overtakes them' (2002: 47–8). This 'fantasy land' was strikingly recreated in American film of the new millennium, even in films that attempted to depict real-life events. This mythologisation process, which reached far beyond the cinema, had dangerous ramifications, as Susan Faludi asserted in *The Terror Dream: Fear and Fantasy in Post-9/11 America*: 'No doubt, the fantasy consoled many. But rather than make us any safer, it misled us into danger, damaging the very security the myth was supposed to bolster. There are consequences to living in a dream' (2007: 289). Faludi's criticism is of a culture that wholeheartedly refused to confront the troubling realities of 9/11, instead preferring platitudes and comforting narratives of legitimate revenge, retribution and moral superiority.

We can see a vivid manifestation of this dilemma realised in Ang Lee's 2012 adaptation of Yann Martel's *Life of Pi* (2001). After losing his family when the ship they are travelling in sinks, the eponymous Piscine 'Pi' Patel is cast adrift in a life boat. Understandably the event is a profoundly traumatic one for the young man, and the film proceeds to offer two rival narrative accounts of his experience, leaving the audience to decide for themselves which may be true. The first, which takes up the majority of the film's running time, is a fantastical tale of Pi's survival on board a small boat for 229 days with only an orang-utan, a hyena, a wounded zebra and a tiger for company. When the hyena is driven mad by hunger, it kills both the zebra and the orang-utan before being killed itself by the tiger. In this narrative Pi and the tiger, named Richard Parker, develop between each other a fragile sense of understanding, and they witness sights of tremendous natural beauty. When this account proves unsatisfactory for the ship's insurance agents who interview Pi after he is found alive, they demand to know 'what really happened'. In response Pi offers a second version of his experience that is a much more disturbing one and recounted only in an extended close-up of his anguished face. He tells them that, in actual fact, his mother had initially survived and made it onboard the life boat alongside the ship's cook and a wounded Buddhist sailor. When the cook is driven mad by hunger, he kills both the sailor and then Pi's mother (in order to use them as bait and then later to eat them himself), before he is killed by Pi in an act of revenge. Pi asks those listening to his story which of the two versions they prefer. It is clear he has chosen the first, even though he seems to acknowledge that this incredible tale is a fabrication and a self-defence mechanism that he has constructed in order to insulate himself from the awful reality of the traumatic deaths of his family (acts that find themselves strikingly replicated in allegory in the first version). Despite this acknowledge-ment, Pi's embrace of the 'fictional' narrative has enabled him to overcome his trauma and lead a happy and prosperous life with seemingly no adverse effects at all. Yet what are the implications of such a choice, whether conscious or otherwise, to willingly choose fantasy over reality? Is a repressed and rewrit-ten trauma truly a trauma that is 'worked through' or one that continues to be 'acted out' (LaCapra 2004: 11)? To 'act out' one's trauma is to fail to come to terms with it, to continually recreate the original traumatic moment without a sense of perspective or understanding. To 'work out' one's trauma is much more demanding; it is to confront and recognise it, and in the process to come to terms with it. Like Pi, America chose to construct a fantasy after 9/11, one that became subsumed in the majority of its cinematic narratives that were overwhelmingly dominated by conservative political paradigms. Certainly to provide a narrative to a trauma is to gain mastery over it; as Jay David Bolter suggested, 'an event that has not been narrativised constitutes a source of anxiety' (2005: 11). However, such a narrativisation is an inherently problematic process and one that is returned to in the course of The 'War on Terror' and American Film: 9/11 Frames per Second. The history of post-9/11 American cinema is the story of this narrativisation, frequently a disavowal of trauma and an embrace of the mythologisation that emerged in its place; it is a story of a cinema that largely preferred to 'print the legend' in the words of Maxwell Scott, the newspaperman at the conclusion of John Ford's The Man who Shot Liberty Valence (1962). Yet the trauma of 9/11 was too powerful to be entirely contained and disavowed. Just as a bright image continues to appear on one's retina long after the original has disappeared, 9/11 is the quin-tessential after-image of the new millennium and has continued to linger on the frames of American film ever since.[10]

In the first decade of the new millennium 9/11 became much more than a singular event; it evolved into an ideological concept, a discourse in itself (see Melnick 2009). The 'War on Terror' and American Film: 9/11 Frames per Second postulates that the post-9/11 era provides us with another such culturally impactful 'allegorical moment', one that in many ways came to define the American film industry as much as it defined the nation itself. It became common in the months and years after September 11th to suggest that 9/11 'changed everything', a phrase that echoed from politician to commentator and back again. Yet this contentious expression was soon justly criticised as exposing the First Worldist nature of those living in contemporary Western democracies. However, without a doubt, 9/11 certainly changed political discourse and American cinema in the subsequent decade. *The 'War on Terror' and American Film: 9/11 Frames per Second* is a survey of the extent of that change.

NOTES

1. In an interview conducted for this book Gregor Jordan continued, 'It was clear that Americans were not ready to examine themselves at all and even though this film had nothing to do with the current conflict it was seen as highly undesirable' (Jordan 2012). Another Miramax film, *The Quiet American* (2002), the second film adaptation (following one in 1958) of the Graham Greene novel of the same name, experienced the same fate. Harvey Weinstein commented, 'I showed the film to some people and staff, and they said: "Are you out of your mind? You cannot release this now; it's unpatriotic. America has to be cohesive, and band together." We were worried that nobody had the stomach for a movie about bad Americans any more' (cited in Thompson 2001).
2. A few years later the complete opposite occurred in the period-set films *Munich* (2005), *Miracle* (2004) and *Rent* (2005). To make them historically accurate the World Trade Center was digitally added.
3. Many witnesses recounted something similar. The newsreader Ron Insana said, 'And we heard it and looked up and started to see elements of the building coming down and we ran. And honestly, it was like a scene out of *Independence Day*' (cited in Monahan 2010: 60).
4. There is a succession of Christian iconography present in the film, the most resonant of which is when Jimeno is shown having a vision of Christ with a water bottle, in an image reminiscent of one from *Ben-Hur* (1959), as if Jesus is watching over him and by extension the United States. There is a suggestive dissolve between Jesus and Kearns, adding further weight to the suggestion that it depicts a righteous America endorsed by God.
5. Sean Redmond wrote, 'Since 9/11, I keep seeing planes falling out of the sky. In film and television, particularly, the image of the aircraft in flames, breaking up, hurtling toward the earth keeps cropping up' (2008: 34).
6. *The 'War on Terror' and American Film: 9/11 Frames per Second* concerns itself with fictional and popular cinema. For a more detailed analysis of American documentary film after 9/11 see Markert's excellent *Post- 9/11 Cinema: Through a Lens Darkly* (2011).
7. See Robert Jay Lifton and Greg Mitchell, *Hiroshima in America: A Half Century of Denial* (1996), John H. Morro, *Taken by Force: Rape and American GIs in Europe during World War II* (2007) and Richard R. Flores, *Remembering the Alamo: Memory, Modernity, and the Master Symbol* (2002).
8. The term was coined by Leon Festinger in *When Prophecy Fails: A Social and Psychological Study of a Modern Group that Predicted the Destruction of the World* (1956).

9. It is important to remember here that these reactions to culturally unpalatable events are mirrored everywhere, not just in the United States. Witness the problematic relationship between England and the British Empire, Germany and the Holocaust, Japan and the Nanking Massacre, Turkey and the Armenian Genocide.

10. Joshua Hirsch's book on cinematic accounts of the Holocaust was called *Afterimage: Film, Trauma, and the Holocaust* (2004). He wrote, 'an image that formally repeats the shock of the original encounters with atrocity – both the original eyewitnessing of the atrocities themselves, and the subsequent cinematic encounter with the images of atrocity' (19).

1. THE LIVES OF OTHERS: VULNERABILITY IN POST-9/11 AMERICAN CINEMA

Most Americans have probably experienced something like the loss of their First Worldism as a result of the events of September 11 and its aftermath. What kind of loss is this? It is the loss of the prerogative, only and always, to be the one who transgresses the sovereign boundaries of other states, but never to be in the position of having one's own boundaries transgressed. The United States was supposed to be the place that could not be attacked, where life was safe from violence initiated from abroad, where the only violence we knew was the kind we inflicted on ourselves.
Judith Butler, *Precarious Life: The Powers of Mourning and Violence*

The reason for fighting
I never got straight
But I learned to accept it
Accept it with pride
For you don't count the dead
When God's on your side
Bob Dylan, 'With God on our side' (1963)

It is only to be expected that the art a nation produces primarily engages with the issues that preoccupy that nation. Furthermore, in all likelihood, those texts that a nation produces will privilege the experiences of its own people, whether out of cultural relevance or economic necessity. It hardly needs to be said that for the most part the Italian film industry tends to make films about the Italians, the Japanese film industry about the Japanese and the American film industry about the Americans. However, the way that these texts articulate both the experiences of their own people and the people of other nationalities is of central importance to understanding the culture in which they are made. The following chapter explores the representation of identity and vulnerability in American film of the post-9/11 era. By looking at American cinema of this decade one is able to discern the presence of patterns in dominant cultural representation practices. Throughout its history American cinema has rarely offered sympathetic images of the Other, those figures who do not correspond to what a society defines as its 'norm' whether in terms of race, nationality, gender or sexuality. A study of post-9/11 American film sees a continuation of this practice of failing to recognise or portray the essential humanity of alternate lives; Judith Butler's *Precarious Life: The Powers of Mourning and Violence* asks the question, 'What can be the cultural impact of such an approach?' – a system that places greater value on the lives of individuals from the First World than the lives of others. The films that have emerged from the American film industry charting the war on terror, even the self-consciously liberal ones, have continued the trend of dehumanising individuals who transgress ideas of racial normativity, which arguably makes their fate in the real world easier to ignore. These ideas are literalised in John Tirman's *The Deaths of Others: The Fate of Civilians in America's Wars* (2011). Tirman wrote, 'One of the most remarkable aspects of American wars is how little we discuss the victims who are not Americans. The costs of war to the populations and common soldiers of the "enemy" are rarely found in the narratives and dissections of conflict, and this habit is a durable feature of how we remember war' (3–4). Tirman's findings confirm what the likes of a broad range of theorists from Louis Althusser, Michel Foucault, Noam Chomsky and Franz Fanon have concluded, that we live in an ideological system which inculcates a strict cultural hierarchy through its production and dissemination of meanings and values. Accordingly, post-9/11 American films privilege American subjectivity, humanity and moral authority at the expense of these Others, perpetuating the idea that suffering is a First World privilege by both marginalising and even excluding non-Westerners from the cinema screen. Thus, the story of the American journalist Daniel Pearl tragically kidnapped and killed by Pakistani militants, filmed by Michael Winterbottom in *A Mighty Heart* (2007), is just one of a multitude of narratives to portray the effects of the war on terror almost exclusively on Americans (and most often white Americans), and in doing so exclude the lives of the hundreds of thousands of those non-Westerners killed and displaced as a result of the conflict. Judith Butler wondered about the effects of such inculcation when she asked whether 'those lives in Afghanistan, or other United States targets, who were also snuffed out brutally and without recourse to any protection', will ever be 'as human as Daniel Pearl' (2004: 37).[1]

When Arabs or Muslims (the two are often conflated as if they are the same thing) are depicted in American cinema, they tend to be heavily stereotyped and limited in the spectrum of their characterisations compared to those offered to citizens from the First World: they are framed as either violent or victimised, both conveniently reducible and disposable stereotypes lacking humanity and agency in their own way. These Others become the subject of a controlling and objectifying imperial gaze, viewed through the symbolic and literal lens of the West. With this in mind, it is useful to turn the work of Emmanuel Lévinas (as Judith Butler also does) and his compelling metonymy of 'the face' in a disquisition of how notions of the Other are constructed by dominant ideologies. Lévinas's face is not a literal one; it is an embodiment of the Other in its potential aliveness and humanity and in the precarity it is able (but rarely allowed) to reveal in 'us'. Lévinas stated, 'To expose myself to the vulnerability of the face is to put my ontological right to existence into question' (1986: 24). It can be seen that American cinema has historically refused to represent the Lévinasian face of the Other in all its intricacies, both as a way of negating its humanity and as a rejection of its inherent ability to remind us of our own ethical responsibilities. The illusion that hegemonic American film maintains is that life outside of the First World is not as valuable and therefore not as human as 'ours'. This ideological construction of Otherness has been a durable one and existed long before General William Westmoreland's infamous articulation in Peter Davis's Vietnam War documentary *Hearts and Minds* (1974), that '[t]he Oriental doesn't put the same high price on life as does a Westerner'. This reductive stereotype was shown to be alive and well in 2004, as President George W. Bush's comments on the campaign trail revealed. He commented, 'Today, if you noticed, there was a car bomb near a school. These people are brutal. They – they're the exact opposite of Americans. We value life and human dignity. They don't care about life and human dignity. We believe in freedom. They have an ideology of hate' (Bush 2004). Jack Shaheen, the author of *Reel Bad Arabs: How Hollywood Vilifies a People* (2009), an extensive analytical survey of the representations of Arabs on the American screen, argued that this racism is systemic, and that according to American film:

> Arab Muslims are fanatics who believe in a different god, who don't value human life as much as we do, they are intent on destroying us (the .[W]est) with their oil or with their terrorism; the men seek to abduct and brutally seduce our women; they are without family and reside in a primitive place (the desert) and behave like primitive beings. The women are subservient — resembling black crows — or we see them portrayed as mute, somewhat exotic harem maidens. (Shaheen cited in Harrickton 2008)

While Lévinas's face is a symbolic rather than a physical one, it is revealing to consider the literal faces of the Other in post-9/11 American cinema. Which films contain the actual faces of Iraqis or Afghanistanis in anything beyond a physical presence? Which films offer portrayals of Arabs outside of the realm of caricature? Where are the films that replace the stereotypes of 'bombers, belly dancers, or billionaires' (Shaheen 2009: 13) with hearts that beat – as fathers, mothers, daughters or sons? To deny someone of a face is to deny their right to life; and it is a denial with disturbing implications, as Michel Foucault observed in his contention that cultural demonisation and racism are 'the precondition that makes killing acceptable' (2011: 132). Unlike in *A Mighty Heart* where Daniel Pearl *is* given a face, an identity and a sense of meaning, post-9/11 American cinema is populated by the monstrous Muslim terrorists of *Body of Lies* and *Traitor* (2008) who are motivated only by a desire to take innocent American lives; or the sexually deviant sheikh in *Taken* who purchases young American virgins to defile; or the crowds of threatening Muslims in *Zero Dark Thirty*, *The Hurt Locker* and *Argo* (2012), each of whom are portrayed as potential suicide bombers waiting for a moment to murder even more innocents.

What will audiences of future generations make of films like *Zero Dark Thirty*, *United 93* and *Syriana*, each of which is discussed in this chapter? How may these texts function as examples of Alison Landsberg's prosthetic memories? Landsberg suggests that prosthetic memories *can* function as socially progressive acts, because they encourage empathetic responses to the experiences of Others, that through them we are able 'to feel connected to, while recognizing the alterity of, the "other"' (2004: 9). Yet the majority of perspectives represented in post-9/11 American cinema are emphatically not those of the Other, whose stories and lives are marginalised, if not completely erased. Films are able to decisively reconfigure how historical events come to be understood and remembered by the public at large: witness the cases of *Platoon*, *JFK*, *Schindler's List* (1993) and *Saving Private Ryan* (1998), each of which traced and arguably even influenced shifts in the understanding of the traumatic events they portray. In a similar way, regardless of their political perspectives, the films produced by the American film industry in the first decade of the new millennium provide a compelling and influential testimony of the era.

'Partial information will be treated as a lie!': The Discourse of Absence and Presence in *Zero Dark Thirty*

A lot of my friends have died trying to do this. I believe I was spared so I could finish the job.
Maya, *Zero Dark Thirty*

Zero Dark Thirty, directed by Kathryn Bigelow and written by Mark Boal, is an account of the decade-long hunt for Osama bin Laden that culminated in his assassination in Operation Neptune Spear in Abbottabad, Pakistan on 2 May 2011. On its release the film was embraced by the majority of critics in much the same way that Bigelow's previous film (also scripted by Boal), *The Hurt Locker*, had been.[2] Mick La Salle's (2013) description of it as being 'one of the most innovative and best made films of the past year' was echoed by many critics in January 2013. However, a small number of commentators questioned the way that the film represented torture or 'enhanced interrogation'. Indeed, the way the film framed these practices proved so contentious that several writers took to likening Bigelow to that doyen of German National Socialist cinema, Leni Riefenstahl. Naomi Wolf (2013) went so far as to address Bigelow in an open letter, which stated, 'Like Riefenstahl, you are a great artist. But now you will be remembered forever as torture's handmaiden'.[3] Wolf's criticism, and those of many who challenged the film, is that it unequivocally presents torture as an effective, moral and necessary tactic for obtaining evidence from detained combatants, and that it is shown as being absolutely instrumental in locating the whereabouts of Osama bin Laden. Boal and Bigelow made it explicitly clear in several interviews that they felt that the film did *not* endorse torture at all, and nor did it suggest that torture was of critical importance in finding Osama bin Laden. Bigelow said, 'I think that it's a deeply moral movie that questions the use of force. It questions what was done in the name of finding bin Laden' (cited in Winter 2013: 32). In a similar response, Boal argued, 'I think that what the film does over the course of two hours is show the complexity of the debate' (cited in Mayer 2012). Therefore, Bigelow and Boal offer a film that, in their understanding, both 'questions' and attempts to 'debate' one of the defining issues of the post-9/11 decade.

Zero Dark Thirty begins with a black screen over which the real-life voices of the victims of the terrorist attacks on 9/11 can be heard frantically calling their loved ones in the final moments before their deaths.[4] Like many other American films it chooses not to directly recreate the impact of the two hijacked jet airliners on 11 September 2001, as if the event is simply too traumatic to portray (see *World Trade Center, United 93* and *Fahrenheit 9/11* (2009)). As E. Ann Kaplan and Ban Wang suggested, intensely traumatic moments can produce 'a shattering of a culture's meaning-making scheme and representational modes'; they are 'as many critics insist, beyond the reach of representation' (2004: 8). As powerful as these moments are, opening the film at this particular point deliberately aligns its narrative with the prevailing understanding that 9/11 brought about an 'end of innocence' for the United States and that what followed was rendered necessary and legitimised by the terrorist attacks on 11 September 2001. The narrative formerly begins with the scene that immediately follows, an extended sequence of the torture of a young man named Ammar al-Baluchi (Reda Kateb) with the palpable sense of grief and loss, and the voices of those murdered on 9/11, still lingering. The torture sequence (with other brief, connected scenes) takes up the first twenty-eight minutes of the film and creates a direct correlation between it and the events of 9/11, an act of juxtaposition that sets the tone for the exculpatory narrative that follows and both naturalises and legitimises the actions of the officers attempting to procure information from Ammar, with an implicit understanding that the attacks of 9/11 were so monstrous that it was essential that the 'gloves came off' in order to prevent another attack.[5] The acts of torture are perpetrated by the charismatic Central Intelligence Agency (CIA) operative Daniel ('Dan') (Jason Clarke) and observed by the inexperienced Maya (Jessica Chastain), a fellow CIA agent, who emerges as the protagonist of the film and the audience's point of identification. In Boal's original script Maya is described as 'beautiful' with 'pale, milky innocence and bright blue eyes' (2). Dan is also given a detailed description and later it is nonchalantly dropped into the conversation that he has a PhD in a calculated attempt to distance him from the casual brutality of the treatment of prisoners in Guantánamo Bay. Yet the object of their attention, Ammar, is not regarded as important enough to be described *at all* in the script even though he plays a fundamental role in revealing the information that will ultimately lead them to bin Laden at the climax of the film more than two hours of screen time and eight years of diegetic time later. In these initial scenes Maya is shown as a reluctant observer of the torture of Ammar – we even see her wincing at the sight, but as the film progresses she embraces the use of torture wholeheartedly. Neither Maya nor Dan nor anyone else on-screen ever doubts the legitimacy or efficacy of torture during the film's 157-minute running time and throughout Maya is continually shown to be resourceful, tenacious and heroic.[6] Forced to share her perspective we are conditioned to empathise with her, and thus her actions become progressively legitimated by our intimate relationship with her and her cause.

On the issue of whether the film shows torture as being instrumental to the finding of evidence that eventually leads to the discovery of the whereabouts of bin Laden, Mark Boal stated:

> We're trying to present a long, 10-year intelligence hunt, of which the harsh interrogation programme is the most controversial aspect. And it's just misreading the film to say that it shows torture leading to the information about Bin Laden. If you actually watch the movie, the detainee [Ammar] doesn't say anything when he's waterboarded. He gives them some information that's new to them over the civilised setting of a lunch – and they go back to the research room and all that information is already there. (Boal cited in Gupta 2012)

While Boal is factually correct in his assertion that Ammar does not reveal any information during the scenes when he is being waterboarded, he is certainly being disingenuous. The 'civilised setting' of lunch that he describes comes directly after Ammar has been beaten, sexually humiliated, denied food, forced to wear a dog collar and deprived of sleep. Furthermore, he is led to the table hooded and then shackled to the floor. When Ammar once again proves reluctant to divulge further information Dan almost casually remarks, 'I can always go and eat with some other dude and hang you up to the ceiling.' It is at this point that Ammar is tricked into revealing the name of bin Laden's personal courier, Abu Ahmed, the person who will eventually allow Maya to locate bin Laden many years later. While Ammar is not being physically abused at the point when he reveals this information, is it really accurate to suggest that torture has not directly led to this breakthrough? The lunch is a brief respite from his torture, with the threat of more torture, at any moment that Dan should choose, lingering fairly explicitly.

The character of Ammar himself is denied any sense of motivation for his actions; the purpose of his cause is never mentioned, and he is dehumanised through the violence perpetrated against him. Dan and Maya are ironically shown to be his intellectual and moral superiors despite the fact that they are the ones torturing him.[7] While he is shown suffering, any empathy derived from his situation is an example of what E. Ann Kaplan described as 'empty empathy', which she characterised as 'empathy elicited by images of suffering provided without any context or background knowledge' (2005: 93). This 'empty empathy' is something that became a common trope in representations of alterity in post-9/11 American cinema. For Bigelow and Boal, Ammar is simply an Other who deserves his treatment. In a Lévinisian sense he is denied a face, as are the vast majority of Arabs in Zero Dark Thirty: they are terrorists and evil-doers who are determined to take the lives of innocent Americans (and others) for no reason the film cares to explain, a potent and literal manifestation of Jack Shaheen's 'bombers, belly dancers, or billionaires' (Shaheen 2009: 13). Later in the film Bigelow's camera lingers on the demonstrators outside the Embassy of the United States in Pakistan, taking part in protests against the deaths of those killed by American drone strikes in the region. Yet those protesting are portrayed as a violent, threatening horde like the hostile crowds of Arabs in films like Rules of Engagement (2000) and Argo. Inside the embassy it is revealed that these protests have forced the CIA to relocate the station chief Joseph Bradley (Kyle Chandler). It may be seen as highly ironic (and revealing) then that the victim of these scenes is unequivocally presented as Bradley himself rather than the thousands of civilians (including children) killed or wounded in the hundreds of US drone strikes in Pakistan since 2004.[8] These attacks have proved so contentious that in June 2010 the United Nations Human Rights Council (UNHRC) issued a report suggesting that the United

States was the 'most prolific user of targeted killings' in the world (Philip Alston cited in Cloud 2010). The fact that those protesting are denied a sense of legitimacy and are presented as a vicious mob eager for American blood is yet another example of the film's inability to provide a political and historical context, as Zero Dark Thirty offers a view of the world not just from the perspective of America, but through the highly politicised and subjective prism of the CIA.

In contrast to these portrayals of Arabs, every single member of the ethnically and gender diverse CIA is shown to be industrious, ethical and patriotic. As if to emphasise both their commitment and vulnerability, the agents are constantly under threat. Maya is attacked twice in the course of the film – once when she is present at the Marriott Hotel bombing in Islamabad on 20 September 2008, and then later in an assassination attempt outside her residence in Pakistan. Her colleague and only friend Jessica (Jennifer Ehle) pays the ultimate sacrifice for her country, as she is one of several CIA operatives killed during the Khost bombings in 2009. In scene after scene the film portrays violent acts perpetrated *against* Americans (and others from the West) and not *by* Americans, as if to remind us as to why the tortures and the detainee programme are vital and justified in the first place.

What the film chooses to exclude from its narrative proves just as significant as that which it portrays. Correspondingly, its aggressive expurgation of any sense of perspective casts serious doubts on Bigelow's and Boal's assertions that they have made a balanced film that attempts to question or debate these most contested of issues. Rather, as Jane Mayer (2012) argues, the film 'milks the U.S. torture program for drama while sidestepping the political and ethical debate that it provoked'. Zero Dark Thirty does not show, on any occasion, a single character arguing against torture whether on legal, ethical or practical grounds, even though this was certainly happening both inside and outside of the CIA at the time (see Coll 2004; Soufan 2011). There are no moments of self-doubt by Maya, Dan or their bosses Joseph Bradley and George (Mark Strong) on the morality or efficacy of the detainment programme. While Dan blames himself for the Saudi attack it is because he was personally unable to secure the information from Ammar, rather than due to the fact that the torture process itself is ineffective. The film also erases from its narrative those who resigned from their positions because of their belief that the programme was immoral, illegal or did not produce reliable, actionable intelligence, such as the Federal Bureau of Investigation (FBI) director Robert Mueller who removed his staff rather than participate in such brutal and illegal treatment of prisoners (see Department of Justice, Office of the Inspector General 2008). The film chooses not to portray the physicians from the CIA's Office of Medical Services (OMS) who were frequently present during enhanced interrogation sessions and who measured detainee vital signs in order to advise on whether the prisoners were well enough for the interrogations to continue and who offered counsel as to the capabilities of the human body to resist extreme pressure (see Taylor 2009). Would this have suggested that the process was too clinical and organised? Rather, Dan's acts of torture seem more spontaneous and even a masculine battle of wits against his ideological enemy Ammar. There is no mention of the more than one hundred detainees who died in captivity, of the frequent failures to get the desired information from prisoners or of the veritable cavalcade of mistakes made in the process, like the egregious abductions of the likes of Khaled el-Masri (who had the misfortune of having a name almost the same as Khaled al-Masri) or that false information gained from the torture of Ibn al-Shaykh al-Libi was used to make the fraudulent case for war against Iraq. In the world of *Zero Dark Thirty* it appears that everyone who is tortured has information vital to American national security interests, although of course this was certainly not the case. One of the many who complained about the lack of 'high-value' captives and the information they possessed was Major General Michael E. Dunlavey, who commented that Guantánamo Bay was full of 'Mickey Mouse' prisoners rather than hardened terrorists with any useful information (see Millar 2002).

Despite these factors, the journalist and author Mark Bowden was able to agree with Mark Boal and Kathryn Bigelow that the film was not pro-torture. He suggested:

> The charge that the film is pro-torture is easy to debunk . . . The agency is shown to be not only failing to find bin Laden and dismantle al-Qaeda, but on the losing end of the fight. In case the point hasn't been made clearly enough, a visit from an angry CIA chief to the U.S. Embassy in Pakistan in the next scene underlines it: 'There's nobody else, hidden away on some other floor,' he says. 'This is just us. And we are failing. We're spending billions of dollars. People are dying. We're still no closer to defeating our enemy.'(Bowden 2013)

While Bowden is correct that the agency is, at this point in the narrative, shown to be failing to find bin Laden, there is no suggestion at all that this is because torture is ineffective; in fact, the complete opposite has been shown to be true by then. In one interview with Maya a man named in the screenplay only as 'Ghul' immediately agrees to tell her anything she asks, saying, 'I don't want to be tortured any more.' Later, when Maya reviews hundreds of hours of interrogations of prisoners, many of whom have obviously been tortured, she finds a key piece of evidence that has been overlooked: once again the implication being that the detainee programme with its harsh interrogation methods was instrumental in the hunt for bin Laden. The 'angry CIA chief' who Boal mentions is George who later complains that the agency's ability to pursue bin Laden has been directly compromised by the removal of the programme:

'We lost the ability to prove that when we lost the detainee programme. Who the hell am I supposed to ask? Some guy in Gitmo lawyered up? He'll just tell his lawyer to warn bin Laden.' The only scene in the film that offers anything approaching a dissenting voice is when President Obama can be seen on the television in the background during a low-key CIA meeting. In footage taken from his first post-election interview on *60 Minutes* (CBS), recorded on 16 November 2008, Obama is heard to say, 'I have said repeatedly that America doesn't torture. And I'm gonna make sure that we don't torture.' Not only do those present at the meeting ignore their newly appointed commander-in-chief, there are even slight, resigned sighs. When the programme is brought to an end by Obama, George is not the only one to criticise President Obama's decision and its negative effects on the effectiveness of the CIA doing their jobs. Dan warns Maya, 'You don't wanna be the last one holding a dog collar when the oversight committee comes.' As a result of these scenes Peter Bergen (2012) suggested, 'In the film, Obama's opposition to torture comes off as wrong-headed and prissy.' The combination of these aspects certainly does not equate to a film, which in Mark Bowden's understanding, presents torture as 'at best only marginally useful, and both politically and morally toxic'.

In some post-9/11 American films that portray torture the act is seen to have a corrosive psychological impact on those conducting it (see *Rendition*, *Traitor* and *Body of Lies*), as the CIA agents (or soldiers) become traumatised by their actions and come to realise that not only is the process ineffective but also ethically dubious. Joshua E. S. Phillips in *None of Us Were Like This Before: American Soldiers and Torture* (2012) offers a disturbing insight into the effects of the enhanced interrogation programme on those tasked with implementing it. Phillips discusses some of the hundreds of cases of those who suffered from pronounced feelings of guilt and even PTSD that frequently led to substance abuse, violent episodes, depression and in some severe cases even suicide (2012: xi). There are no such revelations in *Zero Dark Thirty*; operatives like Dan and Maya are never in any doubt about the morality or the usefulness of the detainee programme and they both remain largely unaffected by participating in acts of torture over a number of years. The only partial concession the film makes is that Dan decides to return to Washington, which he explains with the glib comment, 'I've seen too many guys naked.' The only moment that Dan shows *any* emotion in the film is when he learns about the deaths of his pet monkeys, which took place at one of the CIA's undisclosed black sites. There is no evidence to suggest that the scene is to be regarded as an indication of Dan's dehumanisation, questioning the fact that he would care more about monkeys than the human beings he tortures on a day-to-day basis, or an evocation of Hannah Arrendt's observation on the 'banality of evil' (see Arrendt 1965). Rather, Dan is one of those tasked with, in the words of Jose Rodriguez, Jr, the Director of the National Clandestine Service (D/NCS), putting their 'big boy pants on' and doing what needed to be done (cited in Alvarez 2012) and subsequently he returns to Washington with no apparent blemish to his psychological profile or career.

When Kathryn Bigelow was challenged about the portrayal of torture in the film she insisted:

> As a lifelong pacifist, I support all protests against the use of torture, and, quite simply, inhumane treatment of any kind. But I do wonder if some of the sentiments alternately expressed about the film might be more appropriately directed at those who instituted and ordered these U.S. policies, as opposed to a motion picture that brings the story to the screen. Those of us who work in the arts know that depiction is not endorsement. If it was, no artist would be able to paint inhumane practices, no author could write about them, and no filmmaker could delve into the thorny subjects of our time. (Bigelow 2013)

Yet the persistent criticism of the film in the media was certainly not about whether the film *should* have depicted torture, but rather *how* it was depicted. Peter Maas (2012) offered a cogent explanation of Bigelow's and Boal's disconnection from reality when he suggested that the film 'represents a troubling new frontier of government-embedded filmmaking'. His assertion is that the high levels of access to the CIA that Bigelow and Boal received distorted their perspective on the events and thus correspondingly influenced the shape of the film (see Child 2013). However, there is little new about the collaboration between the CIA and the makers of *Zero Dark Thirty*, as the institution has historically only agreed to participate in film projects that portray it in a positive light, while refusing assistance to texts that offer more critical views of their practices. Tricia Jenkins provides a compelling account of the history of the CIA and its relationship with the media in her book *The CIA in Hollywood: How the Agency Shapes Film and Television* (2012). Jenkins traces the involvement of the CIA in a diverse range of films: from the adaptation of *The Quiet American* (1958), where it demanded changes in order to make Graham Greene's novel about the early American intrusion into Vietnam more patriotic, to post-9/11 films like *The Sum of all Fears*, *The Recruit* (2003) and the Academy Award-winning *Argo*, each of which provide flattering portrayals of the agency and thus received substantial access and assistance.[9] Jenkins wrote that 'those seeking initial CIA consultation and advice are often treated to a whitewashed version of the Agency, where valid criticisms are downplayed or even ignored' (2012: 134), a process that she describes as raising serious 'legal and ethical concerns' (136). Like *Zero Dark Thirty*, *Argo* rewrites history to produce a hagiographic portrayal of CIA bravery and ingenuity: erasing CIA complicity in the 1953 Iranian coup d'état and portraying almost all Iranians as mindless fanatics eager to kill entirely innocent Americans for no apparent reason. From this perspective, the disclaimer at the start of *Zero Dark Thirty*, which informs audiences that it is 'based on firsthand accounts of actual events', is both true and ironic, as it is a statement suggestive not only of veracity, but of subjectivity. When Bigelow commented in an interview that she had 'an obligation to remain faithful to the material', the material to which she was remaining faithful may not be the events themselves, but the accounts of the CIA officers with a vested interest in emphasising the successes of their programme and erasing its many failures (cited in Filkins 2012). Yet to what extent can such reliance on first-hand accounts of those who designed, approved and participated in the torture programme produce a film that foregrounds issues of balance and objectivity, or one that debates and questions this most important of issues? What about the voices of those who opposed the programme, questioned its legitimacy and efficacy, or those who were victims of it?

The film climaxes with the raid on the bin Laden compound in Abbatobad, which is offered as the culmination of national desire intertwined with Maya's personal revenge drama. Maya informs the audience, '*I'm* gonna smoke everyone involved in this op [the Khost bombing], then *I* am gonna kill bin Laden'. The film's moral certainty is embodied in the righteousness of her drive which has fuelled the narrative and is presented as a distinctly divinely ordained one, articulated in her anagogic admission that a lot of her 'friends have died trying to do this. I *believe* I was spared so I could finish the job' (emphasis in original). When bin Laden is assassinated, one of the members of the United States' Navy's Sea, Air, Land Teams (one of the Navy SEALs) transmits the message, 'For God and Country', the agreed confirmation signal to inform the authorities of bin Laden's death, which had also been the film's working title.

Zero Dark Thirty is perhaps the defining American film of the post-9/11 era, an emblematic narrative of American exceptionalism and a dramatisation of the idea that America is a uniquely (and divinely) chosen country somehow distinct from others, one that has no obligation to follow international laws and precedents. For the film (and America at large) these transgressions are simply irrelevant and are thus elided from its narrative. Bin Laden's killing is given no context and there is no debate about the legitimacy of an extrajudicial assassination or the legality of an unsanctioned intrusion onto Pakistani soil. Still US Attorney General Eric Holder stated that the mission was 'lawful, legitimate and appropriate in every way' (cited in Vicini and Pelofsky 2011) and Obama himself claimed that 'justice has been done' (cited in Cohen 2011). Others offered an opposing view, like Professor Steven Ratner, who argued: 'A lot of it depends on whether you believe Osama bin Laden is a combatant in a war or a suspect in a mass murder . . . [Y]ou would only be able to kill a suspect if they represented an immediate threat' (cited in Longstreth 2011).

The film's final scenes provide us with a startlingly literal manifestation of the film's conceptualisation of the Other and the Lévinasian concept of the face discussed earlier in this chapter. Given her expertise and her presence on the ground Maya is asked to identify bin Laden's body; she unzips the body bag and gazes at the face of the corpse inside, but it is not shown to the audience during the scene nor was it clearly seen during the raid itself, as it is imperative that bin Laden is only allowed to function as a symbol and not a person. Shortly after, Maya boards a large aeroplane in which she is the only passenger. In a line positively loaded with metaphorical resonance the pilot asks her, 'Where do you wanna go?' The camera cuts to an extended close-up of Maya's face which is the final image of the film and a shot that lingers for almost a full minute. Boal's screenplay describes it as a moment when '[t]hose luminous eyes become pools of relief and pain' (2013: 111). Maya's tears and Chastain's superbly modulated performance in the shot are calculated in their ambiguity, emblematic of how the film has erased moral uncertainty from its narrative and replaced it with highly subjective and pathic dilemmas. What are the tears for? Are they for the thousands who have died since 9/11 and the tens of thousands more displaced and injured in the war on terror? Or only for the American friends she has lost and those who died in the attacks on 11 September 2001? Are they tears of relief after completing the task she had dedicated so much of her life to? Or are they for the loss of America's standing after having transgressed international laws regarding the ethical treatment of prisoners in the detainee programme? Jessica Chastain commented, 'To end the film on that question is far more interesting than providing an answer' (cited in Rothman 2013). But for more than two hours, despite Bigelow's and Boal's protestations to the contrary, the film has gone out of its way to avoid a sense of ambiguity to its narrative and provided *only* answers rather than questions. Regardless of how we interpret the final image, what is less ambiguous is that even with the tens, if not hundreds of thousands, dead around the world, the film would have us believe that Maya is the film's true victim and in this way she may be the quintessential symbol of America's understanding of the war on terror. Boal solidified this interpretation of the burden Maya shoulders when he suggested, 'There's a little bit of Joan of Arc' (cited in Cameron 2013) in her characterisation (see Figure 8).

Since the film's release, Bigelow and Boal have shown a pronounced incredulity that *Zero Dark Thirty* has been interpreted by some as a justification and a legitimisation of torture, unable to reconcile themselves to the validity of the criticisms directed towards it. This is reflected in Bigelow's mistaken assertion that critics have challenged the film for depicting torture, rather than the manner of its portrayal, and Boal's glib comments at the New York Film Critics Circle (NYFCC's) awards that 'apparently the French government will be investigating *Les Mis*' (cited in Brooks 2013). Arguably *Zero Dark Thirty*

Figure 8   The true victim of the war on terror? The face of the West in *Zero Dark Thirty* (2012).

will become even more significant as the years progress, distancing us from the immediacy of the events themselves. It is, perhaps, the single most vivid encapsulation of the prevailing interpretation of the war on terror and the most expressive example of American cinema's (and by extension US society's) tendency to erase, forget or disremember those elements that are the most troubling in favour of simplistic and quasi-mythological narratives of revenge and justification. This is a process of selective amnesia in which film and the media play a central role by influencing which issues are focused on, which stories remain untold and which characters are presented as worthy or unworthy of a voice. As a film, *Zero Dark Thirty* disremembers much of the first decade of the new millennium, just as American culture has selectively marginalised distressing events from its own collective narrative. Instead, *Zero Dark Thirty* lingers in the viscerality of the present – often with a striking lack of context or self-awareness. Of course, this is not exclusively an American process: the systematic erasure or rewriting of unpalatable truths from the collective narrative of the national imaginary can be seen in every nation. In the particular case of the United States it is imperative to remember the erasure of the holocaust of Native Americans in the nineteenth century, the use of the atomic bomb at the end of World War Two, the internment of Japanese-American citizens and the execution of Japanese soldiers for waterboarding US prisoners of war during World War Two, and the attempts to rewrite the Vietnam War as a noble failure. An awareness of the tremendous power of the cinematic image led US Senators Dianne Feinstein (D-CA), John McCain (R-AZ) and Carl Levin

(D-MI) to write an open letter to Sony Pictures in December 2012 in which they expressed the fear that *Zero Dark Thirty* 'has the potential to shape American public opinion in a disturbing and misleading manner'. *Zero Dark Thirty* is undoubtedly a film of exceptional power and artistry, but its single-minded and distorted vision is almost synchronic in its desire to rewrite the recent past.

THE POLITICS OF REALISM: PAUL GREENGRASS'S *UNITED 93*

We [the victims' families] think it's a worthwhile project, and so we wanted to cooperate and do our very best to assure that the project told the story, that they got it right, because this is a way not only for this generation, but for generations to come to understand what a group of Americans did when confronted by an enemy on that horrible day.[10]

David Beamer, father of Todd Beamer who died on Flight United 93

When *United 93* was released in April 2006, it's director Paul Greengrass went to significant lengths to stress that it was profoundly apolitical, emphasising how he sought to transcend ideological concerns and create 'a film of complex truths wrapped in a cloak of terrifying and compelling reality' (cited in Fleming Jnr. 2013). It was a response echoed by many critics: Roger Ebert stated, 'The movie contains no politics. No theory' (2007: 733) and James Bone (2006) wrote, 'Filmed in real time and shot with handheld cameras, it has the urgency and grit of a documentary rather than a big-studio movie.' *United 93* is one of the most profoundly affecting American films of the post-9/11 decade, but the way that it has been embraced as an icon of realism, as if it creates an unmediated window on to the events of Flight United 93, is problematic to say the least. *United 93* uses a variety of cinematic techniques to emphasise its realist credentials: from the meticulously detailed re-creation of the United Airlines' aircraft, its casting of unknowns (or actual participants on the day in the case of Ben Sliney, the national operations manager of the Federal Aviation Administration (FAA)), to the widely publicised contact with relatives for details as to what the real-life passengers were likely to have been reading and wearing. Its utilisation of a handheld cinematographic style, which deliberately evokes news or documentary footage, even led to Douglas Kellner, the author of *Cinema Wars*, to call it 'ultra-realistic' (2010: 101). Yet a cinéma vérité style and strikingly replicated mise en scène does not make a film any more inherently 'real' than filming on a studio backlot, it only creates the *appearance* of reality. To confuse realism with apoliticism is certainly naive, as John Fiske reminds us; realism is just as much an aesthetic conceit as other modes of artistic expression.

> The conventions of realism have developed in order to disguise the constructedness of the 'reality' it offers, and therefore of the arbitrariness of

the ideology that is mapped onto it. Realism is beguiling for audiences who are like to confuse such mimetic stylistic techniques with some sort of ideological neutrality. Grounding ideology in reality is a way of making it appear unchallengeable and unchangeable, and thus is a reactionary political strategy. (Fiske 2011: 36)

Slavoj Žižek was a rare dissenting voice that disagreed with Greengrass's claims (and those of Oliver Stone who made similar comments about *World Trade Center*) of apoliticism.

[B]oth films are restrained from taking a political stance and depicting the wider context of the events. Neither the passengers on United 93 nor the policemen in WTC grasp the full picture . . . The result is that the political message of the two films resides in their abstention from delivering a direct political message. It is the message of an implicit trust in one's government: when under attack, one just has to do one's duty. (Žižek 2006: 30)

On the surface *United 93* appears to be an ideologically neutral depiction of a profoundly traumatic event, but it becomes readily apparent that the narrative and the cinematic techniques employed serve to mask its highly fictionalised and politicised account of 9/11. One must ask the question, as Paul Farhi did in *The Washington Post*, 'How far can a dramatic movie go in imposing its own reality before it distorts the public's understanding of the event?' (2006: A1). Greengrass offers a Herodotusian gnomê presented as fact in his mythologised portrait of an America populated by honest, everyman heroes, individuals who selflessly put aside their differences and come together in defence of their nation at a time of great need. It is a film that once again disconnects itself from political or historical context in its portrayal of America as a righteous victim, targeted by a Muslim Other for no discernible reason. Rather than being, in Greengrass's terms, a 'meticulous re-enactment' (cited in Wolf 2006), the film is a vivid manifestation of George W. Bush's post-9/11 rhetoric, one that was used to mobilise the American public to support the upcoming wars in Afghanistan and Iraq. Thus, it is imperative to look more critically at such a culturally significant text, especially one that was praised by many for being 'as much journalism as art' (Edelstein 2006). *United 93* creates the compelling illusion that it offers an unbiased re-creation of events. However, as Comolli and Narboni persuasively argued, this can never be the case. They stated, 'What the camera registers in fact is the vague, unformulated, untheorised, unthought-out world of the dominant ideology . . . reproducing things not as they really are but as they appear when refracted through the ideology' (1976: 25). The film tells a very particular version of the events that occurred on

United Airlines Flight 93, one that, on close observation, involves a very selective process as to how these events are framed.

The passengers of *United 93* are introduced quickly and effectively at the beginning of the film, each given a brief moment of detail for us to remember later. Rather than being given names they are presented as types: the sporty guy, the businessman, the grandmother, and so on. Greengrass deliberately does not linger on the characters or use their names, as it is imperative that they function not as individuals, but as a collective hero, which is one of the fundamental aspects of the film's narrative and the mythology around Flight 93.[11] They are almost all friendly and seem strangely eager to chat, most especially about their children and grandchildren. One flight attendant talks about how she would rather 'be home with [her] babies', and the pilot discusses his children and how much he is looking forward to his upcoming wedding anniversary. Even in these quieter moments, Greengrass's camera shakes with a jagged intensity, the quintessential new millennial marker of authenticity and a self-conscious device to emphasise both the film's spontaneity and authorial transparency. This cinematic style projects an aura of credibility onto the film that gives it a sense of legitimacy and facticity based on its connection to a real-life historical event.

Slavoj Žižek stated, 'What fascinates me about disaster films is how circumstances of vast catastrophe suddenly bring about social cooperation' (cited in Yuran 2003). While this is true for the majority of the passengers onboard the flight, and indeed their unity has become a synecdochal moment for American solidarity on 9/11, it is certainly not true for all of them. One particular character is conspicuous in his cowardice, and the fact that he happens to be the only non-American passenger on the flight (apart from the terrorists) is a significant one. Christian Adams (Erich Redman), a German businessman, is repeatedly singled out as a terrorist appeaser who cries out, 'We should not interfere!' Adams later tries to warn the terrorists of the imminent fight-back by the passengers. However, there is no evidence to suggest that the real Christian Adams behaved in such a way, yet Greengrass sees fit to depict him like this in a film that aims to 'look clearly and unflinchingly at a single event, [where] you can find in its shape something precious, something much larger than the event itself . . . the DNA of our times' (cited in Fleming Jnr. 2013). One may ask why does it have to be the only other foreign passenger on the flight who is cast as a terrorist appeaser? Why is it not an American citizen shown to be acting in such a way, something that would be statistically much more likely to have happened? The portrayal of Christian Adams was rarely addressed by critics, a worrying fact in itself that audiences and reviewers would accept such a characterisation and behaviour as natural – so conditioned have they been after decades of such depictions of foreigners (especially Germans). One can almost hear the loud boos directed towards Adams by American cinema audiences. The whole Adams' incident is invented for dramatic effect with absolutely no evidence that it ever happened, but it is given the aura of credibility and believability by Greengrass's appropriation of the documentary style and his comments about the film's verisimilitude.[12] About this, Greengrass makes a partial concession: 'We don't know, no, but you have to set the parameters of the film as they actually are and explore it, and in the end, audiences have to make their own minds up about whether that's a credible, believable portrait' (cited in Harris 2010). On the DVD commentary track recorded by the normally loquacious Greengrass, there is a lingering, almost embarrassed, silence during the Christian Adams' episode. Cosmo Landesman suggested:

> The film doesn't want to deal with the possibility that there were Americans who opted to stay silent and seated. Greengrass wants it both ways: he wants to pose both as the objective documentarist who just presents the facts as they unfolded, and as the dramatist who presents an upbeat portrait of American bravery that makes everybody look good. And he wants us to see the passengers as uncommonly wise as well. He has said they were the ones who first realised they were living in a post-9/11 world; and what's more, they, unlike the bumbling army, unsure of the rules of engagement, knew what to do. I suspect they were simply people motivated by panic and a desire to survive. (Landesman 2010)

In contrast to the portrayal of Adams, the American passengers are given hard-edged lines of dialogue like, 'I don't give a fuck if that thing [the explosive device shown to be strapped to the chest of one of the terrorists] is real or not. See, I'm gonna get his arm and I'm gonna break his arm' and, 'Hey, this is a suicide mission; we have to do something', which would not sound out of place in any thriller or, perhaps, one of Greengrass's two *Bourne* films (explored in Chapter 3). By turning many of the American characters into unambiguous heroes, Landesman suggests that Greengrass moves into ideologically motivated territory. He mentions Greengrass's comments that, 'by examining this single event something much larger can be found – the shape of our world today' (cited in Wolf 2006), which suggests that Greengrass regards the film not just as a realistic account, but as a project with more ideological significance, and an event that he called 'the perfect metaphor of our times' (cited in Fleming Jnr. 2013).

Critics frequently pointed to the even-handed representation of the terrorists as evidence of the film's apoliticism. It is true that Ziad Jarrah (Khalid Abdalla) is the closest the film has to an individual characterisation: he is the one who sits on the hotel room bed thoughtfully reading the Koran at the start of the film and who, at the airport, telephones someone hesitantly to tell them in German, 'I love you' – an act that later connects him to the passengers who

Figure 9   Constructing a heroic mythology for the new millennium in *United 93* (2006).

frantically call their loved ones to tell them the same thing. It is Jarrah who is shown to have a crisis of faith before taking over the plane, when once again there is no evidence to suggest this was or was not the case. However, given his quasi-realistic approach, demonising the terrorists by making them evil Muslim stereotypes like Salim Abu Aziz in *True Lies* (1994) or El Sayad Jaffa in *Executive Decision* (1996) would not have fit the film's attempt at verisimilitude. Despite these moments of intimacy, they are never given any sense of motivation for their actions and any empathy for them is of the 'empty empathy' outlined by Kaplan and commented on in the previous section. Even so, some were appalled that Greengrass dared to show the terrorists as human beings at all. Mick La Salle wrote:

> Most of my anger was directed at the murderers depicted onscreen, but some of it had to do with the way they were initially presented. Writer-director Paul Greengrass does something in *United 93* that invites controversy. He begins his film not with the passengers but with the terrorists praying in their rooms. Then he cuts to an American skyline, while prayers in Arabic are uttered in voice-over. Later, when we meet the passengers, it's almost as if through the eyes of the terrorists. This is a mistake in every possible way – an aesthetic lapse, a lapse in taste

and judgment, and something that raises the question: Does Greengrass understand the moral nature of the event he's depicting? (La Salle 2006)

References to the Bush administration are almost entirely absent from the film, and if *United 93* does offer any criticism of Bush, it is in the fact that he remains inaccessible at the time he is needed most. Peter Bradshaw commented, 'The film is at any rate fiercely critical of Bush and Cheney, who are shown being quite unreachable by the authorities, desperate for leadership and guidance' (2006: 11). This inability to contact Bush is shown only briefly and certainly does not amount to a text that is 'fiercely critical' by any stretch of the imagination.

United 93 concludes with its quintessential myth-making moment, as the passengers break into the plane's cockpit and, while proving unable to prevent the terrorists from crashing the plane, do succeed in preventing the plane from hitting another heavily populated target and become those who Tom Ridge, former US Secretary of Homeland Security, called 'citizen soldiers' (cited in Doss 2012: 167). Yet this event, perhaps the defining moment of the flight and one that has generally come to be accepted as fact, is itself intensely disputed. The *9/11 Commission Report* states that the cockpit recorder reveals Jarrah shouting, 'They want to get in here. Hold, hold from the inside. Hold from the inside. Hold' (Anonymous 2006; dialogue at 9:58:57), which certainly suggests that there was a concerted attempt to get into the cockpit, an act itself that must have required a tremendous amount of effort and bravery on the part of the passengers, but there is no explicit evidence to suggest that the passengers actually got inside. The *9/11 Commission Report* concludes: '[T]he hijackers remained at the controls but must have judged that the passengers were only seconds from overcoming them' (ibid.). However, this is not a dramatic and cathartic enough ending for such a culturally resonant event, and the families of the victims maintained that the passengers of United 93 did actually make it into the cockpit. Of course, this may be comforting to the bereaved, thinking that their loved ones did not die in vain, but is this reason enough to decide that such insubstantial evidence equates to a historical truth? Greengrass elects to believe the families and, in doing so, creates a much more potent and mythological denouement (see Figure 9). Ron Rosenbaum (2006) suggested that Greengrass chose to 'Print the legend' in the words of the newspaper man in *The Man Who Shot Liberty Valence* and perpetuate the myth that America needed to be as much true in 2006 as it did in 2001. He wrote, 'Could it be that [*United 93* and other adaptations of the Flight 93 story] are a symptom of our addiction to fables of redemptive uplift that shield us from the true dimensions of the tragedy? Redemptive uplift: It's the official religion of the media, anyway. There must be a silver lining; it's always darkest before the dawn; the human spirit will triumph over evil.' On its release journalists and writers for the most part conveniently ignored this, the film's most speculative moment; in fact Anne Hornaday remarkably even called the dramatisation of the breaking into the cockpit a 'meaningless detail' (2006: C1).

Greengrass's film is a remarkably affective text, but like *Zero Dark Thirty* its highly politicised re-creation of reality is a problematic one, made even more disconcerting by its filmmakers' persistent claims of veracity and apoliticism. By using the conventions of realism it binds itself to a highly visible and traumatic cultural event and legitimises its depiction. Yet these very conventions, as Fiske suggested, 'disguise the constructedness of the "reality" it offers, and therefore of the arbitrariness of the ideology that is mapped onto it' (2011: 36). While Greengrass maintained that his film 'won't press sentimental buttons. Be judgmental. Or exploitative' (cited in Fleming Jnr. 2013) by stabilising such an inherently traumatic event, *United 93* presents an uncritical reification of what happened to United Airlines Flight 93 and creates a text, in the words of David Beamer, father of Todd Beamer, 'not only for this generation, but for generations to come' (cited in Anonymous 2006). Greengrass stated that he saw making the film as a 'chance to write a burnished page in history', (ibid.) and this is exactly what he has achieved; it is a film that subtly embraces myth over reality, but contends that its mythology *is* reality. Like *Life of Pi*, the narrative Greengrass offers in *United 93* is the preferred one, more palatable to the United States' conception of itself, its history and its values, and, therefore it is the version that becomes memorialised in film and accepted by the public at large.[13]

DIFFERENT PERSPECTIVES ON THE GEOPOLITICAL ARENA:
STEPHEN GAGHAN'S *SYRIANA*

One of the rare American films that does attempt to provide some sense of political and historical context to its depiction of the complicated geopolitical world post-9/11 (those aspects we have seen largely absent from *Zero Dark Thirty* and *United 93*) is Stephen Gaghan's *Syriana*, a film loosely based on former CIA officer Robert Baer's memoir *See No Evil: The True Story of a Ground Soldier in the CIA's War Against Terrorism* (2002). *Syriana* is an example of what has come to be described as a 'hyperlink narrative', with its multi-stranded storyline, globe-hopping plot and diverse cast of characters that range from analysts, lawyers and businessmen, to sheikhs, CIA agents and lobbyists.[14] It adopts a transnational perspective on the imbrication of the political and oil arenas, but frequently refuses to offer simple explanations or moral certainties on the issues that arise. As Kfir Cohen (2012) argued, this sense of complexity is even encoded into its narrative as 'viewers often leave the film with a sense that they have been offered an intelligent lesson about global power relations, yet such a lesson seems almost impossible to articulate given the intricate relations between agents, interests, and events'. The title of the film is derived from a term used to describe the imagined reshaping of the Middle East to suit American interests, not a *Pax Americana*, but a potential *Pax Syriana*, which would ensure future indefinite American access to oil on the Arabian Peninsula where, it is thought, more than 60 per cent of the world's remaining oil resources remain. The catalytic event that sparks the progression of its sprawling narrative is the decision of the heir to the emirate of the unnamed country, Prince Nasir Al-Subaai (Alexander Siddig), to award a lucrative new oil contract to China instead of the United States, instigating worries by the United States over continued American influence in the region. Prince Nasir emerges as one of the film's most compelling characters, a progressive and idealistic Arab who studied at the University of Oxford and who wants to improve the political and social infrastructure of his country. He tells the energy analyst, Bryan Woodman (Matt Damon), who becomes his economic advisor,

> I want to create a parliament. I want to give women the right to vote. I want an independent judiciary. I want to start a new petroleum exchange in the Middle East and cut the speculators out of the business. Why are the major oil exchanges in New York and London anyway? I'll put all of our energy up for competitive bidding. I'll run pipe through Iran to Europe, like you proposed. I'll ship to China. Anything that achieves efficiency and maximizes profits for my people. Profits, which I'll then use to rebuild my country.

Yet it proves more complicated than that, as he continues, 'Except your president calls my father, says, "I've got unemployment in Texas, Kansas, Washington State." One phone call later we're stealing out of our social programs to buy overpriced airplanes.' The film shows how the US Government and the oil industry are threatened by the social, political and economic reforms that Nasir proposes and the impact it would have on American access to oil. The United States prefers Nasir's younger brother, Prince Meshal Al-Subaai, who cares little for reform and would continue existing and profitable relations with the United States. Nasir's deviation from American interests sees him quickly labelled a 'terrorist', just as those 'enemies' of America during the Cold War were demonised by being called 'Communist' for putting the interests of their country before that of the United States, whether they had any true connection to communist ideologies or not.

Running parallel to this is the Department of Justice's investigation into an American company, Killen Oil, which was awarded a lucrative Kazakhstani oil contract. Jimmy Pope (Chris Cooper), the owner of Killen Oil, is determined to maintain a global American hegemony that has been very profitable to him and those like him. He suggests to the lawyer, Bennett Holiday (Jeremy Wright), tasked with looking into the situation, 'China's economy ain't growing as fast as it could because they can't get all the oil they need. I'm damn proud of that fact.' American imperialist values are espoused by the figure of Danny Dalton (Tim Blake Nelson), the Texas oil man, who justifies his unlawful behaviour as being in the best interest of the United States: 'Corruption? Corruption ain't nothing more than government intrusion into market efficiencies in the form of regulation. That's Milton Friedman. He got a goddamn Nobel prize.' The film exposes the gritty realities of the symbiotic relationship between oil and politics that are far from the mythologised ideals of the City upon a Hill: Killen Oil only manages to secure the Kazakhstani contract through a seventy million dollar bribe to the President of Kazakhstan. Dalton is the film's most divisive character: depending on one's political perspective, he is either an industrious patriot securing America's future, or a criminal wilfully ignoring international law. However, the film does not offer an entirely balanced portrayal of big business and Dalton is certainly a stereotypical 'ugly American', who is not given the same sense of complexity and sensitivity as Prince Nasir. The same is true for the other representatives of the oil industry: Jimmy Pope is shown hunting African wild game on his estate, a rather clunky metaphor for his company's colonialist enterprises, and the Machiavellian Dean Whiting, played by Christopher Plummer, is an unscrupulous capitalist very similar to the one Plummer played just a year later in *Inside Man* (2006). The film may have been more non-partisan if it had cast the more sympathetic figures of Matt Damon or George Clooney (who plays CIA agent Bob Barnes) in the role of Dalton, offering a challenge to the stereotypes of shady capitalists that have been pervasive in American cinema.

The film shows how the Emir's decisions have far-reaching ramifications after two young Muslims, Wasim and Saleem, lose their jobs when a Chinese firm takes over Connex's operations. Facing the possibility of being deported because of their unemployed status, they join an Islamic school to study Arabic (but also to get better food) and come under the influence of a charismatic fundamentalist cleric who slowly persuades them to embark upon a jihad that will see them target a Connex oil tanker. The portrayal of Wasim challenges the prevailing images of Arabs in American film as stereotypical vengeful jihadists, and he is a far cry from Ammar in *Zero Dark Thirty*, Al-Saleem in *Body of Lies* or Fareed in *Traitor*. His naivety is manipulated by those who promise him everlasting life in heaven and financial security for his family in this world after he has gone. Even Wasim's father, a very minor character, is registered as a human being in the small amount of time he is on the screen, given a poignant farewell to a son who, unbeknown to him, has agreed to become a suicide bomber. So while the Arabs in the film are still examples of Jack Shaheen's 'bombers, belly dancers, or billionaires' (2009: 13), they are thought-provoking variations or even deconstructions of these stereotypes. However, this sense of perspective was met with hostility by some reviewers who questioned the portrayal of Wasim. Charles Krauthammer (2006) stated,

'The most pernicious element in the movie is the character at the moral heart of the film: the beautiful, modest, caring, generous Pakistani who becomes a beautiful, modest, caring, generous . . . suicide bomber. In his final act, the Pure One, dressed in the purest white robes, takes his explosives-laden little motor-boat headfirst into his target.' To suggest that Wasim is the moral heart of the film is certainly disingenuous, yet there is some validity to Krauthammer's charge that the film may be as unbalanced towards the left of the political spectrum as we have charged that *Zero Dark Thirty* is to the right. The film's greatest strength is that it does what Bigelow and Boal claim they set out to do with *Zero Dark Thirty*: to question and debate. The moral certainty found in *Zero Dark Thirty* is replaced by a profound sense of moral equivalency and ambiguity in *Syriana* that is rare in popular American film of the post-9/11 era. Gaghan's film is one that continually asks questions rather than answers them. George Clooney, who also produced the film, suggested, 'We didn't answer anything in *Syriana*. It isn't a film about what nice kids suicide bombers are, but we do examine the elements that create them as opposed to just labelling them' (cited in Jaafar 2006: 17).

Clooney's jaded operative Barnes, based on Robert Baer himself, is a CIA agent who has spent decades on the ground in the Middle East but who falls out of favour with the new administration when his nuanced accounts do not coalesce with the simplistic 'big picture' that the government wishes to promote, regardless of whether it matches with reality or not. Clooney effectively deconstructs his usual suave persona that has seen him widely described as an 'embodiment of perfect masculinity' (Moss 2007: 22), appearing as the overweight, bearded and ageing Barnes who becomes progressively disillusioned with America's continued intrusion into the Middle East, something he has played a large role in himself, and sets out to warn Prince Nasir that his life is in danger. Barnes's arc is a familiar one in post-9/11 cinema from fervent believer and patriot, to critic (see Hank Deerfield in *In the Valley of Elah* (2008), Douglas Freeman in *Rendition*, Roger Ferris in *Body of Lies* and Stanley Phillips in *Grace is Gone*). When Barnes is captured and tortured by the mercenary Masawi (Mark Strong who played George the senior CIA staff member in *Zero Dark Thirty*), the techniques used against him are seen to be monstrous, but they follow the same methodology of violence used against Ammar and the detainees in *Zero Dark Thirty*. The major difference is in the ambiguity with which it portrays the torture perpetrated against Americans, which is typically portrayed as grotesque and immoral. However, when Bob is tortured we empathise with him, but are simultaneously forced to acknowledge the fact that he too he has committed these acts. We have seen Barnes kill in the film's opening explosion, in which he sold missiles to Muslim extremists only to later deliberately detonate them with little concern as to whether or not there are innocent bystanders around. Ironically, it is one of these weapons sold by Bob at the start of the film that finds its way into the hands of Wasim who uses it to destroy the Killen tanker, as the film emerges as perhaps the fullest approximation of Chalmers Johnson's 'blowback' of the decade. This embrace of multiple perspectives is a striking embodiment of Žižek's seemingly impossible call to transcend reductive binaries of good and evil, and 'adopt both positions simultaneously' (2004: 62). Massawi had earlier been described by one of Barnes's colleagues as 'a soldier . . . just like you'. This sense of moral equivalency raises its head frequently in American cinema, but is habitually disavowed, as its recognition would be a fundamental challenge to the moral certainty that America has historically embraced and the master narrative of 9/11 and the war on terror. However, Barnes himself does not ignore it, and *Syriana* is a rare film that offers an acknowledgement that the practices of the United States may not be as far removed from those of the Other than we have been led to believe.[15]

Elizabeth Ezra highlights the fundamental illogical and hypocritical nature of these distinctions, which are so firmly embedded in our cultural understanding that they appear to be natural:

> If a white male traveler acts violently, it is likely to be in the guise of an action hero, with whom audiences are meant to identify, while similar actions performed by a brown-skinned character are usually signs of the violence and villainy that the narrative is devoted to eradicating. As the film franchise *Mission Impossible* [1996] makes clear, subterfuge and disguise may be associated either with an 'international man of mystery' or with an international terrorist, according to the vagaries of pigmentation. (Ezra and Rowden 2005: 11)

Syriana is rare antidote to this: a site of contesting perspectives and a narrative that gives a voice and a Lévinasian face to non-Western peoples who have traditionally been ignored. The film ends with the deaths of Prince Nasir, Wasim and Bob Barnes, but none are regarded as any more important or grievable than the others, a shared vulnerability infrequently acknowledged in US cinema. The deaths of these characters are tragic and will be mourned regardless of the nationality of those left behind. Stephen Gaghan himself suggested:

> We are living in complex, difficult times and I wanted *Syriana* to reflect this complexity in a visceral way, to embrace it narratively. There are no good guys and no bad guys and there are no easy answers. The characters do not have traditional character arcs; the stories don't wrap up in neat little life lessons, the questions remain open. The hope was that by not wrapping everything up, the film will get under your skin in a different way and stay with you longer. This seemed like the most honest reflection of this post 9/11 world we all find ourselves in. (Gaghan cited in Maslin)

Syriana dares to acknowledge unspoken truths about US foreign policy that have been conveniently ignored since 1945, and in so doing it embraces an awareness of historical context and causality that is absent from the majority of post-9/11 films. To equate the practices of the United States with those of the terrorist groups they are committed to fighting caused ire among several reviewers, so conditioned are we to stereotypical representations of the Muslim Other and American moral superiority. Krauthammer ended his review with the sentence, 'Osama bin Laden could not have scripted this film with more conviction.' It is much easier to see the world through the prism of films like *Zero Dark Thirty* and *United 93*, or as we shall see in the next chapter, *Act of Valour* and *The Hurt Locker*. These are texts that offer sanitised and unproblematic depictions of the globe beyond the borders of the First World, rather than engaging with the complicated reality of the transnational, which is at the heart of *Syriana*.

NOTES

1. Can we also see this reflected in Clint Eastwood's *Hereafter* (2010) and Juan Antonio Bayona's *The Impossible* (2012)? To date they are the only two Western films about the Asian tsunami of 2004. They centre their narratives of loss and redemption on middle-class, white Westerners and ignore the plight of the nearly quarter of a million indigenous people who died in the tragedy. (See David Cox's (2013) article 'Attempting the impossible: Why does western cinema whitewash Asian stories?')
2. As clumsy and unscientific barometers as they are, Metacritic.com interprets that *Zero Dark Thirty* has 95 per cent 'positive' reviews and Rotten Tomatoes interprets that it has 93 per cent.
3. John Pilger (2012), writing in the British cultural and political magazine *New Statesman*, described Kathryn Bigelow as 'the Leni Riefenstahl of our time, promoting her master's voice as did the Führer's pet filmmaker'.
4. Some families of the victims complained about this unauthorized use. See Cieply (2013).
5. Cofer Black testified to the United States Senate in 2002 that after 9/11 'the gloves came off' (cited in Clarke 2004: 276).
6. The idea of sending aid workers to try to find deoxyrinoclueic acid (DNA) evidence of bin Laden is portrayed as an ingenuous scheme concocted by the CIA, but the practice has been subsequently heavily criticised by a variety of aid agencies. As a result of using aid workers undercover many legitimate workers were killed, and there is a significant lack of trust of aid programmes in the region. See Walsh (2012).
7. One may take a moment to consider how differently torture is portrayed when what is being shown is its use against Americans: whether in the World War Two – *The Bridge on the River Kwai* (1957), the Vietnam War – *The Deer Hunter* (1978) and *Rambo: First Blood Part II* (1985) or the war on terror – *Brothers* (2009), *Body of Lies*, *Mission: Impossible 3*, and *Act of Valour*, which is explored in Chapter 2.
8. The Bureau of Investigative Journalism suggests that there have been 370 drone strikes in Pakistan since 2004 and from 411 to 890 civilians have been killed with 168 to 197 children killed and 1,177 to 1,480 injured. See Serle and Woods (2001).

9. Witness how some contemporary films about the CIA have attempted to sidestep the dubious morality of the actions perpetrated by the CIA after 9/11. In *Jack Ryan: Shadow Recruit* (2014) the titular hero (who quits his studies after 9/11 to join the Marines) remarks to CIA agent William Harper (Kevin Costner), 'You know people don't like you guys that much these days . . . waterboarding, rendition.' To which Harper replies, 'Not my unit.'

10. Cited in Anonymous (2006) and in Muntean (2009).

11. W. Bryan Rommel-Ruiz praised this aspect of the film's narrative and its refusal to focus on individual heroes. He stated: 'Often we associate the American character with the attributes of possessive individualism: in the United States individuals have the opportunity to be whatever they want to be, and control the course of their lives' (2011: 240). It is a statement of almost breathtaking naiveté for a renowned historian.

12. In an interview conducted for this book, the actor Erich Redman, who played Christian Adams, was very reflective about his portrayal. He said, 'I saw on the Internet some people's reaction to the film. Some people were saying "How dare Paul Greengrass portray the German as the only coward on the plane?" or, "Typical Germans, always the cowards." Some time has now passed and I feel a little bit ashamed that I suggested to play him the way I did. I was a bit younger then and I was still very ambitious and desperate to find a way to stand out from the crowd as I thought otherwise I am just going to look like an extra. During one of the rehearsals I thought about the Mogadishu incident of 1977 [hijacking of Lufthansa Flight 181]. The lesson the German public was told after this incident was that if ever you get into this kind of situation you should always comply with terrorists and the German secret service will bail you out. All Germans believed that whatever happened you should always comply with the terrorists and hope for the government to take care of you. I am pretty sure Christian Adams would have thought of this; any German of my age group would have been aware of Mogadishu and would have thought of it in the situation. Whether he actually got up and attempted to cooperate with the terrorists and therefore said, "I don't want to die; I am not an American," is very doubtful. To be honest I wanted to be noticed and I feel ashamed now for his wife. I am sure that Mr. Adams's widow has seen it and seen the press. For me to portray her husband as a coward is very regrettable; I wish I hadn't been so selfish at the time. I think it would have been OK to mention Mogadishu but there was no need to say, "I am not American. Please don't kill me. I don't want to die.' We don't know he said it; to be honest he probably didn't, because he looked very big in the picture I have of him. He was probably one of the people who helped attack the hijackers. I have thought about trying to get redemption and contacting the widow and expressing my apology but on the other hand I don't want to make things more difficult than they are already. But this is what I am feeling now' (Redman 2012).

13. Paul Greengrass's 2013 film *Captain Phillips* faced similar challenges about its authenticity (see Tricia Escobedo (2013)).

14. See Quart (2005). Other examples are *Babel* (2006), *21 Grams* (2003) and *The Three Burials of Melquiades Estrada* (2005).

15. The portrayal of the CIA in *Syriana* was vociferously criticised by the agency itself. Tricia Jenkins wrote, '*Syriana* violates almost every criteria the CIA requires of scripts before it will offer assistance: it depicts the CIA in a negative light, it works to undermine employee morale, and it certainly fails to generate positive interest in the agency' (2012: 123).

2. BOOTS ON THE GROUND: THE NEW MILLENNIAL COMBAT FILM AS CULTURAL ARTEFACT

Lurking beneath the surface of every society, including ours, is the passionate yearning for a nationalist cause that exalts us, the kind that war alone is able to deliver. It reduces and at times erases the anxiety of individual consciousness. We abandon individual responsibility for a shared, unquestioned communal enterprise, however morally dubious.
                     Chris Hedges, *War is a Force that Gives Us Meaning*

After the attacks on 11 September 2001 the Bush administration quickly arranged extensive meetings with top Hollywood executives, some even at the White House itself, in a concerted effort to help market the war on terror through the medium of film, just as President Franklin D. Roosevelt had sought to mobilise Hollywood during World War Two through the Office of War Information (OWI). Many promptly got onboard; Bryce Zabel, the chair of the Academy of Television Arts & Sciences, declared, 'We are willing to volunteer to become advocates for the American message' (cited in Cooper (2001)). From the very beginning George W. Bush sought to define the American response to 9/11, as the administration's mantra became, 'You are either with us or you are with the terrorists' (Bush 2001) with little room for nuance or historical awareness. The war on terror was not only to be a military one, it was also to be a war of 'hearts and minds', with not just Iraqis and Afghanistanis as the target, but American citizens as well. This chapter explores combat films made in the war on terror era and asks how the first American wars of the new millennium have been represented on-screen when compared to films made about

World War Two and the Vietnam War. While films about the Vietnam War did not emerge (with one or two notable exceptions) until after the conclusion of the conflict in 1975, a substantial number of films about the conflict in Iraq and Afghanistan were released *while* the war was being fought, even as early as 2005 with the release of Sidney J. Furie's *American Soldiers: A Day in Iraq*. Prior to the new millennium, the Vietnam War had been a national point of crisis which filmmakers had periodically returned to in an attempt reconcile it to the national imaginary. However, after 9/11 Vietnam effectively disappeared from the cinema screens, to be replaced by films about Iraq and Afghanistan, a new symbolic rupture in discourse about national identity. Yet the Vietnam War continued to cast a shadow over not just the Iraq War but cinematic representations of it. Despite the Bush administration's concerted effort to symbolically connect the war on terror to the 'Total War' of World War Two, leapfrogging the more contentious Vietnam War in the process, as the conflict progressed, it was more Vietnam to which the media and the public compared the war in Iraq. Senator Ted Kennedy was one of many to call the conflict 'George Bush's Vietnam' (cited in Phillips 2007), and General Tony Zinni stated, 'I have seen this movie. It was called Vietnam' (cited in Brigham 2006: 50). Paul Haggis, the writer and director of *In the Valley of Elah*, saw the Iraq War film as heavily influenced by films about Vietnam. He stated, 'There's a freedom I think that we got from the folks who made the films about Vietnam. We started learning from that, and we're standing on their shoulders.' He continued, 'I think if the nightly news was doing its job, we wouldn't have to do some of these films. Because we aren't getting the news of what's truly happening to our men and women' (cited in Anonymous 2007).

Indeed films about the Vietnam War function as an effective template for the war on terror era combat film. In his article 'The articulation of memory and desire: From Vietnam to the war in the Persian Gulf', John Storey provides a sustained analysis of the tropes of Vietnam War cinema that offer striking parallels to modern combat films. He argues that films depicting the Vietnam War are characterised by the following: a) their sustained disconnection from a political or historical understanding of the conflict being fought, b) a committed disavowal of the extent of the US military advantage over the Vietnamese, c) an absence of anti-war sentiment to the extent it was present at the time, d) a predisposition towards forgetting Vietnamese casualties or an almost exclusive focus on American casualties, e) Americanisation of narratives including the pronounced exclusion of Vietnamese who are constructed as an unambiguous Other, f) atrocities committed *are* portrayed (which gives the appearance of the films being more challenging than they are) but they are presented as isolated acts of madness often brought about by the intense pressure that soldiers are placed under, and g) the victimisation of the US soldier and by extension the US as a whole (2003: 105–7). Thus, while the public at large understood films like

Platoon, *Full Metal Jacket* (1987) and *Apocalypse Now* to be critical of the Vietnam War, the primary ideological function of these films was actually to 'address and alleviate this trauma in order to restore American self-belief and credibility' (Westwell 2006: 57). It is quite clear to see that the majority of the films made about the wars in Iraq and Afghanistan fit into this paradigm, often with the simple substitution of Iraq or Afghanistan for Vietnam. Thus, films about both Vietnam and Iraq attempt to construct (or, in rare examples, deconstruct) a Foucauldian 'regime of truth' in the creation of meanings connected to the war (see Foucault 1970).

By 2006 and 2007 there was a veritable wave of films about the wars in Iraq and Afghanistan, most of which proved commercially underwhelming despite the presence of big name stars like Matt Damon, Tobey Maguire and Channing Tatum. This lack of success saw the Iraq War cycle of films labelled as 'box office poison' or even 'a toxic genre'.[1]

- Paul Haggis's *In the Valley of Elah* begins with the discovery of the dismembered body of a young American soldier, Mike Deerfield, on leave in the United States after completing a tour of duty in Iraq. Mike's father, Hank Deerfield (Tommy Lee Jones), a former soldier himself, embarks on his own investigation into his son's death after becoming dissatisfied with the official one. Hank is an old-fashioned patriot who initially shows unquestioning support for the war. Near the start of the film when he sees a Salvadorian janitor inadvertently hanging the American flag upside down he helps him change it, explaining to him that an inverted flag is a traditional signal of distress. The film slowly reveals that Mike was actually murdered by his own squad mates after a violent altercation at a strip club. So desensitised to violence have the young men become, that they turn on one another with shocking brutality, and then attempt to cover up the crime by callously disposing of Mike's body. Hank is forced to confront the fact that Mike is not the bright young boy he remembers; in fact, his squad mates referred to him as 'Doc' because of his predilection for abusing Iraqi prisoners. In many studies that emerged from Iraq this proved to be a disturbingly frequent practice: two-thirds of marines and one half of regular soldiers said that they would not report a team member for abuse and 10 per cent said that they had participated in such acts themselves (see Ricks 2009: 7–8). Hank realises that his government has not been honest with its people, and the film concludes with him deliberately hanging his own US flag upside down, a clumsy but potent metaphor for an America in crisis.
- A similar impact is felt in Jim Sheridan's *Brothers*, which shows how the war affects a single family and spreads through the surrounding

community. When US Marine Captain Sam Cahill (Tobey Maguire) is reported killed in Afghanistan, he leaves behind a wife, Grace (Natalie Portman), two young daughters and two grieving parents. Into this void steps Sam's underachieving brother Tommy (Jake Gyllenhaal), a good-natured ex-con who hesitantly takes on a larger role in their family dynamic – becoming a reluctant father figure to the girls. Tommy had found it hard to live in his brother's imposing shadow, especially because of his unforgiving father, an alcoholic Vietnam veteran and strict disciplinarian. However, unbeknownst to them, Sam is not dead, but has been held captive, tortured by insurgents and even forced to kill fellow American soldiers to survive. When he returns home he is a changed man: where once he was open and good-humoured, now he is disengaged and prone to violent mood swings that lead to him being institutionalised for the sake of his own family's safety.

- Kimberly Pierce's *Stop-Loss* features three traumatised Iraq war veterans, who return to a heroes' welcome in their home town of Brazos County, Texas. When one of their number commits suicide, their intensely patriotic squad commander, Brandon (Ryan Phillippe), feels responsible. Having served his country honourably and completed his tour of duty, Brandon expects to be discharged and begins to make plans for his future outside of the army, but he is shocked to hear that he has been stop-lossed, that is, involuntarily ordered to extend his commission. Brandon believes that what the army is asking of him is unlawful and refuses, preferring instead to go AWOL. His reasons for originally joining up are echoed by many soldiers portrayed in post-9/11 films about Iraq: 'I signed up thinking I was gonna go over there and protect my country, my family. We wanted payback for 9/11, and when you get there, and you realise the war wasn't even about any of that. The enemy isn't out in the desert. They're in the hallways and rooftops, living rooms and kitchens. Everybody's got a weapon. Everybody. Nobody knows who's who.' However, wrestling with his own post-traumatic stress disorder, Brandon finds that it is impossible to live as a fugitive, which sees him labelled as unpatriotic and a coward, and so he reluctantly returns to the army.

The cumulative effect of these portrayals is the depiction of the American soldier as the principal victim of the war on terror, not, as one might expect, the Iraqis and Afghanistanis who died and were wounded in their hundreds and thousands. Those soldiers who do survive their tours of duty often go home injured or traumatised, returning to a country that cannot (or does not want) to understand or acknowledge them; as Sergeant Will Foster in *The Messenger* (2009) suggests, 'It's like coming home to a different planet.' Despite their relative failure at the box office, these films have played a substantial role in how the conflict has been viewed in the West, reaffirming the power of film to define concepts of national identity. Taken together they form a compelling tapestry of how the war on terror became a central part of American consciousness in the first decade of the new millennium. Films about a nation's wars are important in a variety of ways; they crystallise an image of the conflict that remains influential at the time of their release and for generations to come: World War Two for many is now embodied in films like *The Sands of Iwo Jima* (1949) and more recently *Saving Private Ryan*, just as the Vietnam War has become encapsulated within *Apocalypse Now*, *Platoon* and *The Deer Hunter*. In this way contemporary films about current conflicts provide a battleground for interpretations of a war, how it is viewed now and how it will be seen in the future.

The Heroic Mythology of a New 'Good War' in Act of *Valour* and *The Hurt Locker*

Remember, you have warrior's blood in your veins. The code that made your father who he was is the same code that'll make you a man he would admire, respect. Put your pain in a box. Lock it down. Like those people in the paintings your father liked, we are men made up of boxes, chambers of loss and triumph. Of hurt and hope and love. No one is stronger or more dangerous than a man who can harness his emotions, his past.

Chief Dave, *Act of Valour*

Act of Valour portrays a team of US Navy SEALs charged with tracking a group of ferocious Islamic terrorists around the globe in order to prevent them striking the United States in a series of attacks that would make '9/11 look like a walk in the park'. Co-directed by Mike McCoy and Kurt Waugh, the film presents a very particular vision of the war on terror, which can be read as a close approximation of how the conflict was viewed by the Bush administration, a fact that may explain the significant input and assistance that the film received from the Pentagon.[2] David L. Robb's *Operation Hollywood: How the Pentagon Shapes and Censors the Movies* (2004) describes a similar process to that which we observed with *Zero Dark Thirty* and the CIA in the previous chapter in his analysis of how films that offer favourable depictions of the military are given extensive support (see *Top Gun* (1986), *Independence Day* and *Black Hawk Down* (2001)) and those that depict the military in a negative light are denied access to materials and personnel (see *The Last Detail* (1973), *Apocalypse Now*, *Born on the Fourth of July* (1989) and *Thirteen Days* (2000).

McCoy and Waugh went to extraordinary lengths to emphasise the realism of their film even presenting screenings with an on-camera prologue that saw the directors themselves explaining how they used authentic weaponry, tactics and operational SEALs instead of actors. Yet the film is so simplistic in its re-creation of complicated geo-political affairs, that it emerges as something akin to a video game, a live action version of the long-running *Call of Duty* franchise (Activision, 2003–) right down to its cardboard-cut-out Islamic terrorist villains, prominent use of point-of-view (POV) shots (a style that video games call the First Person Shooter) and its narrative, which progresses almost as if from level to level via an intensely ludic world map, an approximation of what Garett Stewart regarded as the 'instantaneous videography' of twenty-first century warfare (2009: 48). The film's quasi-eroticisation of war and technology combined with its jingoistic nationalism and portrayals of a dehumanised Other make it one of the most striking examples of cinematic 'War porn' in recent years.

The film dramatises the war on terror as a momentous battle between the virtuous United States against the insidious evil forces of the world, with America portrayed as constantly under siege from a predatory (and most frequently Muslim) Other. The antagonists are crudely drawn and illogical stereotypes: like the Chechen jihadist, Abu Shabal, who is privately funded by his millionaire best friend, the Jewish playboy Christo, or the Mexican drug cartel gangs who join forces with Islamic jihadists. Once again the motives of these characters are absent, superficially defined or reduced to them only being seen as 'enemies of freedom'. The film proceeds to combine many fears of American political conservatives into one amorphous threat: from Muslim terrorists and illegal immigrants to disparate America haters all over the globe, all of whom conspire against a righteous America for no reason other than it being the 'brightest beacon for freedom and opportunity in the world' (Bush 2001). To show how truly evil Shabal is, the film has him target an ice-cream truck in Manila in the Philippines. As the explosion fills the background, killing dozens of children, the camera moves to a tight close-up of his darkly penetrating eyes. It is revealed that Shabal has devised a cunning plan to smuggle terrorists into the United States over the Mexican border wearing high-tech suicide bomber vests that will not show up on X-ray screens; once they are on US soil they intend to target Las Vegas in order to create another 9/11.

The SEALs themselves are portrayed as all-American heroes with conspicuously large and adoring families. They are men who regard themselves as 'watchmen standing guard while the world sleeps'. The film is narrated by one of their number, Dave (for national security reasons no names of the real-life soldiers are given, even further emphasising the film's quasi-mythic approach to the military), as he writes a letter to the unborn son of his best friend and fellow SEAL, Rorke, who will later die in their mission.[3] Dave suggests, 'You don't expect your family to understand what you are doing; you hope they understand that you are doing it for them.' *Act of Valour* reveals that virtues like honour and justice are uniquely American preserves not to be found elsewhere around the globe (see Figure 10). Their first mission is to Costa Rica to rescue a female CIA

Figure 10   *Act of Valour* (2012) reduces complicated geo-political issues to a
             shooting gallery reminiscent of a video game. In doing so it becomes the
             closest approximation the war on terror era had of John Wayne's jingoistic
             The Green Berets (1968).

officer who has been tortured by terrorists in order to force her to reveal clas-
sified information; she is beaten, her hands are drilled and the threat of sexual
violence is ever present if not shown. While the film lingers on her abuse, it is
framed with a very different perspective to that of the torture portrayed in *Zero
Dark Thirty*. Even though both sets of torturers are attempting to secure the
same thing from their victims, *Act of Valour* is able to hypocritically suggest that
this torture (that which is committed against Americans) is a heinous act perpetrated by an inhuman enemy with a lack of morality, whereas the *other* type of
torture (that which is committed by Americans) is moral, legal and justifiable.

Dave and his team finally prevent the terrorists entering American soil
through Rorke's noble sacrifice for his SEAL brothers and his country when he
throws himself on top of a live grenade.[4] This scene is one of many that makes
a concerted effort to connect the war on terror to the 'Good War' of World War
Two by suggesting that the values for which the modern-day SEALs are fighting
are shared with those of the 'Greatest Generation'. Peter Ehrenhaus asserted
that Steven Spielberg's *Saving Private Ryan* performed a similar act by attempting to erase the Vietnam War from American collective memory. He stated:

> Here we see the consequences of leapfrogging back over Vietnam to the
> Second World War. Our inheritance in the present becomes a reconsti-
> tuted national identity grounded in uncontested and incontestable moral
> clarity and commitment, an identity whose stature is measured in by the
> enormity of the horror it sought to end. We can only wonder whether
> a reinvigorated national identity such as this carries with it the germ of
> another Vietnam. (2001: 335)

This process is vividly dramatised throughout *Act of Valour* and its portrayal of the war on terror as a just and necessary war. Rorke's sacrifice is directly equated to that of his grandfather, a pilot in World War Two, who managed to keep his burning bomber plane aloft just long enough to save his comrades, but in the process lost his own life. By connecting Rorke's heroic death with that of his grandfather, the film self-consciously erases this father's war, the more politically troubling Vietnam War, from the narrative.

This notion of quasi-christomimetic self-sacrifice recurs so frequently in American cinema that it has become one of its foundational tropes. In American film to give one's life for one's country is the very pinnacle of masculinity and patriotism. Yet its valorisation – while the very same sacrifices of those of the Other are declared to be monstrous and inhuman – is certainly problematic. In *Welcome to the Desert of the Real*, Žižek reminds us of the young American girl who was reluctantly willing to sacrifice her father for her country after 9/11 by allowing him to go and serve in the Armed Forces, something that was 'perceived as a "normal" outburst of American patriotism' (2012: 54). Žižek then proposes a thought experiment; 'imagine an Arab Muslim girl pathetically reciting into the camera the same words about her father fighting for the Taliban' (ibid.). Such relativism would be preposterous and grotesque for Americans and is symptomatic of a lack of moral equivalency demonstrated by American cinema and society at large.[5]

The film ends with a dedication to all those who have died fighting 'fear and tyranny, and those who will be called on in the future', appealing not just to this generation but those in succeeding generations, like Rorke's unborn son, who may be called to fight and die for the United States in its never-ending war on terror. Reaction was divided on the film's release, but both sides of the political spectrum compared the film to John Wayne's Vietnam War film *The Green Berets* (1968). From the left it was 'an Xbox *Green Berets* for the New American Reich' (Fairclough 2012). But the right read it as a 'tribute to our troops. It is indeed the most positive flick out of Hollywood about our military since *The Green Berets*' (Russo 2012). Like *The Green Berets* and its rewriting of the war in Vietnam, *Act of Valour* turns a decidedly complicated conflict into a simplistic battle between good and evil, drawing more from the tropes of Hollywood cinema by evoking films about World War Two (and even the Wild West) rather than establishing any authentic connection to a political or historical reality. As Gary Wills wrote about *The Green Berets*:

> People who did not want to know about the actual Vietnam War could feel that the national unity and resolve of World War II might turn around this strange new conflict in the far-off jungles of the East. Wayne was fighting World War II again, the only way he ever did, in make-believe;

and that make-believe was a memory of American greatness that many still wanted to live by. (Wills 1997: 233)

Act of Valour fulfils a very similar function: it attempts to erase the ruptures and tensions caused by 9/11, by assuring Americans of both their military and moral superiority, by fashioning a link between the war on terror and the mythology surrounding World War Two.

On the surface *The Hurt Locker* appears far removed from the jingoistic patriotism of *Act of Valour*. Directed by Kathryn Bigelow and written by Mark Boal, the director/writer team behind *Zero Dark Thirty*, explored in Chapter 1, the film is certainly the most acclaimed war film of the era and it won several Academy Awards, including Best Picture, Best Director, and Best Original Screenplay. Many critics widely praised the veracity of its tale of a year in the life of a United States Army explosive ordnance disposal (EOD) unit and its apparent lack of a moral agenda: one wrote, 'It's a nonpolitical film about Iraq. Many films about the Iraq war have fallen into a trap of appearing preachy or at least having a strong point of view' (Anonymous 2010a). It was even held up as an example of an anti-war film precisely because it does not contain the overt histrionics that define *Act of Valour*. *The Hurt Locker* is certainly a visceral portrait of war, frequently filmed in tight, atmospheric close-ups with a striking multilayered aural soundscape. Barry Ackroyd's impressive cinematography once again places the spectator within restricted and subjective spaces, as he had done so effectively with his work on *United 93*. The utilisation of numerous close-ups with the intermittent use of POV shots is a powerful and immersive cinematic technique, but this intimacy comes in the form of a shared burden of victimisation and the suturing of spectator and protagonist experience. Beneath its detailed and intimate narrative is a rather reactionary treatise that emphasises the humanitarian role of the American military in Iraq and detaches itself from any sense of political and historical context. Therefore, while the film may not be 'preachy', it offers a particularly ideological approach to the war that is not as far removed from *Act of Valour* as it first appears.

The film begins with a quotation from Pulitzer Prize-winning journalist Chris Hedges – 'The rush of battle is a potent and often lethal addiction, for war is a drug' – and proceeds to acknowledge the simple fact that despite its manifest horrors, there are a certain breed of men who thrive on the intensity of war.[6] The narrative is comprised of episodic vignettes, their loosely connected nature evocative of the fragmented lives of the deployed soldiers themselves. A. O. Scott suggested that this structure produced a kind of 'hyperbolic realism, [which] distils the psychological essence and moral complications of modern warfare into a series of brilliant, agonizing set pieces'. At its centre is the reckless, yet charismatic and heroic Sergeant First Class James (Jeremy Renner) who replaces Staff Sergeant Matthew Thompson (Guy Pearce), surprisingly killed off in the film's intense prologue. By disposing of the film's biggest star in its opening scene the audience is assured that celebrity is no guarantee of safety in the world of *The Hurt Locker*.

The location of the narrative in a bomb disposal team allows the film to disconnect itself from the day-to-day realities of combat and portray a war in which the United States are not combatants but peacekeepers, committed to saving Iraqi lives rather than taking them, the popular impression that many Americans had about the war. By concentrating on the profound pressure of their daily life, the film narrows 'the war to the existential confrontation of man and deadly threat' and the audience is free to enjoy the destruction 'without ambivalence and guilt' (Denby 2009). In doing this, *The Hurt Locker* presents a very conservative ideological approach to the conflict, as the American mission in Iraq is framed as a distinctly humanitarian, even altruistic, one, as James is charged with preventing insurgents from killing Iraqi civilians and destroying Iraqi buildings. The target of the bombs is rarely shown as being the Americans themselves, which, of course, was the overwhelming reality on the ground. This transformation of a contentious political narrative into a more personal one initially seems to be a retreat from ideology, but it is in the perceived absence of a political perspective that Žižek finds that *The Hurt Locker* contains 'ideology at its purest'; he asserts that 'the focus on the perpetrator's traumatic experience enables us to obliterate the entire ethico-political background of the conflict' (Žižek 2010). If we briefly return to John Storey's categorisations of the Vietnam War film charted at the beginning of this chapter, we see a remarkable correlation and a film that participates in the creation of its very own 'regime of truth' about the Iraq War. The danger that James and his team faces is a constant one; the camera jerks between one threatening Iraqi face to another, each a potential terrorist and the latest in a long line of dehumanised Others.

The closest that the film comes to an overt criticism of the war is through the neurotic, yet sympathetic Eldridge and his rather muted, even comical comments about the army's poor strategic planning: on the presence of tanks in the desert he says, 'Yeah, but they don't do anything. I mean, anyone comes alongside a Humvee, we're dead. Anybody even looks at you funny, we're dead. Pretty much the bottom line is: if you're in Iraq, you're dead!' There is no mention of the purpose of the war, or why the Americans may be meeting such vociferous contempt and aggression from the locals, and no Iraqi is allowed to speak of their own experience. Once again the mighty behemoth of the US Army is depicted as a plucky underdog cautiously making its way through the dangerous streets of Iraq. In the world of *The Hurt Locker* the victims are predominantly American in great contrast to the reality of the war that saw in the region of 100,000 to 200,000 Iraqis dead as opposed to approximately 5,000 Americans (Rogers 2012).[7] Furthermore, when Iraqis are killed, it is mostly other Iraqis who perpetrate the crimes and rarely Americans. For Mamoon Alabassi, this disconnection from any context or sense of reality disqualifies *The Hurt Locker* from being considered as an Iraq War film at all: 'It would be more accurate to say that *The Hurt Locker* is an action movie that uses Iraq as a background than to brand it as an "Iraq War movie", and less so as the "Iraq War drama".'

James strikes up a relationship with a young boy called Beckham who is the closest the film comes to having an Iraqi characterisation, and their interactions produce the film's most intimate, but also its most disturbing, moments. When James comes across an insurgent bomb factory, he finds the dead body of a young boy, who he believes to be Beckham, seemingly murdered by insurgents who have filled his corpse with explosives intending to use him as an improvised explosive device (IED). The fact that there is no recorded evidence of such a scheme ever being used reveals more about the film's desire to imagine monstrosities that continue to demonise Iraqi insurgents while at the same time glorifying James's singular humanity and heroism. Beckham's 'death' becomes a symbol of the need for American intervention and, perhaps, the 'most extreme example of the trope of the dead child, innocence destroyed by the chaos of war that will linger in the consciousness of the soldiers sent to fight it' (Peebles 2011: 168). After the incident James goes AWOL from the base, looking to enact revenge on those who killed the boy; but on his return the next day somehow Beckham is there again and in the film's most ambiguous moment James refuses to recognise him. What is this act of misrecognition and what can it mean for the film's representation of an Iraqi Other? Robert Kolker rather generously reads the boy reappearing as a 'gesture of the futility of passion in this horrendous war' (2011: 301). However, the African–American Sergeant J.T. Sanborn's earlier comment that 'they all look the same' lingers. It is in this scene of misrecognition that the ideological contradictions and ruptures of the film's depiction of a 'Good War' force their way to the surface. To misrecognise the Other is to deny his/her humanity, and for James to acknowledge that Beckham is alive and that the dead boy was someone else would be to concede that his judgement is flawed and that 'they all look the same' for him. The former soldier Stan Goff wrote,

> When I was in Vietnam, we were taught to refer to the Vietnamese as gooks. This name calling is always part of any military aggression because soldiers have to be brought along in their dehumanization of those they are obliged by conditions and ignorance to abuse, dominate, and kill. Social psychologists tell us that we are overcoming 'cognitive dissonance' when we do that. (Goff 2004: 147)

James is confronted with a superlative example of his own cognitive dissonance but it is too difficult for him to process; his only reaction is to refuse to acknowledge it and to turn his head the other way.

The Hurt Locker is one of many Iraq War films in which the true victim of the war is shown to be the American soldier: if he kills (*Brothers*, *In the Valley of Elah* and *Stop-Loss*) or even if he does not (*Jarhead* and *The Messenger*). Despite his recklessness James is framed as a distinctly masculine hero, an archetypal maverick movie construction who takes down the protective boards from his hut, removes his protective blast suit in moments of great danger and refuses to use the bomb disposal robot that disconnects him from the immediacy of his highly dangerous job. He is called a 'wild man' by a visiting colonel, and while Sanborn and Eldridge challenge his behaviour and even consider 'fragging' him, he is the film's hero: a throwback to the hard-bodied maverick icons of the 1980s and an embodiment of the real man whose return was called for after 9/11 (see Chapter 3). However, it is the mythic construct of the cowboy figure that he most resembles, a 'rugged "he-man," strong, resilient, resourceful, capable of coping with overwhelming odds' (Balswick and Peek 1976: 55), with Iraq cast as his new millennial frontier. James's instinctive manly approach (much like Michael played by Robert De Niro in *The Deer Hunter*) is contrasted with the likes of the sensitive 'new man' figures of 'Doc' Cambridge and Eldridge who prove unable to cope with the war, which is portrayed as something of a challenge to their masculinity, devoid of a political landscape and bled of ethical considerations. In James's portrayal we witness a reaffirmation of military power, framed from a righteous and ethical perspective. He may be unorthodox and break the rules, but he saves lives and gets the job done. The final bomb sequence of the film, in which James is tasked with removing an explosive device locked on to the unwilling body of an innocent Iraqi civilian functions as a telling metaphor for Bigelow's vision of the American role in Iraq. James desperately tries to save the man – he even puts himself in great danger, but he simply cannot do it, as the man's fate has already been decided by the internecine fighting between Iraqis, who, as the film suggests, put such little value on human life compared to 'us' in the West.

When his tour of duty is finished, James returns home to his loving wife and infant son, but he soon realises that the pleasures of domesticity can never be enough for him. How can changing nappies and shopping for soap powder compare to the adrenaline rush of bomb disposal? In a clumsy but potent image of the emasculating potential of modern consumerist society James is framed among the long aisles of a supermarket confronted with literally hundreds of different varieties of cereal: he is paralysed by the surfeit of choice and looks more disoriented and ill at ease than we have ever seen him in the war zone (see Figure 11). Shortly after he recounts a story about Iraq to his wife that evokes both his recent trip to the supermarket and the film's portrayal of Beckham: 'Some guy drove this truck to the middle of an Iraqi market. He starts passing out free candies, all the kids come running up, the families and stuff. He detonates . . . You know they need more bomb techs . . .' Once

Figure 11   Sergeant James in *The Hurt Locker* returns home to be confronted with the stultifying and emasculating effects of modern consumer capitalism.

again violent acts are perpetrated by Iraqis on Iraqis, especially children, with Americans cast as the unambiguous saviours and the only barrier between Iraq and chaos. James cannot articulate this hunger to his wife and he volunteers for another tour of duty in Iraq, as many characters in the war on terror films do (see, for example, *Stop-Loss* and *The Lucky Ones* (2008). Thus, the call that he answers is a call to a just war, which is as uncritical an approach to the conflict and as devoid of historical or political context as the transgenerational call for war that concluded *Act of Valour*.

'WHAT DO YOU WANNA KNOW?': DISCURSIVE MODES OF REALITY IN *BATTLE FOR HADITHA* AND *REDACTED*

It is not history, because both the war in Iraq and the court case are still going on. It is not fiction, because it actually happened. But it is not documentary, either. It is a blend of all three, for an age that does not pause for judgment.

David Hearst, on *Battle for Haditha*

The two films discussed in this section offer very different perspectives on the combat film in comparison to *Act of Valour* and *The Hurt Locker*. Both *Battle for Haditha* (2007) and *Redacted* were severely criticised by some in the mainstream media for their pronounced anti-war sentiments, and both found themselves accused of being anti-American. In an ironically titled review,

'One-sided battle', *Battle for Haditha* was described by Kyle Smith (2008) as 'an exposé only of a filmmaker's senseless contempt for the military'. *Redacted* was on the receiving end of similar criticisms and was even called 'an awful aberration' by Joel Morgernstern (2007). One may suggest that the primary reason for these criticisms, for the most part, is not the quality of the films, but actually their political perspectives, as they both deviate considerably from the conventional stylistic and ideological template of the combat film. Both are loosely based on contentious real-life incidents. Nick Broomfield's *Battle for Haditha* is a fictionalised exploration of the 'Haditha killings' that took place in Iraq in November 2004, when twenty-four unarmed Iraqi men, women and children were allegedly killed by a unit of United States Marines in an incident described in the media as 'Bush's My Lai' (see Parry 2006). Brian De Palma's *Redacted* is a fictional account of the 'Mahmudiya killings' of March 2006, also in Iraq, when a small group of American soldiers allegedly proceeded to rape a fourteen year-old girl and then murder her and several members of her family in order to hide evidence of the crime. In both events the military appeared initially reluctant to investigate the crimes or they issued inaccurate accounts of what had happened until prompted to undertake further investigations by the media. In the case of the Haditha killings an initial report published by the military suggested that fifteen Iraqis had been killed by a bomb blast and eight had been shot by the marines in a protracted gun battle. It was only after an investigation by *Time* magazine reporter Tim McGirk exposed inaccuracies in the report that the army started a formal investigation into the incident. Similarly the Mahmudiya killings were originally reported by the authorities as being perpetrated not by American soldiers, but by Sunni insurgents. A more accurate version of the events only came out when one of the soldiers admitted to the crime during psychological counselling.

Like many contemporary war films *Battle for Haditha* begins with a series of intimate confessionals to camera. It's very first lines are offered as a conspicuous challenge to the spectator: 'What do you wanna know?' The question is asked by Corporal Elliot Ramirez (Elliot Ruiz), already on his third tour of duty in Iraq, even though he is only twenty years of age. From the opening scenes it is immediately apparent that *Haditha* is distinctly influenced by Broomfield's prior work as a documentarian, and his use of a documentary-style aesthetic is reminiscent of the footage of embedded journalists filmed during the war. The film's use of non-professional actors, many of whom are either ex-marines or Iraqi refugees, gives it a sense of verisimilitude not seen in many larger budgeted Iraq War films. Yet, as we observed in the discussion of *United 93*, these cinematic devices can only give the appearance of realism rather than any objective sense of reality. However, unlike *Act of Valour* and *Zero Dark Thirty*, which seem to embody a concerted need to convince the audience of their authenticity, *Haditha* and *Redacted* repeatedly acknowledge their own construction – and this awareness of the highly subjective nature of 'reality' becomes a key thematic and stylistic motif in both films. They offer no coherent totalising view of the conflict and they become defined by their attempts to transcend the traditional hegemonic perspectives of the American war film.

Haditha proceeds to show the huge pressures on the marines and the unrelenting dangers they are exposed to on a day-to-day basis. Ramirez is certainly shown, even before the central event of the film, to be suffering from some form of post-traumatic stress disorder, but he is informed by his commanding officer that he cannot seek counselling until after his tour of duty is complete. Ramirez is a professional soldier, but he is conflicted and has doubts about why his unit is stationed in Iraq. He sees his allegiance as primarily to his squad mates rather than his country, and provides quite a different vision of the contemporary American soldier when compared to the rugged machismo of James in *The Hurt Locker* and the patriotic Rorke from *Act of Valour*.

In a conventional war film Ramirez and his unit would have been at the centre of the narrative, but instead *Haditha* offers three parallel and intersecting narrative strands of which Ramirez's perspective is only one. The second follows two insurgents, Ahmed and Jafar, who are paid to place an IED on a road in order to target an American military vehicle. In *Haditha* the target of Iraqi insurgents is not other Iraqis, as shown in *The Hurt Locker*, but the American military. The third narrative perspective is of an Iraqi family, including a young woman called Hiba and her fiancé Walied, who happen to live near the road where the IED is placed. These three narrative strands intertwine when it is revealed that the unit that is targeted by Ahmed and Jafar is Ramirez's and as Hiba and Walied's family become caught in the ensuing chaos.

In providing three contrasting perspectives of the occupation of Iraq, *Haditha* becomes a rare example of an American film that breaks free of an America-centric view of the war and in doing so destabilises the habitual privileging of American subjectivity and authority. The insurgent named Ahmed is a complicated figure, not a stereotypical jihadist seeking only blood and revenge or a shallow caricature designed to evoke the 'empty empathy' described by Kaplan. The film reveals that he has joined the insurgency as much out of economic necessity than as a result of nationalism or religious beliefs. A veteran of the disbanded Iraqi Army, he reluctantly turns to the insurgency as a way to provide financial support for his family. He is certainly antagonistic towards the Americans, but he also regards the leaders of the insurgency themselves with deep suspicion and is fearful of what the future holds for his country. Likewise, the family who become caught between the Americans and the insurgents are similarly humanised. Broomfield moves his camera into the Muslim domestic sphere, revealing the essential humanity of its occupants and also the precarious conditions under which they live. Hiba and Walied are not the shrieking and faceless victims of a conventional Iraq War film; they offer a sharp contrast to stereotypical depictions of Muslim couples, as Broomfield portrays them as loving and even sexual partners. When Hiba sees the IED being planted on the roadside near their house, she is not sure what she should do. It seems they are as afraid of the local al-Qaeda (whom they call terrorists), as they are of the Americans. The family goes to their sheikh, the local authority figure, and reveals their predicament: 'If we tell the Americans, the terrorists will kill us; if we keep quiet, the Americans will say we're cooperating with the insurgents. What should we do?' The sheikh's answer is a simple one, but it is unsatisfactory for them: 'Pray to God, he will help us.' By endeavouring to show the perspectives of the insurgents and the Iraqi families caught in the conflict, the film reverse focalises the traditional approach to combat films by giving a voice to the Other that has been habitually marginalised or even erased from the genre.

The incident that sparks the reprisal killings is prompted by one of Ramirez's marines being killed in the IED explosion set up by Ahmed. Ramirez is then assigned the difficult task of finding those responsible in the form of a vague order from his commanding officer back at the base to 'take whatever action is necessary'. The marines become progressively more and more frustrated and vent their anger on the nearby buildings that contain the innocent families of Hiba and Walied, who, Ramirez believes, surely *must* know who planted the IED. After an altercation with a group of young men who the marines shoot and kill, they enter the Iraqi homes – that they class as being filled with enemy combatants – and in the ensuing chaos proceed to kill twenty-four people including women and children. Yet even in their barbarous act the marines retain a sense of humanity and the film even suggests that shots *were* fired from the Iraqi houses before the slaughter. Yet unbeknownst to Ramirez they came from an elderly Iraqi shooting an antique weapon, distraught and furious at having seen the deaths of the young men who were completely unconnected to the IED bombing. While the marines are shown committing the atrocity in some detail, within the context of the event and what has led to it, it becomes understandable why such a tragic incident might have taken place.

After the incident, Ramirez is physically sick on the street, but he pulls himself together when a commanding officer arrives who tells him, 'You handled yourself like a true professional out there. I'm gonna promote you to sergeant and recommend you for the bronze star.' However, when the details of the incident come out, Ramirez is quickly scapegoated and punished by the very same commanding officer who had ordered the actions. These officers are shown to be disconnected from the war on the ground, ordering operations from the safety of their headquarters miles behind the front line and only viewing the conflict through the satellites that hover above the cities. In one sequence an officer orders a drone strike to kill an unarmed Iraqi man walking through the street carrying a shovel. To the Americans he looks as if he has just planted (or is going to plant) an IED, but we have seen him plant nothing more dangerous than an olive tree. The sequence not only evokes the WikiLeaks' 'Collateral Murder' attack video, but the allegation that American soldiers routinely placed 'drop shovels' on innocent Iraqis victims in order to make them look like enemy combatants (see Washburn 2008: 22).

The end of the film shows al-Qaeda (including the sheikh to whom the family went to for advice) positively welcome such brutal retaliations from American soldiers, which act as fuel for the fire of resentment felt by the general population towards their occupiers and leads to increasing numbers of people joining the insurgency. In a scene that even brings the veracity of *Time* magazine report into the discourse, the only survivors of the Haditha incident are told to recall the traumatic event on videotape, especially a little girl, Safa, who is pressured into recounting how the Americans struck her: 'Say the Americans hit you over the head!' In doing so, *Haditha* interrogates the prevailing narrative of the killings from a variety of perspectives: offering a direct challenge to spectator complicity in the events and the war at large. An American TV news headline 'Ramirez: Hero or Bad Guy?' reveals how the American media quickly simplifies complicated issues in order to make them more accessible to the public. Yet the film has deliberately attempted to do the opposite of this and thus offers a counter-hegemonic narrative to the traditional representations of the war in Iraq, not because it portrays the contentious incident (here we see an echo of Kathryn Bigelow's earlier disingenuous comments that portrayal is not endorsement) but because of *how* it is depicted. *Haditha* is a rare film that portrays Iraqis as human beings, not as the lifeless enemies of a video game, and by reinstating the humanity of the Other, it calls into dispute the very reasons that the war was fought for and derails the prevailing 'us versus them' narrative that was so pervasive in the post-9/11 years.

Battle for Haditha saves its most remarkable moments for its final scene, an epilogue in which Ramirez recalls the event itself. The sequence lasts for a minute and a half and is ambiguously presented: shot in a crepuscular light, with a static camera and no audible dialogue, its oneiric nature is striking in a film that has endeavoured to create a sense of naturalism throughout. It shows Ramirez taking the small girl, Safa, out of the bathroom where she had been hiding when the marines stormed her family home. Whether it is a memory, a dream, a vision of what actually happened or what Ramirez wished had happened is never entirely clear. Is it another return to the trope of the symbolic child as cultural battleground like Beckham in *The Hurt Locker*? Yet, none of these interpretations are prioritised, and it is only in this final scene that the meaning of the film's title becomes clear: the *Battle for Haditha* is not the blood shed in Iraq on 19 November 2005, but the battle for meanings that still continues to resonate in films produced about the war in Iraq today.

These issues of representation, subjectivity and culpability are also at the centre of Brian De Palma's *Redacted*, which confronts the complicated relationship between spectator and screen in a much more explicit fashion than other texts about the Iraq War, even *Battle for Haditha*. The film deviates from the long-established naturalistic aesthetic of the combat film in favour of a bricolage of contrasting styles that alternate between a POV video diary, a soldiers' wives' website, psychological evaluation camera footage, an insurgent website, an Arabic news channel, a Skype-style videoconference, closed-circuit television (CCTV) cameras and even a pretentious French documentary called *Checkpoint* replete with classical music and pretentious symbolism. This fragmented approach destabilises and ruptures the subjective spectatorial position that films like *Act of Valour* and *The Hurt Locker* work so diligently to reinforce. De Palma insisted, 'The movie attempts to bring the reality of what happened in Iraq to the American people' (cited in Jaafar 2008: 16) and he finds this sense of 'reality' not in the quasi-documentary style of films like *United 93* and *The Hurt Locker*, but in a deconstruction of their reliance upon the codes and conventions that create the appearance of realism and authenticity, while at the same time perpetuating highly politicised ideologies. This is not to say that *Redacted* itself offers any approximation of an objective sense of reality; Joel Morgernstern (2007) may have been correct to suggest that it is 'a work of propaganda in its turn'. However, its deviation from mytho-poetic accounts of combat, that have been regarded as the norm for portraying war on-screen, prove a compelling antidote to such uncritical discourses on the Iraq War that dominated the media. While *Redacted* centres on the events of the Mahmudiya killings, it is actually more concerned with how they are mediated and received by audiences at home. In this way the process of redaction becomes the film's central thematic motif and metaphor. Needless to say, this highly critical perspective on the war caused concern among mainstream critics. Conservative host and political pundit Bill O'Reilly, to whom we will return more than once in the course of this book, said that the film was so irresponsible that it 'endangered the lives of American servicemen' (cited in Fellerath 2007).

The film follows a unit of US soldiers stationed at Camp Carolina near Samarra in Iraq. The soldiers themselves are largely stereotypical characters, the likes of which have populated the combat film for decades: the good-natured everyman (McCoy), the bookish nerd (Blix), the cocky and self-confident joker (Salazar), the brash redneck who only joined up in order to escape jail (Flake) and even the grizzled veteran sergeant (Sweet). Unlike James in *The Hurt Locker*, the soldiers have all become jaded by their service for their country, rather than energised by it, and they are disillusioned with the conflict and the reasons for which it is being fought. Anyone who tries to talk about politics is silenced by the loud boos and hisses of his squad mates. The audience is initially provided with a surrogate in Salazar, who is making an amateur film he calls *Tell*

Me No Lies about his tour of duty, which he hopes will get him into film school on his return to America. He claims it will be a truthful account of the war and warns his squad and the audience, 'Don't be expecting no Hollywood action flick; there's not gonna be any smash cuts, no adrenalin-pumping soundtrack, no logical narrative to help make sense of it. Basically here shit happens.' De Palma quickly shows that Salazar's assertion that 'the camera never lies' is a fallacy by revealing the power of the image to alter one's perspective on any given event just by the way it is presented. In these early scenes in which Salazar is filming himself, he comes across as impetuous and shallow, but when he is returned to in the French documentary *Checkpoint*, he is transformed into a consummate soldier and professional, his stature enhanced by the choice of mise en scène, camera angle and Handel's 'Sarabande' on the soundtrack. Similarly, as the film moves between aesthetic styles audience perspectives are continually challenged as they are forced to come to terms with the highly mediated nature of the images on the screen they have long taken for granted.

The racism that remained in the liminal spaces of *The Hurt Locker* and *Act of Valour* (or perhaps was redacted) is placed in the foreground of De Palma's film, where soldiers refer to the Iraqis by a wide range of racist epithets from 'midget Ali Babas', 'ragheads' and 'mother-fucking haji' to 'sand niggers' and 'johnny jihads'. After an Iraqi car fails to stop at the intersection manned by the recidivist Flake, he follows the prescribed 'Rules of Engagement' and shoots to kill, only to later discover that the driver and his pregnant wife thought that they were being waved through rather than being asked to stop. Flake is congratulated by his commanding officers and De Palma shows how he expresses no remorse at his actions, describing killing Iraqis as just like 'gutting catfish'. The film reveals how the troops have become progressively dehumanised by the conflict and how this is deliberately fostered by the military with a conspicuous lack of awareness as to what it may lead to. After their long promised leave is cancelled and their mentor Sergeant Sweet is killed by an IED the protagonists become progressively more resentful of the Iraqi civilians that they are charged to protect. Like many other Iraq films the war is presented as a sustained challenge to the masculinity of the soldiers (see *Jarhead*, *Stop-Loss* and *The Hurt Locker*) and the target of their frustrations becomes a young Iraqi girl who Flake and Brush inform the rest of the unit is to be regarded as a 'spoil of war'. When Blix tries to dissuade them from going AWOL from the base and sexually assaulting the girl he is labelled as 'gay' and a 'pussy' for not wanting to go along. McCoy too tries to prevent them from carrying out the crime, but when they threaten him with violence he can only stand outside the house where the young girl lives, powerless to do anything about it. Throughout all this, Salazar keeps his camera running (now mounted on his helmet), insisting that he is only a dispassionate observer and a 'fly on the wall'; but McCoy calls him nothing more than a 'jackal'. Yet Salazar, too, becomes overwhelmed by his proximity to the crime and even joins in the sexual attack on the girl. Through Salazar's actions De Palma challenges our own voyeuristic appetite for such images and asks how we can so readily disconnect ourselves from personal responsibility for a war fought in our name.[8]

After the girl is raped and murdered, her family are killed and their house burned down in order to destroy the evidence of the crime. Flake and Brush blame the destruction on the internecine fighting in the area between Sunnis and Shiites and their story is unquestionably accepted by the authorities who either do not want to know the truth or have little awareness of the realities on the ground. However, the Iraqi community know exactly what happened and the truth is broadcast on local TV news, but these reports are summarily dismissed by the army and the US media in a compelling metaphor of how Iraqi perspectives on the war have been largely disregarded. Later, Brush offers a moral equivalence rarely explicitly stated in the Iraq War film: 'What – bombing and killing them's OK but fucking them isn't?' Flake adds, 'You prosecute guys like us – you're just aiding the terrorists.' The heinous crime escalates rising tensions in the area and as an act of reprisal Salazar is kidnapped and then beheaded by members of the Mujahideen Shura Council and al-Qaeda, an act that is shown on-screen via a videotape filmed by the perpetrators and then broadcast on an insurgent website. It is a shockingly brutal scene, filmed in an almost exact replication of the beheadings of American journalists Daniel Pearl and Nick Berg.

Redacted presents a protracted challenge to not only the films about the war in Iraq, but the combat film in general, as it questions how texts like *Black Hawk Down* and even *Saving Private Ryan* are valorised for their realism but are in actual fact highly mediated faux-realist texts, which continue to legitimate violence and promote a distinct hierarchy of the value of human life. In one striking scene in *Redacted* a young woman known only as 'Internet girl' verbalises this discourse in her online diatribe about Flake, after the truth about the incident has come to light. 'This is the same monster that is immortalised in every fucking movie about Vietnam . . . That doesn't stop them making another movie about 9/11 because in America an American life is worth so much more than a Vietnamese, a Palestinian, a Lebanese or an Iraqi life.' While *Redacted* lacks the multiple perspectives of *Haditha* and there are no Iraqi characterisations, it is a film that deconstructs the pervasive myth of American altruism and moral certainty in its international conflicts. Jim Frederick, author of *Black Hearts: One Platoon's Descent into Madness in Iraq's Triangle of Death* (2010), a non-fiction account of the Mahmudiyah killings and their aftermath, wrote: 'Rape and murder have been by-products of warfare since the beginnings of time. Soldiers today, however, suffer mightily under the burden of "the Greatest Generation" mythos and the sanitization of Hollywood depictions of World War II' (xx). Yet the estimated 14,000 rapes committed by US soldiers in the European Theatre from 1942 to 1945 have been redacted from our memory in favour of sixty years of mythic-poetic accounts of a 'Good War'. Like *Haditha*, *Redacted* rejects the mythology of the 'Good War' and attempts to deconstruct the language of the combat film.

Brian De Palma had told a similar story before in his Vietnam War film *Casualties of War* (1989) about the abduction and rape of a young Vietnamese girl in 1966 (also a fictionalised account of a real-life incident). The parallels between it and *Redacted* are deliberate and sustained; even the tagline of *Redacted* drew a self-conscious connection between the two: 'Truth is the first casualty of war'. Yet the differences between the two films are telling. Despite its brutality, *Casualties of War* adopts the conventional form and aesthetic of a traditional combat film (replete with an operatic Morricone soundtrack), and being made fourteen years after the end of the war in Vietnam, it is able to provide its protagonist Max (who has a similar experience to McCoy) with a sense of closure and the opportunity to finally move on from his traumatic past. *Redacted* is a more formally experimental reproduction of the fragmentary narratives of the Internet age and, given that it was made *during* the Iraq War, it cannot offer such a reconciliation for its characters or for the audience. It ends with McCoy's return to America after his tour of duty and with the homecoming party that has been thrown for him by his wife and friends. They ask him for a war story, anticipating a tale of courage under fire, much like the narratives of *Act of Valour* and *The Hurt Locker*, but McCoy's experience of war is not one of heroism or daring battles in which he proves himself against ruthless enemies. The tale he recounts to his friends is about the rape and murder of a fourteen year-old Iraqi girl, but it is one that proves impossible for them to process, so far is it disconnected from their reality and their understanding of the war. After an awkward silence they quickly change the subject and turn their heads away from him, just as James turned his head away from Beckham in *The Hurt Locker*.

Redacted concludes with a series of real-life still photographs of dead Iraqis in a sequence called 'Collateral Damage', images that were denied to the American public in the drive to mythologise the war and the reasons why it was being fought. In one final irony these images were themselves redacted by the producers of the film consequent of fears of legal culpability. De Palma sought to present them in full, but perhaps this closing act of censorship, whatever its reason, suits the themes of the film in an entirely apposite way. In a similar fashion to how McCoy's story was rejected by his friends, *Redacted* was ignored by American audiences when it was released in only fifteen cinemas in the United States, even though it won the prestigious Silver Lion for Best Direction at the Venice Film Festival. Its domestic box office earnings were only $25,628 on a weekend when escapist fantasies like *Beowulf*, *Bee Movie* (2007) and *Fred Claus* (2007) rode high in the charts. One year later in 2008,

Battle for Haditha failed to even achieve this; released in two cinemas it earned just $1,982 in its opening weekend, when it debuted in 112th position.

NOTES

1. Ann Thompson (2008) used the phrase 'a toxic genre' and Bill Everhart (2009) used the phrase 'box office poison'.
2. Kurt Waugh also contributed to the script of *300*, which is discussed in Chapter 7.
3. In a move that is symbolic of American cultural cherry-picking of colonial histories, Rorke's name evokes the 1879 battle of Rorke's Drift in the Anglo-Zulu War when approximately 150 British troops mounted a spirited defence against more than 3,000 Zulu warriors. The film ironically culminates with the famous poem from the leader of the Shawnee, Tecumseh, who was killed opposing US imperialism at the Battle of the Thames in 1813.
4. Rorke's act mirrors the death of US Navy SEAL Michael Monsoor who received the Medal of Honour for doing the same in Iraq on 29 September 2006. Monsoor was killed but saved many members of his platoon from death and injury.
5. Peter Berg's *Lone Survivor* performed a similar feat for another group of US Navy SEALs in a film based on the novel of the same name by Marcus Luttrel. While the film was praised by the majority of reviewers, some challenged the film's ideological perspective and its historical accuracy. The veracity of one scene in particular caused concern in which the mission is compromised by local civilians and the SEAL team debate about whether to let them go or terminate them. When they elect to set them free, the fleeing civilians inform the local Taliban of their location and a firefight ensues that kills all but one of the SEALs. Keith Uhlich (2013), writing for *Time Out New York*, called it 'war porn of the highest order' and Amy Nicholson at *The Village Voice* described it as a 'jingoistic snuff film'. The film joins Berg's other films *The Kingdom* and *Battleship* (2012) in its uncritical valorisation of American moral superiority and humanity while marginalising or demonising America's enemies. The film mythologises the SEALs and finds victory even in their defeat. One of the soldiers laments, 'I'm sorry that we didn't kill more of these motherfuckers.' It even concludes with a four-minute montage of real-life photographs of the SEALs over which a thoroughly ill-conceived, mournful cover version of David Bowie's "Heroes" performed by Peter Gabriel can be heard.
6. Bigelow conveniently ends her quotation of Hedges here, but it continues as follows: ' . . . one I ingested for many years. It is peddled by myth-makers – historians, war correspondents, filmmakers, novelists and the state – all of whom endow it with qualities it often does possess: excitement, exoticism, power, chance to rise above our small stations in life, and a bizarre and fantastic universe that has a grotesque and dark beauty. It dominates culture, distorts memory, corrupts language and infects everything around it' (Bigelow 2013: 3). In an episode of Al Jazeera's *Empire* Hedges himself commented that he was disappointed with *The Hurt Locker*, arguing that it had little to say about the war and that the reason it was given the Academy Award was that it was the first notable film about the Iraq war not to be critical of the conflict. See Jazeera (2010).
7. Some recent sources have suggested that the death toll may have been as high as 500,000 (Vergano 2013).
8. In a tragic footnote that attests to the film's power, in March 2011 a man killed two servicemen at an army base in Germany after having seen a clip from the film on the Internet and believing that what he saw was real.

3. 'MASTERS OF OUR OWN SECURITY': REDEMPTION THROUGH VIOLENCE IN THE POST-9/11 ACTION GENRE

The intrusions of September 11 broke the dead bolt on our protective myth, the illusion that we are masters of our own security, that our might makes our homeland impregnable, that our families are safe in the bower of our communities and our women and children are safe in the arms of their men.

Susan Faludi, *The Terror Dream: Fear and Fantasy in Post 9/11 America*

We must take the battle to the enemy, disrupt his plans, and confront the worst threats before they emerge. In the world we have entered the only path to safety is the path of action. And this nation will act.

George W. Bush (2002b)

In the wake of the terrorist attacks on 11 September 2001 it was widely speculated that film genres built on excessive and gratuitous violence would become redundant, rejected by audiences who had no further desire to receive vicarious thrills from entertainment that continued to glamorise brutality or trivialise the loss of human life. Yet the decade that followed revealed this to be only partially true, as American cinema refused to forgo depictions of violence. Rather than eschewing 9/11 and the subsequent war on terror, the action genre subsumed the prevalent fears and anxieties of the new millennium into its narratives, which manifested themselves primarily as threats to the nation and the family, the erosion of traditional forms of masculinity and patriarchy, and the traumatic effects of violence not just on the victims, but also its perpetrators. This chapter attempts to ascertain how far the action genre incorporated the discourse of the war on terror into its narratives. Certainly not all of the films of the genre are explicitly connected to 9/11 and the war on terror (although a great many are), but emerging post-9/11 debates on masculinity, the legitimacy of revenge and America's role in international affairs provide context for the genre just as the aftermath of the Vietnam War had served as a framework for action cinema twenty years before. As Susan Jeffords and many others have observed, the defining action films of the 1980s, starring the likes of Sylvester Stallone, Arnold Schwarzenegger and Chuck Norris, can be persuasively seen as an articulation of and an engagement with Reaganite political philosophies and muscular representations of American power. Jeffords wrote, 'The depiction of the indefatigable, muscular, and invincible masculine body became the lynchpin of the Reagan imaginary; this hardened male form became an emblem not only for the Reagan Presidency but for its ideologies and economies as well' (1994: 25).

The attacks on September 11th 2001 were almost immediately gendered by the media who swiftly categorised them as an assault on the very masculinity of the nation. Wolfgang Schivelbusch stated that they were aimed not just at buildings, but nothing less than the quintessential symbols of American 'power, control, hardship, and mastery' (2001: 292). Some even went as far as to assert that the destruction of the World Trade Center was akin to a symbolic castration, with the Twin Towers cast as consummate phallic symbols, 'not just in the crude sense of being towering monoliths that penetrated the sky, [but] because they, along with [The] Pentagon, represented attitudes associated with political, economic, and cultural hegemony' (Ducat 2004: 225). The blame for this defeat, in the eyes of the media and many cultural commentators, was not only to be found in those who perpetrated the acts, but those who had allowed them to happen. However, those deemed guilty were not George W. Bush and his administration who had repeatedly ignored warnings of an impending strike on the United States by al-Qaeda, but a demasculinised America, those 'masses of weak-chinned BlackBerry [sic] clutchers [who] had left the nation open to attack and wouldn't have the cojones for the confrontation ahead' (Faludi 2007: 8). Or as Kim Du Toit infamously commented in his widely publicised article entitled 'The Pussification of the Western Male' (n.d.s.), America had become 'a nation of women'.

Such paranoid fears of a nationwide demasculinisation are far from new; in fact they have appeared intermittently throughout American cultural history, most often at times of national crisis, whether real or imagined. More than fifty years before 9/11, at the start of the Cold War, the historian Arthur Schlesinger Jr articulated the very same concerns as Du Toit:

What has happened to the American male? For a long time, he seemed utterly confident in his manhood, sure of his masculine role in society, easy and definite in his sense of sexual identity. The frontiersmen of James Fenimore Cooper, for example, never had any concern about masculinity; they were men, and it did not occur to them to think twice about it . . . Today men are more and more conscious of maleness not as a fact but as a problem. The ways by which American men affirm their masculinity are uncertain and obscure. There are multiplying signs, indeed, that something has gone badly wrong with the American male's conception of himself. (Schlesinger Jr 2008: 292)[1]

Schlesinger Jr's comments reveal that the 'masculinity in crisis' trope is not something uniquely connected to the new millennium, but rather a persistent anxiety. However, 9/11 certainly acted as a fissure point in debates about shifting definitions of gender identity, as the roles of both the 'traditional' and the 'new man' became interrogated by media texts produced in the era.

Definitions of masculinity have always been mediated by the cinema screen: just as the 1980s came to be embodied by the hard-bodied heroes played by the likes of Sylvester Stallone and Jean-Claude Van Damme, the 1990s offered more complicated articulations of maleness, perhaps best exemplified by the ascendance of stars like Johnny Depp, Brad Pitt and Keanu Reeves. In fact, these contested notions of what constituted masculinity often found themselves compellingly realised *within* individual star personae: witness the evolution of Arnold Schwarzenegger from *Conan the Barbarian* (1982) to *Kindergarten Cop* (1990) or even inside the same franchise as he moved from a dehumanised killing machine in *Terminator* (1984) to a softer-edged paternal substitute in *Terminator 2: Judgement Day* (1991). Similarly, the decade of the war on terror emerged as a cultural battleground upon which competing depictions of masculinity were contested. In the wake of 9/11 the mainstream media cried out for a return of the 'manly man', a man ready and able to protect his family from harm. Peggy Noonan in her article 'Welcome Back, Duke: From the ashes of Sept. 11 arise the manly virtues' lamented the loss of this traditional brand of masculinity, which she saw embodied in John Wayne. The kind of men who

push things and pull things and haul things and build things, men who charge up the stairs in a hundred pounds of gear and tell everyone else where to go to be safe. Men who are welders, who do construction, men who are cops and firemen. They are all of them, one way or another, the men who put the fire out, the men who are digging the rubble out, and the men who will build whatever takes its place. (Noonan 2001)

However, Noonan (2001) saw the spirit of John Wayne returning after 9/11: 'But now I think . . . he's back. I think he returned on Sept. 11. I think he ran up the stairs, threw the kid over his back like a sack of potatoes, came back down and shovelled rubble. I think he's in Afghanistan now, saying, with his slow swagger and simmering silence, "Yer in a whole lotta trouble now, Osama-boy."' Noonan's article was certainly part of a sustained backlash against the prevailing image of the caring, sharing, sensitive 1990s male, and John Wayne provided a looming shadow over new millennial depictions of masculinity, emblematic of a call for a renewed ideological conservatism in the politics of gender and nation. In fact, Wayne's most iconic role of Ethan Edwards in John Ford's *The Searchers* (1956) proved to be a continued inspiration to filmmakers of the 2000s, as much as it had been to the likes of Paul Schrader, George Lucas, Steven Spielberg and John Milius in the 1970s (see Byron 1979). *The Searchers* is a film self-consciously referenced by *War of the Worlds*, *Rambo* (2008) and *Taken*, and even partially remade in Ron Howard's *The Missing* (2003).[2] This image of Wayne as an icon of masculine prowess and even as a symbolic substitute for the United States periodically returned throughout the decade: in *Battle: Los Angeles* (2007) a euphoric marine yells, 'That was some real John Wayne shit!' after a display of heroism by the beleaguered Staff Sergeant Nantz (Aaron Eckhart). The meta-textuality of the moment is dizzying even without considering Wayne's reputed draft evasion during World War Two. Nantz is one of many ageing and disillusioned men in post-9/11 cinema given the opportunity to once again prove their worth in narratives of heroic redemption in the face of crisis. The spectre of John Wayne returns in *The Boondock Saints II: All Saints Day* (2009) where the character of Rocco yells, 'Fuck it! Do it all I say! Do you think Duke Wayne spent all of his time talking about his feelings with a fuckin' therapist?' and Ben Affleck's *Argo*, set in 1979, has the movie producer Lester Siegel (Alan Arkin) despairingly observe in the wake of the Iran hostage crisis, 'John Wayne in the ground six months and *this* is what is left of America' (emphasis in the original). Senator Chuck Hagel, Secretary of Defense under Barack Obama and a Vietnam veteran, was more critical of the influence of John Wayne on America's perception of war and itself when he informed President George W. Bush, 'If you think you're going to drop the 82nd Airborne in Baghdad and finish the job, I think you've been watching too many John Wayne movies' (cited in Anderton 2011: 111).

In the early years of the decade President Bush himself seemed to fit the bill of the man of action that Noonan and Du Toit called for. The Bush administration certainly recognised the affective power of the image, constructing artful photo opportunities that aligned the president with numerous Hollywood icons of the past and present. Bush channelled John Wayne and Clint Eastwood with his frequent evocations of the Old West; just one week after 9/11 he demanded that Osama bin Laden be taken 'Dead or Alive' (cited in Harnden 2001). He later suggested that the best technique for finding terrorists was to '[s]moke them out' (cited in Knowlton 2001). In July of 2003 Bush sounded like a character from a 1980s Stallone or Schwarzenegger movie when he challenged militants who sought to attack the United States with his cry of 'bring them on' (cited in Murphy 2003). It was an assertion he later admitted to regretting (see Anonymous 2008a). His most iconic photo opportunity, however, was the deliberately constructed *Top Gun* landing on the deck of the USS *Abraham Lincoln* on 1 May 2003 with Bush cast as Tom Cruise's heroic United States Naval Aviator Lieutenant Pete 'Maverick' Mitchell. On seeing this, MSNBC's Chris Matthews stated, 'Americans love having a guy as a President, a guy who has a little swagger . . . The women like this war. I think we like having a hero as our President' (cited in Anderton 2011: 136). In a characteristic moment of hubris and wishful thinking, Bush went on to deliver his speech in front of a banner that declared 'Mission Accomplished', announcing major combat engagements in Iraq to be at an end. It was another incident he later admitted to regretting (see Hurwitz 2008).

The notion that the action genre is little more than disposable entertainment for the masses remains pervasive even though it has been challenged by a variety of authors. Yvonne Tasker argued that action films are commonly regarded as 'dumb movies for dumb people' (1993: 98). Yet she also commented that the apparent straightforwardness of the genre is illusory; 'the supposed obviousness of the action movie is founded on what is a deceptive simplicity' (2004: 3). Tasker's primary assertion is that the action film engages in a reciprocal dialogue with the cultures and the times in which it is produced with contemporaneous debates encoded into their texts. Thus, it is entirely appropriate to ask the question, 'What do action films offer to our understanding of post-9/11 political discourse?' While Mathias Nilges proclaimed that 9/11 heralded the death of the white male action hero 'as the anthropomorphised narrative of protection in the present world' (2010: 28), this was only ever partially true. The role of the invincible, wise-cracking protagonist of Hollywood action cinema was certainly challenged in the years after 9/11 more than ever before, but while he was down, he was never quite out (and he was almost always still a *he*). Like in any other decade, no single definition or articulation of masculinity emerged and this battle of conflicting perspectives became manifested on the screen, often within a single character, like the complicated masculinities of the new millennial James Bond or Jason Bourne, which certainly problematise simplistic binaries such as the 'traditional' and the 'new' man. On the one hand many action heroes seemed to embody George W. Bush's assertion that '[o]ur nation enters this conflict reluctantly – yet our purpose is sure' (Bush 2003a) and typified a discernible sense of moral certainty and righteousness felt among many Americans in the immediate aftermath of 9/11 (see *Taken*, *Rambo* and *The Expendables*). These films offer narratives of wish-fulfilment fantasies, desirous of a return to the pre-9/11 era, before everything became so 'complicated'. However, many action heroes transformed into something much more human and vulnerable: gone were the days when they could be beaten, bruised or shot in one scene only to miraculously appear unscathed in the next. New millennial action heroes often displayed their wounds, both internal and external, conspicuously, making them an extended site of ambiguity and fallibility, a marker of how stereotypical notions of masculinity became progressively challenged both in society and in the films it produced. These shifting coordinates are most clearly seen in film franchises that existed before 9/11 and were returned to again after (see *James Bond* (1962–), *Rambo* (1982–) and *Mission: Impossible* (1996–)) or in films based on existent sources like the adaptation of Robert Ludlum's novels beginning with *The Bourne Identity* (1980). Thus, it is possible to witness an abrupt change of tone in the *Mission: Impossible* franchise, to which Tom Cruise returned as both star and producer for the first time after 9/11 with *Mission: Impossible III* (2006). The film largely eschews the glibness of both the high-tech De Palma original and its flamboyant sequel directed by John Woo in favour of a more plausible, quasi-realistic narrative that attempts to engage with the real world (at least on some levels) more than its predecessors ever did. Rather than the almost superhuman solo agent of before, Ethan Hunt works as part of a distinctly human team, adding an element of vulnerability that was lacking in the previous films, which were largely glossy exercises in action-movie excess. The film's two villains are also framed in markedly contemporary geo-political terms and both are Americans revealed as traitors to their country. One is Owen Davian (Philip Seymour Hoffman), an international arms dealer, who trades fusion materials with North Korea and Islamic fundamentalist terrorists. Davian acquires a biochemical WMD code-named 'the Rabbit's Foot' and wishes to sell to the highest bidder regardless of where they come from or what they intend to do with it. The second villain, and the surprise twist of the film, is that Hunt's boss, the uber-patriotic International Monetary Fund (IMF) Operations Director John Musgrave (Billy Cruddup) is revealed as being in cahoots with Davian in order to create financial and strategic opportunities for the United States. Musgrave is one of those neoconservative hawks willing to transgress international law in order to advance US interests abroad that became a permanent feature of post-9/11 cinema. He suggests, 'Our country will do what it does best. Clean up. Democracy wins', evoking Naomi Klein's *The Shock Doctrine: The Rise of Disaster Capitalism* (2007) and the role that the United States has played in destabilising global democracy for profit throughout the twentieth century and beyond.

The effectiveness of torture is also explored in *Mission: Impossible III* as it was in many post-9/11 films. Seeing the charismatic and attractive Ethan Hunt/ Tom Cruise, one of many heroic protagonists who perpetrate the act in the interests of national security both naturalises and legitimises it, which is made even further morally permissible because of the 'ticking time bomb' scenarios he is frequently placed in. Yet in *Mission: Impossible III* Hunt is seen to suffer real pain: his bruises do not disappear from scene to scene; and when his wife is kidnapped, tortured and murdered by Musgrave in front of him, the film touches on human drama rarely encountered in the genre. However, moments later it is revealed that the woman killed in front of Hunt's eyes was not in fact his wife, but a double, wearing one of those remarkable masks that have come to define the series. The idea that life in Hollywood cinema is fragile is just a momentary illusion; only in a Hollywood film could someone experience the trauma of the violent death of a loved one, just for it to be disavowed moments later and normalcy be reconstituted. Here Hunt is able to realise what many longed for in post-9/11 America, but were only able to achieve in the movies, a return to the moment before the traumatic event – a return to the past.

In this post-9/11 period Hollywood tough guy and star of *Die Hard* (1988) and *The Expendables*, Bruce Willis, frequently seemed to confuse himself with the action heroes he portrayed on-screen: he once famously offered a million dollars to the person who would capture Saddam Hussein and give Willis a few seconds alone in the room with him. On another occasion he insisted he had telephoned President George W. Bush and asked what he could do to assist the war on terror, only to be dismayed to learn he was too old to join the Special Forces (see Biskind 2007). Mark Wahlberg, the former underwear model and rapper turned actor, who had famously been booked on, but missed, one of the flights hijacked on 11 September 2001, had a similar identity crisis while publicising his 2012 thriller *Contraband*. During an interview Wahlberg stated, 'If I was on that plane with my kids, it wouldn't have went down like it did. There would have been a lot of blood in that first-class cabin and then me saying, "OK, we're going to land somewhere safely, don't worry"' (cited in Hedegaard 2012). He later issued a strained apology stating, 'To speculate about such a situation is ridiculous to begin with, and to suggest I would have done anything differently than the passengers on that plane was irresponsible' (cited in Schreffler 2012). But Willis's and Wahlberg's inability to reconcile reality with fantasy was not so far removed from the narratives of the Hollywood films that they starred in, populated by American heroes unapologetically killing bad guys and saving the day in wish-fulfilment fantasies set in worlds much less complicated than the ones their audiences actually resided in.

THE RETURN OF OLD SCHOOL MASCULINITY AND THE CAPTIVITY
NARRATIVE: *RAMBO*, *THE EXPENDABLES* AND *TAKEN*

You live in your little bubble, here behind your wall, with your maids and chauffeurs and servants; you have no idea what the world is like . . .
Bryan Mills, *Taken*

Almost immediately after 9/11 a succession of conservative and patriotic films were released; many of these had been made prior to 11 September 2001 but fitted perfectly with the prevailing mood of the times. They embodied the call for military intervention and revenge as espoused by the likes of the democratic senator from Georgia, Zell Miller, who cried, 'I say bomb the hell out of them. If there's collateral damage, so be it. They certainly found our civilians expendable' (cited in Mitchell and Berke 2001). Kevin Hermening, who had been the youngest hostage in the Iran hostage crisis, called for a 'prompt and massive military response to include total physical destruction of the capitals of the following nations – Afghanistan, Iran, Iraq, Lebanon, Libya, Sudan, and Yemen' (cited in Feingold 2012: 35). Or even Cofer Black, CIA counter-terrorism deputy, who stated, 'We're going to kill them. We're going to put their heads on sticks. We're going to rock their world' (cited in Woodward 2002: 52, 103). Films like *Behind Enemy Lines* (2001), *Collateral Damage* (2002) and *Black Hawk Down* were released into the waves of nationalistic fervour engulfing the country, and their release coincided with Bush's stratospheric approval ratings of ninety per cent at the end of 2001, the highest ever for a President since records began during the Roosevelt administration (Gallup 2001). These films depict the world as a Manichean place, in which America is an unambiguous force for good and all that opposes it as unquestionably evil. America's enemies are ready and willing to violate international law in order to kill innocent people, making it, therefore, necessary and morally just that America sometimes transgresses its own laws to enable it to keep its citizens (and the citizens of the world) safe. In doing so, these films reproduce the Bush administration's assertions that the war on terror was both an ethical and a just war (proclamations that were loudly echoed by the conservative media) and offer a distinctly uncritical celebration of US power and autonomy. As a group these films present a firmly Western-centric approach to complex geo-political affairs and they may be termed 'necessary intervention' films. Moreover, they portray America as a reluctant participant, drawn into international conflict despite unequivocally striving to avoid it; as Bush said about the attacks on September 11th 2001, 'I went from being a President primarily focused on domestic issues, to a wartime president – something I never anticipated, nor something I ever wanted to be' (cited in Anonymous 2011). The violence that these films depict is a sanitised one, and the victims are largely disposable, that is until they are American, and then the deaths are framed as a tragic loss that often necessitates immediate military action.

- Ridley Scott's *Black Hawk Down*, an account of American intervention in Somalia in 1993, was originally due for release in the spring of 2002, but was rushed into cinemas in order to tap into the interest in the burgeoning war on terror. Its hyper-kinetic aesthetic proved hugely influential throughout the decade, when film after film adopted its frenetic visual style. Yet the film's deliberate avoidance of political context and its collective characterisation of Somali soldiers as monstrous in comparison to the sympathetic – simultaneously ordinary *and* heroic Americans – justifiably opened it up to criticisms of First World bias. The narrative does not concern itself with why the United States may have decided to send troops to Somalia or why Somali troops would react in such a way to American soldiers, instead it is the spectacularly realised battle and its effects on the American soldiers that hold the greatest interest for Scott.

- *Behind Enemy Lines* was released only two months after 9/11 and used the atrocities committed in the Bosnian War (1992–5) as a backdrop for a patriotic military fantasy that legitimises continued American participation in the international sphere. At the start of the film maverick US Navy pilot Chris Burnett (Owen Wilson) expresses his boredom and dissatisfaction with America's involvement in the conflict: 'At least give me a fight I can understand' he pines, a just war, a war with a purpose and the moral clarity of World War Two. Evoking the clarity of the 'Total War' of World War Two he laments, 'Everybody thinks they're gonna get the chance to punch some Nazi in the face at Normandy, and those days are long over. They're long gone. I used to think I was going to get a chance to do that. Now I realise I get to eat Jello,' and he hands in his resignation. When Burnett accidentally strays into a demilitarised zone, he is shot down by genocidal Serbian nationalists and pursued hundreds of miles behind enemy lines. The film almost dispassionately shows the deaths of hundreds of the local Muslim population, but when Burnett's American co-pilot is killed, he reassesses both his and America's role in the conflict. The conservative ideology of the film is confirmed at the film's climax, where Burnett retrieves proof of Serbian atrocities and reaffirms both his and the audience's faith in America's mission abroad and the importance of its continued role as global police officer.

- *Collateral Damage* offered a similar ideological message in its depiction of a Los Angeles' firefighter, Gordy Brewer (Arnold Schwarzenegger), whose wife and son are two of many victims killed by a terrorist bomb planted in the Columbian Embassy in Los Angeles by the infamous terrorist, El Lobo, who is motivated by a desire to force Americans out of Colombia. The film was originally due to be released on 5 October 2001, but given its themes and its images of civilians killed in a terrorist attack it was delayed until 8 February 2002. In the wake of 11 September, certain adverts for the film were quickly removed, including a mocked-up newspaper with Schwarzenegger's face declaring,

'What would you do if you lost everything?' Like in *Behind Enemy Lines*, the deaths of Americans are used as a catalyst to motivate and legitimise unilateral action and, in Brewer's case, revenge. The film's conclusion has Brewer intercept and kill El Lobo before he can detonate another bomb, the metaphorical equivalent of finding and killing Osama bin Laden just before he could have perpetrated another 9/11. This was just the first use of a motif that would become regularly recreated in Hollywood films after 9/11, which saw terror attacks repeatedly rewritten in order to provide wish-fulfilment fantasies of what may have been, or what could happen next time.

Towards the end of the post-9/11 decade, Sylvester Stallone, one of the preeminent icons of hard-bodied masculinity that dominated the cinema screens throughout the 1980s, returned to his most culturally significant character, John Rambo. Rambo's potency as a cultural icon in the 1980s was unrivalled; the decade even saw itself described as 'the age of Rambo' (Tasker 2004: 92). Rambo was co-opted by President Ronald Reagan on a number of occasions. Commenting on the release of thirty-nine American hostages from Lebanon, Reagan was reported to have said, 'After seeing *Rambo* [*Rambo: First Blood Part II*] last night, I know what to do next time this happens' (cited in Christensen 1987: 203). Yet while the character has routinely (and justifiably) been equated with American militarism and the glorification of violence, Rambo has always been much more than that. In interviews Stallone expressed a disdain for these unproblematic connections. In 1986 he suggested,

And in *Rambo* [*Rambo: First Blood Part II*] I didn't sit there and say that every Communist should die. What did I say? What did I say? I put America down at the end! I put my own country down. I said I wanted it to love me as much as I love it. Don't they [the critics] listen to the end of the movie? Do they leave before it's over? (cited in Broeske 1986)

Both of Stallone's iconic characters of the 1980s, Rocky Balboa and John Rambo, embody the paradoxical desire of the United States to see itself simultaneously as world number one *and* a plucky underdog. It was no coincidence that Stallone returned to them as writer, director and star in the 2000s and in the process reinvigorated his ailing career, which had languished in direct-to-DVD titles for the majority of the decade. Unlike Schwarzenegger, Stallone had found the transition from the hard-bodied masculinities of the 1980s to the more sensitive action heroes of the 1990s much more difficult, as attempts to soften or complicate his image in films like *Oscar* (1991) and *Stop! Or My Mom Will Shoot* (1992) proved to be critically and commercially underwhelming.[3]

The Rambo franchise combines gratuitous and spectacularly orchestrated violence with a deliberate and ironic strain of anti-war sentiment that manifests itself in an exploration of the effects of conflict on the ultimate veteran and survivor, John Rambo. Having been so much a part of the Cold War with his first three films, many wondered how Rambo would fare after 9/11. Although some hoped he would pursue al-Qaeda and Osama bin Laden directly, the fourth film in the series was set in Myanmar (formerly Burma), which had been plagued with violent internal conflict since democratic rule was overthrown by a military junta in 1962. In the way he is self-consciously constructed as an archetypal brooding masculine hero, Rambo is a symbolic and literal embodiment of the calls for a return to traditional masculinity that writers like Noonan and Du Hoit demanded. On the release of *Rambo* Brian Lowry wrote that the character had still retained his symbolic power:

> In a sense, the timing is strangely appropriate, inasmuch as *Rambo* [*Rambo: First Blood Part II*] wound up being a kind of referendum on Vietnam, advancing the theory that the war was winnable if only we'd let Rambo do his job, leaving him to pay (and pay and pay) for all his countrymen's sins back home. Given the current debate over Iraq, this latest bloodbath perhaps wisely steers clear of those landmines, though they remain unavoidable subtext to anybody who knows the character's history. (Lowry 2008)

The film opens with an ageing and world-weary Rambo living in self-imposed exile in Thailand, earning a living as a snake catcher. When a group of Christian missionaries ask to be ferried into Myanmar, which has been a war zone for more than fifty years, the staunchly isolationist Rambo refuses, as he knows that they can make little difference to the oppressed people there. However, an attractive blonde Christian missionary, Sarah, manages to persuade him with her passionate desire to make a difference, 'Maybe *you've* lost your faith in people . . . But trying to save a life isn't wasting your life, is it?' Rambo reluctantly agrees to take them, but soon after he drops them off, the missionaries are captured by the villainous Major Tint, so Rambo joins a team of mercenaries tasked with rescuing them. Rambo is portrayed as a decidedly unwilling participant in the conflict, having seen the horrors of war many times first-hand. Yet he, as we will see in many of the characters of post-9/11 action films, has a history of violence and when the conflict begins, despite his protestations, there is a sense that he thrives on it. Like the films about Iraq and Afghanistan discussed in the previous chapter, *Rambo* gives the indigenous Karen people of Burma no voice of their own, and we are never given any historical context for their suffering, as the film focuses exclusively on

Figure 12   *Rambo* (2008): the iconic figure of American masculinity and military prowess in the 1980s re-emerges in the post-9/11 decade as the epitome of the 'necessary intervention' narrative.

Rambo's status as both their saviour and, somewhat ironically, a victim of his own deep-seated need for violent redemption. The message of the film seems to be that America has a moral requirement to combat the forces of evil in the world, despite the high price it has to pay (see Figure 12). The missionaries try to make a difference with their diplomatic solutions and aid, but such a liberal approach, the film suggests, is doomed to failure, as the only answer to injustice is violence.

At the end of the film, Rambo is excluded from the community of the surviving missionaries like Ethan Edwards from *The Searchers* (who Stallone has frequently compared the character to), even though it is only because of him that they are alive (see Knowles 2007). In doing this Stallone acknowledges that the burden of responsibility can be a heavy and unpopular one. In an epilogue Rambo returns to his family ranch in the United States; but whether there is a place for him there the film wisely chooses not to reveal, as doing so would detract from Rambo's enduring status as a perpetual outsider and 'the last real soldier in America and the only hope for a return to freedom and Conservative Republican values' (Simon 1999: 165).

Stallone's career renaissance continued with *The Expendables* and *The Expendables 2* (2012), which had a combined worldwide gross of more than

$500 million. In both Stallone plays Barney Ross, the leader of a band of cynical mercenaries, who rediscover their humanity by liberating an oppressed Latin American country from its villainous dictator. The narrative provides American audiences with a fantasy of what the liberation of Iraq may have been like if only it had been scripted, produced, directed by and starred Sylvester Stallone. *The Independent* memorably called *The Expendables* 'Tea Party cinema: Manichean in its worldview, pissed off in a directionless, agitated way, and eager for immediate and definitive solutions' (Anonymous 2010b). The fictional country of Vilena is ruled by General Garza who, despite Stallone's protestations to the contrary, is clearly envisaged as a Hugo Chávez figure (with shades of both Augusto Pinochet and Manuel Noriega): his private army wear red berets, and he is characterised by his anti-American diatribes, during one of which he promises to expel 'this American disease' from the shores of Vilena. The idealised mercenary band Ross heads has a change of heart after years of profiting from the misfortunes of others in countries like Somalia and Bosnia (the very countries in which *Black Hawk Down* and *Behind Enemy Lines* are set), each name-checked in the film's dialogue. Ross's friend Tool (Mickey Rourke) gives a long speech that is a veritable paean to interventionism, 'We don't stand for shit; we used to but that all dried up.' He describes how he once let a woman commit suicide in front of him: 'She looked at me and I knew she was gonna jump. You know what I did man? I just turned around and I kept walking until I heard that splash. What I realised later on was if I had saved her I might have saved what was left of my soul.' Like Barney Ross, Bush undoubtedly saw himself as a man of action eager to assert his country's dominance in the guise of altruism. Bob Woodward in *Bush at War* stated that after 9/11 'Bush was tired of rhetoric. The President wanted to kill somebody' (2002: 105). *The Expendables* shows the reluctant Ross, who somewhat revealingly uses antiquated six shooters like the heroes of the Wild West, eschewing his isolationist credo in order to 'do the right thing' and in the process remasculinise America, ushering in the return of an old-fashioned, omnipotent brand of hyper-masculinity that many had desired after 9/11.

By abandoning the vagaries of many thrillers set in the real world in favour of almost nostalgic evocations of moral clarity, the film became a throwback to a pre-9/11 age, before everything became so contentious. Like *Rambo* the film's depiction of masculinity is a distinctly conservative one. Each of the mercenaries engage in a perpetual performance of one-upmanship; obsessed with proving their masculinity to one another, in the process they attempt to disavow both the lingering spectre of homosexuality and the advancing ages of the stars playing them by killing the never-ending succession of Latin American enemies that fill the screen. In an effort to normalise their pathological lifestyle, one of their number is presented as deviant: Gunnar (Dolph Lundgren), an unstable alcoholic who has taken to enjoying the killing too much. However,

Gunnar is not too far removed from Ross and the others, his only distinction being that he breaks the taboo by verbalising his satisfaction. Ross tells him, 'This isn't how we work,' but in the course of the film the Expendables kill so many faceless and nameless brown-skinned Others that his protestations ring hollow.[4] Like much of the contemporary action genre, which for the most part excludes women, the all-male environment is permeated with a discernible sense of homoeroticism that has to be disavowed, displaced and denied for fear of challenging the heteronormativity of its protagonists. As Christine Holmlund wrote about one of Stallone's previous films, *Tango & Cash* (1989), the characters 'look at each other long and hard and, although their looks signal competitiveness, they convey more than a little affection, admiration, and appreciation as well' (220–1). In one of the film's most revealing moments this homoeroticism bubbles to the surface, as the three iconic action heroes of the last decades of the twentieth century, Bruce Willis, Arnold Schwarzenegger and Sylvester Stallone, occupy the screen together for the first time in their careers. Within moments of the scene beginning, Mr. Church (Willis) turns to Ross and Trench Mauser (Schwarzenegger) and asks, 'You guys aren't gonna start sucking each other's dicks are ya?' The overt puncture of the very issue the genre goes to such great lengths to deny is conspicuous, and the two rival action stars look at each other with a puzzled and then disgusted expression on their faces.

Barney Ross is provided with a woman to romance and rescue, Sandra Garza, who becomes a personification of her country's need of saving by the American heroes, one in a long line of foreign 'damsels in distress' offering a justification for American intrusion into foreign countries from *Casablanca* (1942), through *The Alamo* (1960), to *The Quiet American* (2002) and *Tears of the Sun* (2003). At the end of the film Ross not only saves Vilena, but he gets the girl and gives his fee back to the country – a potent manifestation of how many had fantasised that the conflict in Iraq would play out – with American soldiers greeted in the streets as liberating heroes rather than as neo-colonial invaders.

Both *Rambo* and *The Expendables* are compensatory fantasies of American pre-eminence and muscularity framed with a sense of justification and an acknowledgement of the burdens of 'necessary intervention'. They are also variations on one of the foundational American literary tropes, 'the captivity narrative', which has been returned to again and again in the course of the last two centuries. In the 1970s Richard Slotkin wrote, 'The great and continuing popularity of these narratives, the uses to which they were put, and the nature of the symbolism employed in them are evidence that the captivity narratives constitute the first coherent myth-literature developed in America for American audiences' (1973: 95). In the post-9/11 era American cinema once again frequently turned to the captivity narrative as a telling metaphor of all that

America hoped to protect from a predatory and deviant Other. Whether in the form of biological daughters (*Taken*, *Live Free or Die Hard* (2007), *Gone Baby Gone*, *Mystic River* (2003), *Prisoners* (2013)) or daughter substitutes (*Man on Fire*, *Spartan* (2004), *Rambo*), they are most commonly white, and often virginal, girls. The frequency of these narratives in post-9/11 Hollywood was so remarkable, that one may ask whether it has to be a young, white, virginal American girl in order for audiences to care about their plight. Are audiences more invested in these characters than the loss of black or Asian children?

This captivity narrative found its most striking embodiment in Pierre Norrel and Luc Besson's hyper-violent action film *Taken*, which centres on a seventeen year-old blonde American girl, Kim (Maggie Grace) and her father Bryan Mills (Liam Neeson), a retired CIA agent. Bryan was divorced by Kim's mother Lenore (Famke Janssen) because he spent too little time with his family when Kim was growing up in what would have been the immediate post-9/11 period. Realising that he is losing his daughter, Bryan quits his job in order to spend more time with her, but he finds it very difficult to reconcile himself to the fact that Kim no longer needs him the way she once did and he fears that he has been replaced by Kim's affluent step-father, Stuart. When Lenore asks Bryan to provide permission for Kim's upcoming trip to Europe he is reluctant as his work has made him sceptical of the many dangers outside America. He criticises Lenore with the paranoid tirade, 'You live in your little bubble, here behind your wall, with your maids and chauffeurs and servants; you have no idea what the world is like.' However, the two women emotionally blackmail him into agreeing to the trip, and of course, just as Sarah in *Rambo* and Sandra in *The Expendables* are captured, within hours of arriving in Paris, Kim is kidnapped by Muslim Albanian sex traffickers and sold into slavery to a grotesquely overweight and sexually deviant Arab sheikh who pays a much higher price for her because she is a virgin – revealing that daddy was right to be paranoid after all. The French setting proves a convenient location given that American opprobrium for France re-emerged during the post-9/11 era because of the country's failure to support the war in Iraq, which was regarded by many Americans as a betrayal. As a result, for the next few years anything remotely connected to France became toxic to large sections of the American public: from French fries being renamed as 'Freedom Fries' or John Kerry being repudiated as the 'French' candidate when running against Bush because of his ability to speak the language. In this climate a range of jokes emerged on American television that viciously targeted the French. Dennis Miller joked, 'I would call the French scumbags, but that, of course, would be a disservice to bags filled with scum. I say we invade Iraq, then invade *Chi*-rac' (emphasis in original) (Anonymous, 'French jokes'). David Letterman quipped, 'A lot of folks are still demanding more evidence before they actually consider Iraq a threat. For example, France wants more evidence. And you know I'm thinking, the last time France wanted more evidence they rolled right through Paris with the German flag' (ibid.)[5]

The overt racism of the revenge narrative that follows in *Taken* is so hysterical that there remains a lingering suspicion that Besson and Norrel may have considered the whole thing a parody of the action genre rather than an embrace of it, but the dubious racial and sexual politics of Besson's prior work and the fact that *Taken* was hugely successful at the United States' box office indicates that it may have been taken at face value by the majority of audiences. *Taken* (and the other films discussed in this chapter) taps into very particular fears and fantasies of Americans in the post-9/11 decade when the United States seemed to many Americans to be a fortress largely besieged by the outside world. Liam Neeson, the film's star, was under no illusions as to why *Taken* became so popular on its release:

> That's when the whole financial debacle happened and I really think with *Taken* audiences saw a guy who's not going to call authority figures when he's in trouble, because they were not to be trusted anymore. I think that's what everybody felt. I certainly felt that in 2008. You can't trust anybody. You certainly can't trust your bankers, certainly not politicians. And here's a guy that will not call the police when something happens. He'll do something about it himself. I think people rooted for that individuality. (Neeson cited in Anonymous 2012b: 17)

Bryan quickly travels to Paris and allows nothing to stand in the way of retrieving his daughter as he proceeds to shoot, kick and punch his way through what feels like the whole of Paris's Muslim community. His righteousness is never questioned throughout the narrative and his mission is portrayed as an entirely legitimate and justified one. Capturing one of the Albanians responsible, Bryan tortures him while delivering a speech about the history of US rendition practices:

> You know, we used to outsource this kind of thing. But what we found was the countries we outsourced to had unreliable power grids. Very Third World. You'd turn on a switch – power wouldn't come on, and then tempers would get short. People would resort to pulling fingernails. Acid drips on bare skin. The whole exercise would become counterproductive. But here, the power's stable. Here, there's a nice even flow. Here, you can flip a switch and the power stays on all day.

The film was one of an increasing number of popular culture narratives to dramatise torture in the decade and a Human Rights First study showed that representations of torture on television went from four examples a year before 2001 to more than one hundred after (see Anonymous (n.d.s.)). Just as important as the increased frequency was the change in how these acts were portrayed: prior to 9/11 it was the norm for antagonists to be shown as the ones doing the torturing, but after 9/11 the overwhelming trend was for the protagonist to commit torture in the name of national security. In the world of *Taken* violence and torture practised by Americans is both legitimate and effective. *Taken* ends with Bryan finding and saving Kim before the monstrous sheikh has been able to have his wicked way with her. When he returns Kim to her mother he is welcomed back into the family having proved his worth as a father and a husband once more (the sequel *Taken 2* (2012) shows them to be reconciled). However, rather than be traumatised by her ordeal, which included being forced to take drugs, seeing her best friend murdered and being sold into sex slavery, in the epilogue Kim is revealed to have suffered no after-effects that a meeting with her favourite celebrity pop star could not cure.[6]

If John Wayne's characterisation of Ethan Edwards was indeed the template for the characters who inhabited these films, as he was for many in the 1970s, there is a fundamental erasure of the complexity that was arguably a key aspect of Ford's film. Bryan Mills and Barney Ross experience little impact of their murderous professions on their characters as the violent acts they commit are framed largely as an opportunity for them to prove themselves to those around them and gain personal redemption. These films offer a nostalgic return to the invulnerability of the action hero of the 1980s and in the process they attempt to reconsolidate and reinforce hegemonic power relations. Rambo, while certainly marked by trauma, is able to negate its effects through violence and also redeems himself through the murder of hundreds while saving a beautiful young American girl in the process. Despite the racism of *The Searchers*, which has been commented on in detail (see Buscombe 2008), Edwards is almost as monstrous as he is heroic and is excluded from the community at the end of the film as emphatically as Mills is welcomed back into it. *The Searchers* even tacitly acknowledges the fact that Edwards is in some ways a mirror image of his nemesis Scar, something that *The Expendables* and *Taken* are unable to recognise in their depictions of a strict moral dichotomy between their heroes and the evildoers they battle against. Rambo kills Asians, Ross kills Hispanics and Mills kills Muslims, and each is redeemed through violence in narratives that reconsolidate their world views rather than challenge them, and their dramas function, as Frederic Jameson suggested, by 'inventing imaginary or formal "solutions" to unresolvable social contradictions' (1981: 79).

'YOU START DOWN THIS PATH. WHERE DOES IT END?': THE NEW MILLENNIAL
MASCULINITIES OF JAMES BOND AND JASON BOURNE

*It is typical of an imperial people to have a short memory for its less
pleasant imperial acts, but for those on the receiving end, memory can
be long indeed.*

Chalmers Johnson, *Blowback: The Costs and Consequences of
American Empire*

Everything I found out, I want to forget.

Jason Bourne, *The Bourne Identity*

Although Pierce Brosnan continued his tenure as the iconic secret agent James
Bond until November 2002 with the release of *Die Another Day*, his final film
was conceived and written before 11 September 2001 and followed the familiar trajectory of the Brosnan-era films with few concessions to the post-9/11
world. Despite grossing in the region of $431 million at the worldwide box
office, making it the most successful Bond film ever made at the time, producers Michael G. Wilson and Barbara Broccoli decided to reboot the franchise
and refashion it into something more relevant to the new millennium. The
Brosnan years had shown great promise with *Goldeneye* (1995), but they
had quickly moved into the realms of fantastical action and outlandish plots,
becoming almost a parody of themselves with their invisible cars and exaggerated gadgets, centred on a Bond who seemed more and more invulnerable.

It has long been argued by Bond scholars that the Fleming novels and their
cinematic counterparts can be read as a prolonged attempt for England to
negate its readily apparent declining imperial status and fantasise about continued pre-eminence in the international sphere (see Baron 2009). Umberto Eco's
interpretation of Bond narratives as encapsulating a decidedly Manichean
formula of binary oppositions, revolving around simplistic concepts of good
versus evil, Bond versus villain, and the Free World versus the Soviet Union, has
been an influential one (2003: 34–55). Thus, Bond has consistently provided
an unsophisticated way for Western audiences to make sense of the turbulent
political realities of the eras in which they are produced. After a four-year
break, Bond returned to the screens in *Casino Royale* (2006), quickly followed
by *Quantum of Solace* (2008) and then four years later in *Skyfall* (2012).
Many had thought that there would be no room for the spectacular and gratuitous excesses of James Bond post-9/11, but the retooled *Casino Royale*
became the most financially successful film (until *Skyfall*) in the history of the
long franchise and in the process substantially rewrote some of the essential
tenets of the Bond universe, immersing the character in real-world geo-politics
more than ever before, supporting Bennett and Woollacott's claim that Bond is

'a mythic figure who transcends his own variable incarnations, Bond is always identified with himself but is never quite the same – an ever mobile signifier' (1987: 274). The opening minutes of *Casino Royale* introduce a much more visceral Bond universe: a grittier world, one in which every punch, kick and bullet is felt in contrast to the suave glamour and invulnerability which characterised the Brosnan era. In the first few scenes Bond messily earns his double O status, that is, his famous licence to kill, by brutally murdering an assailant in a grimy men's bathroom, crashing through stall after stall before drowning his desperate victim in a urinal. There is no witty one-liner or sly smile at the camera, a far cry from the knowing irony of Brosnan's dispatch of an assailant into a printing press with 'They'll print anything these days' from *Tomorrow Never Dies* (1997) or Connery's famous disposure of a thug in an electrified bath with 'Shocking, absolutely shocking' from *Goldfinger*.

Rather than the fully formed Bonds of the pre-9/11 era Daniel Craig's interpretation of the character is very much a work in progress, a truly new millennial creation, whose masculinity is an extended site of paradox and ambiguity – rooted in reality, tortured by his past and his continued role in the deaths of others (see Figure 13). Bond's psychological and physical wounds remain visible throughout the narrative, progressing to a severe case of post-traumatic stress disorder in *Skyfall*, which threatens to end his career; they do not disappear from scene to scene, unlike Brosnan's Bond, tortured in North Korea in the opening of *Die Another Day* who emerges from years of incarceration with his trauma immediately erased, a pot belly and nothing that a shave and a hot shower could not fix. In contrast to this, Craig's Bond is both hyper-masculine *and* sensitive: he kills or incapacitates his enemies, but he is traumatised by the experience and washes their blood from his hands while staring at himself in the mirror as if shell-shocked. While Bond is still the causal agent of these new narratives, he often stumbles through the plot failing to grasp any sense of the 'big picture', and even though it is through his eyes that we continue to see the world, he too is offered up as an object for our visual pleasure unlike any Bond before him.

The three films repeatedly connect themselves to new millennial anxieties in a variety of ways. In *Casino Royale* the Bond trope of a central diabolical mastermind (à la Ernst Stavro Blofeld or Dr. No) is replaced by a mysterious group known only as Quantum, a huge corporation that is shown to be able to manipulate international markets, but to what end Bond is never quite sure. Even when Bond apprehends a high-ranking figure within the organisation, Quantum has him swiftly killed by a double agent they have been able to place inside MI6 before he can reveal anything. The head of MI6, M (Judi Dench), is frustrated by the lack of information they have about Quantum: 'Who the hell is this organisation, Bond? How can they be everywhere and we know nothing about them?' The former head of MI5, Dame Stella Rimington, on whom

Figure 13   Shaken *and* stirred: the reconfiguration of an icon in *Casino Royale* (2006). The new James Bond is more vulnerable and human than ever before.

Judi Dench's incarnation of M was based, considered the post-9/11 era of terrorism in a remarkably similar fashion, categorising new emerging threats as 'networks of individuals . . . that bled into society . . . who live normal, routine lives until called upon for specific tasks by another part of the network' (cited in Barker 2011: 193). Both Rimington and her fictional counterpart lament the loss of the certainties of the Cold War, when at least one knew who one's enemy was. M locates Quantum in the very real world of post-9/11 terrorism when she observes, 'When they analysed the stock market after 9/11, the CIA discovered there had been massive shorting of airline stocks. When the stocks hit bottom on 9/12, somebody made a fortune.' The implication is that Quantum was aware of the impending attacks and that the group was able to profit from them financially. In the film's blistering post-credits sequence, in a parkour-style chase scene set in the fictional African country of Nambutu, Bond shoots and kills a terrorist bomb-maker only to be chastised by M: 'We're trying to find out how an entire network of terrorist groups is financed and you give us one bomb-maker. Hardly the big picture, wouldn't you say?' The big picture that would have traditionally been revealed to Bond in a rambling monologue by the film's antagonist is nowhere to be found in *Casino Royale* or *Quantum of Solace* (but it does return in the more traditional *Skyfall*). The closest *Casino Royale* has to a main villain is Le Chiffre (Mads Mikkelsen), a private banker for terrorists, but a relatively minor player in Quantum's grand scheme. Like many Bond antagonists he seems as much attracted to Bond as he is repulsed by him: at the high-stakes poker table Le Chiffre neglects his own beautiful blonde partner, jealously looking at Bond while he kisses Vesper Lynd (Eva Green). The film also features the most homo-erotic scene (until the release of *Skyfall*) in the history of the franchise. In order to force Bond to reveal the password to access the money that he has won from the poker tournament, Le Chiffre strips Bond nude and ties him to a chair. 'You've taken good care of your body,' he comments, admiring Bond's physique, before he repeatedly strikes Bond's testicles with a large knotted piece of rope. The film revels in the sadomasochist pleasures that were the hallmark of Fleming's original novels but only flirted with in previous film versions and reveals that even in the 2000s homosexuality still lingers as the great Other in the action genre. After torture at the hands of Le Chiffre, Bond worries if the experience will have caused him irreparable damage, but the audience and Vesper is quickly reassured that Bond's status as a legendary ladies' man is still apt. Le Chiffre had reminded Bond that he could kill both him and Vesper and still be accepted by the British Government: 'Because even after I slaughtered you and your little girlfriend, your people would still welcome me with open arms . . . because they need . . . what I know.' Bond's silence affirms that he knows that Le Chiffre is telling the truth, and this awareness of the harsh reality of geo-politics is the closest Bond ever comes to an understanding of the illusive big picture.

One of the series' most interesting aspects is its continued dramatisation of the 'special relationship' between Britain and the United States, which was repeatedly emphasised by Tony Blair, who was still in office when *Casino Royale* was produced. After the attacks on 9/11 Blair stated, 'This is not a battle between the United States of America and terrorism, but between the free and democratic world and terrorism. We therefore here in Britain stand shoulder to shoulder with our American friends in this hour of tragedy, and we, like them, will not rest until this evil is driven from our world' (cited in Jones 2001). Yet the film makes it clear that the two countries are far from shoulder to shoulder. Despite Bond's status as the pre-eminent agent, it is the United States that is emphatically the dominant superpower. When Bond loses all of his money in the poker tournament, it is the CIA agent Felix Leiter (Jeffrey Wright) who buys him in again with US cash, on the understanding that America gets the credit when the terrorists are captured. Bond bickers with the Americans in *Quantum of Solace* about whose country is the most imperialistic, but both governments are revealed to be complicit in global arms' deals and illegal coups that their populations will never be aware of. Arguably, for the first time in the history of the series the audience is forced to question the role of England in international affairs, and while Bond does not have a Jason Bourne-like revelation that he is a tool in the hands of his government, he does not always relish his job as a hired assassin as his predecessors had often done.

After an extended hiatus caused by the bankruptcy of MGM, the longest ever between films without a change of actor, Daniel Craig's Bond returned in a film directed by the Academy Award-winning Sam Mendes. *Skyfall* is certainly the most character-driven movie in the history of the franchise, as one might expect from the director of *American Beauty* (1999) and *Road to Perdition*

(2002), and it is a film that continued the post-9/11 trend for humanising Bond while at the same time reverting back to some of the long-standing formula of the series from which *Casino Royale* and *Quantum of Solace* had deliberately deviated. In *Skyfall* Bond is revealed to be ageing, shown to have drug and alcohol dependency issues and even be suffering from PTSD. In the film's frenetic pre-credits sequence, Bond chases Patrice (Ola Rapace) who has stolen a disk drive containing vital national security secrets through (and above) the streets of Istanbul. Bond is told that if he does not apprehend his target, the names and identities of every MI6 agent on active duty all over the world will be revealed on the Internet and compromised. When it looks like the mission is slipping out of Bond's hands, M orders MI6 agent Eve (Naomi Harris) to take a risky shot to kill Patrice, but when she misses it is Bond who is struck and falls hundreds of feet from the top of a speeding train to his apparent death, leaving Patrice to escape with the valuable information. Later, when M ordered in front of a public enquiry for her role in the loss of these state secrets, *Skyfall* reveals how the British security services changed in the years after 9/11 and how they became more accountable and visible than they ever were before in the wake of the real-life WikiLeaks' scandals and cases like those of Edward Snowdon and Bradley Manning. She states,

> Today I've repeatedly heard how irrelevant my department has become. 'Why do we need agents, the Double-0 section? Isn't it all antiquated?' Well, I suppose I see a different world than you do, and the truth is that what I see frightens me. I'm frightened because our enemies are no longer known to us. They do not exist on a map. They're not nations, they're individuals. And look around you. Who do you fear? Can you see a face, a uniform, a flag? No! Our world is not more transparent now; it's more opaque! It's in the shadows. That's where we must do battle. So before you declare us irrelevant, ask yourselves, how safe do you feel?

Almost exactly a year after the film's release, MI5 Director-General Andrew Parker and Head of MI6 John Sawyers were questioned in a remarkably similar fashion in an inquiry session that saw the spy chiefs broadcast live on television for the first time. Sawyers also stressed how the world had changed since 9/11: 'What I would say is that with the benefit of hindsight, we were not configured, in 2001, for the scale of the terrorist threat that this country faced after 9/11. Our people were not trained for it. We did not have the experience for it. We did not have the resources for it. And it took us some time to adapt to the scale of the threat that we faced' (Anonymous 2013). The two previous on-screen Ms (played by Robert Brown from 1983 to 1989 and Bernard Lee from 1962 to 1979) were never held up to such public scrutiny and they, like the secret service they presided over, remained largely in the shadows.

The credits sequence of *Skyfall*, which follows Bond's on-screen 'death', is certainly the most foreboding in the franchise history, populated not by the habitual naked young women and exaggerated phallic symbols, but rather menacingly placed skulls, tombstones (of his former victims and, perhaps, all those women who ever got close to him) and images of a conflicted Bond shooting likenesses of himself, which foreshadow a narrative that sees him wrestling with his identity, his past and even his mortality. When Bond resurfaces he finds solace in the bottom of a tequila bottle and seems to be considering his permanent retirement from the service, wondering whether, in his traumatised and broken state, he has it in him to perform the role of 'James Bond' any more. But when he discovers that an unknown terrorist has blown up MI6 headquarters, in what seems like a personal vendetta against M, he returns to London. On his arrival he is a pale shadow of his former self: aching, ailing and ageing, it is apparent he has lost his edge, and having failed the required test for field agents it is clear that he is mentally and physically unfit for active duty.

The narrative slowly reveals that the cyber-terrorist responsible for the attacks is Silva (Javier Bardem) a former MI6 agent, who believes he was betrayed by M and sold out to the Chinese during the handover of Hong Kong from the United Kingdom to China in 1997. During his time in a Chinese prison he was tortured for months and after an unsuccessful attempt to commit suicide using standard agent issue cyanide, he was left disfigured and obsessed with revenge. Played with a charismatic flair by Javier Bardem, Silva is certainly one of the most memorable Bond villains in decades, even if his homosexuality is alarmingly reactionary and feels reminiscent of the Connery-era characters of Mr. Wint and Mr. Kidd from *Diamonds are Forever* (1971). This, combined with the return to disturbingly one-dimensional characterisations of women, is an indication that the small steps forward for female characters in both *Casino Royale* and *Quantum of Solace* were aberrations rather than the beginning of a new attitude towards women in the series. It is not as if the first two films in Daniel Craig's tenure as James Bond were feminist texts, but at least in Vesper Lynd and Camille Montes (Olga Kurylenko) there was some attempt to situate the film in the changing gender landscape of the new millennium. While Vesper did ultimately betray Bond, she proved that she was his equal in verbal ripostes, and she even saved his life twice. Instead of Vesper and Camille, in *Skyfall* we are given a nameless and topless Greek model with whom Bond wiles away the hours of his drunken exile, a former sex slave in Severine (Berenice Marlowe) who Bond sleeps with just once before she is killed by Silva in part of a voyeuristic and misogynistic game that he demands Bond participate in – leading Bond to utter the disturbing one-liner, 'What a waste of good whisky' – and Eve Moneypenny who, after almost killing Bond in the film's prologue, decides that being a secret agent is a man's job and instead becomes M's secretary/personal assistant.

Despite this, Silva's rails against Bond's blind patriotism are potent and timely. It is tempting to see him as yet another post-9/11 manifestation of Chalmers Johnson's 'Blowback' and the dubious reality of illegally intervening in the affairs of other countries. Silva is a mercurial cyber-genius with an air of Heath Ledger's Joker about him, able to manipulate the stock markets or hijack satellites all over the world with the press of the button. There is a sense that Bond may recognise Silva as being not too far removed from himself, as they were both 'sold out' by M who always puts the mission before the lives of her agents. But it seems that Bond is much more pragmatic than Silva and accepts this as part of the reality of their chosen profession. Like Silva, Bond is a man forged in violence and the film explores that recurring theme of post-9/11 cinema – how the past continues to impact on the present. Indeed, Bond is forced to come to terms with his own past, as the relevance of the film's title only becomes evident at the climax of the film. Skyfall is Bond's ancestral family home, a place to which he has not returned since his parents died when he was a boy, but it is where he retreats with M in full knowledge that Silva will pursue them there for a final confrontation. A shot of Bond's parents' gravestone acknowledges Bond's fragile relationship with the past, as does M's admission that orphans 'always make the best recruits'. Daniel Craig's third performance as Bond continued to redefine the icon and struck a chord with new millennial audiences because, unlike the suave and infallible perfection of Connery and Moore, he was a more human figure and all the more resonant for it. Correspondingly, Bond's on-screen failures in the Craig-era far outweigh his successes: in *Casino Royale* alone he is unable to capture the bomb-maker Mollaka, he is humiliated by his initial loss to Le Chiffre and he fails to recognise that Vesper is betraying him until it is too late. *Skyfall* too ends with yet another failure, his inability to save his mentor, M, as she is shockingly killed by Silva, leading Bond to lose yet another person he had become close to. When Bond pulls her dead body close to him in the same church where his parents are buried, it is, perhaps, the most human moment in the history of the franchise.

Despite the financial and critical success of Daniel Craig's reinvention of Bond, the defining action hero of the decade was undoubtedly Jason Bourne, played by Matt Damon and directed by Doug Liman in *The Bourne Identity* (2002) and then by Paul Greengrass in *The Bourne Supremacy* (2004) and *The Bourne Ultimatum* (2007). The series follows the premise of the original Robert Ludlum novels (1980–90) on which they are based; however, they are substantially updated from their Cold War concerns to the much more contemporary and culturally relevant post-9/11 world. Liman's *The Bourne Identity* begins with a lifeless body being pulled unconscious from the Mediterannean Sea. On waking, the man realises that is suffering from extreme memory loss, and the only clues as to his identity are two bullets lodged in his back and details of a Swiss bank accountant concealed in a device embedded *inside* his skin. The narrative slowly reveals that the amnesiac man, Jason Bourne, was an elite government operative who quit the agency after becoming disillusioned with the questionable morality of the missions he was tasked to perform in the name of US national security. In retrospect, Matt Damon seems perfectly cast as the reluctant hero, but at the time it was hard to believe that the harmless, blond college boy of *Good Will Hunting* (1997) could convincingly portray a traumatised killer like Jason Bourne. Damon's casting gives Bourne an every-man quality; it is a far cry from the extravagant excesses of the action heroes of the 1980s embodied by the hard-bodied icons of Stallone and Schwarzenegger. Remarkably for an action film, Bourne shies away from violence when he can, and he refuses to use handguns unless absolutely necessary. This reluctance made him even more attractive to audiences in the wake of 9/11, given free rein to indulge in fantasies of violent omnipotence free from guilt. As Cosmo Landesman (2007) wrote in *The Sunday Times*, Bourne was the perfect liberal hero and 'the John Rambo of the liberal intelligentsia'. With more than a touch of sarcasm he asserted:

> This is a great and liberating day for liberal-kind. For them, spy heroes have always been suspect: Bond was too much of a sexist, Schwarzenegger (*True Lies*) too right-wing and Vin Diesel (*XXX* (2002)) too dumb. But Bourne allows liberals to enjoy all the forbidden pleasures of the espionage block-buster: they can see him kick ass, break necks, smash faces and shoot fellow human beings, and not complain about civil liberties because the victims work for the CIA. Bourne is the perfect liberal hero – he doesn't have a fantastic secret-agent body, a tuxedo or a taste for martinis and one-night stands. He is fluent in five languages, drives brilliantly in any city and, as we see here, even reads *The Guardian*. More important, he blames the system for his sins and is consumed with liberal guilt for what he has done. Perfect.

Bourne emerges as a profoundly empathetic figure whose backstory is slowly revealed throughout the trilogy, leading the audience to frequently share his fractured and harrowing memories as they return to him. Like Daniel Craig's incarnation of Bond, Bourne is a much more human figure, rendered vulnerable and traumatised by his violent past. Bourne's memory loss is a form of psychogenic amnesia brought on as a result of a traumatic incident. On the surface it seems to be the result of the gunshot wounds inflicted during his final mission for the agency where he found himself unable to carry out the assassination of the exiled African dictator Nykwana Mombosi. On the mission Bourne was presented with the perfect opportunity to complete his objective, but seeing Mombosi with a sleeping child on his lap, his once inhuman target is rendered human again and he is unable to pull the trigger. It is later

Figure 14   The existential crisis of a contemporary action hero and a projection of
how liberal America sees itself? The ever-mobile Jason Bourne in *The Bourne Ultimatum* (2007).

revealed that Mombosi was targeted by the agency for threatening to expose the involvement of the CIA in his rise to power – evidence of their continued and unlawful interference in overseas affairs. Yet there appears to be more to Bourne's amnesia than physical trauma alone: when his memories slowly begin to return, he is confronted with the realisation that he does not like the person he once was and the illegal and immoral acts of violence he perpetrated. Challenged by evidence of his own cognitive dissonance, his amnesia is framed as an unconscious attempt to repress the reality of what he has participated in. While amnesia is a recurring trope of the formulaic narratives of the action genre, here it becomes part of a thematic strain about identity and personal responsibility more akin to the narratives of *Memento* (2000) and *Eternal Sunshine of the Spotless Mind* (2004). Bourne's amnesia functions as an effective metaphor for United States' foreign policy in the post-World War Two era, a materialisation of what Gore Vidal (2004) memorably called 'the United States of Amnesia'. Is it too much to suggest then, as Vincent M. Gaine does, that Bourne becomes a surrogate for American audiences, suffering a trauma 'much as Western society, specifically the United States, was by 9/11' (2011: 160)? Gaine continues, 'Just as those who saw the collapse of the Twin Towers either in person or through the media are likely to be haunted by the images, so is Bourne haunted by the images of his past experiences' (ibid.). Bourne struggles to come to terms with his past, just as America has never been able to come to terms with its own history, the truth about which contrasts greatly to its own claims for moral authority around the globe (see Figure 14).

The Bourne trilogy finds its antagonists not in the forms of jihadists, neo-Nazis or North Korean generals, but devoted if misguided Americans like Alexander Conklin (Chris Cooper), Ward Abbot (Brian Cox) and Noah Vosen (David Straithairn) who see themselves as patriots unafraid to transgress international law in order to consolidate American power abroad – a far cry from the whitewashed depictions of the CIA in *Zero Dark Thirty* and *Argo*. The branch of the CIA that Bourne worked for, Treadstone, is a secret organisation tasked with carrying out deniable operations that are never officially endorsed by the authorities. Treadstone is shown to target foreign dignitaries who stand in the way of American geo-political interests, like the aforementioned Wombosi or the Russian politician Vladimir Neski assassinated for knowing too much about the CIA's profitable and illegal involvement with high-ranking Russian oligarchs. The film's premise of an amnesiac agent seeking redemption is a familiar one; however, the series taps into a rich vein of anxiety about the US Government and its actions around the world that resonated with audiences in the decade after 9/11 especially after the public became aware of the systematic mistreatment of prisoners in Abu Ghraib, the CIA's policy of extraordinary rendition and the extent of its hidden surveillance programmes. It is not until the third instalment of the franchise that it is revealed that Bourne was not pressured into joining Treadstone, as audiences had been led to believe, but he had in fact volunteered, eager to play his role in defending his country like many of the American soldiers in post-9/11 war films. This explicit criticism of US foreign policy angered many on the right of the political spectrum and led Bill O'Reilly to suggest that 'the America-haters will love *The Bourne Ultimatum*' and that 'this is harmless nonsense to those of us who understand the hero and villain business, and realize the simplistic bias that permeates Hollywood. But to impressionable audiences, the anti-American theme could resonate' (O'Reilly 2007).

Those that attempt to kill Bourne throughout the series like Vosen and Abbot are equated to the reckless policies of the Bush administration and its short-term methodology in the war on terror. Vosen proudly describes the lack of legal restrictions on his team:

> Full envelope intrusion, rendition, experimental interrogation – it is all run out of this office. We are the sharp end of the stick now . . . No more red tape. No more getting the bad guys caught on our sights, then watching them escape while we wait for somebody in Washington to issue the order.

Like many of the Bush administration's neo-cons, Vosen sees 9/11 as an opportunity to pursue America's enemies and strengthen national interests abroad, but this commitment and their willingness to transgress international law reveals them to be disconnected from the changing realities of the post-9/11 world. When he orders the assassination of an innocent British journalist whose only crime is that he is investigating Treadstone and then targets another of his own agents who he suspects has been compromised, Vosen's deputy Pamela Landy (Joan Allen) believes that he has crossed the line. She asks, 'You start down this path – where does it end?' To which Vosen replies, 'It ends when we've won.' In situating itself in such a politicised and contemporary geo-political arena, the Bourne franchise is certainly the most political series of action films in the history of American cinema. Landy's arc is a familiar one and in her conversion we can see an embodiment of the transition that many Americans experienced in their attitudes to the war on terror in the years since 2001. At first she is utterly loyal to the agency and accepts the accusations against Bourne, believing him to be a dangerous threat to national security; she later realises that it is not Bourne who is the menace, but rather the likes of the neo-cons Vosen and Abbot who use the agency to pursue their own extreme ideological agenda.

While the Bourne series seems to be politically progressive, far removed from the overt revenge dramas of *Rambo* and *Taken* in its sustained criticism of American foreign policy, it still embodies a narrative in which personal redemption is achieved through violence and features highly stereotyped (if more human than in the Bond series) representations of women. The trilogy contains only three notable female characters in Bourne's girlfriend Marie, Nicky Parsons (a Treadstone officer) and Pam Landy. Both Marie and Nicky frequently require protection and saving by Bourne, and even though Marie is killed very early on in *The Bourne Supremacy* at the hands of a Russian assassin, her presence lingers throughout the series in the familiar trope of the female as source of redemption. Bourne refuses to kill Abbot and the Russian assassin responsible for her death, because he believes that Marie would not want him to. However, this romanticism is undercut when Abbot tells Bourne that he only has himself to blame for Marie's death in a literalisation of culpability that is rare in the genre: '*You* killed Marie the minute you climbed into her car. The minute you entered her life she was dead'. It is a charge that Bourne is unable to deny. Pam Landy, despite being a strong individual, certainly reminiscent of Maya from *Zero Dark Thirty*, is endowed with traits that are coded as distinctly feminine, namely her empathy and diplomatic skills as opposed to the decisive hyper-masculinities of the likes of Vosen and Abbot. The old-fashioned masculinities of these characters are juxtaposed with Bourne's more sensitive and empathetic 'new man' style – revealing Bourne as a cultural battleground not just for memory and accountability, but also for new millennial masculinity. The defining scene in the trilogy appears at the end of *The Bourne Supremacy* and surprisingly it is one of its most understated. An injured Bourne meets the daughter of one of the many men he killed in his career as an agent/assassin, the Russian politician Vladimir Neski. Bourne reveals the truth to the girl – that he killed her father under orders from the CIA – but he does not expect forgiveness as he cannot even forgive himself. He comments, 'It changes things, doesn't it?', before leaving her with a simple, 'I'm sorry.' This recognition of responsibility provides American audiences with the fictional catharsis of the United States apologising for its aggressive foreign policy and the acknowledgement of the reality of the ramifications of the war on terror. Bourne's apology for his, and by extension America's, past interference in global affairs, is an act that was strikingly replicated in President Obama's interpretation of recent American history that he repeatedly espoused throughout his election campaign in 2008. Obama stated, 'I personally would want to see our tragic history, or the tragic elements of our history, acknowledged' (cited in Au 2008) and was vociferously criticised for his reflections by many conservatives. Yet this is something the characters of Abbot and Vosen are unable to admit. When confronted with his crimes, Abbot can only say, 'I'm a patriot!', yet he proceeds to kill himself. Likewise George W. Bush, Dick Cheney and Donald Rumsfeld have steadfastly refused to move from the moral clarity of their positions on the war on terror or acknowledge the most serious of mistakes made in the aftermath of 9/11.

The trilogy ends with Vosen arrested and facing a tribunal, the suggestion being that the bad guys are being brought to justice and that the system, while flawed, works as long as there are people like Bourne and Landy there to 'do the right thing'. Ironically, it is in this denouement that the franchise departs most from reality. *The Washington Post* reported that projects like Treadstone had actually existed at times during the Bush administration, and CIA Director Leon Panetta stated that many plans had been hidden from the United States Congress at the recommendations of Dick Cheney (see Shane 2009). Nancy Pelosi, former speaker of the House of Representatives, asserted that the CIA deliberately and repeatedly misled congress about waterboarding programmes and other matters long after 9/11 (see Anonymous 2009). Yet despite this, not a single individual was ever prosecuted; only in the realm of a Hollywood thriller could such things happen.

All of the films discussed in this chapter function on one level as popular action films, delivering the prerequisite thrills of the genre, the likes of which have filled American cinemas (and those around the globe) for decades. But on another level they articulate the very particular fears and fantasies of the post-9/11 world with vivid clarity, embracing the paradoxical relationship American cinema has with violence in its depiction of America's enemies at home and abroad during the war on terror era. The action genre has been long decried by critics, but it has always been able to collectively represent and project American neuroses on-screen. In this way each of these texts becomes inextricably bound to the post-9/11 era regardless of their political perspectives. As we move further into the twenty-first century those fears and anxieties will certainly shift and ebb, but no matter how much they change they will always be reflected on the cinema screens.

NOTES

1. After the exposure of the treatment of prisoners at Abu Ghraib, Schlesinger Jr, then in his late eighties, commented, 'No position taken has done more damage to the American reputation in the world – ever' (cited in Mayer 2008: 8).
2. *The Searchers* was even used as inspiration for the end to the award-winning *Breaking Bad* (AMC, 2008–13) (see Acuna 2013).
3. Stallone even poked fun at Rambo in another film that attempted to deconstruct his star persona, *Tango & Cash* (1989), by having his character, the art-loving and bespectacled intellectual cop, Ray Tango, declare, 'Rambo is a pussy!'
4. As a frame of reference courtesy of moviebodycounts.com, *The Expendables* has 221 on-screen deaths, *The Expendables* 2 has 489, *Rambo* has 247 and *Taken* has 'only' 35.
5. Some years later Letterman denounced the war in Iraq. See Baker (2006).
6. *Taken* is strikingly similar to Tony Scott's *Man on Fire* in which ex-CIA agent Creasy (Denzel Washington) is charged with finding a kidnapped nine year-old American girl Pita (Dakota Fanning) in Mexico. Like Bryan Mills, Creasy is not bound by the laws of the land and he too is not averse to torture. Scott portrays the whole country as corrupt; from the media, the police and the judges, even the Mexican father of the girl is revealed to have played a part in her abduction, whereas her mother, a beautiful white American woman, is completely blameless. It is left to the vigilante American Creasy to do for Mexico what it could never do for itself. A friend of his remarks, 'He'll deliver more justice in a weekend than your courts and tribunals do in ten years. Just stay out of his way!'

4. TURNING TO THE DARK SIDE: CHALLENGING AMERICAN MYTHOLOGY IN THE SUPERHERO GENRE

We of the twenty-first century, although unable to believe in the literal reality of such heroes, nevertheless still dream our myths onward, clothing them in modern dress . . . We dream them onward, give them colorful costumes, and pseudoscientific origins, but we no longer consider them real. Or do we?

Don LoCicero, *Superheroes and Gods: A Comparative Study from Babylonia to Batman*

We also have to work, though, sort of the dark side, if you will. We've got to spend time in the shadows in the intelligence world. A lot of what needs to be done here will have to be done quietly, without any discussion, using sources and methods that are available to our intelligence agencies, if we're going to be successful. That's the world these folks operate in, and so it's going to be vital for us to use any means at our disposal, basically, to achieve our objective.

Dick Cheney, appearance on NBC's *Meet the Press*

It is possible to discern a great deal about a society from its heroic mythology. Just as the Ancient Greeks had tales of Hercules, Achilles and Theseus, late nineteenth-century America turned to mythologised stories of Wyatt Earp, Davy Crockett and Jesse James. In the twentieth century and into the twenty-first, contemporary Western culture found its heroic ideals embodied in comic-book heroes like Superman, Batman and Spider-Man.[1] These icons authenticate and endorse prevailing social values and behaviours in texts that both reflect *and* influence the cultures in which they are produced. As Richard Slotkin observed, 'The mythology of a nation is the intelligible mask of that enigma called the "national character". Through myths the psychology and world view of our cultural ancestors are transmitted to modern descendants, in such a way and with such power that our perception of contemporary reality and our ability to function in the world are directly, often tragically affected' (1973: 3). Slotkin's use of the term 'tragically' indicates an awareness of the power that mythology, in its disparate forms, has over society. In this chapter we consider perhaps the most explicit manifestations of contemporary mythology – the superhero film. Indeed, the first decade of the new millennium saw itself described as the 'superhero decade' due to the sheer number and influence of these narratives (Gray and Kaklamanidou 2011: 1). While they offer portrayals of universal values and concerns, they also function as embodiments of a quintessentially American mythology that John Shelton Lawrence and Robert Jewett have described as 'the American monomyth' (1988). Lawrence and Jewett argue that American incarnations of heroic narratives differ considerably from Joseph Campbell's accounts of common mythological tropes in *The Hero with a Thousand Faces* (1949). Like Slotkin, Lawrence and Jewett see the problematic nature of such redemptive narratives that offer 'vigilantism without lawlessness, sexual repression without resultant perversion, and moral infallibility without the use of intellect (2002: 47–8).

In the immediate aftermath of 9/11 it seemed that the United States no longer needed fictional heroes, having found real-life counterparts in the first responders to the attack on the World Trade Center on 11 September 2001, like the firefighters, ambulance crews and police officers, many of whom gave their lives to save others on that tragic day. In the weeks after, George W. Bush's popularity ratings rose to stratospheric levels and when he called out to America (and the rest of the world) from the rubble of Ground Zero, many began to see him in a distinctly heroic light: Peggy Noonan said she expected him to 'tear open his shirt and reveal the big "S" on his chest' (2003). Some of Bush's rhetoric itself seemed overtly mythological or at least reminiscent of a comic book: his quest to 'rid the world of the evil-doers' in 'a monumental struggle of good versus evil' (Bush 2002c) is a superlative example of what Jewett and Lawrence (2003: 28) describe as the 'Captain America complex' that has beguiled many American Presidents.

Susan Faludi found this emerging trend and its implications troubling:

> [W]hy were our serious media insisting on portraying us and our leaders with such comic hyperbole? The implications of that heightening were a bit unnerving. Superheroes are fantasies for a particular type of reader: someone, typically a prepubescent boy, who feels weak in the world and

insufficient to the demands of the day and who needs a Walter Mitty [from Thurber's 'The Secret Life of Walter Mitty'] bellows to pump up his self-worth. Was the same now true for the national audience, the American people, whose elected and appointed officials were being inflated with imaginary grit and guts into the Heat and the Protector and Tower of Strength? (Faludi 2007: 51)[2]

While this glorification of politicians like George W. Bush and Rudy Giuliani continued, fictional superheroes almost universally experienced the complete opposite, becoming progressively more humanised in the comic books and films that emerged after 9/11. In the comic *Heroes*, published in December 2001, many of Marvel's most famous characters like Spider-Man, Captain America and the Incredible Hulk were shown alongside the firemen, police officers and other rescue workers among the detritus of 9/11. In one of the panels, Captain America looms over the dust-filled skyline of New York, holding up his hand to cover his weeping face.[3] As Spiderman walks through the ruins, he is asked, 'Where were you? Why didn't you stop this?' Of course, he is unable to answer, not only because he is a fictional character intruding upon the 'real' world, but also because cinematic incarnations of superheroes, which would soon become some of the most commercially successful films in the history of American cinema, would never allow him to interact with real-life tragedy so explicitly. This tendency was revealed just forty-eight hours after 11 September 2001, when the trailer for the upcoming *Spider-Man* showing a pre-9/11 World Trade Center was removed from cinemas, and in the years that followed superhero films were only able to allude to the war on terror without ever confronting it directly. Despite this, the war on terror and 9/11 influenced the genre profoundly in its themes and even in the construction of its mise en scène. Grant Morrison, the award-winning comic book writer, observed this change and suggested:

> Stories had to be about 'real' things. As a result, more and more Marvel comics, including some of my own, had scenes set in the Middle East or on board hijacked aircraft. The emphasis veered away from escapist cosmic fantasy, nostalgia and surrealism toward social critique, satire, and filmic vérité wrapped in the flag of shameless patriotism. (Morrison 2011: 355)

This change of focus is revealed quite startlingly in the transition from Bryan Singer's *X-Men* (2000) to *X-Men 2* (2003). *X-Men* is a resolutely pre-9/11 text and functions primarily as a vivid allegory of race relations, which has been one of the enduring interpretations of the comic-book series since its original release in the 1960s (see Dipaolo 2011: 219–47). It is set in a world in which super-powered mutants struggle for equality but are continuously denied equal rights and mistrusted by humans. In protest at this treatment the powerful mutant Magneto (Ian McKellen) builds a device able to blast radioactive energy from the top of the Statue of Liberty that will turn all humans into mutants. Magneto's plan, an audacious act of terrorism taking place on one of America's greatest landmarks, is not viewed as such in the film's diegesis and the word 'terrorism' is never used. However, just three years later the political climate in America had changed considerably, and the frame of reference for the franchise (and the majority of superhero films) had undergone quite a remarkable transformation. Instead of the fairly delineated battle between good and evil apparent in the first film, *X-Men 2* features a much more ambiguous and timely conflict with sustained and explicit references to the contemporary political arena. The mutants are now repeatedly referred to as 'terrorists', and Magneto himself is 'one of the terrorists from the Liberty Island incident'. Thus, the attack on Liberty Island is retroactively connected to the attacks on the Twin Towers, and in the narrative of the film it is used as a rallying cry by political conservatives for a wave of anti-mutant hysteria. Of course, the Liberty Island incident was perpetrated by just a small band of mutants, but many humans in the film regard it as a symbol that no mutant can be trusted. Therefore, in the space of a few short years Magneto had gone from being framed as a Malcolm X-type figure (he even says in *X-Men* that he will fight the Mutant Registration Act 'by any means necessary') to an Osama bin Laden-esque terrorist in *X-Men 2*. Intriguingly, Magneto is not the primary villain in the film; that role is afforded to the patriotic but misguided and duplicitous government operative Stryker (Brian Cox, who played the similar role of Wade Abbot in *The Bourne Supremacy*). Stryker manipulates the conflict in order to engineer even more hatred for mutants that will lead to increased public support for their eradication. Stryker tortures the mutants he captures in order to get information, an act that was completely absent from the first film, and, in particular, he does it in order to learn the whereabouts of Xavier's Mutant School, which he hopes to destroy, thereby killing all the mutants in one strategic pre-emptive strike. As a result many implore the President to 'declare a state of emergency and place every mutant in the country under arrest' in striking echoes of the anti-Muslim fervour that swept the United States after 9/11.

This chapter argues that superheroes and the films that feature them perform a distinct cultural and sociological function by embodying myths in conspicuously realised forms. However, rather than being simply wish-fulfilment fantasies for pre-pubescent teenagers, as Faludi suggests, they frequently deconstruct as well as reproduce our desires. By revealing how we dream ourselves to be, they become a manifestation not just of the fantasies of individuals, but of entire nations: accordingly, Spider-Man, Batman, Iron Man and Superman can persuasively be seen as reflections of American values and ideals. Thus, rather than provide texts to enable Americans to 'escape from the very real horrors of international unrest and terrorism whose epic moment was September 11, 2001' (Roberts 2004: 210), superhero films are actually deeply immersed in and engage with that moment.

Interestingly, Superman, perhaps the most iconic American superhero of all, struggled to find his cinematic identity in the first decade of the new millennium. One may have thought that this nostalgic and unquestionably patriotic figure would have been the perfect hero in order to galvanise American unity in the post-9/11 years, just as he had embodied the American spirit of resistance during World War Two. In one early post-9/11 charity comic this looked to be the case, as Superman was shown among the ruins of the Twin Towers clutching the Stars and Stripes, looking to the skies, and whispering, 'First things first. Then we come for you.' Superman, like most superheroes, has undergone distinct ideological shifts in personality throughout the decades: he was markedly isolationist and anti-war as late as 1939, but as soon as the United States entered World War Two, he quickly joined the war effort and fought against both the Germans and the Japanese. In the post-9/11 era, like Spider-Man, he begrudged his fictional status and lamented that he was unable to break free from the pages of the comic books and, by association, the cinema screens that restrained him. In Bryan Singer's *Superman Returns* (2006) Lois Lane asks him, 'Where did you go?' referring to his extended absence from Metropolis not his inability to intervene on 9/11, but one cannot help see her question filtering into the 'real' world. Yet American audiences failed to embrace Singer's reboot of the *Superman* franchise that only just managed to earn more money than the original *Superman* (1978) without even adjusting for inflation. While Superman has historically been considered as the pre-eminent personification of American ethics and values, it may be more accurate to suggest that it is Batman, especially in his new millennial incarnation, who more readily encompasses the complicated and polarised post-9/11 American psyche, and this may be one of the reasons for the phenomenal success of Christopher Nolan's interpretation of the character in the decade after the attacks on 11 September 2001. While America may wish to see itself as the principled and noble Superman, in reality it resembles more closely the conflicted and much more morally ambiguous Batman. As Michael Caine, who starred as Alfred in Nolan's Batman trilogy was said to have remarked, 'Superman is the way America sees itself, but Batman is the way the world sees America' (cited in Svetkey 2008). Certainly the concept of standing for 'Truth, justice and the American way' had markedly different associations for much of the world in the wake of the war on terror. In Singer's film the most striking sequence is when Superman rescues a space shuttle full of passengers and the crowd at the stadium where it is about to crash. While heroic scenes like this certainly occurred prior to September 11th 2001, it is tempting to see this as a symbolic attempt to rewrite the events of 9/11, only with Superman there to save the day. It is a scene that is regularly returned to in the superhero genre, with a distinctly different emphasis in the post-9/11 years. Was Singer's old-fashioned, nostalgic fantasy an uneasy fit for a country divided by its reaction to the abuses in Abu Ghraib, the intrusions of the USA Patriot Act and the ongoing wars in Iraq and Afghanistan? Could the invulnerable Superman even resonate any more in a world in which 'unrestrained capitalism always wins, where politicians always lie, where sports idols take drugs and beat their wives, and where white picket fences are suspect because they hide dark things' (Waid 2006: 5). However, these are the very motifs at the heart of *Batman Begins*, *The Dark Knight* and *The Dark Knight Rises* (2012), texts that eschew Superman's Manichean morality in favour of something much more complicated. The new millennial Batman replays the events of the fractious era just as *Superman Returns* does, but it offers no such unproblematic resolutions and in doing so it is one of many films from the superhero genre that seem to beat with the very pulse of the decade.[4]

'WHAT ABOUT ESCALATION?' BATMAN, 9/11 AND THE 'WAR ON TERROR': THE RETURN OF THE (VERY) DARK KNIGHT

I think Gotham's a fantastic hyper-real arena in which to discuss contemporary ideas without being pretentious about it, without being overly political or anything. I enjoy having that parallel universe.

Christopher Nolan, director of *Batman Begins*, *The Dark Knight* and
The Dark Knight Rises (*The Complete Screenplays*)

Christopher Nolan's three-pronged assault on the superhero film arguably left an indelible mark not just on the genre, but even on popular culture and society at large. The first film in the trilogy, *Batman Begins*, set a template for the dark and gritty comic-book adaptations that engaged with reality as much as fantasy that came to dominate the domestic and international box office for the rest of the decade. This turn towards 'reality' is certainly not unprecedented in American genre cinema, as Leo Braudy has observed, many stagnant genres over the years have become revivified with an 'injection, usually of "realism"' (2002: 111). Nolan's Batman trilogy immerses itself in the key events of the fractious decade and offers timely meditations on the efficacy and ethics of torture, revenge, vigilantism, pre-emptive violence and extraordinary rendition, with the war on terror as a compelling and ever-present metaphorical backdrop to its narrative (see Figures 15 and 16).

Christopher Nolan was given the daunting task of rebooting the Batman franchise after the disastrous *Batman & Robin* (1997) had turned Tim

Burton's vision of the Dark Knight back towards the cartoony kitsch of the 1960s' television show replete with camp villains, groan-inducing one-liners and an exaggeratedly benippled bat suit. Much of the resonance of Nolan's depiction of Batman is due to its quasi-realistic setting and context. His Gotham City is not the dayglow Metropolis of the Salkind-era *Superman* or the cartoonish world of Joel Schumacher's Batman years; rather, it is a grim and decidedly contemporary world with its own iconic landmark in the imposing Wayne Tower that, like the Twin Towers, comes under attack by a terrorist intent on bringing a decadent city to its knees. The terrorist in question is Ra's al Ghul, who states, 'Gotham's time has come, like Constantinople or Rome before it, the city has become a breeding ground for suffering and injustice, it is beyond saving and must be allowed to die.' At the start of the trilogy Gotham is a hotbed of corruption, virtually owned by the amoral crime boss Carmine Falconi who controls the police, the lawyers and even the judges. This corruption is so pervasive that Bruce Wayne is morally compelled to step outside of the law and take matters into his own hands by becoming the masked vigilante Batman. The film explicitly suggests that his actions are not only necessary, but that it is almost his moral duty to do so as a concerned citizen and patriot.

Bruce Wayne, like many superheroes, is a man marked by the violent trauma of his past, in his case the murder of his parents, Thomas and Martha Wayne, when he was a child. He holds himself personally responsible for their deaths, as he had begged them to leave the performance of Arrigo Boito's opera *Mefistofele* that they were attending, when he became disturbed by the Bat-like images on the stage. Years later when their murderer is set free after serving only fourteen years of his sentence, Wayne considers killing the man but cannot bring himself to do it. Instead he gives up his identity, his billionaire status and his First World privileges and turns his back on civilisation to travel through Asia, living for the first time in his life on just his wits and not on his vast inherited fortune. After a spell in a Chinese prison (for stealing Wayne Industries' products) he is recruited and trained by the enigmatic Ra's al Ghul who is framed as a distinctly Osama bin Laden figure on a quasi-jihad style mission to destroy Gotham City. Writer David S. Goyer made this comparison explicit when he stated, 'We modelled him after Osama bin Laden. He's not crazy in the way that all the other Batman villains are. He's not bent on revenge; he's actually trying to heal the world. He's just doing it by very draconian means' (cited in Ryan 2005).[5] Al Ghul even has his own training camp in a mountain hideaway where he instructs a cadre of elite terrorists in the art of war, each of whom is prepared to sacrifice everything, including his life, for the cause.

To complete his initiation Wayne is assigned one final task: to kill a local petty thief and murderer, but he cannot agree, as this would violate his most fundamental code. On his return to Gotham after seven years away Wayne creates Batman as a powerful symbol able to strike fear into the hearts of the criminals who have for so long had the run of the city. They fear Batman because they know that unlike the police he is not restricted by the law. Batman operates in a world in which Gotham's criminals freely break society's rules and this necessitates that he must do the same in a similar way to how Dick Cheney asserted in 2001 that many long-standing legal precedents prevented America from fighting an effective war on terror. Cheney stated, 'We also have to work, though, sort of the dark side, if you will . . . That's the world these folks operate in, and so it's going to be vital for us to use any means at our disposal, basically, to achieve our objective.' Batman's own war on crime is a brutally effective one; unrestrained by the law and due process, he quickly clears the streets and is welcomed as a hero by the residents of Gotham City.

However, it soon becomes apparent that there is a larger conspiracy afoot as Ra's al Ghul has created a virus that induces people to hallucinate that which they fear the most and intends to spread it throughout Gotham with a Microwave Emitter – a weapon of mass destruction manufactured by Bruce Wayne's own company, Wayne Industries – including its use on the home of the very man who produced it. Al Ghul's primary target is Wayne Tower, Gotham's imposing symbol of hope for the future and a renewed economic prosperity. He anticipates its destruction and that the fear that the virus generates will make the citizens of Gotham tear their own city apart. But Batman is able to prevent him from completing his mission, as Nolan provides audiences with a powerful wish-fulfilment fantasy and one of the quintessential 'what if' moments in contemporary American cinema by showing what Batman might have done in New York on 9/11 if only he had been able to tear himself free from the bounds of the cinema screen.

Batman Begins depicts its hero's unlawful vigilante crusade as an entirely moral and successful one: he cleans the streets of crime, apprehends those who are responsible and saves the city from certain destruction. He joins the ranks of icons of cinematic vigilantism uncritically celebrated within their own dieges for their necessary transgressions of the law like Harry Callahan in *Dirty Harry*, Buford Pusser in *Walking Tall* (1973), David Sumner in *Straw Dogs* (1971) and Paul Kersey in *Death Wish* (1974), each of whom can be similarly seen as a manifestation of the prevailing anxieties of the era in which they were rendered large on the cinema screen.[6] Framed like this it is hard not to see the film as some sort of a reaffirmation of the Bush administration's policies after 9/11, consciously designed to be so or not, a justification of the measures taken – whether the transgressions of international law or the restrictions of civil liberties – and a legitimisation of Cheney's decision to work on 'the dark side'. Justine Toh even saw the Batman of *Batman Begins* not just as an allegory for the Bush era but for George W. Bush himself. She wrote, 'In this frame, Batman's righteous task is to clean up Gotham by removing its corrupt elements, a fictional parallel for the righteousness of the US's campaign to promote democracy in the Middle East' (2010: 132). Like Bush, Batman is compelled to go outside the law to do what he instinctively knows is right, even though many will disapprove. Yet despite the reactionary nature of what has gone before, the film ends on a note of caution as James Gordon (Gary Oldman) asks Batman, 'What about escalation?' It is a question the sequel, *The Dark Knight*, spends most of its narrative interrogating.

The sequel resumes in a Gotham City almost entirely free of crime, a fact that frustrates the remaining impotent crime bosses beyond measure. Furthermore, a new and impeccably honest district attorney, Harvey Dent (Aaron Eckhart), seems to have made Batman almost redundant as he is able to fight crime effectively without breaking the law: he is the 'White Knight' to Batman's 'Dark Knight'. Even Bruce Wayne comes to admire Dent and he considers hanging up his cowl for good, seeing no reason for Batman to exist while someone like Dent can do his job for him. In this time of apparent peace and prosperity the public begin to turn against Batman: with the streets free of crime they forget why he was ever needed in the first place. But Dent understands the continued importance of Batman as a symbol and he calls on the Roman Empire as a metaphor: 'When their enemies were at the gates, the Romans would suspend democracy and appoint one man to protect the city. It wasn't considered an honour; it was considered a public service.' To which Rachel (Maggie Gyllenhaal), who was once romantically involved with Bruce Wayne and who is now engaged to Dent, comments, 'The last man who they appointed the Republic was named Caesar and he never gave up his power.' The second film takes Rachel's observation as the starting point for a disquisition on the ramifications of the vigilantism that was so emphatically endorsed in *Batman Begins*. By acting the way he has, even in the defence of a moral ideal, Batman has unwittingly created an environment that fosters more and more extreme forms of violence. As Bruce's trusted butler Alfred observes, '*You* crossed the line first'.

Gordon's fear of escalation is realised in a new and even more dangerous threat to Gotham, the anarchic and nihilistic Joker (Heath Ledger) who holds the entire city to ransom with his random acts of destructive terrorism. He embarks on a campaign of violence, murder and intimidation that paralyses the city with fear; however, it remains unclear what he actually wants, as he seems to have no desire for money or power. The Joker is clearly identified by Nolan as a terrorist: from his suicide bomber's vest to his use of the media as a weapon to spread his message of terror throughout the city. Dana Stevens suggested 'Nolan turns the Manichean morality of comic books – pure good vs. pure evil – into a bleak post-9/11 allegory about how terror (and, make no mistake, Heath Ledger's Joker is a terrorist) breaks down those reassuring moral categories' (Stevens 2008).[7]

The first film had repeatedly presented Batman's transgression of the law as necessary and effective: when a corrupt policeman in the pay of Falconi had refused to talk, Batman intimidated and beat him until he gave up the exact information he required. In *The Dark Knight* this simplistic causal relationship is problematised as the effectiveness of such a sustained violent approach is repeatedly questioned. In a visceral representation of Alan Dershowitz's infamous 'the Ticking Bomb Scenario' that came to dominate media depictions of terrorism in the post-9/11 years, the Joker is apprehended and shown to have information that could save the lives of both Rachel and Dent who he has captured and placed near bombs that are primed to explode (see Dershowitz 2008). If Batman does not quickly get the information that he needs from the Joker then it seems they will both die. Gordon allows Batman to be alone in the room with the Joker, who is in police custody, thereby endorsing his actions, and Batman proceeds to violently beat him, effectively torturing him, to reveal their whereabouts. Initially the torture seems to have worked as the Joker tells Batman their location, but Batman is forced to choose who to save and who to entrust to the Gotham police. When he arrives where Joker had informed him Rachel would be, instead he finds Harvey, and Rachel is killed in the ensuing explosion. In the world of *The Dark Knight*, unlike in *Batman Begins*, violence, intimidation and torture tactics do not always get the results they once did. Here the film challenges what Stephen Faller called the 'false dichotomy choice' (2010: 259) that superheroes are often confronted with, where they are forced to decide between saving one innocent party or another, before in the end figuring out a way to save both (see *Spider-Man*, *Iron Man 3* (2013), *Superman Returns* and so on). Batman's failure to save Rachel, the love of his life, is a rare moment of gravity in the superhero genre and an indication of how Nolan's trilogy differs from many of its genre counterparts.

As the Joker's reign of terror sweeps through the city, the people turn more and more against Batman, blaming him for the escalation of violence. An angry crowd chants at him, 'It's because of you these guys are dead!' Of course, this is something the Joker had wished for and he is pleased to see the city turn against the man who was once their beloved hero. The Joker even demands that Batman unmask himself and reveal his true identity or he will continue to target even more innocent people. While it is hard to gauge what the Joker hopes to achieve, it seems by orchestrating the fall of Batman and then Harvey Dent he will prove that even the best among us are fallible and that beneath the superficial veneer of civilised society, man is little more than a brutal and savage animal. In the wake of his traumatic loss Dent becomes a changed man, bitter and twisted, seemingly proving the Joker to be correct. While he had once been the 'White Knight' to Batman's 'Dark Knight', he becomes an even

Figure 15   'The things that worry us these days': Christopher Nolan's *The Dark Knight* (2009). Despite being 'just' a comic-book movie, the film engages with the tumultuous decade in a sustained and interrogative fashion.

Figure 16   The extent of the destruction at the site of the World Trade Center. Public domain image. Taken by Andrea Booher ©.

more exaggerated and morally ambiguous version of the vigilante Batman in his thirst for revenge on those who played a role in Rachel's death. His revenge is motivated by his all-consuming rage and it is tempting to see Nolan using Dent as a commentary on America's confusion of revenge with justice in the post-9/11 years. Batman also undergoes a change: in order to apprehend someone like the Joker he is forced to go against his own strict code of ethics that has always distinguished him from the villains he fights. He asks Lucius Fox (Morgan Freeman), the head of research and development at Wayne Industries, to help him find the Joker by using a highly advanced yet illegal high-tech surveillance technology that takes over the mobile phones of every citizen in Gotham City in a fairly explicit reference to the USA Patriot Act and UK's anti-terror laws. Fox protests that it is 'too much power for one person', but agrees to do it only once, after which he insists he will resign.

The film concludes with Batman finally apprehending the Joker, having proved to him that Gotham's citizens are not as inherently bestial as he had suggested. The Joker had planted two bombs on two separate boats in an inspired variation of a well-known problem in Game theory by Merrill Flood and Melvin Dresher called the 'prisoner's dilemma'. The passengers on each boat are told that they can only save themselves by blowing up the other boat. The Joker, given his cynical perspective on human behaviour, believes that they will quickly do so, but he is surprised to see that neither boat decides to destroy the others in order to save themselves.[8] The Joker reveals to Batman that he never wanted his adversary dead: 'You complete me,' he adds in a humorous nod to *Jerry Maguire* (1996). Like the finest Batman villains, Joker is a distorted mirror image of Batman with exaggerated aspects of his personality, a process that sees Batman in a continuous psychological battle not only with his enemies, but even with himself. Both Batman and Joker have traumatic pasts and personalities that have been forged in violence, both operate outside the law and both trade in fear in order to achieve their goals. The Joker's assertion is that it is through our enemies that we come to define ourselves, and the parallel he draws between himself and Batman is too powerful for either the audience or Batman to ignore. Yet even though he has been apprehended, Joker's scheme is not yet over. His orchestration of Harvey Dent's fall from grace is his final gambit, turning one of Gotham's finest citizens into a twisted monster desirous only of revenge. When Dent threatens to murder Gordon's family because of the role the senior police officer played in Rachel's death, Batman is reluctantly forced to kill Dent and transgress his own moral code. But Batman recognises that if the citizens of Gotham learn about Dent's turn to the dark side, their faith in law and justice will be ruined forever, so he decides to take the blame for the murders that Harvey committed and offers up Batman as the villain that the people need in order to maintain their belief in the system. In the end Batman endorses the legend of Harvey Dent and sacrifices himself, his reputation and maybe even his life for Gotham in another return of the maxim from *The Man Who Shot Liberty Valence* and the commitment to 'Print the legend' rather than reveal the truth to the public.

The final part of the trilogy, *The Dark Knight Rises*, picks up the story eight years later, that is, eight years after the Joker's reign of terror has come to an end and the death of Harvey Dent. The film, released just over ten years after the attacks on 9/11, explores the aftermath of a traumatic event that transpired almost a decade ago, the reverberations of which are still being felt throughout Gotham City. In the wake of his death, Harvey Dent has become a martyr with a city-wide holiday held every year in his honour. Politicians in Gotham have also instituted the Dent Act, which has cleaned the streets of Gotham by enabling lawmakers to send suspected criminals to jail without observing due process. Thus, the peace that has come to the city in Dent's name is a false one, used by those in power to reinforce their fragile social order, built on the convenient lie that Dent died a hero.

Batman has been absent from Gotham for the eight years in-between the two films; partly because the Dent Act has made his presence unnecessary and also because he is reviled by the residents of Gotham who blame him for the death of their heroic saviour. Additionally Wayne has retired his cloak because of his grief at Rachel's death who he believed was his only chance for a normal life away from Batman and because, ageing and wounded, he just does not have it in him to be the Batman any more. The film makes it clear that Gotham is now a peaceful city and there is no place left for wartime relics like Batman and Commissioner Jim Gordon, who have both sacrificed a great deal but are now forgotten, or in the case of Batman, reviled. The seductive cat burglar Selina Kyle (Anne Hathaway) tells the reclusive Bruce Wayne, who has become a Howard Hughes-like hermit closeted away in his mansion disconnected from the world, 'There's a storm coming, Mr. Wayne. You and your friends better batten down the hatches, because when it hits, you're all gonna wonder how you ever thought you could live so large and leave so little for the rest of us.' The storm emerges in the shape of yet another terrorist figure to join the ranks of Ra's al Ghul and the Joker. Bane (Tom Hardy) is a hardened mercenary who inspires fanatical devotion from his followers, a literal and figurative underground army of revolutionaries taken from the city's underclasses – a horde of 'have nots' eager to take revenge on Gotham's 'haves'. Bane's followers have the hardened resolve of jihadists and are committed to die for their master and their cause. Whereas the Joker was an anarchic nihilist, Bane is very particular about what he wants; he calls himself 'Gotham's reckoning' and informs the city elite, the wealthy and the powerful one per cent of Gotham who have long lived off the sweat and labour of those less fortunate, 'I am the borrowed time you've all been living on.' Bane marches his army into Gotham with the pointed and familiar declaration, 'We come here not as conquerors but as liberators.' His intention to return the city to the hands of the people gives the film a perspective that resonates not just with the war on terror but the new millennial global financial breakdown and fears over its potential effects on society. In one of the film's most exhilarating sequences, Bane targets the Gotham Stock Exchange and bankrupts Bruce Wayne, turning him from billionaire to pauper at the press of a button. Wayne is not the only person in Gotham to lose his privileged status, as Bane's army attacks the city's wealthy, evicting them from their palatial homes and trying them in kangaroo courts where the only sentence is death. While the film revels in giving the rich their comeuppance, it is just as critical of the ninety-nine per cent as it is of the one per cent they seek to replace. Despite his proclamations and his dedication to ushering in the 'next era of Western civilisation', Bane cares little for the people he claims to represent; he is a tyrant who thirsts only for power and revenge. It transpires he was trained by Ra's al Ghul himself and hopes to complete his surrogate father's work by killing Batman and destroying Gotham, bringing the trilogy full circle from its opening in the mountains of China. The film portrays the fears of both the elite, wary of losing everything they have had for so long, and the disenfranchised who are quickly taken in by the lure of such demagoguery. Thus, the film's political message is as ambiguous as *The Dark Knight* and enables audiences to see either their own beliefs or their own fears reflected in it. As Scott Tobias (2012) suggested, 'There's a catchall quality to the politics of it – the Occupy movement could be viewed here as unifying force or order-upending menace – but Nolan seems content to let his popular entertainment double as a Rorschach test.' Ultimately, the film continues to mythologise Batman in both life and in 'death'; while his and Gordon's desire to hide the truth about Dent from the public is questioned, their decision is finally sanctioned. As Gordon explains, 'There's a point far out there where the structures fail you and the rules aren't weapons any more; they're shackles letting the bad guy get ahead.' What is far from ambiguous, however, is Nolan's deliberate and ongoing attempts to vividly dramatise the fears of the post-9/11 era. Bane steals a clean energy fusion reactor built by Wayne Industries that could have solved the city's energy problems forever and turns it into a four megaton nuclear weapon primed to explode if Gotham does not do his bidding. Once again a device built by Wayne himself becomes a potential WMD used on his own city. Bane traps the city's police underground and takes out Gotham's major landmarks and bridges, trapping its citizens within the city, and insists that if anyone tries to leave, he will detonate the bomb. The scene in which Bane blows up Gotham's American football stadium is a powerfully realised and visceral example of how destructive a terrorist attack can be – both physically and psychologically. The scene was described, somewhat inappropriately, by Joe Williams (2012) writing in the *St. Louis Dispatcher*, as '9/11 squared'. In fact, many reviewers found it hard not to mention 9/11 while writing about the film: from Scott Tobias's assertion that the film 'plunges headlong into the abyss, as seemingly every grim, paranoid post-9/11 fantasy comes to pass' (2012) to Manohla Dargis's (2012) emotional contention that 'because of the explosions, the dust, the panic and the sweeping aerial shots of a very real-looking New York City – invokes the Sept 11 attacks. It's unsettling enough that some may find it tough going'. The film continues the series' use of 9/11 and the war on terror as both a thematic and visual influence with its explosions, its dust and debris and in one sequence where Bane orders for dead police officers to be hung upside down from a bridge, reminiscent of the notorious incident in Fallujah in March 2004 where four Blackwater civilian contractors were killed, mutilated, burned and hung from a bridge to the cheers of the on-looking crowds.

Batman is once again needed by Gotham despite the citizens having turned their backs on him. He is forced to confront his own fears and limitations and, for the first time, face an enemy that is more powerful than he is. After being initially defeated, he returns some months later with a new-found realisation of his own mortality and purpose that he had lost after Rachel's death. He then manages to retrieve the nuclear bomb and take it outside of the city just before it detonates, saving the lives of millions but seemingly sacrificing himself in the process. An understated epilogue reveals that somehow he managed to escape, and now that everyone thinks he is dead, he can finally lay Batman to rest and for the first time since his parents' deaths live an ordinary life. So, once again, while the film criticises many of Batman's choices, it also mythologises him and his transgression of the law as a necessary and just action, albeit one that comes at a great price.

The message of Nolan's Batman series is an ambiguous one: they can persuasively be read as both an endorsement *and* a critique of the Bush administration's policies that are dramatised in the quasi-mythic tale of a conflicted superhero. Do they support Bush's war on terror by suggesting that unilateral violent action is both necessary and moral? Or do they expose how violence can only lead to more violence, exploring the effects of Chalmers Johnson's concept of 'blowback', an idea that came to define many people's critical attitude to American foreign policy in the post-9/11 era? Gotham is located in a mythical America 'permanently scarred in a way Osama bin Laden could only dream about' (O'Hehir 2012); however, it is a place very much connected to the real world that engages with fears very similar to those that permeated America in the first decade of the new millennium. The film is, as Nolan, who rarely comments on his work in detail stated, about 'the things that worry us these days' – and his description is certainly an apposite one (cited in Jensen 2012). Never in the history of popular cinema has a trilogy offered such a sustained interrogation of the anxieties that defined the era in which it was produced. Christine Muller suggested, 'In effect, *The Dark Knight* instantiates and leaves unresolved the kinds of moral quandaries Sept 11 has posed, exploring and implicating its audience in the culturally traumatic complexities of agency and responsibility under conditions of constrained choice and shattered meaning and subjectivity' (2011: 58). The fact that the trilogy speculates on the ramifications of such actions in a way that many films set in the real world were unable or unwilling to do, might be the final highly resonant irony of a simple comic-book film about a man who chooses to prowl the streets at night dressed like a bat.

If Christopher Nolan's Batman trilogy functions as an allegory for some of the ethical dilemmas America faced as a nation in the decade after 9/11, Marvel's cinematic output in these years trod a distinctly similar path. The success of *Iron Man* (2008) and its sequel *Iron Man 2* (2010), which had a combined gross of more than $1.2 billion, surprised many, elevating what had once been a second-string Marvel hero to the status of Spider-Man, Superman and Batman.[9] At the start of the series Tony Stark (Robert Downey Jr) is a genius American arms' manufacturer and a playboy icon who sells his weapons of mass destruction all over the world. As the film opens, he is an arrogant, thinly veiled reflection of an aggressively hegemonistic United States pursuing global dominance through a combination of military and economic power. The turbulent geo-political climate of the 2000s is a profitable time for Stark's business, and peace holds no interest for him: 'I'd be out of a job with peace,' he wryly comments. When displaying his latest death-dealing invention to a rapturous crowd he asks, 'Is it better to be feared or respected? I say is it too much to ask for both?' slyly subverting Machiavelli's famous maxim. The patriotic Stark is connected to both contemporary America and the America of the past through his deceased father, Howard Stark, who had once been a part of the Manhattan Project tasked with creating the atomic bomb. The ebulliently self-confident Stark suggests, 'That's how Dad did it and that's how America does it!' and clearly sees himself as continuing his father's mission. While he is an undeniably attractive protagonist, he is also glib and irresponsible and he sees the furthering of a *Pax Americana* as his role only as long as there is profit in it for himself, and he is referred to by newspapers as 'The most famous mass murderer in the history of America'.

Yet Stark experiences a traumatic event and undergoes a transformation that forces him to reconsider his role in the world – and by extension the role of the United States. While testing his new advanced missiles in war-torn Afghanistan, he is blown up and almost killed by one of his own weapons that have found their way into the hands of the insurgents, as, unbeknownst to him, his creations are being sold to America's enemies all around the globe. With a disquieting sense of directness for what might be regarded as merely a 'comic-book movie', Stark laments America's role in the escalation of global conflict: 'I saw young Americans killed by the very weapons I created to defend and protect them. I saw I had become part of the system that was comfortable with zero accountability.' In dramatising his complicity in how Stark Industries (and by association America) eschewed ethical considerations in favour of economic profits, the film briefly enters real-world geo-politics. Whether Stark did not know or did not care to know of the actions being undertaken in his name, his reaction evokes that of many Americans confronted with the reality of America's continued wars abroad. In this, Stark becomes one in a long line of characters to have their world view altered by their trauma, whether 9/11 or a fictional substitute for it. As Anthony Peter Spanakos observes, 'Stark is the fly in the ointment that shakes the viewers out of the idea that the events of September 11 created an ongoing condition of lawlessness in which the U.S. state could act as sovereign without regard to the fundamental liberties and rights that constitute the authentic legitimacy of the state' (2011: 22).

The villain of the film is not a Middle Eastern terrorist but another misguided American patriot, Obadiah Stane (Jeff Bridges), Stark's mentor and a surrogate father figure who, the film reveals, arranged Stark's kidnap in order to gain a controlling interest in Stark Industries. The father–son relationship is one of the most dominant motifs of the superhero genre, where absent or domineering fathers cast long shadows over their sons: from Thomas Wayne's brutal murder in front of the young Bruce Wayne, to David Banner, a genetic researcher who passes his mutant deoxyribonucleic acid (DNA) on to his son, Bruce, who later becomes the Incredible Hulk in *The Hulk* (2003). It is Stane who had facilitated the sale of Stark's weapons all over the globe and is a representative of the Military Industrial Complex that emerges as the central villain throughout the post-9/11 Marvel cycle, whether they seek to weaponise the hulk in *The Incredible Hulk* (2008) or create an intergalactic WMD in *Marvel Avengers Assemble*. When Stark returns to America with a more humanitarian and less profit-oriented vision of Stark Industries, Stane informs the world that Stark is suffering from PTSD as a result of his kidnap and violent trauma, and takes over the company himself.

Stark proves a compelling character to centre a film on, and *Iron Man* continues the post-9/11 trend of placing superheroes into quasi-realistic settings instead of the more traditional fantasy landscapes. This connection to the real world in Nolan's *Batman* trilogy and *Iron Man* is a far cry from the superhero films of the 1980s and 1990s that seemed to exist in a dream-like, apolitical vacuum. About *Iron Man* Joey Esposito (n.d.s.) wrote, 'What unravels is a tale of global and corporate espionage, tying into the current War on Terror and some social commentary on WMDs.' Stark discovers the error of his ways and transforms himself from an irresponsible and arrogant 'merchant of death' to a flawed but sensitive hero, while retaining his audience-pleasing sarcasm and mistrust of authority. In this respect it is no coincidence that it is his heart that is damaged and replaced, like a new millennial version of the Tin Man from L. Frank Baum's *The Wonderful Wizard of Oz* (1900).

Iron Man was just one of several Marvel characters brought to the screen in the post-9/11 years: the Hulk was featured twice in *Hulk* and *The Incredible Hulk*, and the Asgardian demigod Thor appeared in *Thor* (2011) and *Thor: The Dark World* (2013). Yet of all the Marvel heroes given cinematic adaptations throughout the decade, it may be argued that Captain America was the most challenging to transfer on to the cinema screen. How would the unambiguous heroics of a superhero who wears a costume adorned with an American flag fare at a time when America was viewed with considerably more scrutiny by the international community than ever before? In the foreword to *Captain America and the Struggle of the Superhero* (2005) by Robert Weiner, published before the release of the 2011 film, John Shelton Lawrence wrote, 'Since Captain America's writers traditionally compelled him to engage in the discourses of power within his eras, consider the strong implications of his playing a role in the Global War on Terrorism. Remaining true to his own character, as well as the genre conventions, how could he fight in this war?' (cited in Weiner 2005: 5). In 2007 the comic writer Ed Brubaker observed, 'What I found is that all the really hard-core left-wing fans want Cap to be standing out and giving speeches on the street corner against the Bush administration, and all the really right-wing [fans] all want him to be over in the streets of Baghdad, punching out Saddam' (cited in Harkaway 2011). In the world of superheroes, Captain America certainly has an intrinsic connection to American propaganda that is matched only by Superman. Indeed, he was originally created by Jack Kirby in 1941 explicitly to be a propaganda tool, just nine months before Hitler declared war on the United States. Despite Avi Arad suggesting that 'Captain America stands for freedom for all democracies, for hope all around the world' (cited in Sanchez 2007), he is a literal embodiment of the American Dream and an encapsulation of a very particular set of American values. The resulting film, Joe Johnston's *Captain America: The First Avenger* (2011), mediates these concerns and attempts to play down the jingoistic nationalism that has often been associated with the character. Its narrative follows a patriotic young man, Steve Rogers (Chris Evans), who repeatedly tries to enlist in the US Army in 1941, but is continually rejected and declared unfit on the grounds of his frail stature and numerous health problems. Yet his unrelenting determination and integrity leads to him being given the opportunity to participate in an experiment that gives him superhuman strength, speed and agility. Part of Captain America's appeal is that he is not a tortured soul like Batman, but an earnest and relatively untroubled character. However, Captain America's cry of 'I don't like bullies' is an ironic one for contemporary audiences and the film's portrayal of World War Two is a nostalgic fantasy of a time before America was regarded as the quintessential bully of the modern era. M. Keith Booker argued that it was no coincidence that during the post-9/11 decade 'many comics returned to imagery from World War II, presenting the ambiguous war on terror in terms of the certainties associated with the earlier conflict' (2010: 440). *Captain America: The First Avenger* portrays America as it would like to be remembered, certainly not as it was, in its fantastical rewriting of World War Two that goes to great lengths to be a distinctly depoliticised one. Not only are Adolf Hitler and the Nazis replaced with the Red Skull and his Skull troopers, but Captain America's small elite unit features both a Japanese-American and an African-American, two ethnic groups that suffered considerably during the war even while serving their country.[10] The film ends with Captain America selflessly sacrificing himself to save the United States and by extension the free world. Frozen and presumed dead for seventy years, he is revived in the film's epilogue, set in the modern era, but not only have all of his friends and loved ones are now dead, but the world around him has changed irrevocably and he must come to terms with his new life.[11]

The culmination of Marvel's decade-long strategy of setting their heroes in a coherent and interconnected world was Joss Whedon's *Marvel Avengers Assemble*, which brought every one of these individual heroes into a single film. If even one of the previous stand-alone adventures had been a financial failure, it would have thrown the entire project into jeopardy, but *Marvel Avengers Assemble* had the biggest opening weekend in the history of American film with more than $200 million dollars at the US box office alone. The film manages to effectively integrate the separate narrative and thematic threads of the previous Marvel films and combine them with spectacular mayhem, the likes of which have rarely been seen on such a scale. The film also functions as a compelling conclusion to the post-9/11 decade of superhero cinema in the way it symbolically recreates and rewrites 9/11 and the war on terror in an attempt to perform some sort of closure by reconciling America with the divisive events of its recent past. Philip French (2012: 22) was dismissive of the film in *The Guardian*, where he wrote, 'Karl Marx could have been antici-pating 9/11 and this movie [*Marvel Avengers Assemble*] when he said that history repeats itself first as tragedy, then as farce'. *Marvel Avengers Assemble* certainly does replay America's response to 9/11 via the fictional guise of a genuinely apocalyptic terrorist threat, 'real' enemies of freedom that George W. Bush claimed al-Qaeda to be in the war on terror. Yet al-Qaeda did not target the United States because it was the 'brightest beacon for freedom and oppor-tunity in the world', as George W. Bush claimed, but because of America's continued presence on the Arabian Peninsula and its perceived hostile treat-ment of Muslims all over the world (Bush 2001a). The malevolent God Loki, brother to Thor, who returns to Earth with an alien army and a supernatural WMD looking for revenge, *is* fighting for this reason – to subjugate America and enslave all humans around the globe. While the film successfully manages to juggle its large roster of characters who work for S.H.I.E.L.D. (that once stood for 'Supreme Headquarters, International Espionage, Law-Enforcement

Division', and then in the 1990s for 'Strategic Hazard Intervention Espionage Logistics Directorate', but in the post-9/11 era was altered to the more contemporary sounding 'Strategic Homeland Intervention, Enforcement and Logistics Division'), Captain America emerges as the moral centre of the film, dismayed at how much the world has changed since he was frozen during World War Two. He says, 'They say we won – they didn't tell me what we had lost,' referring to the changes that America has undergone since the clarity of the Total War of World War Two he had participated in and even came to embody. This lack of a sense of purpose and moral accountability is for him epitomised by the flamboyant Tony Stark, Iron Man himself, who despite his heroic status is a selfish and egocentric narcissist. Stark is one of the most self-aware of new millennial superheroes and recognises the absurdity of what he calls the 'terrible privilege' of their situation, a phrase more readily used to describe the burden of hegemonic superpowers than superheroes (see Chambliss 2012). Captain America doubts that a 'hero' like Stark would sacrifice himself for his country, as many did during World War Two. He says, 'The only thing you really fight for is yourself. You're not the guy to make the sacrifice play, to lay down on a wire and let the other guy crawl over you.'[12]

Nick Fury (Samuel L. Jackson), the leader of the Avengers Initiative, takes on the seemingly impossible task of forming the world's greatest superheroes, each with their own motives, rivalries and histories, into a single team in order to combat Loki's threat of global genocide. When Fury reluctantly admits to Captain America, 'We've made some mistakes along the way ... some very recently,' his comment lingers. Is he talking about the use of the Tesseract (a source of unlimited energy) to create WMD within the film's diegesis, or America's ill-considered and ill-conceived post-9/11 war on terror? It is not just the loss of community spirit and solidarity that Captain America recognises as having characterised the US during World War Two, but the unity that occurred once again briefly between America and the international community after the attacks on September 11th 2001, a unity that was quickly lost in the Bush administration's rush to war in Iraq. Captain America looks at his own costume, coloured red, white and blue, and asks Agent Coulson (Clarke Gregg), 'Aren't the Stars and Stripes a little old-fashioned?' But Coulson knows that, in the wake of Loki's attacks and the apocalyptic battle that is still to come, 'everything has changed'. He comments, 'With everything that is happening and things coming to light people just might *need* a little old fashioned'. Captain America's out-of-time status and his nostalgic connection to a simpler, bygone era was why Thomas Foster regarded the character as the perfect antidote to twenty-first century cynicism. He suggested, it was 'precisely this immediate symbolic burden, this allegorical flatness and lack of psychological depth, and this lack of distance between character and nation, that make Captain America a perfect 9/11 icon for a culture dominated by cynical reason' (2005: 262).

This evocation of the 'Total War' of World War Two continues with Loki's arrival in, of all places, Germany, in order to retrieve material to make a second supernatural WMD. In an ostentatious display of his supremacy he demands that the crowd kneel before him, informing them that he will free them from their obsession with the idea of freedom, which he calls 'life's glorious lie'. The members of the crowd all fall to their knees except for one white-haired old man, the implication being that he is a survivor of the Holocaust who has seen such tyranny before: 'There are *always* men like you,' he calls out to Loki, his new oppressor. The power-hungry Norse God turns his weapon on the old man, seeking to make an example of him, but, as Loki's supernatural blast of energy fires, Captain America arrives just in time to protect the old man with his shield adorned with the US flag. Captain America gazes up at Loki with disdain and says, 'The last time I was in Germany and saw a man standing above everyone else, we ended up disagreeing.'

Captain America initially accepts the orders given to him by Nick Fury without question; he even seems energised with a new sense of purpose: 'We have orders; we should follow them.' Later when he is informed by Stark and Bruce Banner of the existence of suspicious weapons' development programmes built by the US Government, he discovers that instead of using the unlimited power of the Tesseract to build self-sustaining energy sources that could have solved the world's energy problems, the government was instead making WMDs. Fury and those above him suggest that the seriousness of the threats have forced them to pursue more militaristic uses of the technology, but Thor warns them, 'Your work with the Tesseract is what drew Loki to it . . . and his allies. It is a signal to the Realm that Earth is ready for a higher form of war.' When Agent Coulson dies at the hands of Loki, once again Fury manipulates Captain America by handing him a pack of blood-stained vintage trading cards, telling him that they were found on Coulson's lifeless body. Moments later Agent Hill reveals to the audience that the cards were not on Coulson at all when he died and that Fury had only said they were in order to galvanise Captain America and the group into action.

Thus, the stage is set for the heroes to overcome their differences and unite to meet Loki and his huge intergalactic army in an extended forty-five minute battle through the streets of New York, replete with fleeing civilians, crashing debris and falling structures: symbolically and literally a manifestation of Bush's suggestion that '[l]ike generations before us, we have a calling from beyond the stars to stand for freedom' (Bush 2004a).[13] So while the film warns that the United States can be both manipulative and destructive, ultimately it rehabilitates its global role as a necessary one – as without these very Americanised superheroes the world would be lost to those like Loki. The battle ends with Iron Man sacrificing himself in a way that Captain America suggested he would never be able to do, a new generation of hero embodying the spirit of the

Figure 17   Superheroes at Ground Zero: *Marvel Avengers Assemble* (2012) attempts to mediate the changed perception of America between World War Two and the post 9/11 era.

'Greatest Generation'. Many critics observed the film's numerous self-conscious references to 9/11 and the war on terror. Richard Brody (2013) at *The New Yorker* described the film as a 'post-9/11 revenge fantasy', and J. Hoberman (2012) stated that the film 'recasts 9/11 in the Bush years' dominant movie mode, namely the comic book superhero spectacular – albeit with a heavy dose of irony and added stereoscopic depth ... Bombs away: [*Marvel*] *Avengers Assemble* is 9/11 as you've never seen it!' (see Figure 17). These connections were further underlined when both Kevin Feige and Robert Downey Jr dedicated the film to New York firefighters, police officers, paramedics and other real-life heroes of 9/11. Feige said, 'It's our real-life heroes who save the world every day by making it a better place for all of us' (see Figure 17).

After Iron Man miraculously survives, Whedon shows the responses from the members of the public who have just witnessed the apocalyptic battle in New York: one says, 'It's just really great knowing that they're out there. That someone's watching over us.' Another witness states, 'I don't exactly feel safer with those things out there.' A third says, 'It just seems like there's a lot they're not telling us.' While each of the comments is a reaction to fictional comic-book superheroes saving New York from an intergalactic threat, they are certainly evocative of the range of responses that the international community (and American citizens themselves) have had towards the United States throughout the first decade of the new millennium.

Heroic tales have always been a cultural battleground with a much greater capacity to engage the public than any number of philosophical tomes written by the likes of Noam Chomsky or Slavoj Žižek. It is distinctly possible that *The Dark Knight* caused Americans to discuss vigilantism more than any book ever did, or that *Spider-Man* defined the plucky coming together of people in New York in vastly superior ways than many serious attempts to define the occasion. Not all superhero films mined real life for inspiration; Hollywood continued to produce overtly fantastical superhero films like *Catwoman* (2004), *Fantastic Four* (2005), *Ghost Rider* (2007) and *Green Lantern* (2011), but I would argue that those that did place their narratives among the concerns of the decade were without a doubt the most successful, both critically and commercially. Gray and Kaklamanidou were correct in their assertion that the malleability of the superhero genre makes it a perfect barometer for reflecting changing concerns. They wrote, 'Due to the fact that superheroes have been perpetually subject to revisionism, they become signifiers of contemporary consciousness and thus can serve as embodiments of specific needs in a given time' (2011: 33–4). The events of 9/11 and the war on terror certainly did influence the superhero genre in profound ways, and those superhero films that take place in a recognisable world cannot help but filter their narratives through the prism of 9/11, such was its influence on the American consciousness of the 2000s, and this is why these films prove to be such powerful cultural artefacts and will continue to be compelling in decades to come. If the superhero genre revealed anything to new millennial audiences, it was that we in the real world need fictional superheroes just as much as the diegetic populations of the films that they feature in.

NOTES

1. In fact, as Danny Fingeroth suggests, 'Biblical and mythological heroes are clearly precursors of superheroes' (2004: 16).
2. The James Thurber character Walter Mitty was brought to the screens for the second time in Ben Stiller's *The Secret Life of Walter Mitty* (2013).
3. This image became later directly replicated in a scene from *Marvel Avengers Assemble*.
4. *Man of Steel* returned Superman to the screens once more in 2013 in a film directed by Zack Snyder and produced by Christopher Nolan. The film was less critically successful than Singer's but earned significantly more money.
5. Ra's al Ghul's speeches are certainly reminiscent of bin Laden's, which often talk of injustice and suffering. In a speech reported in *The Washington Post*, 30 October 2004, entitled 'Bin Laden speaks to the American people' he said, 'God knows it did not cross our minds to attack the towers. But after the situation became unbearable and we witnessed the injustice and tyranny of the American-Israeli alliance against our people in Palestine and Lebanon, I thought about it . . . In those difficult moments, many emotions came over me that are hard to describe, but that produced an overwhelming feeling to reject injustice and a strong determination to punish the unjust' (Anonymous 2004b: A16).

6. These films are just four from the early 1970s' texts that function as a reaction against the counter-culture movement of the previous decade by portraying the actions of their heroes as legitimate. Michael Ryan and Douglas Kellner in *Camera Politica: The Politics and Ideology of Contemporary Hollywood Film* (1990) see this as an era in which America was engulfed by a crisis in confidence (49–75).

7. To locate the Joker, Batman must first find a Chinese money launderer, Andy Lau, who flees to Hong Kong to evade prosecution by the Gotham police. Residing in Hong Kong he is way outside of the jurisdiction of the United States and there is nothing that Dent can do about it. Yet Batman has no jurisdiction and no qualms about violating international law, so in a startling example of extraordinary rendition he kidnaps Lau from Hong Kong and deposits him on the steps of Gotham's court building.

8. While the boats do not explode, it may also be considered that the Joker was actually proved correct in some ways as Nolan shows that the vote for detonation receives 340 votes for and only 196 against. It is only prevented by the actions of a large convict known in the script as the 'Tattooed Prisoner' who throws the detonator out of the window of the ferry.

9. *Iron-Man 3*, which is discussed briefly in the conclusion of this book, made more than $1.2 billion dollars at the worldwide box office, making it the fifth most successful film of all time. This remarkable success indicates that the character has now replaced Batman, Superman and Spider-Man as the most popular cinematic superhero in the world.

10. While a significant number of Japanese-Americans fought during World War Two their loyalty was questioned and they were forbidden from being deployed in the Pacific Theatre: whereas no such restrictions were placed on Italian-Americans or German-Americans who fought on the Western Front. A figure of about 110,000 Japanese-Americans were interned by the United States Government because of fears of anti-American activities and sabotage, an act that President Reagan apologised for in 1988 when the United States Congress stated that the internment was a decision based on 'race prejudice, war hysteria, and a failure of political leadership' (see the Civil Liberties Act of 1988). African-American soldiers were largely segregated from whites and kept separate in parades, canteens, church services and transportation. Despite this more than 100,000 African-Americans served in the US military, many with distinction.

11. In 2014 the sequel, *Captain America: Winter Soldier*, continued to explore these very same themes. It is revealed that HYDRA has infiltrated S.H.I.E.L.D. and sown global chaos for decades, watching humanity exchange freedoms for the pretence of security. It has constructed gigantic drones, called Hellicarriers, which can identify and eliminate individuals who are deemed a threat. One of the film's directors, Anthony Russo, commented, 'We are all reading the articles that were coming out questioning drone strikes, pre-emptive strikes, civil liberties – Obama talking about who they would kill, y' know? We wanted to put all of that into the film because it would be a contrast to Cap's greatest generation [way of thinking]' (cited in Lovece 2014).

12. This exact same moral choice was also present in *Cabin in the Woods* (2012), which was co-written by Joss Whedon. The slacker Marty (Fran Krantz) is given the choice of sacrificing himself to save the whole world, but he chooses not to do so and the whole world, including himself, dies.

13. *The Hollywood Reporter* consulted disaster experts at Kinetic Analysis Corporation who speculated that the destruction wreaked on New York in the film would have cost $160 billion to clean up. In comparison, the recovery operations for 9/11 and Hurricane Katrina cost $83 billion and $90 billion respectively (see Zakarin 2012).

5. REMAKING 9/11:
IMAGINING THE UNIMAGINABLE IN
THE ALIEN-INVASION FILM

Robbie: What is it? Is it terrorists?
Ray: These came from someplace else.
Robbie: What do you mean? Like, Europe?
Ray: No, Robbie, not like Europe!

War of the Worlds (2005)

If I thought we were safe from attack, I would be thinking differently. But
I see a gathering threat.

George W. Bush (Anonymous 2003a)

The New York events have radicalized the relation of images to reality, in
the same way as they have radicalized the global situation. While before
we dealt with an unbroken abundance of banal images and an uninter-
rupted flow of spurious events, the terrorist attack in New York has res-
urrected both the image and the event ... But does reality really prevail
over fiction? If it seems so, it is because reality has absorbed the energy
of fiction, and become fiction itself. One could almost say that reality is
jealous of fiction, that the real is jealous of the image ... It is as if they
duel, to find which is the most unimaginable.

Jean Baudrillard, *The Spirit of Terrorism*

In the preceding chapters we have seen how American cinema has been reluctant to represent the terrorist attacks on September 11th 2001 directly on

the screen and how, when the events have been portrayed, it has been in a very particular fashion, thematically and aesthetically. Dramatisations of the two hijacked airliners striking the World Trade Center and the extent of the death and destruction experienced on 9/11 have remained a persistent taboo in American film. If depicted at all, the moments of collision themselves have been portrayed through the use of a black screen and original sound recordings of the real-life transmission (see *Zero Dark Thirty* and *Fahrenheit 9/11*) or authentic news footage recorded on the day (see *United 93* and *World Trade Center*). This erasure is almost certainly an expression of the prevailing understanding that 9/11 was such a traumatic event that it could never be accurately portrayed, very much akin to the belief that it is impossible to truthfully represent the inconceivable trauma of those who experienced the Holocaust. In his foreword to Annette Insdorf's *Indelible Shadows: Film and the Holocaust* (2003), Nobel Peace Prize-winner and Holocaust survivor Elie Wiesel wrote, 'One does not imagine the unimaginable, and in particular, one does not show it onscreen' (xi). Despite this unwillingness to confront the traumatic event of 9/11 directly, it is clear to see that images of planes colliding with skyscrapers, tall buildings collapsing, debris falling from the skies and scenes of dust-caked, panicked crowds fleeing disaster became an indelible part of the cinematic landscape in the post-9/11 era in ways they had never been before.

The alien-invasion films discussed in this chapter, primarily *War of the Worlds* and *Cloverfield*, but also the likes of *Battle: Los Angeles, Transformers, Signs* (2002), *Knowing* and *Monsters* (2010), fill their screens with barely coded images and situations so self-consciously designed to evoke 9/11 and the war on terror that Kyle Buchanan felt compelled to ask, 'Is it possible to make a Hollywood blockbuster without evoking 9/11?' Manohla Dargis (2013) wondered about the ethics of American cinema's compulsion to return to images reminiscent of 9/11 as convenient shorthand for trauma and a dubious source of entertainment. She suggested that it was remarkable 'just how thoroughly Sept. 11 and its aftermath have been colonized by the movies'. The ensuing decade witnessed a decisive shift in the depiction of apocalyptic disasters on-screen. Whereas pre-9/11 films invited audiences to take guilt-free, vicarious pleasure in their spectacles of devastation in 'enjoyable fantasies of destruction, enjoyable because they are meant to belong to the territory of fantasy' (King 2005: 49), science-fiction and disaster cinema of the post-9/11 era presented spectators with much more challenging 'remakes' of September 11th 2001, both in their striking replications of the aesthetic of 9/11 and in the traumatic situations that the characters find themselves in. This is not to say that post-9/11 apocalyptic films eschew spectacle; this is, after all, the age of 'disaster porn' extravaganzas like *2012* and *The Day After Tomorrow* (see Corliss 2009). Yet, as the likes of Jean Baudrillard, Slavoj Žižek and E. Ann

Kaplan suggest, 9/11 functioned as an epoch-defining 'image-event' with far-reaching implications for the relationship between spectator and image and that between reality and fiction. Are these films to be understood solely as a cynical re-packaging of cultural trauma designed to sell movie tickets? Or as a palpable manifestation of that very same trauma and an attempt to come to terms with it in ways deemed socially acceptable by society at large? E. Ann Kaplan suggested a similar dichotomy: 'Arguably, being vicariously trauma-tised invited members of a society to confront, rather than conceal, catastro-phes, and in that way might be useful. On the other hand, it might arouse anxiety and trigger defense against further exposure' (2005: 87). Thus, accord-ing to Kaplan, these texts may be further evidence of a disavowal of trauma *or* a productive engagement with collective anxieties in which re-creations function as a catachristic substitute for the unspeakable realities of the original traumatic event itself.

This chapter argues that science-fiction films, especially those that feature alien-invasion narratives, prove themselves as distinctly culturally relevant and their potent realisations of an alien Other (both figuratively and literally) provide yet another manifestation of the particular fears and fantasies that characterised the decade. David Simpson was one of many to evoke the 'alien' nature of the attacks on September 11th 2001, when he suggested in his book *9/11: The Culture of Commemoration* that the day itself 'looked to many of us . . . like the work of agents so unfamiliar as to seem like aliens' (2006: 6). In the absence of meaningful and interrogative cinematic accounts that portrayed 9/11 explicitly, allegories fulfilled a powerful social function in the first decade of the new millennium and made a significant contribution to the discourse of the war on terror era in a similar way to how the likes of *The Day the Earth Stood Still* (1951), *The Thing from Another World* (1951) and *Invasion of the Body Snatchers* (1956) engaged with the turbulent political climate of the first decades of the Cold War. In fact, Stephen Prince's assertion that living 'in the age of terror is comparable . . . to living during the Cold War and under its continuing nuclear threat' (2009: 306) was one that was repeated by many cultural commentators. Melvin E. Matthews argued, 'In the immediate after-math of the 9/11 attacks, the B-movie genre received a new lease on life', which he states is explained partly 'by the fact that, for the first time since the Cold War, the notion of an attack on the United States was a very real possibility' (2007: 142). Don Siegel's *Invasion of the Body Snatchers*, based on the Jack Finney novel *The Body Snatchers* (1955), is a pertinent example of how cin-ematic texts are able to address prevailing fears, as it was adapted three more times in the subsequent decades with each version offering a vivid engagement with the particular political climate in which it was made. From Siegel's anti-communist allegory (or anti-HUAC allegory, depending on how one reads it), through Philip Kaufman's cynical post-Vietnam, post-Watergate *Invasion of the Body Snatchers* (1978) to Abel Ferrara's *Body Snatchers* (1993), which is certainly an example of the Body horror cinema of the 1980s and early 1990s. Given the pervasive remake culture that has come to dominate the American film industry, it was not surprising that another version found its way to the screen in 2007 as *The Invasion*, directed by Oliver Hirschbiegel, one of many alien-invasion texts permeated with self-conscious allusions to 9/11 and the war on terror.

- As early as the summer of 2002 M. Night Shyamalan's *Signs* offered numerous allusions to the experience of September 11th 2001. On its release Philip French (2002), writing in *The Guardian*, suggested that 'everything about *Signs* reflects and responds to the confused spirit of universal threat, the need for national unity and the search for a renewed faith aroused by the events of 9/11'. The first day of its production had begun on 12 September 2001, leading its director to comment, 'It was very difficult, difficult and meaningful. It made the metaphor of the movie more real for us' (cited in Johnston 2004: 142). The film sets a readily identifiable template that the majority of alien-invasion narratives were to adopt throughout the rest of the decade by restricting its narrative focus to a small group, more often than not a single family, rather than the planetary-wide scope that had been the norm for the genre pre-9/11. The characters who populate the films are no longer the scientists, soldiers and experts who were routinely at the centre of pre-9/11 science-fiction cinema; rather, they are ordinary people thrust into the midst of a terrifying ordeal, struggling not to overcome the threat, but to survive it. The only glimpses the audience sees of the global scale of the invasion are through the television set, which continuously plays in the family living room hour after hour, intensifying the personal and claustrophobic nature of drama, as the family seem alienated from the world around them. Merrill Hess (Joaquin Phoenix) becomes fascinated with the image of a huge alien spaceship hovering above Mexico City on the TV, and he cannot tear his eyes away from it. He knows the image is real, yet somehow he can hardly bring himself to believe what he is seeing; 'This is like *War of the Worlds*,' he comments, as a lifetime of movies about alien invasions have made the image appear false to him – in a distinctly similar fashion to the disbelief that many viewers felt while watching the Twin Towers collapse on 9/11.
- In Gareth Edwards's low-budget *Monsters* a National Aeronautics and Space Administration (NASA) space probe crashes in Mexico, bringing with it extra-terrestrials that grow to such huge proportions that they are regarded as a serious threat to US national security. As a precau-

tionary measure America erects a huge wall along the border between the two countries. Despite the fact that the authorities have informed everyone that the aliens are dangerous they actually seem quite docile unless provoked. It is only when they are attacked by the US military that they respond with violence. There is also a sense that America uses the alien invasion as a pretext to exert their influence over the region, utilising the aliens to legitimise their foreign policy decisions in Mexico just as many believe 9/11 served as a pretext for increased presence in the Middle East. The camera slowly pans over the burning candles of a midnight vigil commemorating the loss of about 200,000 people killed in the conflict, not by the aliens as one may expect, but by the US bombings of the area. Gareth Edwards observed, 'I started to explore the idea of creating a film that was set years after most monster movies normally end. The crude way to explain it is if *Godzilla* were like a 9/11 event, our film would be more like the war on terror' (cited in Crozier 2010). The film's title emphasises this ambiguity, leading the viewer to ponder who, in fact, are the monsters of the title. Is it the aliens or, perhaps, humans themselves?[1]

• Michael Bay's hugely successful but critically reviled trilogy of movies about an intergalactic war between a race of sentient robots that began with *Transformers*, continued with *Transformers: Revenge of the Fallen* (2009) and concluded with *Transformers: Dark Side of the Moon* (2011) is an extended paean to the hegemonic status of United States and its self-appointed role of global peace officer.[2] The invasion of the evil Decepticons is described by one news reporter as 'the worst attack on the United States since 9/11'. Coming to Earth's aid are the noble and virtuous Autobots, who are quickly subsumed into the American military and seek out hiding Decepticon terrorists throughout the globe. The leader of the Autobots, Optimus Prime, whose battle cry is, 'Let's Roll', takes on his nemesis Megatron, who is presented as an Osama bin Laden-like terrorist, shown brooding in the desert, planning his revenge attacks on the United States.[3] At the end of the first film when Megatron is killed, the United States Secretary of Defence John Keller (Jon Voight) states, 'Gentlemen, it is the direct order of the President that Sector Seven be terminated, and the remains of the dead aliens be disposed of. The Laurentian Abyss is seven miles below sea level. Deepest place on the planet. The aliens will be deposited there, where the intense pressure coupled with sub-zero temperatures will crush and entomb them . . . leaving no evidence.' The United States drops Megatron in the ocean in order to prevent his followers using him as a martyr for their cause, several years before President Obama controversially ordered the real-life

US military to do exactly the same thing with Osama bin Laden. The point being not that the film is prescient, but that the United States dispatches its 'bogeymen' in similar ways whether in reality or in fantasy. The director of *In the Valley of Elah*, Paul Haggis, asserted that, despite being based on a range of children's toys about battling races of alien robots, the *Transformers* franchise depicts America in a very similar way to how it perceives itself in the real world: as a benevolent and virtuous hegemon committed to spreading freedom around the globe. He stated, 'We're living a fantasy where the message is that if we can't win over there, we can win at home on our screens. To make a film like *Transformers* at a time of war is a political act' (cited in Jaafar 16). Haggis's argument that even seemingly inconsequential narratives can contribute to political discourse links popular culture to ideology in a way that many have been reluctant to do. The final words of *Transformers: The Dark Side of the Moon* are by Optimus Prime and they are a plea for continued vigilance much like that at the conclusion of *Act of Valour*: 'In any war there are calms between storms. There will be days when we lose faith. Days when our allies turn against us. But the day will never come that we forsake this planet and its people.' In Optimus Prime, a fictional alien robot, we hear the voice of conservative Americans offering a warning not only to the diegetic America of the *Transformers* franchise but to the real America that they should never be complacent as the terrorist threat remains ever present.

- The modestly budgeted thriller *The Forgotten* (2004) struck a chord with American audiences when it somehow managed to top the US box office on its release almost exactly three years after 9/11 in September 2004. Its protagonist, Telly Paretta (Julianne Moore), is a traumatised and grieving parent whose son, Sam, was killed alongside ten of his school friends in a tragic aeroplane crash. Telly obsesses about her son, spending hour after hour in his room going through his things, even though her psychiatrist tells her she must let go and carry on with her life. After Telly's condition worsens, the doctor explains that her son is actually a figment of her imagination, the result of manufactured memories after a miscarriage. Telly cannot believe that her son never existed, but on returning to his room she finds that all of his possessions are gone as if he were never there. Telly suffers from a traumatic event in the past that she cannot come to terms with, evoking the ordeal of the surviving families of the 9/11 victims and, on a broader scale, the nation as a whole. The film's New York setting and its themes evoke the pervasive 'always remember' slogans of 9/11. Its spectacular narrative twist is that Telly and numerous others have been forced to participate in an alien experiment that tests the bond between mothers and their children. The government knew and were complicit in the experiments, but for some unexplained reason chose to do nothing about them. Telly is the only subject of the experiments whose memory could not be erased, so strong was the bond between her and her son, and therefore the entire experiment is deemed a failure. The film climaxes with Telly returning to the playground to find that Sam is there too, and that everything is back to the way that it was before 'everything changed'. Telly recieves what many wished for after 9/11, both in film and in reality, yet it is a fantasy of reconciliation that could only be achieved in the movies.

'Is it the Terrorists?' *War of the Worlds* (2005) as 9/11 allegory

Think about it. They defeated the greatest power in the world in a couple days. Walked right over us. And these were only the first. They'll keep coming.

Harlan Ogilvy, War of the Worlds

Three days after 11 September 2001 the journalist and New Yorker Lance Morrow (2001) recounted his own experiences during the terrorist attacks. He described that the images he had witnessed 'might have been shot for a remake of *War of the Worlds*'. Morrow could not have known then that an actual remake of the classic H. G. Wells alien-invasion novel would be released just four years later and that the film would self-consciously frame itself as a re-imagining of 9/11 in its thematic motifs and its extensive appropriation of 9/11 iconography. The film's director, Steven Spielberg, gave an insight into his approach to the material when he remarked, 'In the shadow of 9/11 I felt *War of the Worlds* had a special significance; I mean this film touches mostly on how this much catastrophe can bring about that much healing' (cited in 'Revisiting the Invasion' on *War of the Worlds* DVD special features 2005). Spielberg has consistently and effectively re-packaged cultural trauma for the consumption of mainstream audiences throughout his career: whether it is the Holocaust (*Schindler's List*), the D-Day landings (*Saving Private Ryan*), slavery (*Amistad*, 1997) or the 1972 Munich Olympic assassinations (*Munich*), his ability to connect his oeuvre to the zeitgeist has arguably been like no other in the history of American cinema, and Robert Kolker's description of his work as producing 'images and narratives that respond to or give shape to the current ideological needs' (2011: 274) is a pertinent one.

The fact that Spielberg's version was only the second major film adaptation of Welles's 1898 novel belies how influential the text has been since its publication. From Orson Welles's infamous 1938 radio adaptation, which reputedly caused a wave of mass hysteria to engulf the United States, to the historian Niall Ferguson's use of the book as a telling metaphor for the inhumanities of twentieth-century conflict, in which he reads it as a work of 'singular prescience' (2007: xxxiii) and a precursor to the bloodiest century in the history of humankind. The co-writer of Spielberg's version, David Koepp, directly commented on how adaptations of the text have been able to reflect the prevailing fears and anxieties of the times in which they were made:

> As for 9/11, certainly this story [*War of the Worlds*] has vast political implications. In the late 1890s, it was about British imperialism; in the late 1930s, it was about the fear of fascism; in the early 1950s, it was the Commies are coming to get us; and now it can be read two ways – it could be post-9/11 American fear of terrorism, which is certainly there in the movie, but I bet if you see the film in France, it will be about Iraq and the fear of an American invasion. (Koepp cited in Friedman and Koepp 2005: 143)

Koepp reflects on the malleability of *War of the Worlds*, in particular how Spielberg's adaptation can simultaneously be experienced as an allegory of the terrorist attacks on America and an anti-imperialist tale that warns of the destructive effects of colonialist expansion. For American audiences, the vicious and merciless aliens of Spielberg's *War of the Worlds*, who are quite intentionally framed to evoke Islamic fundamentalists, are very different to the peaceful extra-terrestrials of his earlier *Close Encounters of the Third Kind* (1977) and *E.T. the Extra-Terrestrial* (1982). Spielberg addressed this change of perspective in several interviews where he often returned to the phrase 'in the shadow of 9/11'. He stated, 'It seemed like the time was right for me as a filmmaker to let the audience experience an alien that is a little less pleasant than E.T. Today, in the shadow of 9/11, I think the film has found a place in society' (cited in Hard 2005). Spielberg's comments frame the film in a distinctly contemporary socio-political context, and his version is permeated with a range of such sustained and deliberate allusions to 9/11 that it almost functions as a 'remake' of September 11th 2001 seen through the prism of an alien invasion. *Cahiers Du Cinema* somewhat surprisingly regarded *War of the Worlds* as one of the greatest films of the decade (see Anonymous n.d.s) and Emmaneul Burdeau (2005) suggested that it was a rare American film that attempted 'to pull 9/11 out of its localization nonetheless irreducible in History' and while, as a science-fiction film, it was unable to offer 'access to the truth of the event', at least it provided 'fidelity to the confusion that it [9/11] arose, and still arouses'. While *War of the Worlds* received mixed reviews on its release it was the fourth highest grossing film of the year at the domestic box office, and subsequently some have suggested that it may be much more than a disposable pop cultural artefact, rather, in a range of intriguing ways it evokes and avows September 11th 2001 and 'literalizes a metaphor for the experience of 9/11' in a way that few American films of the decade ever attempted to do (Wetmore 2012: 27).

The film is centred on the experiences of a working-class crane operator from New Jersey, Ray Ferrier (Tom Cruise). While Ray is one of Peggy Noonan's (2001) 'real men', those who 'push things and pull things and haul things and build things', it is quickly apparent that he is something of an irresponsible parent who has become alienated from his two children following his divorce from their mother, Mary Ann, and her subsequent remarriage. Ray has become disconnected from his recalcitrant teenage son, Robbie, who refuses to call him 'Dad' and his neurotic pre-teen daughter, Rachel, who is practically a stranger to him. In contrast to her relationship with Ray, Rachel is quite specifically shown lavishing affection on her step-father, the affluent and middle-class Tim. A large part of Ray's anxiety throughout the film is the fear that his position as the patriarch of the family has been usurped: initially by Tim, who seems to have replaced him as both protector and provider for the Ferrier family (something made even more palpable by the fact that Mary Ann is pregnant), and later by a variety of other characters and events in the film's narrative. Yet, for Ray, Tim is clearly one of Kim Du Toit's 'pussified' males and a 'BlackBerry clutcher' (Faludi 2007: 8) who he sarcastically derides for driving a 'safe-looking vehicle' as opposed to his own hyper-masculine

Figure 18 Remaking 9/11: Spielberg re-packages 9/11 imagery and trauma for mainstream consumption in *War of the Worlds* (2005).

all-American classic 1966 Shelby Mustang. The film spends the majority of its running time rehabilitating Ray's status as the head of his fractured family in what Joshua Gunn has described as a battle for 'paternal sovereignty' (2008: 1), as Spielberg shows that being a father is not about being there for your children on a day-to-day basis or knowing what allergies they suffer from, but rescuing them from danger and, if necessary, killing for them. In this way *War of the Worlds* joins the range of films discussed in Chapter 3 that offer fathers (or father figures) the opportunity of reconstituting the traditional family unit through their redemptive acts of violence. Rachel emerges as an encapsulation of all that America sought to protect from a predatory Other in the wake of 9/11, yet she is a figure that has already been compromised by her controlling mother, her touchy-feely step-father and their 'modern' style of parenting. While the implication is that this may be the result of Ray's absence, he is not shown as being to blame; rather it is through him that Rachel may, in fact, be saved from both the aliens and her overly nurturing mother and step-father. By the end of the film Ray has proved himself not to be a 'deadbeat dad' at all, but a traditional all-American hero.

The film opens with a prologue deliberately evocative of a pre-9/11 America blissfully ignorant of what is about to befall it. A God-like narrator (fittingly Morgan Freeman who played God twice in *Bruce Almighty* (2003) and *Evan Almighty* (2007) and an African-American President in *Deep Impact* (1998) ten years before Obama was elected) states, 'With infinite complacency, man went to and fro about the globe confident of our empire over this world.' The aliens choose to invade on one of the rare weekends that Ray is tasked with 'looking after' his children, and their attack is one that is unprovoked and brutal. After a protracted and intense lightning storm, Ray leaves his pre-teen daughter alone at home as he gathers with the majority of the local community in the town square where everyone is drawn because of the loud noises emanating from cracks in the pavement (see Figure 18). When a giant tripod-like alien bursts out of the ground, instead of immediately running away, many gravitate towards it, brandishing their cameras and cell phones in anticipation. As the tripod turns its advanced weaponry on the crowd, the ensuing chaos is filmed in a particularly gritty, handheld style with a deliberate eye on the images of 9/11, which was described by Spielberg himself as being 'as ultra-realistic as I've ever attempted to make a movie, in terms of its documentary style' (cited in Hoberman 2007). As Ray flees, bodies are vaporised around him, leaving their dusty residue all over his body, evoking the clouds of dust from the collapsing Twin Towers on September 11th. N. R. Kleinfield (2001) witnessed this wall of dust on 9/11 first-hand, but he could have also been describing scenes from *War of the Worlds* when he wrote, 'People began running, chased by the smoke. The air rained white ash and plaster dust, coating people until they looked ghostlike.'[4]

Figure 19 *War of the Worlds* offers perhaps the most potent synecdochal image of the war on terror being brought into the homes of 'normal' Americans produced in the post-9/11 era.

Ray manages to return home and gazes blankly in the mirror at his ash-covered face and body in a potent subversion of Cruise's habitually narcissistic persona. In a profound state of shock he is unable to express to his children the nature of the unimaginable events that he has seen and cannot answer their questions. This direct visualisation of September 11th is the first in a range of unambiguous evocations of 9/11 throughout the film, and it is hard not to see the events that transpire through the prism of the 2001 terrorist attacks. David Koepp suggested that these references to September 11th 'were put in because we all lived through 9/11. We all come out of the same set of experiences, and we just decided not to censor ourselves, because that's not realistic, that's not the world we live in' (Friedman and Koepp 2005: 143). Later when Ray and his children seek refuge in the basement of their mother's house in the seemingly unaffected New Jersey suburbs, they are woken by a Boeing 747 crashing in the street right outside. The detritus of the crash reaches as far as the eye can see. Ray picks up Rachel and shields her eyes from the devastation, a more potent synecdochal image of the war on terror being brought into the homes of 'normal' Americans would be hard to find (see Figure 19).

As Ray and his family flee, New Jersey is obliterated behind them in spectacularly realised scenes of destruction. Rachel asks him, 'Is it the terrorists?', as she has been raised to view terrorism as the defining fear of her young life. Pre-9/11 alien-invasion films rarely framed their attacks through the prism of terrorism, and, unlike Ray's sometimes desperate bid for survival, their heroes often sought to find a way to put an end to the disaster rather than just endure it. It is important to note that Rachel's question is not 'Is it terrorists?' but 'Is it *the* terrorists?' Her inclusion of the definite article indicates that she has in mind a specific set of terrorists who wrought devastation on her country only four years before. The aliens themselves are quite consciously framed as an Islamic Other: from the observation that they have been lying dormant under-ground, waiting to attack an unprepared community like terrorist sleeper cells, to their commitment to wipe out their innocent foes without mercy, whether civilian or not, and take over the world.[5] As David Sterrit (2010) observed, 'In *War of the Worlds*, fear and loathing of the Other is explicitly based on dread of an older, smarter culture that's eager to wipe out "real humans" as ruthlessly and callously as possible. Given the movie's 9/11 links, it's hard not to see Islamic militancy as the metaphoric foe.' The film was praised by arch-conservative anchorman and cultural commentator Bill O'Reilly whom we have seen criticise both *Redacted* and *The Bourne Ultimatum* in previous chapters. O'Reilly saw something quintessentially American in its portrayal of plucky underdogs attacked by legions of interstellar terrorists. He stated, 'Influenced by the death and destruction visited upon us by the Islamic killers . . . *War of the Worlds* actually reflects the view of everyday Americans rather than a few Beverly Hills pinheads' (cited in Hoberman 2007). For O'Reilly the attacks of 9/11 were perpetrated by vicious and inhuman killers who may just as well have been from another planet. His praise for the film finds its counterpart in Douglas Kellner's opprobrium from the left of the political spectrum. Kellner described the film as 'repellant and largely reactionary' (2010: 122). Yet both Kellner and O'Reilly ignore the film's sustained depiction of the failure of American institutions: the ineffectuality of the police, the impotence of the army and the destruction of the church, which is shown ripped in half in the opening tripod attack scene described above. While humanity does prevail at the end of the film, it is only because the aliens prove susceptible to Earth bacteria that humans have developed immunity to over millennia. The American military's methods of combating the unconventional warfare of the intergalactic terrorists prove useless (thereby providing a striking echo to the problems that the military encountered in combating insurgents in the war on terror – see Eldridge's comments in Chapter 2's discussion of *The Hurt Locker*). The film shows visceral and highly subjective scenes of 'shock and awe' being perpetrated *on* Americans rather than conveniently distant Others in faraway lands, and, perhaps most importantly, it does not portray harmonious communities unified by the crisis, but an American society breaking down in the face of tragedy and hardship. In one particularly brutal scene, the members of a desperate crowd turn savagely against one another as they try to steal Ray's car, threatening him and his family. The scene is far from the idealised depictions of how 9/11 brought a nation together in films like *World*

Trade Center and *United 93* or the pre-9/11 alien invasion depicted in the jingoistic *Independence Day*, where American pluck and ingenuity unites the world by its example. These violent scenes in *War of the Worlds* were criticised by Stephen Prince who argued that the 'panic, disorder, anger, and anti-social violence, as people turn on one another in a fight for scarce resources' did not reflect the 'spirit of cooperation' that actually took place on 9/11 (2009: 88). So while the film saw itself criticised by many for appropriating 9/11, Prince challenges it for not imitating it closely enough. Regardless of its political viewpoint, *War of the Worlds* is certainly emblematic of the sustained shift in perspective from pre-9/11 alien-invasion (and disaster) films that were largely 'enjoyable fantasies of destruction, enjoyable because they are meant to belong to the territory of fantasy', to much more confrontational dramas mired in traumatic imagery and situations deliberately designed to evoke 11 September 2001 (King 2005: 49).

The film's portrayal of Ray is also initially far from heroic. At first he is a selfish, indecisive and refreshingly human figure, a far cry from Tom Cruise's customary masculine persona in his career-defining roles as Ethan Hunt, Lieutenant Pete 'Maverick' Mitchell or Frank T. J. Mackey. Yet, in its third act a significant transformation occurs erasing this sense of humanity and vulnerability that is illustrative of the very same process that occurred in discourse about 9/11 in the United States. When Ray and Rachel seek to evade detection by hiding in the basement of an abandoned house, Ray is forced to kill the deranged Harlan Ogilvy (Tim Robbins) who has lost his own family and threatens to reveal their position to the aliens. Despite his unbalanced nature, Ogilvy certainly is Ray's alter ego, a glimpse into the future at what Ray may become if he were to lose Rachel and Robbie, and another of the film's challenges to Ray's paternal authority. While it is Ogilvy's noisy digging and loud curses that attract the attention of the nearby aliens, his greatest crime is suggesting to Rachel that 'if anything happens to your daddy, I'll take care of you'. Once again Ray shields Rachel's eyes and then kills Ogilvy in a legitimised act that will save his daughter's life. Shortly after, the previously distinctly fallible Ray takes on a giant alien tripod and single-handedly destroys it as if he were participating in some 1980s Schwarzenegger or Stallone film in a scene so jarring and out of place that it initially resembles a dream sequence. Earlier Robbie had commented, 'If we had any balls we'd go back and find one of those things and kill it!' But although this statement of ludicrous bravado is rejected by both Ray and the audience, this is exactly what happens towards the end of the film. In doing so, Ray is transmogrified from an ineffectual father who had lost the respect of his children, to their almost superhuman heroic saviour and protector. He may not know what food Rachel is allergic to, but like a 'real man' he will kill to protect her. Whereas to begin with Rachel had turned to her brother Robbie for security (she is once seen asking him,

'Who's gonna take care of me if you go?' with Ray standing right next to her), she comes to again see Ray as her father, and Robbie is finally able to recognise Ray's ascension and once again call him 'Dad'. Like many male protagonists in post-9/11 cinema, the tragic events, whether those of 9/11 or a substitute for them, are presented as an opportunity for a very specific type of masculine redemption that is achieved through the use of reluctant, yet legitimate and necessary, violence in order to re-establish the patriarchal order.[6]

The film concludes with Ray, the 'citizen soldier', reuniting his family by returning Rachel to her mother in Boston, America's 'Cradle of Liberty', while he remains outside (framed in yet another self-conscious reference to *The Searchers*). Even Robbie, who the audience had last seen running off to join the fight against the aliens, in a scene in which Ray is confronted with the Spielbergian equivalent of a *Sophie's Choice* (1982) moment, is alive and present. Forced to choose whether to let his teenage son head off to battle or lose sight of his daughter in the fleeing crowds, Ray reluctantly allows Robbie to leave and fulfil his own ascent towards manhood. Hurriedly returning to Rachel, who is almost taken away by two well-meaning strangers, Ray repeats to them, 'I'm her father, I'm her father,' as if to convince himself as much as them. The calculated harmony of this fantastic reconcilement of the family unit is at odds with much of the devastation that had preceded it and led Ty Burr to rail, 'If you are going to take us back to 9/11 – and even amp it up to 11 – you can't try to flatter us by pretending that everyone comes back alive. To do so condescends to audiences and trivialises the real event, and some of us may even find that offensive' (2005: E1).[7] This ending is certainly a challenge to the writer David Koepp's claim that 'we decided not to censor ourselves, because that's not realistic, that's not the world we live in' (Friedman and Koepp 2005: 143). However, the denouement wholly corresponds to Spielberg's oeuvre and his classification of 9/11 as an event that is defined not by its traumatic effects or political ramifications but by 'how this much catastrophe can bring about that much healing' (cited in 'Revisiting the invasion' on DVD special features 2006). *War of the Worlds* is one of a range of films in which the vulnerability initially exposed by the proximity of the narrative to 9/11 is progressively erased in favour of the mythical reconstruction of masculine authority and the affirmation of the inviolability of the American heroic male that, for a brief moment was called into question by the events of 9/11, but has been systematically reconstituted by American cinema and culture in a variety of guises since.[8]

THE SPECTACLE OF REALITY AND THE REALITY OF SPECTACLE IN *CLOVERFIELD*

My name is Robert Hawkins. It's 6:42 a.m. on Saturday, May 23rd. Approximately seven hours ago, some . . . thing attacked the city. I don't

*know what it is. If you found this tape, I mean if you're watching this
right now, then you probably know more about it than I do.*

Rob, *Cloverfield*

*They say there is always a witness for history. I guess that day we were
chosen to be the witness.*

Jules Naudet, *9/11* (2002)

Matt Reeves's *Cloverfield* is one of the most significant films to emerge from
post-9/11 America. Despite being 'just' a contemporary incarnation of a classic
monster movie, in this case about a twenty-five storey-tall beast rampaging
through New York, it has certainly become the urtext for many film scholars
writing about contemporary American cinema, and to date it has been on the
cover of three books published about the relationship between 9/11 and film
(see Wetmore 2012, Pollard 2011, Comer and Vayo 2013). Like *War of the
Worlds* before it, *Cloverfield* effectively 'remakes' 9/11, and its narrative is as
bound to the events of September 11th 2001 as the Toho Company's original Shōwa *Godzilla* series of films (1954–75) are to post-Hiroshima Japan.[9]
Without a doubt 9/11 is the film's traumatic referent, as *Cloverfield* offers
repeated evocations of 9/11 in scene after scene of people fleeing in confusion
from destruction and devastation, with New York once again cast as Ground
Zero. These are profoundly auratic images that move beyond the film's frames
in the way they resonate with the non-diegetic world. Even its mode of address,
the 'found footage' film, might be regarded as the logical extension of the
restricted perspectives of *Signs* and *War of the Worlds*. Such close proximity to
the iconography of 9/11 led to the film being accused of cynical opportunism.
Stephanie Zacharek suggested that

> *Cloverfield* harnesses the horror of 9/11 – specifically as it was felt in New
> York – and repackages it as an amusement-park ride. We see familiar
> buildings exploding and crumpling before our eyes, and plumes of smoke
> rolling up the narrow corridors formed by lower-Manhattan streets,
> images that were once the province of news footage and have now been
> reduced to special effects. (Zacharek 2008)

Zacharek, perhaps somewhat understandably, wonders about the ethics of
actualising such imagery for the vicarious pleasure of viewers. However,
Cloverfield is much more than 'an amusement-park ride'; it is a film that both
displaces the traumatic events of September 11th 2001 and dares to quite
explicitly recreate and engage with them in a way that was extremely rare in
post-9/11 American cinema. By transgressing this taboo of representation, at
least in allegorical form, *Cloverfield* in its 'visual and experiential references to

9/11' (Wetmore 2012: 51) emerges as a significant and timely cultural artefact. It goes even beyond the allegorical perspective adopted by *War of the Worlds*, as Steffen Hantke argued, when he suggested that it 'is a film that not only depicts but affectively re-enacts, recreates, and reproduces the massive devastation caused by the collapse of the Twin Towers' (2010: 237).

For the first twenty minutes of its slight eighty-five minute running time very little actually happens in *Cloverfield*. Reeves focuses on the leaving party of Rob, an affluent twenty-something New Yorker who is emigrating to Japan for a lucrative corporate position. Rob's best friend, Hud, reluctantly agrees to record the video testimonies of the guests in order to mark the occasion. Rob's evening is upset by the arrival of his childhood friend, Beth, with another man, as not so long before the two had indulged in a brief fling which was reluctantly broken off by Rob because of his imminent departure. Frustrated and a little drunk, Rob clumsily insults Beth, causing her to abscond from the party, but before he has too much time to dwell on his actions the building is rocked by what seems like an earthquake and the guests rush to the roof with Hud's camera still recording everything they witness. In the distance they see a large explosion and, like Rachel and Robbie in *War of the Worlds*, their first frame of reference is terrorism; 'Think it's another terrorist attack?' one of the crowd of onlookers asks before they are forced to flee as debris begins to rain down on their building. The sixty minutes that follow presents the audience with a dizzying succession of intensely visceral images and situations that are deliberately and almost continuously suggestive of 9/11. The screen is filled with ash and debris from explosions; news reports state 'Panic in Manhattan'; large structures are shown collapsing; pieces of paper slowly drift from the skies; and in one moment that is highly reminiscent of the collapse of the World Trade Center, one of the towers from the Time Warner Center is shown leaning precariously against the other. In one remarkable scene, the terrorised and dazed citizens of New York are shown running in order to evade a giant huge wall of dust as it sweeps through the streets (see Figure 20). These images, in particular the 'wall of dust' sequence, are not just designed to be an approximation of 9/11 (as in *War of the Worlds*) but a direct experiential realisation of it: so much so that they appear to be taken *directly* from footage recorded on 11 September 2001 like Jules and Gedeon Naudet's *9/11* (2002). Nathan Lee concurred, suggesting, 'Street-level 9/11 footage would fit seamlessly into *Cloverfield*'s hand-held, ersatz-amateur POV; the initial onslaught of mayhem, panic, plummeting concrete, and toxic avalanches could have been storyboarded directly from the CNN archive' (2008). However, unlike the Naudet brothers, who performed acts of self-censorship by at times deliberately panning their camera away from some of the most disturbing images (like the bodies falling from the World Trade Center), Hud does not pan away from the unimaginable in *Cloverfield*;

Figure 20   Is *Cloverfield* (2008) simply a reincarnation of a B-movie monster,
a cynical manipulation of traumatic imagery, or a film that provides
audiences with an opportunity to both vicariously experience and
deconstruct the spectacle of 9/11?

in fact, he keeps his camera running throughout and even records his own
death. As if to emphasise these sustained connections to 9/11 a brief extra on
the DVD release of *Cloverfield* entitled 'Wall of Dust' sees members of the
crew mention 9/11 as an inspiration not once but twice in the space of just
a few minutes. Special Effects Coordinator David Waine states, 'We're doing
a wall of dust. Basically it's supposed to be the leading edge of the building
exploding and collapsing just like in the Trade Towers.' Then Niamh Murphy,
the film's textile artist says, 'We looked through a lot of 9/11 photos and we
noticed certain things – like some people were completely covered, and they
looked just utterly vulnerable.'[10]

One of the primary ways that *Cloverfield* attempts to physically recreate the
experience of 9/11 is through its utilisation of an exclusively first-person point
of view of unbroken and seemingly unedited footage, a stylistic device that has
come to be known as 'found footage'. This aesthetic instigates an intriguing
suture of spectator and image as the entire film is viewed through Hud's digital
video camera.[11] At the start of the film Hud is a decidedly reluctant videog-
rapher, but when he realises the importance of the event they are experiencing, he becomes obsessed with recording it. When he says, 'People are gonna
want to know how it all went down,' Rob remarks 'You can just tell them.'
But Hud knows that in our image-obsessed age the spoken word is no longer
sufficient: 'No, that wouldn't work; people *need* to see this. This is gonna be

important, people are gonna watch this'. The found-footage device connects the film to both the documentary tradition and also video-game culture, in which many popular games adopt the same first-person perspective (FPS). While this style can be dated back to *Cannibal Holocaust* (1980), the trend experienced a renaissance post-9/11 arguably consequent of the emergence of a pervasive camera culture, where images can now be recorded and disseminated to millions of spectators all over the globe within minutes. The found-footage experience is a seemingly unmediated replication of real-time, but one that simultaneously forces the audience's recognition of the fact that they are watching a film. Geoff King observed this paradox: 'If a limited view and problems of access signify authenticity, something not set up for the cameras, such qualities also tend to draw our attention to the process of mediation' (2005: 54). Not only does the film eschew the ironic tone of the pre-9/11 alien/creature feature (see *Godzilla* (1998) *Tremors* (1989) and *Independence Day*), but the spectator is placed in the middle of a real-time event self-consciously designed not only to invoke 9/11 but, perhaps even more importantly, challenged to be exhilarated by the experience. The producer of the film, J. J. Abrams himself, described *Cloverfield* as a commentary on:

> the YouTube-ification of things, the ubiquity of video cameras, cell phones with cameras. The age of self-documentation felt like a wonderful prism through which to look at the monster movie. Our take is what if the absolutely preposterous would happen? How terrifying would that be? The video camera, we all have access to; there's a certain odd and eerie intimacy that goes along with those videos. (Abrams cited in Winters Keegan 2008)

In this respect *Cloverfield* implements this aesthetic conceit into its narrative very successfully, even utilising flashbacks presented as if fragments from the digital tape had not been erased, managing to maintain the illusion of authentic found footage while still moving backwards and forwards in time. Furthermore, the film is deliberately designed to look non-professional: there are no credits or non-diegetic music, the performers are unknown and the cinematography is frequently blurred and shaky as if filmed by an amateur. Hud's commentary is interspersed with phrases like 'Did you see that?!' and 'Are you guys seeing this shit right now?!', which accentuate both his disbelief and exhilaration at what he is seeing. On one level, Hud's interjections are a re-creation of the exclamations of those who saw the planes strike the World Trade Center on September 11th 2001 (whether first-hand or on television), but they are also the reactions of the spectators of the extravagant destruction on display in blockbuster spectacles that are deliberately designed to astonish and provoke a sense of incredulity. Thus, ironically Hud's statements simultaneously break the fourth wall and reinforce it, very much like the found-footage aesthetic itself.

Geoff King argued that while many justifiably commented that the images of 9/11 were 'just like a movie', in actual fact the media event that 9/11 became was not like a traditional science-fiction or disaster film for a variety of reasons. Primarily because there was 'no footage of the first impact at all, a key absence, a guarantor of authenticity (what spectacular disaster flick would leave so crucial an event unseen, other than in the event of severe lack of resources?)' (2005: 50). While this may have been true of pre-9/11 disaster films like *Deep Impact* and *Armageddon*, which both depict the destruction of the Twin Towers, *Cloverfield* provides its own 'guarantor of authenticity' by leaving many crucial events unseen or relegated to the corners of the frame, including the important first impact. King, writing in 2005, had not yet seen the emergence of the post-9/11 science-fiction film and not witnessed its shifts in modes of address. In fact, for the vast majority of *Cloverfield* the monster is absent from the screen or glimpsed in only a fragmentary fashion by Hud's frenetic and mobile camera. Even in what became the film's signature moment, when the head of the Statue of Liberty crashes into the Woolworth Building, the monster is nowhere to be seen. Correspondingly, *Cloverfield* never explains or even addresses the reasons for the appearance of the creature itself and in doing so recreates experiencing a traumatic historical event from within in a variety of ways, rather than from the privileged position of omniscience usually associated with the genre pre-9/11. At the end of the film Rob states, 'I don't know what it is. If you found this tape, I mean if you're watching this right now, then you probably know more about it than I do.' However, he is incorrect; having shared his and Hud's perspective for the entirety of the film we only know what he knows. The ambiguity of this vividly realised perpetual present tense that the found-footage film, and in particular *Cloverfield*, recreates is a compelling materialisation of many of the anxieties of living in a 'presentist' society explored in Douglas Rushkoff's insightful *Present Shock: When Everything Happens Now* (2012). Rushkoff asserts that our obsessive reliance on new media technologies has led to the new-millennial collapse of traditional narratives and the emergence of states of digiphrenia (a dislocation caused by the attempt to live in the real and digital simultaneously) and fractalnoia (an attempt to understand everything only in the present tense). He writes, 'Instead of finding a stable foothold in the here and now, we end up reacting to the ever-present assault of simultaneous impulses and commands' (4). This fractured narrative is replicated in *Cloverfield* and, while it functions as a self-contained film, is also part of a bewildering array of media texts in its status as a transmedia artefact. While the film never reveals where the monster came from (or even what happens to it at the conclusion), the audience is offered the possibility of 'completing' its narrative if they engage with its extra-diegetic texts, in what Reeves described as a 'meta-parallel story' (cited in Kelly 2009). Thus, the film's viral marketing utilised Myspace pages for its fictional characters that revealed that Rob was hired by the Japanese company Tagruato who make the soft drink Slusho! (facts that are not revealed in the film), and it was Tagruato who disturbed the beast from its underwater slumber.[12] This interconnected web of narrative strands started even before the film was released with the premiere of the film's trailer before *Transformers*, which included no title and only a release date '1-18-08' that also secretly acted as a password for the film's cryptic website.

In the absence of any explicit diegetic evidence for why the monster emerges, might it be valid to explore metaphorical accounts for its appearance, as many have similarly speculated about the equally unexplained phenomenon of the avian behaviour in Alfred Hitchcock's *The Birds* (1963)? Just as how the events of Hitchcock's film have been interpreted as a manifestation of oedipal desire or the return of repressed sexual tension, one may turn to Rob's desperate realisation of his affection for Beth, despite having insulted her at the beginning of the film. Is it a coincidence that the beast emerges not long after she flees from the party? Thus, the entire narrative becomes yet another projection of the male's attempt to re-establish order and prove himself to those who he loves (like Ray Ferrier, Bryan Mills, and so forth). On another level, of course, the monster emerges only because J. J. Abrams and Matt Reeves wished to create a national monster for the United States and an embodiment of the prevailing anxieties of the post-9/11 era, just as Godzilla embodied Japanese fears throughout the 1950s and beyond. Reeves suggested, 'There's no question that we were aware of the fact that the monster in that film was really a metaphor for the anxiety of that time. That was definitely the idea here that we wanted to create our own national monster the same way *Godzilla* [1954] did to create a monster of our time' (cited in Kelly 2009).

Despite the fact that Rob does initially save Beth, who unfortunately is little more than a 'damsel in distress', ultimately his gesture is revealed to be a futile one, as unlike *War of the Worlds, Signs* and *The Forgotten, Cloverfield* provides no happy ending for the couple and is a more resonant text because of it. Even though aspects of their narrative arguably offer some social criticism, the majority of post-9/11 alien-invasion texts still induce a catastrophic event only to assuage it in a highly cathartic manner and thus reconstitute a sense of normalcy at their closures. However, *Cloverfield* offers no such unproblematic resolution. Seemingly the last of their friends to survive, Rob and Beth seek cover under a footbridge in Central Park and record a final video testimonial, an ironic echo of the earlier farewell messages to Rob recorded by Hud at the film's beginning, seven diegetic hours before. Wounded, dazed and confused, Beth can only ask, 'Why is this happening to me?' When the military fail to contain the monster they launch a nuclear weapon in a manoeuvre dubbed

'Operation Hammer Down' (almost exactly the same name as used for an operation in Afghanistan in 2007) killing Rob, Beth and, perhaps, millions of others still stuck in New York. In its final image the film offers a brief coda, one last nostalgic flashback to a happier time when Rob and Beth were together, one of many cinematic depictions of a much desired pre-9/11 moment in American cinema during the decade before 'everything changed'. Yet this cannot alter the fact that all of the main characters in the film and countless others are dead.

In the absence of explicit and interrogative portrayals of the experiences of 9/11, films like *War of the Worlds* and *Cloverfield* allowed audiences to relive the trauma of 9/11 vicariously, for good or ill. Stephen Prince wondered why audiences would choose to put themselves through such an ordeal. He observed, 'The notion of collective trauma also fails to account for why large audiences of moviegoers turned out for a film such as *Cloverfield*, which recycled 9/11 imagery of Manhattan's destruction in the context of a monster movie' (2009: 13). Yet Prince is mistaken; it is the notion of collective trauma that is the very reason why audiences were drawn to such allegorical scenes of destruction, scenes that had been erased from the few films explicitly about 9/11 that had been made throughout the decade. By forcing the audience to share the fear and the exhilaration of Hud's experiences (as we share the experiences of Maya in *Zero Dark Thirty* and Sergeant James in *The Hurt Locker*), the film partially confronts the taboo of representing the destruction that ocurred on 9/11, if only through allegory. So while the film certainly is, as Kellner suggests, a '9/11 exploitation flick' (2010: 126), it may be argued that the true 9/11 exploitation films are the likes of *Zero Dark Thirty, United 93* and *World Trade Center*. Post-9/11 cinema sought to erase and sanitise the 'monstrous dose of reality' that was September 11th 2001 or to use it to provide America with justification for the excesses of the war on terror in an endorsement of the subjective hierarchies, uncritical victimisation, dehumanisation of foreign enemies and legitimation of intrusion on foreign soil that characterised the majority of American cinema in the post-9/11 decade. Many of these narratives, whether consciously or not, are a sustained attempt to rewrite reality into a more amenable form, and in a significant way they achieved this. By attempting to recreate the experience of 9/11, *Cloverfield* drew much criticism, but, in a media landscape that has both commodified these images and diluted them of meaning, it is a visceral text that fulfils a powerful social function and will be recognised as such in the years to come.

NOTES

1. In 2014 Edwards directed his own Godzilla film, *Godzilla*, undoubtedly influenced not only by 9/11 but by its legacy as a cultural trauma which is encoded into the narrative in a variety of ways. The sequel to *Monsters, Monsters: Dark Continent*

(2014), set in an unnamed Middle Eastern country, was described as 'The Hurt Locker ... with added giant aliens' (Jolin 2014: 18).

2. The franchise was rebooted by Bay himself in *Transformers: Age of Extinction* (2014).

3. The catchphrase has been used by Optimus Prime since the animated series in 1984, but nevertheless is given added resonance by its proximity to the reported use of the phrase on 9/11 by Todd Beamer on United Airlines Flight 93.

4. The dust imagery has led some to suggest that the film draws not only from 9/11 but also the Holocaust, evoking the scene from *Schindler's List* when the children mistake ash from the skies as snow. About 9/11 one bystander commented to *The Toronto Sun*, 'This is like the Holocaust' (see Warmington 2001: S14).

5. In a scene present in the shooting script but not in the final film, Ray says, 'Let me tell you something I know for sure, okay? Wherever they're from, they have done a *very* stupid thing ... And they pissed us right off. And right now our army has found out about *them*, and they are very, very angry, and they're on their way this very minute to destroy that machine and whatever is running it. And then everything in your life, and mine, and Robbie's, is gonna go right back to exactly the way it was before' (cited in Friedman and Koepp 2005: 49; emphasis in original). With the changing of one or two words Ray may have been talking directly about the attacks on 9/11.

6. Such was the extent to which the film mined contemporary consciousness that even Ray's evolution from irresponsible parent to courageous father was seen in light of the war on terror by J. Hoberman. He perhaps reached a little too far when he called the film 'an allegory of George W. Bush's crisis inspired growth into leadership' (Hoberman 2006: 23).

7. Consider the overly sentimental conclusions of *Minority Report* and *A.I: Artificial Intelligence*, which erase the complexity of the issues raised by their narratives in their unambiguous denouement.

8. The exact same pattern is repeated in one of Tom Cruise's other post-9/11 alien invasion films, *Edge of Tomorrow* (2014). Cruise's glib PR man, Major William Cage, transforms from a vulnerable and incompetent coward to a seemingly indestructible alien killer.

9. Yomota Inuhiko wrote, '[T]he most commonly evoked reading of the concept of Godzilla remains the monster's powerful appropriateness as a metaphor for the nuclear bomb' (2007: 106).

10. Matt Reeves was not afraid of discussing the film's connections to 9/11 in interviews: 'We felt that in doing a monster movie for our country and of our time that it would definitely be reflective of the anxieties we all feel since 9/11. So that was definitely something we were aware of from the beginning although at the end of the day we were also aware that what we were making was a fantasy. That [9/11 anxiety] was an entry point for the film, a way in, but ultimately what we made was a giant monster movie' (cited in Carnevale n.d.s.).

11. Hud's name is a reference to the acronym HUD, short for Heads-Up Display, the visual display used in aeroplanes and, more recently, video games.

12. Slusho! also appeared in *Alias* (2001–6) and *Fringe* (2008–13) both produced by J. J. Abrams. Matt Reeves commented, 'Yet in another way, because of all the viral stuff and the meta parallel story we've had building all along, that's also part of a puzzle. So, in a way, at the center of the whole thing there's this one puzzle piece, which, if you knew nothing about Slusho or Tagruato and all of those things, it would play completely by itself' (cited in Kelly 2009).

6. DECADE OF THE DEAD: ZOMBIE FILMS AS ALLEGORY OF NATIONAL TRAUMA

At some point we may be the only ones left. That's okay with me. We are America.[1]

George W. Bush cited in Woodward, *State of Denial: Bush at War*

The zombies represent the suppressed tensions and conflicts – the legacy of the past, of the patriarchal structuring of relationships, 'dead' yet automatically continuing – which that order creates and on which it precariously rests.

Robin Wood, *Hollywood from Vietnam to Reagan*

The 1990s was arguably a lacklustre decade for American horror, defined by the proliferation of sequel after sequel and ironic meta-narratives that served only to dilute the genre of the visceral power that had characterised the greatest horror films of the 1970s and 1980s. Once ferocious texts like *The Texas Chainsaw Massacre, Halloween* (1978) and *A Nightmare on Elm Street* (1984) saw themselves transformed into franchises, almost parodies of themselves, manufactured to eviscerate and titillate the teenagers who simultaneously populated the films and went to see them at their local multiplexes. The most commercially successful horror films of the 1990s were the ironic *Scream* series (1996–2011), a virtual disquisition and almost parody of the horror genre itself, which was then spoofed in *Scary Movie* (2000) and its four sequels, as the genre seemed to be in danger of virtually consuming itself.[2]

Just as violent action films came under heavy criticism in the wake of 9/11, many also called for an end to the frequently gratuitous and sadistic horror genre (see Brown 2001). However, like the action film, horror did not go away. Indeed, it was positively rejuvenated in the first decade of the new millennium; the fact that this was the war on terror era was certainly not a coincidence. While the trend for sequels and remakes gained an even greater pace, the horror film experienced something of a renaissance in the post-9/11 decade with filmmakers using the genre as a platform to express their concerns about many of the crucial issues of the fractious decade, just as the defining horror films of the 1960s and 1970s like *Night of the Living Dead* (1969), *Rosemary's Baby* (1968), *The Exorcist* (1973) and *The Texas Chainsaw Massacre* had once done before. Kevin J. Wetmore argued that the attacks on 9/11 had a decisive influence on horror film in a variety of ways:

> Several elements, tropes and images dominate post-9/11 horror. No one film has all of these elements and images and no image or trope appears in every film. But together these elements represent ways in which horror cinema has appropriated 9/11 and its imagery, not least of which in order to contain it, understand it and re-experience it under safer conditions or with a different ending. (Wetmore 2012: 24)

While it would be a misnomer to suggest that the horror film experienced a fundamental shift overnight, one can certainly observe some marked changes in emphasis and even the emergence (or re-emergence) of several subgenres: from gorno (otherwise known as torture porn) with its sustained connections to debates concerning the systematic mistreatment of prisoners in Abu Ghraib and Guantánamo Bay, the reinvigoration of the slasher film, the return of 'the fear of the foreigner' film (with Americans becoming lost and tortured in Eastern Europe, Mexico or South America), the found-footage film and the materialisation of the home-invasion sub-genre. Narratively, American horror cinema of the post-9/11 decade became characterised by a renewed embrace of the bleakness of the 1970s' texts where victims seemed to be chosen at random and chances of survival were negligible, as films once again chose downbeat climaxes, as opposed to the knowing irony of the self-referential horror of the 1990s.

One of the most remarkable of these developments is explored in this chapter: the return to prominence of the zombie film which had been largely 'dead' throughout the 1990s. The 2000s saw the zombie rise again as a cultural icon in a veritable avalanche of zombie texts: from films and television programmes, to books and video games. While in the whole of the 1990s only about eighty zombie films were produced, 2007 alone saw seventy-three zombie titles released, and in the entire decade there were in excess of five hundred. The majority of these were straight-to-DVD titles, but a great number of them were released theatrically, ranging from big-budget blockbusters (e.g. *I am Legend* (2007) and *World War Z* (2013)) to video-game adaptations (*Resident Evil* (2002) and *House of the Dead* (2009)), gritty and realistic incarnations (e.g. *28 Days Later* and *The Dead* (2010)) to zombie comedies or 'zomedies' (e.g. *Zombieland* (2009) and *Shaun of the Dead* (2004)) and even soft-core zombie sex films (e.g. *Big Tits Zombie* (2002), *Zombie Strippers!* (2008) and the memorably titled *Night of the Giving Head* (2008)).

What led to the zombie becoming such a compelling presence in the 2000s when it had not resonated in such a way in the 1990s? The 2000s even saw the word 'zombie' become a part of the cultural lexicon, whether as an alcoholic cocktail, a dysfunctional bank, a type of computer virus, part of a philosophical thought experiment or a rather disturbing sex act. The term 'living dead' became part of the terminology in the war on terror when Donald Rumsfeld gave his famous 'unknown knowns' comments, talking about, among other things, the fate of the prisoners in Guantánamo Bay; his implications were that many of the prisoners, although they were alive, were technically 'living dead'. On this subject Slavoj Žižek observed:

> In the debate about the Guantánamo prisoners, one often hears arguments that their treatment is ethically and legally acceptable because 'they are those who were missed by the bombs.' Since they were the targets of U.S. bombings and accidentally survived them, and since these bombings were part of a legitimate military operation, one cannot condemn their fate when they were taken prisoners after the combat—whatever their situation, it is better, less severe, than being dead. This reasoning tells more than it intends to say. It puts prisoners into a literal position of the 'living dead,' those who are in a way already dead. (Žižek 2004)

The zombie found itself explored not just as an allegory but as a real threat by Daniel W. Drezner, professor of international politics, who wrote a serious treatise in *Theories of Internatrional Politics and Zombies* (2011) on what would happen if the zombie threat actually materialised. This level of engagement with a figure once only explored in fantasy continued when the official Centers for Disease Control and Prevention (CDC) produced a document called 'Preparedness 101: Zombie apocalypse' detailing what the public should do in the event of a zombie uprising.

Certainly zombies are one of the most malleable of on-screen monsters and have been uniquely able to encompass allegories of class, race and other forms of social conflict since Val Lewton's *I Walked with a Zombie* (1943). Annalee Newitz suggested, 'Gloopy zombies and entrail-covered serial killers are allegorical figures of the modern age, acting out with their broken bodies and minds the conflicts that rip our social fabric apart' (2006: 2). Zombies are not some distant alien race with no connection to humanity: they are very often even our husbands or our wives (*28 Weeks Later* (2007), *Land of the Dead*), our children (*Night of the Living Dead, REC* (2007), *28 Days Later*), our Presidents (*Dawn of the Dead* (2004), *Zombieland*), or even ourselves (*Warm Bodies* (2013), *Fido* (2006)). In what way may this return of the living dead have been provoked by the turbulent political environment of the post-9/11 decade? Kyle Bishop has argued, as many have done, that the zombie film is inextricably connected to the times in which it is made: 'A post 9/11 audience can hardly help but perceive the characteristics of zombie cinema through the filter of terrorist threats and apocalyptic reality' (2009: 30). Many of the zombie films of the post-9/11 years vividly embody the fears and anxieties of the decade. While George W. Bush categorically stated. 'You are either with us or against us' (cited in Anonymous 2001), many zombie films challenge the certainties of this reductive moral binarism, offering more interrogative portrayals of the Other than mainstream films were able to provide. The idea that horror, in particular the zombie film, may be more than disposable and morally dubious entertainment was given currency by Robin Wood in his influential *Hollywood from Vietnam to Reagan* (1986). Wood maintains that the monster at the centre of the horror genre functions as a manifestation of a Freudian 'return of the repressed', and that this Other is a projection of that that 'is repressed within the Self, in order that it can be discredited, disowned, and if possible annihilated' (73). Wood argues that horror and other allegorical modes are thus the perfect site for social criticism, free as they are from many of the constraints imposed on mainstream film. Therefore, fears that cannot be articulated in mainstream culture become manifested, whether consciously or not, in the horror film. We may ask then what is it that returns in post-9/11 film that has been repressed by American culture at large? Might it be the dissent against the war that was erased from the airwaves in the aftermath of 9/11, or challenges to its mythologisation and the emphatic claims that the war on terror was a just and legitimate war? These issues found themselves redacted from the American cultural imaginary in the post-9/11 decade and thus returned in allegorical form in genre cinema. Nick Muntean and Matthew Thomas Payne suggested that we may consider the zombie genre in its entirety as offering a striking parallel to the events of 9/11 and the war on terror and this may have been why the films became so resonant. The zombie film, with its vividly depicted 'return of the repressed', they suggested, 'functioned according to a logic quite similar to that of the zombie films, albeit with terrifyingly real consequences' (2009: 243).

- Zack Snyder's *Dawn of the Dead* begins with an unnerving credits sequence that intersperses real-life documentary footage intercut with an unexplained zombie outbreak. Crowds of Muslims are shown

praying in a mosque explicitly connecting the zombie outbreak to contemporary fears of Islamic fundamentalism, something that became a
trend in the genre. Kevin J. Wetmore argued that the film suggests that
'[w]e are under assault from without and within, just as on 9/11. The
zombie is a terrorist' (2011: 146). The final shot of the credits is the
White House being overrun by zombies, and it is a provocative image
that was returned to in *Zombieland* and *Resident Evil: Retribution*
(2012).

- The movie *28 Days Later* and its sequel *28 Weeks Later* portray the
progressive breakdown of social institutions that form the fabric of
our culture: the government, the military, the law and even the family.
While it is ultimately the less interesting of the two films, *28 Weeks
Later* opens with one of the most brutally affective scenes in the
history of the genre. Several months after the zombie outbreak, Don
and his wife, Alice, are hiding in an isolated farmhouse with a few
other desperate survivors. When a small boy knocks on the door, the
majority of their group do not want to let him in, fearing that even if
he is not infected, he will attract the attention of the zombies who still
mill around outside in their hundreds. When Alice insists, their fears
are immediately realised as the zombies begin to break into the building with a ferocious intensity. Alice and Don run upstairs where they
have a chance to escape through an open window, but Alice refuses
to leave without the boy. Don faces an impossible dilemma: should
he remain and help his wife and the child, or flee? Before he knows
it, his sense of self-preservation kicks in and he throws himself out of
the window. Sprinting away from the building chased by dozens of
zombies, he turns to look behind only to see Alice's face screaming in
fear and desperation at him. Don's inability to protect his family is
an exploration of the failure of traditional forms of masculinity that
many American films unquestioningly reconstituted and rehabilitated
in the post-9/11 era. Some months later a North Atlantic Treaty
Organization (NATO) force led by the United States Army occupies
London, and the Isle of Dogs is declared a safe area where all survivors are subject to rigorous blood tests. The occupation deliberately
evokes America's intervention in Iraq and, in particular, Baghdad's
Green Zone as the Stars and Stripes wave conspicuously in the breeze
over the secure facilities that are effectively juxtaposed with the deso-
lated London streets outside. While the Americans insist that their
presence is a reluctant one, there is a sense that the United States rel-
ishes the opportunity to interfere in European affairs. Lou Lumenick
(2007) commented, 'The film is not only an unambiguous critique of
the U.S. presence in Iraq, but there also are references to Vietnam (a

napalm shower), the Tiananmen Square massacre, the Holocaust and the World War II London Blitz.'

- Joe Dante's *Homecoming* (2005), produced for the *Masters of Horror* series, was described by Dennis Lim (2005) as 'easily one of the most important political films of the Bush II era'. Somehow American soldiers killed in Iraq return as zombies demanding the right to participate in upcoming presidential elections. At first the Republican Party sees this as an endorsement of their Bush-like President and his war on terror. Reverend Luther Poole, a Jerry Falwell-esque figure, insists that the zombies are evidence of American exceptionalism and that they are 'the hand of God, reaching down to touch our nation and our blessed President'. Later, when it becomes apparent that the zombies neither support the war nor the President and what they actually want is regime change, Poole and the administration quickly change their minds. Poole then states, 'It's as if the bowels of hell have opened to dispel these demons, this Satanic spawn.' They are now described as dissidents and traitors, 'giving aid and comfort to the enemy'. When the administration rigs the vote to ensure that the President gets re-elected, the results cause even more soldiers to return from the dead: this time not only from Iraq but also the Vietnam War, World War Two, and even the American Civil War.

The majority of the zombie films of the decade are post-lapserian tales about the collapse of civilisation, no doubt a perennial fear, but one rendered more potent by the proximity of 9/11 and the war on terror to the American people. When in Snyder's *Dawn of the Dead* the racist and homophobic security guard C. J. gleefully watches US soldiers shooting zombies on the television screen, he patriotically observes, 'America *always* sorts its shit out!' However, the central trope of the zombie film is that the authorities are unable to deal with the outbreak that rapidly spirals out of control, and in film after film America certainly does not sort 'its shit out'. Rather than coming together as a community, as in the mythologised visions of American solidarity like *United 93* and *World Trade Center*, or portraying public servants who valiantly sacrifice themselves for the greater good of the nation (*The Hurt Locker, Act of Valour, Zero Dark Thirty*), many of these zombie texts feature a society that quickly devolves into a state of anarchy and civil war, exploring what happens when the thin veneer of civilisation is fractured, revealing a Hobbesian world underneath, 'solitary, poor, nasty, brutish, and short' (Hobbes 1969: 62). The genre is even sometimes able to provocatively suggest that the world may be a better place *after* the apocalypse, as the destruction of civilisation affords the characters some sense of liberation from the stultifying effects of modern capitalism (see *Zombieland, Fido*), or expose the calculated manipulation of terrorist threats used to control the population often with a state of martial law (*The Crazies* (2012), *Fido*, *ZMD: Zombies of Mass Destruction*). These zombie texts do not shy away from sustained political criticism; they mobilise complicated discourses, and they support one of the underlying contentions of this book, that allegorical films, whether about superheroes, alien invasions or zombies, have been able to expose the entrenched unease and unequivocal phobias that permeated the decade.

BLURRING THE BOUNDARIES BETWEEN THE LIVING AND THE DEAD IN GEORGE ROMERO'S *LAND OF THE DEAD* AND *DIARY OF THE DEAD*

I'm gonna do a jihad on his ass!
Cholo, *Land of the Dead*

It took the Godfather of the zombie genre, George Romero, seventeen years to complete his seminal triptych of *Night of the Living Dead*, *Dawn of the Dead* and *Day of the Dead* (1986). About these three films Robin Wood wrote, 'It is perhaps the lingering intellectual distrust of the horror genre that has prevented Romero's "living dead" trilogy from receiving full recognition for what it undoubtedly is: one of the most remarkable and audacious achievements of modern American cinema' (1986: 267). The first film of the zombie cycle, *Night of the Living Dead*, is often read as an allegory of the tumultuous social climate of 1960s America in the years of the Vietnam War and the Civil Rights Movement. Its sequel, *Dawn of the Dead*, widely regarded as the crowning achievement of the genre and a potent satire of consumerism, is redolent of societal mistrust in the wake of Watergate and Nixon's resignation in the 1970s. The final part in the original trilogy, *Day of the Dead*, reflects a 1980s defined by Reaganomics and the ideological implications of privileging military funding over social care, leading to an almost unremittingly bleak depiction of a humanity that is impossible to save and, perhaps, even not worth saving. When Romero revealed in 2002, just one year after September 11th, that he would be creating a fourth film in the zombie cycle, he said:

> We started sending the [initial *Land of the Dead*] screenplay around right after 9/11, and everyone said, 'Ugh! We want to make soft and fuzzy movies now. Go home.' So I did. Then this post 9/11 mentality started to set in and I thought, 'This might be even better'; so I tried to relate this movie to the post 9/11 head in America. (Romero cited in Rae 2005: 45)

The resulting film, *Land of the Dead*, marked the start of a second trilogy nineteen years after the first concluded. This time it took Romero only four years to complete as it was quickly followed by *Diary of the Dead* (2007) and then *Survival of the Dead* (2009). The new films are just as connected to the era in which they are made as the original trilogy, and like the previous films they explore the most pervasive anxieties in American culture with an at times contemptuous disregard for some of the foundational principles of American national identity. *Land of the Dead* emerges as, perhaps, the most transparent allegory of the attacks on 11 September 2001 in the whole of post-9/11 cinema, even more so than *War of the Worlds* and *Cloverfield* explored in the previous chapter. It is an audacious and provocative film that attempts to desacralise the events of 9/11 by reimagining them through the lens of a zombie film and adopting a much more confrontational ideological perspective than those rare American films that attempted to portray 9/11 directly.

Set several years after the zombie outbreak portrayed in the original films, *Land of the Dead* depicts a privileged elite who reside in a seemingly impenetrable tower, known as Fiddler's Green, replete with still-functioning luxury stores, restaurants and cafes. This security enables the residents of the tower to be entirely disconnected from the suffering of those beyond its heavily fortified walls and defences. Despite the apparent 'end of the world', vestiges of civilisation remain in Fiddler's Green where boundaries of class, race and gender are still as rigidly constructed as ever. On the television inside a nostalgic advertisement plays on a loop, as if trying to convince its citizens that nothing has changed: 'Life goes on at Fiddler's Green. In the heart of one of America's oldest and greatest cities. Bordered on three sides by mighty rivers, Fiddler's Green offers luxury living in the grand old style.' Fiddler's Green is presided over by the Cheney-esque Gerald Kaufman (Dennis Hopper) who refuses to acknowledge that the world outside has been transformed. The way Romero frames the geographical placement of the building and its apparently impregnable status, it is hard not to see echoes of the World Trade Center and America itself before the attacks on 9/11. This was something Romero confirmed in an interview: 'It's about that whole period, immediately before 9/11: feeling safe – protected by water. And then the water gets breached – that's there. We made the tower a little taller' (cited in Berriman 2013: 80).

Outside the imposing tower, but still within the protective enclave of the compound and the river, reside the film's working classes, denied access to the American Dream that Fiddler's Green has come to represent. They are an oppressed underclass forced to beg for scraps from Kaufman's table despite outnumbering their masters many times over. Kaufman employs armed guards and mercenaries ostensibly to guard the community from the zombies outside, but in reality to protect the elites from the disenfranchised proletariat in case they ever decide to do something about their disadvantaged social situation. This underclass is populated by the likes of Slack (Asia Argento), who is refused a position in Kaufman's private army because she is a woman and is instead forced to become a prostitute, and the Hispanic American Cholo (John

Leguizamo), who does dirty work for Kaufman, procuring luxury goods from the outside and quietly killing and disposing of those who voice their disapproval of the status quo. Cholo continues to obey his master under the illusion that he may one day be allowed a much coveted place inside Fiddler's Green, but he is oblivious to the fact that he is twice removed from those that occupy the tower, by both his race and by his class. While some of the slum dwellers protest about their lowly status, the majority are distracted by the illusion of safety and the sex, drugs and gambling Kaufman provides them with. There is even a gladiatorial arena that initially pits zombie against zombie for the entertainment of the masses, but as things become more desperate offers human versus zombie spectacles in Romero's dual allusion to both the Roman Empire and America's ceaseless and increasingly sadistic fascination with reality television (see Pulliam 2009).

Kaufman sends his Blackwater-esque army into the neighbouring zombie-infested areas in order to pillage for supplies. While he claims that it is for necessary provisions and medicine for everyone, it seems it is more often to secure luxuries for him and his privileged friends. On one night-time raid Cholo disturbs a dormant zombie enclave, known as Uniontown, with his unnecessarily violent and riotous incursion, which prompts a large group of the undead to follow their persecutors back towards the city. Romero shows the zombies gazing up longingly at the looming tower of Fiddler's Green in the distance in another powerful literalisation of Chalmers Johnson's theory of 'blowback'. Romero suggests through allegory that America is not to be regarded as such a bastion of innocence and moral clarity but, perhaps, even the architect of the social situation that created the attacks of 9/11, evoking Noam Chomsky's assertion, 'We can think of the United States as an "innocent victim" only if we adopt the convenient path of ignoring the record of its actions and those of its allies, which are, after all, hardly a secret' (2001: 35).

Furthermore, Romero continues to offer a much more sympathetic representation of zombies than the majority of other films from the genre where they have historically been portrayed as a monstrous and unambiguous Other. In *Land of the Dead* (as in his original trilogy) the threat to the protagonists is just as often from the living as it is from the undead, as humans are shown quickly reverting to savagery and selfishness as soon as the certainties of their social structures crumble around them. Near the start of the film one young soldier suggests, 'There is a big difference between us and them,' but the film reveals that humans and zombies are not so distinct from one another at all. While the handsome anti-hero Riley (Simon Baker) may be the ostensible protagonist of the film, its moral centre is ironically a zombie in the form of Big Daddy (Eugene Clarke), who emerges as a much more compassionate figure than Kaufman and indeed many of the other living humans. Through his portrayal of Big Daddy Romero challenges the oft-repeated 'us versus them' canard of the Bush administration as the zombified African-American small business owner is shown expressing a palpable concern for his fellow zombies: he becomes upset when they are killed; he teaches them how to ignore the fireworks, called 'sky flowers', that the soldiers use to distract them in an interesting parallel between the zombies and the living being distracted by the drink, drugs and gladiatorial games); and it is Big Daddy that mobilises them to move towards the object of their oppression, Fiddler's Green. By daring to present the monster as sympathetic, Romero offers a potent exposure of American cultural attitudes towards their enemies and continues the social criticism that became a hallmark of the original trilogy. This refocalisation proved too much for many raised on horror narratives that present the zombie as an inhuman beast, but this process was duplicated in several texts in the post-9/11 era that offered more humanistic depictions of the undead than ever before (see *Fido* and *Warm Bodies*).

When Kaufman finally makes it clear to Cholo that he will never be given an apartment in Fiddler's Green, the estranged subordinate turns terrorist by stealing Dead Reckoning, a mobile WMD truck built on Kaufman's orders, and demands five million dollars from his erstwhile master on the understanding that he will otherwise launch a devastating salvo of missiles directly at the building itself. Riley begs him to stop with the plea, 'You hit that tower straight on you are gonna kill a lot of innocent people!' Romero frames Cholo as a distinctly bin Laden-eque figure, and, if we doubt the connections, he is given the line, 'I'm gonna do a jihad on his ass.' A few moments later Kaufman even tells his board of executives, 'We don't negotiate with terrorists,' one of George W. Bush's defining maxims from the war on terror era. On this particular line, Romero can be heard to remark on the commentary recorded for the DVD release of the film, 'I always thought that was a little too on the nose, but I think that has gone a long way to making sure people understand there is a little politics in this film.'

The film ends with Romero's symbolic re-creation of 9/11, as the zombies assault Fiddler's Green over the water in an attack, which is presented as both a Freudian return of the repressed and a Bhabian return of the oppressed (see Bhaba 1983) (see Figure 21). Those living there are entirely unprepared and quickly overrun as they had been convinced by Kaufman that their fortress was impregnable. Audaciously the attack is portrayed as *both* monstrous in its violence and somehow justifiable, as the film has dared to suggest that America (through the allegorical figures of Kaufman and the elites) has provoked the attack through its intrusive foreign policy and transgression of international law. Here Romero is able to present another rare example of Žižek's challenge to 'reject this very opposition and to adopt both positions simultaneously' (2012: 62). Despite the carnage that he has just witnessed, the film ends with Riley's final recognition of the fact that there is little difference between the

Figure 21 Nearly forty years after *Night of the Living Dead* (1968), George Romero still proves himself to be a 'radical critic of American culture' in *Land of the Dead* (2005), perhaps the most challenging recreation of 11 September 2001 in film of the decade (Shaviro 1993).

zombies and the living and that, 'They are just looking for a place to go . . . same as us.'

Just three years later Romero returned with *Diary of the Dead*, a reboot of the franchise and a return to the immediacy of the original outbreak, shot in the style of the found-footage film discussed in the previous chapter. Robin Wood considered the film 'the series' supreme achievement' and argued that it was the summation of Romero's treatise on the American condition. He stated, '[T]he first four in the series cover and demolish, systematically, the central structures of what we still call our civilization, establishing Romero as the most radical of all horror directors' (Wood 2008). *Diary of the Dead* follows a group of film students who happen to be making a low-budget horror movie when the zombie outbreak happens. Like Hud in *Cloverfield*, the film's director and cameraman Jason insists on keeping the camera rolling in order to document history as it happens in front of him: 'If this turns out to be a big thing, I just wanna record it.' As for many characters in post-9/11 film, it is as if something not viewed through the lens of a digital camera is not really experienced at all. Romero is much more critical of Jason's obsessive need to film than Matt Reeves was of Hud, whose transition from reluctant to ardent documentarian went largely unnoticed. Jason is a much less likeable characterisation who is often more interested in the quality of the images he is recording than the fact that his friends are being killed in front of him. In this, Romero offers a critique of the dehumanising potential of new media technology and the complicity of those that compulsively film and watch it, which connects *Diary of the Dead* more to Brian De Palma's *Redacted* than Matt Reeves's *Cloverfield*. In fact, the film's primary target is not the zombies themselves but the media and our unquestioning dependence on it, in particular, the mainstream media's collusion with politics and big business that results in an industry unable to produce unbiased and objective news, regurgitating partisan support for political parties or sensationalised stories in order to secure higher and higher ratings for its sponsors. With such a constant cycle of spin, spectators find it impossible to discern what 'real' news is. This is vividly realised in the film's prologue, which shows how the zombie outbreak was originally broadcast on television; later the same scene is returned to and presented from a very different and 'unedited' perspective. The disinformation spread by the news and the authorities about the zombie outbreak deliberately evokes the media coverage of the war in Iraq on several occasions. We see a government representative announcing, 'We expect things to return to normal very soon,' when it is clear that society is falling apart and the unnamed President is shown not to be at the White House or the President's Emergency Operations Center (PEOC) but relaxing at his ranch. Jason's professor remarks, 'In war time when the enemy can be marked as this son of a bitch or that son of a bitch the cruelty becomes justified.' Yet Romero is just as critical of the alternative to mainstream media, the Internet, where more than two hundred million cameras upload footage everyday observing the world first-hand. Despite it being metaphorically and literally in the hands of the people, with thousands if not millions of versions of the truth out there, it is impossible to make sense of them all. When Jason is bitten by a zombie and is about to turn into one himself, he groans 'shoot me', gesturing to the floor where both the video camera and a gun lie – leaving the audience unsure of which one he means for his friends to use on him.

Unlike the previous four films in the series, *Diary of the Dead* is not set in an isolated environment like a farm house, shopping mall, missile silo or a skyscraper; for most of its running time it functions as a road movie. It is only in the final third of the film, when Jason's group seeks solace in a mansion belonging to one of their wealthy friends, replete with secure walls and a high-tech video-surveillance system, that it adopts the familiar pattern of Romero's siege narratives. Yet as one may expect in a film by George Romero, who has spent much of his career exploring the fragilities of modern civilisation and the porous nature of physical and psychological borders, they soon become trapped inside with hundreds of zombies blocking their escape. It is entirely fitting, given the themes of the film, that what is left of the group finally retreats into an impenetrable panic room without food or water but with an entire wall full of CCTV monitors for company.

Romero saves his most scathing denunciation of humanity for the final sequence of the film, which features footage posted on the Internet of two rednecks using strung-up zombies for target practice. The film's voice-over concludes with the question, 'Are we worth saving?' The line between zombie and human has become even more blurred, and humanity has become increasingly inhumane. Despite making 'just' horror movies and being the object of scorn by many mainstream critics throughout his career, Romero has tackled through allegory what the majority of films set in the real world refused to do. His two post-9/11 films discussed in this chapter emerge as compelling manifestations of contemporary real-world anxieties, and they offer a similar political message to *Syriana* and *Redacted* in their desire to deconstruct the events of 9/11 and the war on terror rather than perpetuate the mythology surrounding them. Romero's body of work reveals him to be one of America's foremost social commentators and, as Tim Shaviro commented, a 'radical critic of American culture' (1993: 82).[3]

FIXING THE APOCALYPSE:

THE UNDEAD AS ALLEGORY OF NATIONAL TRAUMA IN *I AM LEGEND*

This is Ground Zero. This is my site. I can fix . . . I can fix this.

Robert Neville, *I am Legend*

Francis Lawrence's 2007 adaptation of Richard Matheson's novel *I am Legend* (1954) was the third cinematic incarnation of one of the most compelling post-apocalyptic narratives to emerge from post-World War Two American literature. It had been previously filmed twice as *The Last Man on Earth* (1964) and *The Omega Man* (1971), both films redolent with anxieties pertaining to the Cold War era in which they were made and set. As one might expect, the new millennial *I am Legend* updates these fears to much more contemporary perspectives. The end of the world in Lawrence's version of the tale is certainly viewed through the lens of 9/11 as the film's writer and producer Akiva Goldsman observed: '[T]here is no question that 9/11 is now part of our imaginations . . . it turned out to be impossible to tell a story about the end of the world without this recent catastrophic event that seemed to promise, in our imaginations for a second, the end of the world' (cited in Ulaby 2007). The most recent version of *I am Legend* retains the central premise of the original novel, yet transforms much of its social commentary. While it raises some provocative and compelling questions, it is ultimately unable to reconcile them with the bombastic demands of a big budget star vehicle and, as a result, dissolves into a formulaic rites-of-passage narrative, with some disturbingly reactionary politics, highly reflective of the era in which it was made.

In a brief prologue, scientist Alice Krippin (Emma Thompson) reveals to the world that by genetically engineering a version of the measles virus she has

Figure 22   'The ghosts of place': the spectre of 9/11 haunts the frames of the post-apocalyptic *I am Legend* (2007).

found a cure for cancer. A solemn cut to THREE YEARS LATER reveals the unexpected results of her discovery: a barren and seemingly post-human New York (see Figure 22). What became known as the Krippen Virus quickly spread around the globe killing ninety per cent of the world's population. Of those that remained nine per cent degenerated into grey, zombie-vampire hybrids referred to as Dark Seekers who then turned on the one per cent of humans left alive. In the absence of the nine million people who used to reside there, the once bustling metropolis of New York is in the process of being reclaimed by nature, transformed into a serene ecological landscape occupied only by birds, deer and even mountain lions. Seemingly the only human left in the whole city and, perhaps, even the world, is US Army virologist Robert Neville (Will Smith). In an interview the director commented about the effects of filming on the streets of New York just a few years after 9/11. He stated, 'We would empty the streets [of parts of New York] to shoot and every once in a while there would be somebody walking down the street that would get horribly disturbed because it reminded them of how quiet and empty the city got during 9/11' (cited in Ulaby 2007). While superficially empty, Neville's New York is haunted by the ghostly presence of both the traumatic diegetic incident that led to its desolation *and* the events of 9/11. Michael Bell described this phenomenon as 'the ghosts of place', arguing, 'We moderns, despite our mechanistic and rationalistic ethos, live in landscapes littered with ghosts. The scenes we pass through each day are inhabited, possessed, by spirits we cannot see but whose presence we nevertheless experience' (1997: 813). Bell's 'spirits' are not those of the literal undead (although the film's Dark Seekers are ironically an embodiment of them) but the discernible presence of those who are no longer physically there, yet still palpably present to those who continue to inhabit these spaces. Bell suggests that memories of the past remain present in an almost Proustian sense and contribute to the historical specificity of particularly (but not exclusively) traumatic sites: whether in New York, Hiroshima, Auschwitz or Chernobyl. Thus, Bell's 'ghosts' function as both a metaphor for Neville's traumatic inability to turn away from the past and the lingering, almost palimpsestic, presence of 9/11 iconography and motifs that came to dominate the screens in post-9/11 American science-fiction and horror cinema.[4]

These connections to the harrowing events of the past are reinforced by Neville's intrusive flashbacks to the outbreak. His painful memories of the government's institution of martial law, which failed to stop the spread of the Krippen Virus, culminate in his tortured recollections of the helicopter crash that killed his beloved wife and daughter. Neville holds himself personally responsible both for their deaths and the deaths of millions as he was the military scientist charged with containing the virus. In an act of claiming responsibility, he states, 'Ground Zero. This is *my* site.' The flashbacks that Neville experiences are just one of several symptoms of PTSD he displays throughout the course of the narrative: from hallucinations to pronounced obsessive-compulsive tendencies. Like many characters in post-9/11 films he remains preoccupied by the past, always returning in his mind to the time before 'it' happened. He continuously watches television news from before the outbreak, and the walls of his house are plastered with images from before, including covers and pages from newspapers and magazines, some of which even feature him. One *Time* magazine has his picture with the word 'Saviour', to which he has appended a question mark. However, the film cannot dwell too much on Neville's trauma and his neurosis without derailing its vision of heroic redemption or its status as a fast-paced sci-fi action blockbuster. Therefore, it channels Neville's grief and anger into a hatred for the Dark Seekers and the search for a cure for the Krippen Virus, which at times seems more like a quest to pre-emptively eradicate those infected rather than heal them. During the day Neville calculatedly stalks the city block by block, capturing the Dark Seekers in order to perform his experiments on them. In yet another example of cognitive dissonance, Neville refuses to acknowledge that the Dark Seekers have any remaining human qualities, although it is clear to the audience that they have developed emotional attachments to one another and are capable of at least some rational thought. However, Neville remains oblivious to this and can only record in his video journal, 'Typical human behaviour is now completely absent.' Smith's Neville is an intriguing characterisation; both arrogant and proud, he displays the type of hubris that brought about the destruction of the world in the first place. Yet, Lawrence and Smith frame his anger as a sense of righteous indignation and purpose without ever lingering on his irrational hatred for the Dark Seekers and blindness to their nascent humanity. It is in this refusal that the film departs profoundly from Matheson's original novel in which Neville is never so easily able to ignore the humanity of the Others as they become embodied in the form of his zombified neighbour Ben Cortman, the undead children he comes across who remind him of his own daughter and in his sexual desire for the infected women who lasciviously call out to him night after night. The literary Neville is even able to acknowledge that 'but for some affliction he didn't understand, these people were the same as he' (Matheson 1999: 39). In Lawrence's version the Dark Seekers remain an inscrutable and monstrous Other and Neville's desire to cure them is presented as a quasi-religious quest.

When Neville finally meets another survivor, Ana, he is at first sceptical when she insists that God *told* her how to find him. Neville once was a believer but the 'end of the world' has shaken his faith in God. Ana says, '*He* must have sent me here for a reason. The world is quieter now. We just have to listen. If we listen, we can hear God's plan'. Although Neville initially remarks, 'God didn't do this, Ana, we did,' he ultimately comes to reassess his atheism in favour of a renewed belief in God as many characters did in the decade after 9/11 – like Father Graham in *Signs*, Katherine Winter in *The Reaping* (2007), Elliot Moore in *The Happening* (2008) or John Koestler in *Knowing*. In the film's final flashback, Neville recalls many events that seem to have led him to this moment in time, in particular the butterfly imagery that has permeated his life – from his daughter's drawings, cracks in a glass window in the shape of a butterfly, to Ana's tattoo – bringing him to the realisation that everything had been God's plan after all. Neville turns his back on science in favour of absolute faith in his cause and accepts his role in God's divine plan, yelling at the alpha-male Dark Seeker with a religious fervour, 'Let me save you! Let me save you!' When he realises he has finally found the cure he chooses to sacrifice himself (in a perverse return to the trope we saw in *Act of Valour* in Chapter 2) by 'transforming himself from sceptical scientist to saviour-cum-suicide bomber' in an act regarded as monstrous when perpetrated by those who do not share our ideological viewpoint, but here valorised as one of supreme courage and even framed with shades of christomimeticism (Boyle 2009). Neville kills the leader of the Dark Seekers, in the process ignoring the fact that the he had displayed signs of humanity and intelligence that Neville had refused to recognise. After his 'heroic' death, which reaffirms both the primacy of masculinity and religious faith, Ana is once again led by

God to a colony of survivors in a town named Bethel in Vermont. Through the gates it is clear to see that the town is a pre-industrial Eden, with a white, steepled church and eco-friendly wind turbines in the distance. Therefore, the film's apocalypse is presented not as the end of the world after all, but rather a spring clean for humanity and a chance to start afresh with America at the centre of the world's spiritual rebirth (just as it is in *2012* and *The Day After Tomorrow*). In a Gospel-like closing narration Ana suggests that Neville has become the Christ-like 'legend' of the film's title for finding a cure (from his own blood) and for his great sacrifice for the future of humankind. Lawrence shows that everything was a part of God's divine plan and Neville *was* the saviour that the *Time* magazine had predicted him to be, although not in the way many had originally expected.

The subsequent Blu-ray and DVD release of the film revealed that this ending had not been Francis Lawrence's first choice about how to conclude the narrative and that the original climax had been scrapped after testing negatively with American preview audiences. This original cut would have radically changed the emphasis of the film, bringing its fractures and inconsistencies into startling focus. In the final scenes, instead of blowing up the Dark Seekers and confirming their status as an unproblematic Other, Neville at last recognises their humanity and thus his own deviancy. In doing so the Other that has been demonised throughout, becomes humanised, and it is Neville himself who is revealed to be monstrous. In this challenging reconfiguration of the film's themes, the central events of the narrative are cast in a new light as Neville does not experience a divine epiphany but actually works through his trauma, which enables him to reconcile himself with his traumatic past. In this version the apocalypse was not an act of God and neither was the cure, and God did not send Ana to Neville, nor call for Neville's sacrifice. This conclusion provides an understanding of the self and alterity not present in the theatrically released film and is more in line with the Matheson novel in which, in a striking display of moral equivalency and self-knowledge, Neville comes to understand that *he* is a relic of a former age and a grotesque legend for those infected who remain 'alive', as he has been stalking, tracking and experimenting on them. The alternate ending of the film dares to suggest that one's enemies may not be so removed from oneself, challenging the alluring rhetoric of the Bush administration's war on terror – an ideological perspective that was perhaps just as unpalatable for America on the film's release in 2007 as it had been in 2001.[5]

NOTES

1. One wonders about how this quote was delivered and whether the stress was on the 'We' or the 'Are', recalling the 'We are the people' of a speech delivered by Tom (Albert Brooks) in *Taxi Driver*.

2. Some of the ideas contained in this chapter were initially proposed in McSweeney (2010).
3. The final film of the second trilogy, *Survival of the Dead*, received such a limited release that it was practically a direct-to-DVD title. However, the end result is the weakest film of the series and if it is the final zombie film from Romero then it is a shame that one of the most influential cycles in horror cinema ends so disappointingly.
4. Sean Brayton (2011) sees reflections of Hurricane Katrina in the film.
5. For a remarkable analysis of the representation of religion in the novel and its adaptations see Moreman (2012).

7. THE RISE AND FALL OF EMPIRES: THE 'WAR ON TERROR' AS ALLEGORICAL MOMENT IN HISTORICAL FILM

History is a representation of the past, not the past itself.
Robert Rosenstone, *Visions of the Past: The Challenge of Film to Our Idea of History*

With the barbarism of the U.S intervention in Iraq in all of its aspects increasingly evident, it is more difficult than ever to maintain the illusion of the benevolent imperialism of Pax Americana. The American Empire has truly become a Pox Americana in the eyes of the world.
John Foster and Robert McChesney, 'The American Empire: Pax Americana or Pox Americana?'

People a hundred years from now should be able to grasp the enormity of this attack by visiting this sacred ground. Ground Zero is a cemetery. It is the last resting place for loved ones whose bodies were not recovered and whose remains are still within that hallowed ground. We must respect the role these events play in our history.
Rudolph Giuliani, 'Getting it Right at Ground Zero'

Throughout his administration, George W. Bush, like many Presidents before him, made a concerted effort to link his policies to decisive moments in American history: justifying his decisions, be it to go to war in Iraq or to institute the USA Patriot Act, by connecting them to historical precedents. In doing so, Bush proceeded to appropriate American history, reshaping and remodelling it to suit the ideological perspective of his administration. Bush stated,

> These values must be imparted to each new generation. Our children need to know that our Nation is a force for good in the world, extending hope and freedom to others. By learning about America's history, achievements, ideas, and heroes, our young citizens will come to understand even more why freedom is worth protecting. (Bush 2003b)

This selective adoption of history is what Herbert Butterfield called 'present-minded history' (1950: v), that is, to selectively appropriate elements of the past to validate contemporary political decisions. The logical culmination of this process was the contention that anyone who disagreed with Bush must, therefore, be unpatriotic because they were disputing not only the policies of the current administration, but precedents set by the likes of George Washington, Abraham Lincoln or Ronald Reagan that he evoked. Of course, George W. Bush was not the first President to have adopted such a strategy, but his administration made conscious decisions to 'select, abridge, generalise and interpret in accord with the knowledge of hindsight and the predisposition of a historian' arguably more than ever before (Himmelfarb 2004: 219).

Until relatively recently, critical studies of historical film as a cultural artefact had tended to primarily focus on issues of fidelity and authenticity (see Hughes-Warrington 2009). These issues are perhaps embodied in Maria Wyke's question, 'Is historical film, therefore, a proper object of study for classicists? And should cinema have a place in the investigation of antiquity's reception?' (1997: 3). But this chapter asks not what historical films are able to tell us about the past in which they are set, but rather the present in which they are made. How is the past, and, specifically, cinematic images of the past, mediated and appropriated for use in the present? In this chapter I argue that the historical films that emerged after 9/11, while ostensibly about the period in which they are set, be that second-century Roman Britain in *The Eagle*, fifth-century BC Greece in *300* or nineteenth-century America in *The Alamo* (2004), are actually potent cultural artefacts that engage with the dominant concerns of the decade they are produced in. The war on terror proves to be an allegorical moment that resonates throughout the genre and reveals that history is always viewed through a prism of the present. In this understanding of historical film, a film like *The Birth of a Nation* (1915) is strictly limited in what it is able to reveal to us about the American Civil War of 1861 to 1865, but as a text about early twentieth-century attitudes towards the conflict it is exemplary. About D. W. Griffith's most contentious film, Robert Burgoyne wrote, 'Yet for all its bigotry and offensive stereotyping, the film accurately reflected the prevailing historical understanding and knowledge of the era in which it was produced. Although it was challenged at the time, its depiction of Reconstruction matched the beliefs of the most powerful school of American historians of the era' (2008: 26). In the same way, contemporary historical films both reflect and engage with the era that saw their construction. Thus, Spielberg's *Schindler's List* offers a compelling insight not into the Holocaust itself, but its place in the 'contemporary culture of memory and memorializing' that has arisen in the fifty years since the traumatic event itself (Hansen 1997: 81). Likewise, as Pierre Sorlin argued in *Film in History: Restaging the Past* (1980), the historical film engages in an almost Benjaminian dialogical relationship with the past and the present, symbiotically connecting the two in its vibrant discourse. Therefore, we can look to the genre as a barometer of American cultural concerns of the times, whether reflecting Cold War era anxieties in films like *Spartacus* (1960) and *The Alamo* (1960) or the perception of an American empire of benevolence in films produced in the 1990s like *Gladiator* (2000) and *First Knight* (1995) (see Wilson 2002).[1] These films and others from the genre are easy to dismiss, as many have, given the liberties they often take with recorded history, but it is not so easy to ignore how they have undoubtedly 'played a decisive role articulating an image of America that informs, or in some cases challenges, our sense of national self-identity, an image of nation that is projected to the world' (Burgoyne 2008: 2).

Given that the films discussed in this chapter were produced from 2004 to 2011, it is only to be expected that they engage with and interrogate concepts of national identity with sustained and direct connections to the United States of the early years of the twenty-first century. Whether they are directly about America (for example, *The Alamo, The Conspirator* (2010) and *The New World* (2005)) or other nations (for example, *Kingdom of Heaven, The Eagle* and *King Arthur* (2004)), the United States nevertheless becomes their subject through an allegorical prism: like the extended occupations of Britannia by the Roman Empire in *King Arthur* and *The Eagle*, which explicitly and deliberately parallel those of Iraq and Afghanistan, or the clashes between rival civilisations in *300* and *Kingdom of Heaven* that are created with an eye on strained new millennial tensions between East and West.

The films become what Anton Kaes has called 'discursive events' (1989: x), narratives that are defined by their modern perspectives on the past. A film like *The Conspirator*, despite being set in the nineteenth century, positively reverberates with connections to the post-9/11 era. Its protracted images of prisoners framed as terrorists in all but name – bound, hooded and placed before military tribunals rather than civilian courts – and its portrayal of an America vacillating between the desire for justice and revenge after a traumatic national incident, in this case not 9/11 but the assassination of President Abraham Lincoln – all serve to connect it to contemporary America. Shirley Sealy (2011) asked, 'Sound familiar? Terrorist attacks? Conspiracy theories? A rush to seek revenge? Civilian terrorists being tried in military courts?' After the assassination, Edwin Stanton, the Secretary of War, believes he understands the mood of the nation. With very deliberate allusions to 9/11 the film's director, Robert Redford, has him suggest, 'Someone must be held accountable; the people *want* that'. Is it conceivable that, if the film had been made prior to 9/11 and the war on terror, there would be such a sustained emphasis on terrorism, the suspension of law and of habeas corpus?

Such tensions are palpable in Ridley Scott's *Kingdom of Heaven*. Many wondered how Scott would approach a contentious topic like the twelfth-century Crusades in such politically charged times. George W. Bush had once inadvertently used the word 'crusade' to describe the war on terror, causing such a critical backlash that he never uttered it again (see Ford 2001). Like most of the historical dramas of the decade, *Kingdom of Heaven* uses a past conflict to explore the present, and as Hamid Dabashi concurred, 'The Crusade proves a potent metaphor for contemporary religious conflicts' (2005: 27). The film caused consternation even prior to going in front of the cameras when some writers expressed concerns that the film would show the conflict from a Muslim perspective. One suggested that the film 'panders to Osama Bin Laden', but it was later revealed that the writer of those comments had not even read the screenplay (cited in Edwardes 2004).[2] Professor Khaled Abu el-Fadl, who had read the screenplay, came to the opposite conclusion, that *Kingdom of Heaven* 'teaches people to hate Muslims. There is a stereotype of the Muslim as constantly stupid, retarded, backward, unable to think in complex forms' (cited in Galupo 2005). Yet this is far from the case in the finished film; perhaps, Professor Abu el-Fadl saw what he expected to see in the pages of the script, understandably accustomed to decades of crude Hollywood representations of Arabs. These intensely contradictory opinions continued after the film was released when Professor Jonathan Riley-Smith, Dixie professor of ecclesiastical history at the University of Cambridge, described the film as 'not historically accurate at all. They refer to The Talisman, which depicts the Muslims as sophisticated and civilised, and the Crusaders are all brutes and barbarians. It has nothing to do with reality' (cited in Edwardes 2004). Riley-Smith is mistaken to suggest that the film portrays all Muslims as 'sophisticated and civilised', and neither is it the case that all of the crusaders are portrayed as 'brutes and barbarians'. However, the film does depict a religious tolerance that historically may not have been a part of the times, something that is much more of a late twentieth and twenty-first century concept. Its protagonist, Bailian, states, 'We fight for an offense we did not give against those who were not alive to be offended'; such beliefs are markedly a fabric of the 2000s, not the twelfth century. Amin Maalouf, author of *The Crusades through Arab Eyes* (1984), thought that while the portrayal was balanced, it distorted history by viewing it from new millennial perspectives: 'It does not do any good to distort history, even if you believe you are distorting it in a good way. Cruelty was not on one side but on all' (cited in Edwardes 2004). Is it then a retelling of history in the way that Ridley Scott and screenwriter William Monahan believe it happened, or perhaps the way it should have been? Or, as Arthur Lindley suggested, *Kingdom of Heaven* is more like 'a parable of modern problems, primarily, but not exclusively, those of the Middle East, for twelfth century we must read twenty-first' (2007: 16).

This process of using historical drama to explore the period in which a film is made rather than that in which it is set reached its apogee with Sofia Coppola's *Marie Antoinette* (2006), an almost ahistorical account of Marie Antoinette's marriage to her second cousin the Dauphin of France, Louis XVI. By using a variety of anachronistic devices, including incongruous accents and dialogue and even the use of modern music and Converse trainers, the film transfers twenty-first century concerns to the eighteenth century to such an extent that very little from the original period remains. Such blatant ahistoricism was criticised by many as a wasted opportunity (the film was unsurprisingly booed at screenings in Cannes by French critics) given the almost unprecedented access Coppola had to the Palace of Versailles. Yet the film fits perfectly in Coppola's oeuvre alongside the similarly themed *The Virgin Suicides* (1999), *Lost in Translation* (2003) and *Somewhere* (2010), all of which explore the malaise of the affluent new millennial American. It is this very ahistoricity that defines the film and is a political statement in itself, an assertion that Coppola's generation and contemporary American teenagers are so disconnected from politics and history that, for them, the past does not even exist. Dana Stevens (2006) wrote, 'In neglecting them she has unwittingly taken a political stance.' The majority of the films discussed in this chapter do not take this idea of encapsulating the contemporary world into the historical film to such extremes, but each of them, without exception, is defined by their relationship to the post-9/11 era.

THE DECLINE AND FALL OF THE ROMAN/AMERICAN EMPIRE IN *THE EAGLE* AND *KING ARTHUR*

The Eagle is not a piece of metal; the Eagle is Rome.

Marcus Aquila, *The Eagle*

By 300 AD, the Roman Empire extended from Arabia to Britain. But they wanted more. More land. More peoples loyal and subservient to Rome.

Lancelot, *King Arthur*

In recent decades America and its perceived imperial status has been more and more compared to that of the Roman Empire in its declining years (see

Murphy 2007; Laxer 2008; Hubbard and Kane 2013). These parallels, whether erroneous or not, have tended to focus on America's continued military and cultural dominance, while at the same time foregrounding issues of imperial overstretch, debt and deficit, colossal defence spending and declining international reputation as evidence of the precarious status of the world's only remaining superpower. The veracity of these claims is not up for debate in this book, but one cannot dismiss the fact that these ideas have gained significant cultural currency in the last decade both inside and outside of the United States and articles with titles like 'Will America too fall, just as Rome did?' (Stossel 2013) and 'Is America the new Rome?' (Malcolm 2008) have become regular occurrences in newspapers, magazines and journals. Throughout its history America has frequently sought to see itself through the prism of Ancient Rome, and it has a 'long tradition of borrowing from the Roman past in order to crystallise and critique aspects of American national identity. From the founding years of the nation-state, the imagery of Rome was deployed to link the civic ideals of the fledgling nation to the classical past with readymade connotations of democracy, liberty and nobility' (Burgoyne 2008: 75). Just as the defining historical films of the 1940s and 1950s turned to Rome and saw America reflected in its image, contemporary films depicting the Roman Empire like *The Eagle* and *King Arthur* discussed here are just two texts among many that have once again returned to Rome as a metaphor for debates about contemporary America.[3] Both films are connected to the decade of the war on terror in sustained and intriguing ways and both draw direct analogies between the decline of the Roman Empire and the status of the so-called *Pax Americana*. In their more ambiguous portrayals of empire they mark a departure from the depiction of Rome/America as a benevolent hegemon in films like *Gladiator*, which Rob Wilson argues provides a 'legitimation of the imperial machine' (2002: 71). Scott's film, which re-energised the genre, has Clinton's perceived humanitarian interventions in the former Yugoslavia and Somalia as its metaphorical backdrop in a way that *The Eagle* and *King Arthur* symbolically interact with the occupations of Iraq and Afghanistan. Despite attempts at veracity, both films are predictably unable to offer much of an insight into the historical period. *King Arthur* claims to be 'The true story behind the legend', but it is plagued by a myriad of historical inaccuracies that led Tom Shippey to suggest that its grasp on history 'is at best dubious, and its geography frankly ludicrous' (2007: 310). Yet to focus exclusively on these inaccuracies is to miss the point, as *King Arthur* and *The Eagle* provide a commentary not on the final centuries of the Roman Empire, but on rather the political landscape of the American Empire at the turn of the twenty-first century.

Kevin MacDonald's *The Eagle*, based on the Rosemary Sutcliff novel *The Eagle of the Ninth* (1954), is set in Roman-occupied Britain in AD 140 and follows a young centurion named Marcus Aquila (Channing Tatum) undertaking his first command far away from civilised Rome in a largely forgotten colony teetering on the brink of collapse. It is Aquila's sense of purpose and his patriotism that drives the narrative: he wishes to regain his family's honour (and also that of the nation) as he lives with the burden that it was his father who commanded the infamous Ninth Legion when it disappeared along with its standard, the eponymous eagle of the film's title, somewhere beyond Hadrian's Wall in the wilds of Scotland. This loss is framed as both a personal and a national trauma, and its effects on Aquila are so profound that he experiences vivid dreams/memories of the event that he did not himself witness.

McDonald intriguingly subverts one of the foundational conventions of the Roman historical film, the pronounced English accent habitually adopted by actors playing Romans, as one of a variety of ways of connecting it to the new millennium. Just as Roland Barthes called the prominent fringes of Hollywood epic cinema of the 1950s a 'label of Roman-ness' (1957: 15), so has an unwavering Recieved Pronunciation (RP) English accent been a fundamental trope in the construction of the ancient epic. Yet in *The Eagle* MacDonald has the Romans in the film played by American actors who make no effort to disguise their accents. While initially disconcerting, so indoctrinated have we become to regarding the absurd notion of English accents as being somehow authentic in historical films, the decision proves an effective one, and MacDonald argued that this brought 'a little contemporary symbolism' to the film (cited in Linklater 2009). The casting of Channing Tatum in the role of Aquila further connects the film to America's war on terror given his roles as an American soldier in *Stop-Loss* and *Dear John* (2010), a former US Marine in *White House Down* (2013), and his embodiment of all-American machismo in *G.I. Joe: The Rise of Cobra* (2009) and *G.I. Joe: Retaliation* (2013).[4]

The Romans stationed in occupied Britannia are engaged in a brutal conflict with their enemies, the Picts, who are portrayed as insurgents and vicious barbarians standing in the way of Roman enlightenment and progress. The atrocities committed by the Picts are shown in great detail, particularly the beheading of a Roman soldier, which is portrayed as an act of religious fanaticism, undoubtedly filmed with an eye on the very public beheadings of several American journalists during the war on terror (there is no such scene in the Sutcliffe novel). Although the Pict druid at the start of the film calls out to the besieged Romans, 'You have stolen our lands and killed our sons,' his comments are quickly brushed aside in a demonstration of Aquila's heroism, as the untested centurion proves himself in battle against the bestial and quasi-demonic Picts. It is described that in an earlier engagement the tribesmen 'came at us [the Romans] like animals' and even ripped the hearts out of fallen Roman soldiers while they were still alive. The fact that the Picts are defending their homeland against colonial Roman invaders is ignored, and Rome's actions are ideologically legitimised by their moral (and physical) superiority and the fact that we see the conflict from the perspective of Aquila himself, which initially justifies their actions. Despite his heroism Aquila is grievously wounded and pensioned out of the army with little more than an award for 'conspicuous gallantry'.

When Aquila hears a rumour that the iconic Eagle of the ninth has been sighted far north of Hadrian's Wall, he decides to attempt to retrieve it. When asked why a simple piece of metal is so important, he replies, 'The Eagle is not a piece of metal; the Eagle *is* Rome'. Like the Stars and Stripes has been for America, the Eagle (with its own palpable symbolic links to the United States) is a symbol of Roman pre-eminence and ideological superiority. He takes with him his slave Esca (Jamie Bell) whom he had saved from certain death in the gladiatorial arena. Yet Esca initially makes it clear to Aquila that he despises him for what the Romans have done to his country: 'I hate everything you stand for, everything you are.' He tells Marcus the story of how his father preferred to kill his own wife (Esca's mother) to save her from the Romans, as 'he knew what they would do to her'. This is the film's first indication that, perhaps, the Rome Aquila fights for and holds in such high esteem may not be synonymous with the Rome of his grand declarations, but he quickly shrugs off this challenge to his world view. In their travels north they come across a legionary who had once fought alongside Aquila's father but has now 'gone native' with a Pict family of his own beyond the wall. The man, Lucius Cauis Metellus (Mark Strong), or Guern in his Pict name, adopts an American accent because he was originally a legionary and draws the most explicit parallel to the war in Iraq when he asks Aquila, 'Couldn't they [Rome] have been satisfied with what they have? Do they always have to punish and push on, looking for more territories, more conquests, more wars?' Guern suggests that the Ninth Legion's march north was not one of glorious expansion, but the folly, hubris and greed of a colonial Empire.

Yet despite these admissions Rome's transgressions are largely kept off the screen; in contrast, the cruelties of the indigenous peoples are presented in visceral detail: from the malicious beheading at the beginning of the film to their barbaric propensity for brutal violence as opposed to the 'civilised' Roman way of conducting war. The differences in these portrayals are at their most explicit when the film depicts the deaths of two indigenous children: one killed by Aquila and the other by the Prince of the Seal People (Tahar Rahim) whose tribe had been responsible for the destruction of the Ninth Legion and the capture of the Eagle many years before. In order to stop a young boy revealing their whereabouts to his tribe, Aquila is forced to kill him, an act that is portrayed as regrettable, but ultimately necessary. Later when the prince kills a child who had betrayed their community by deliberately allowing their enemies to escape, the murder is lingered on as a symbol of his (and his tribe's) bestiality, while Aquila's actions and the killing of the first boy are soon forgotten in the march towards restoring honour to his family and country.

When they finally find the location of the missing Eagle, Esca confronts Aquila with a truth he finds hard to ignore: 'Your father came to *kill*. He came to punish us because we would not bow to the name of Rome'. While the location of his father's last stand is a site of great tragedy and loss for Aquila, for Esca 'it is the place of heroes'. Aquila's world view is challenged by this exposure of his cognitive dissonance, and it is too much for him to process. McDonald himself commented, 'We're occupying countries, and one way or another that makes it a war of occupation, which has a parallel with Rome – a nation that steamrolled over cultures, tried to install their own culture in nations and some resisted and fought back. You'd have to be blind not to see some similarity' (cited in Faraci 2011). The more that Aquila is confronted by evidence that Rome may not be as benevolent as it had previously appeared to him, the more he is forced to recognise the humanity of those he has long considered his inhuman enemies. He comes to understand that his perspective, that of the hegemonic imperialist, cannot be reconciled with the views of those his country has invaded in the name of freedom and progress. Aquila even experiences the lives of others directly when he is forced to become Esca's slave in a reversal not featured in Sutcliffe's novel, but one that is a fitting addition to the themes of the narrative.

The Eagle ends with Aquila retrieving the Eagle and defeating the barbaric Seals alongside the remaining survivors of the Ninth Legion who have each 'gone native' but return to the Roman banner in order to give their lives in memory of what they have left behind. In a brief moment which encapsulates Aquila's new-found awareness of the humanity of the Other, he drowns the Prince of the Seal people in a shallow stream only to see the fierce warrior's make-up wash off, for the first time revealing the face of a human being beneath. Aquila returns the Eagle to his superiors and thus restores his family's honour and the honour of Rome, but refuses the offer of command of the newly reformed Ninth Legion, as he has become disillusioned with the contradictions of benevolent imperialism. Instead he seeks refuge outside of the empire with Esca, who he now regards as his equal. Yet the film's uncomfortable oscillation between recognition of the Other as human and its demonisation lingers, as does Esca's betrayal of his own in favour of the Romans who occupied his land and killed his people.[5]

Like *The Eagle, King Arthur* is also set in Britannia in the declining days of the Roman Empire and features a protagonist, Arthur (Clive Owen), who becomes disillusioned with all that Rome has come to stand for. Arthur is honourable and humble, a living embodiment of the Roman ideal, which he initially describes as 'ordered, civilised, advanced . . . [a place where] the greatest minds in all the lands have come together in one place to make mankind free'.

Arthur leads a band of heroic and loyal Sarmatian knights who are forced to fight for the Roman Empire for fifteen years, after which they are promised full citizenship or given freedom to return home. However, just days before they are due to be discharged they are effectively stop-lossed by the Roman authorities and forced to engage in one last dangerous mission. By the time of the film's production in 2003 criticism of the Bush administration's stop-loss policy was gaining much cultural currency. During the 2004 Presidential campaign it was publically challenged by John Kerry and labelled a 'back door draft' (cited in Anonymous 2004a). Lancelot, sounding a lot like Brandon King from *Stop-Loss*, asks Arthur, 'All these long years we've been together, the trials we've faced, the blood we've shed . . . What was it all for, if not for the reward of freedom? Does it all count for nothing?' The Sarmations find themselves fighting a war for a cause they no longer believe in, as the writer David Franzoni (who also wrote *Gladiator*) remarked, they are enduring the 'GI experience – strangers in a strange land, killing to stay alive and hating doing it' (cited in Matthews 2007: 116).

The film pits Arthur (who himself is half-Roman and half-Briton) and his knights against two rival groups of antagonists: the Woads (the indigenous people of Britannia) and the invading Saxons. Both are initially presented as a barbaric Other in contrast to the civilisation and order inherent in the Roman Empire. In the film's opening battle Arthur and his Sarmations heroically defend a convoy containing the carriage of the Roman Bishop Germanius from a Woad ambush. The fact that the Sarmations are tasked with killing *for* those who took them into slavery and are fighting *against* those who are attempting to free themselves from the shackles of the Roman Empire goes unmentioned. Yet Arthur's world view becomes more and more chal-lenged as the film progresses. The pompous Germanius, who in a humourous episode demands to be seated at the head of the table, only to be dismayed when he sees it is the Round Table of Arthurian folklore, betrays Arthur and his knights by sending them on their final mission, even though he knows that many of them will not return. They are tasked with rescuing the Pope's favourite God son Alecto, who may one day be Pope himself, and it is clear that his life is regarded as much more valuable than any of theirs. When they reach their destination beyond the wall Arthur is confronted first-hand with the inequities of Roman rule as Alecto's father, Senator Marius, uses the name of God and of Rome to brutally mistreat and oppress his serfs. When they rescue a young woman, Guinevere (Keira Knightley), she tells Arthur, 'They tortured me with machines to make me tell them things I didn't know to begin with.' Guinevere challenges Arthur's belief in Rome and the values he has held so dear, 'The Rome you talk of doesn't exist except in your dreams,' and calls him, 'The famous Briton who kills his own people'. She confronts him about how illogical his allegiances are: he supposedly fights for freedom but he oppresses his own. He is unable to deny the truth of her words, and when he hears that his tutor and father figure, Bishop Pelagius, has been killed as a heretic for teaching that all men are equal, he finally turns his back on the empire. The Woads he has long seen as his enemy are now recognised as human beings, and he acknowledges that his Rome is 'ideologically burnt out, an imposing, hegemonic state engrossed by its own survival and heedless of the economic and political vulnerability of its subjects and allies, something like the disquieting relationship of the first and third worlds in our times' (Jewers 2007: 93).

After the few surviving Sarmation knights are given their freedom, instead of leaving they choose to stay and join Arthur's battle against the bestial Saxons of their own accord. Thus, Arthur finds that the values that he had exclusively ascribed to Rome may be universal, and not bound to nationalist identities or ideas of exceptionalism. As Susan Aronstein suggested, the film then 'can be read as a direct condemnation of the cold war rhetoric and attitudes that led to the war in Iraq. By figuring Rome, the supposed ambassador of the *Pax Romana*, as a corrupt imperialist force that – in the name of Christianity and under the cover of God's will – offers its subjects not freedom but exploitation' (2009: 168). Franzoni denied that the film was directly about the occupation of Iraq, stating, 'I've been asked over and over if the movie is about Bagdad [*sic*] . . . The obvious answer is that it's not, because I wrote it before that war' (cited in Matthews 2007: 116). Yet its observations on the nature of freedom and empire are timely as they became a central part of national discourse during the first years of the new millennium.

It is no coincidence that both *The Eagle* and *King Arthur* (and Neil Marshall's Britannia-set Roman film *Centurion*) conclude with their protagonists turning their backs on the empire that they once held in such high esteem, much as Brandon King in *Stop-Loss*, Roy Miller in *Green Zone* and Hank Deerfield in *In the Valley of Elah* turn their backs on their own country, disillusioned by the uncomfortable realities they are confronted with. Hank Deerfield turns the Stars and Stripes upside down as a symbol of distress, much like Aquila melts down the Eagle at the end of the original cut of *The Eagle*. If the Roman occupations at the centre of these narratives are metaphors of American imperialism, then their conclusions are potent ones as their protagonists are afforded different perspectives on their supposedly virtuous and glorious nation, which is revealed to be founded on the oppression of others, a fact that they had been able to remain oblivious to until their political transformations in the course of the narrative. The rejection of empire that Aquila and Arthur embody is even more conspicuous than that of King, Miller and Deerfield, as the Romans seek solace among a former enemy: whether in the form of a business partnership (*The Eagle*) or in marriage (*King Arthur* and *Centurion* (2010)). In Arthur's case he marries Guinevere, a former ideological enemy, and is subsequently embraced by her people as one of them; the modern equivalent would be an American soldier deciding to stay in Iraq, converting to Islam and marrying a Muslim.

'EYES AS DARK AS NIGHT, TEETH FILED TO FANGS . . . SOULLESS': THE HOLY CRUSADE AGAINST THE MUSLIM OTHER IN *300*

While *King Arthur* and *The Eagle* can be read as offering a partial criticism of the Roman and, by extension, the American Empire, Zack Snyder's *300*, based on the 1998 graphic novel by Frank Miller, offers a symbolic rebuttal to such ideological criticisms in its portrayal of an event that has become one of the foundational myths of Western civilisation. The Battle of Thermopylae in 480 BC, in which a small number of Greek warriors fought against a vast invading Persian army, has remained a lure for dramatists since Herodotus's account of the battle in the seventh book of his *Histories* (see Herodotus 2013). While the historian Charles Hignett called Thermopylae 'an unsolved riddle' (1963: 378), the idea of a band of resolute heroes and defenders of freedom pitted against a demonic horde of uncivilised enemies has been the pervasive understanding of the battle in popular culture for centuries and repeated in films like *The 300 Spartans* (1962) and books like William Golding's *The Hot Gates* (1965) and Stephen Pressfield's *Gates of Fire* (1998).[6] Snyder's *300* embraces these tropes with a distinctly new millennial twist by portraying the Spartans, led by their warrior King Leonidas (Gerard Butler), as a distinctly Americanised society in their love of honour, liberty and their spirit of self-sacrifice, while their Persian enemies led by King Xerxes (Rodrigo Santoro) are framed as cthnonic quasi-Muslim fundamentalists (even though the film is set nearly a thousand years before the birth of Islam) who outnumber the Greeks by thousands to one. The all-white Spartans, who call themselves 'the world's one hope for reason and justice', form a pre-emptive expeditionary force to sacrifice themselves for freedom and to prevent the hordes attacking them on their own land, mirroring the Bush administration's 'Fight Them Over There So We Don't Have To Fight Them Here' rhetoric.[7] Leonidas goes against the wishes of the Spartan council and their laws because he knows in his heart (as George W. Bush did) that he must 'do the right thing'. When Leonidas's wife, Gorgo, acknowledges her husband's sacrifice for his nation, it sounds like a particularly American declaration: 'Freedom isn't free at all; it comes with the highest of costs, the cost of blood.'[8]

In stark contrast to this, Xerxes's forces are a hideously grotesque Other: uncivilised, primitive, barbaric and literally and figuratively demonic. Xerxes himself is a cruel despot who sacrifices thousands of his men with a wave of his hand. Snyder shows the Persian army made up mostly of slaves and Xerxes's tent full of deformed individuals indulging in all kinds of bizarre, sadomasochistic behaviour. Unlike the noble, stoic and avowedly white heterosexual

Figure 23   Reconsolidating fears of a monstrous and deviant Muslim Other in *300* (2006).

Leonidas, Xerxes is a monstrous characterisation: cruel, dark-skinned, androgynous and clad in earrings and a dog collar; even his voice is digitally altered to emphasise his strangeness and deviant sexuality (see Figure 23). Snyder made his intentions (and his primary audience) explicit when he suggested in an interview, 'What's more scary to a twenty year old boy than a giant god-king who wants to have his way with you?' (cited in Daly 2007). In presenting the Spartans as avowedly heteronormative, the film sidesteps the more complicated attitudes to sexuality that were prevalent at the time throughout Greece; instead, as if to draw attention away from the film's palpable homoeroticism, the Spartans direct homophobic slurs at the Athenians who are called 'philosophers and boy-lovers' and other Greeks are chided for offering their 'backsides to the thespians' (see Solomon 2013). Xerxes demands that Leonidas kneel at his feet as a symbol of his capitulation in a scene with particularly sexual overtones. But Leonidas is a free man, and even though he knows it will mean death for him and his men, he cannot surrender and he is prepared to sacrifice himself for the cause of freedom and liberty like Rorke in *Act of Valour*, Neville in *I am Legend* and Iron Man in *Marvel Avengers Assemble*.

The ensuing battle is certainly framed as an ethnic one and a defence against a quasi-Muslim jihad; the Spartan narrator Dilios states, 'We rescue a world from mysticism and tyranny,' in the process conveniently ignoring the equally barbaric Spartan practices of leaving perfectly healthy babies to die, sending young children into the wilderness to fight wolves or forcing beautiful young virgins into drug-addicted slavery. Snyder's implication, and that of many novelists, historians and filmmakers before him, is that the Greeks (like the Americans) are an exceptional nation, in their essential humanity and embrace of liberty, qualities that the 'backward' Persians were entirely lacking. This is a convenient fallacy that is, in actual fact, far from reality and one that ignores notable Persian achievements in science, mathematics, architecture and engineering. The film's portrayal of Persians was roundly criticised by Iranian journalists, and Omid Memarian wrote, 'Not only does it give the wrong outcomes to battles, it grossly misrepresents the Persians and their civilization' (cited in Joneidi 2007). *300* was perceived by Iranians as part of a wider cultural and ideological campaign by the United States against Iran, a country that Bush had declared part of the 'axis of evil' in 2002 (Bush 2002b). A daily Iranian newspaper *Ayandeh-No* carried the headline 'Hollywood declares war on Iranians' (cited in Joneidi 2007), and President Ahmadinejad himself even entered the fray, 'They are trying to tamper with history . . . by making Iran's image look savage' (cited in Perkis 2007).

While Leonidas and the brave three hundred are all killed, the film cannot conclude its narrative with Leonidas's death and defeat, as this is not the material foundational myths are made of. Leonidas's sacrifice, replete with christomimetic pose, is shown to rally the reluctant city states all over Greece to unite and form an army against their common enemy, defeating the Persians at the subsequent Battle of Platea in 479 BC. It is only at the film's climax that it becomes clear that the narrator of the film, Dilios, has been telling the story to Greeks all across the land in a hortatory narrative to inspire hatred of their dark-skinned enemies. However, his tale is not just directed towards the diegetic Greeks of the film, but also at contemporary Western audiences beyond the frames of the screen. Joanna Paul wrote, 'The Persians are represented in the way that they are because they have *become* so in Dilios' telling; and they have become so for the specific purpose of inflating the story, the enemy, and Leonidas' defeat of them, so that it will inspire the Greeks for the next battle' (2013: 78–9; emphasis in original). Yet even this involves a substantial rewrite of history that ignores the Persian sack of Athens (Book VIII of Herodotus's *Histories*) and the Persian defeat at Salamis, which led to Xerxes returning the vast majority of his forces to Persia, only leaving a smaller army behind to be defeated at Platea.

To the Spartans the Persians are 'beasts' and 'motherless dogs', just as American enemies through the decades have been Gooks, Nips, Rag Heads or Hajis. *300* is a film that glamorises the warrior cult and destruction of one's inhuman foes, not far removed from the likes of *Black Hawk Down*, *Zero Dark Thirty* and *Act of Valour*. Thus, the film functions as a manifestation of the Bush Doctrine in its call for the slaughter of Muslims in the name of freedom, a slaughter that is both necessary and morally justified. It would be hard to find a more potent cultural artefact emblematic of American cultural attitudes towards the Middle East in the era, and, as Hamid Dabashi memorably suggested, 'If we ever forget what G.W Bush's America felt like, it will take only ten minutes of *300* to remind us' (cited in James 2009: 20).

'YOU WILL NEVER FORGET': AMERICAN HISTORY AND MYTH IN THE ALAMO

You will remember this battle! Each minute! Each second! Until the day that you die! But that is for tomorrow, gentlemen. For today, Remember The Alamo!

Sam Houston, *The Alamo*

A number of the cherished stories about the Alamo have no basis in historical fact, but have moved out of the earthly realm of reality into the stratosphere of myth.

David J. Weber (cited in Flores 2002)

There are considerable parallels between the narrative that has been constructed around Thermopylae in 480 BC and that of the Battle of the Alamo in 1836. Not long after it was fought, the engagement at the Alamo even came to be referred to by many as the 'Thermopylae of Texas', and for many years a plaque bearing the same inscription has been placed at the monument to the Alamo in San Antonio, Texas. Like its ancient counterpart, the defining event in the Texas War for Independence is also understood as a heroic defence of freedom against vastly superior numbers, by men willing to give their lives in the pursuit of a noble cause. In both, even though the battle itself is lost, ultimately a greater victory is achieved when the values for which the conflict is fought inspire their fellow countrymen to prevail against their enemies, whether at the Battle of Platea (479 BC) or the Battle of San Jincento (1836). The Alamo even has its own Xerxes in the figure of General Antonio López de Santa Anna, the Mexican dictator who is habitually portrayed as a preening narcissist and sexual predator, commanding an army, not of slaves like Xerxes, but, according to accounts so often repeated that they have become established lore, convicts and young men stolen from neighbouring villages in order to satisfy his thirst for revenge against those that would steal Texas from him.

This is very much how the tale of the Alamo has been told and received by generations of Americans since 1836, and it has become a formative moment in the creation of a national imaginary for the United States and an object of American cathexis almost two hundred years before the events of 9/11. Yet, like 9/11, it is a traumatic event that has been co-opted by a variety of figures and given symbolic status in many ways disconnected from historical reality. Any interpretation that casts doubt on the essential tenets of this sacred narrative has seen itself largely marginalised, ignored or erased from the national discourse. In a similar vein, those who attempted to situate 9/11 in a historical and political context were labelled 'anti-American' or 'terrorist sympathisers'. As Bill Groneman observed, 'The traditional and incorrect view of the Alamo battle is that every man there made a conscious choice to die gloriously in its defense. Any scenario which deviated from that preconceived notion, such as the willing surrender of any of its defenders, has hardly been tolerated over the years' (1994: 88). It is hard to underestimate the cultural importance of the Alamo not only for the state of Texas, but for the whole of the United States. It was described as one of the quintessential 'Master Symbols' of the American experience by Richard R. Flores, and such is its enduring power that this prevailing understanding of the event seems legitimate and almost objective. However, it conceals an acutely ideological discourse on racial superiority, American exceptionalism and moral certainty that has cast a significant spell over many political figures in the years since. In this way the perspective taken on the Alamo is reminiscent of interpretations of 9/11 in the early years of the new millennium: a refusal to acknowledge political and historical context, the acceptance of moral binarism instead of an awareness of complexity and ambiguity, the erasure of dissenting voices and an embrace of more palatable mythic interpretations that offer a highly politicised and restricted understanding of the events themselves.

Representing the history of the Alamo is a precarious task for any historian, novelist or filmmaker given that its shadow loomed over the United States throughout the nineteenth and twentieth centuries. As Mark Cousins (2003) suggested, 'The Alamo will always, for conservative America, be a reminder to be vigilant and, if necessary, fight'. As one may expect, films made about the Alamo have historically tended to embody the prevailing concerns of the decades in which they are made: from the white supremacist *The Martyrs of the Alamo* (1915) to the Cold War rallying cry of John Wayne's *The Alamo* (1960). Randy Roberts and James S. Olson suggested that the 1960 film evoked 'parallels between Santa Anna's Mexico and Khrushchev's Soviet Union, as well as Hitler's Germany. All three demanded lines in the sand and resistance to death' (2001: 474). It has been said that John Wayne even hoped that his interpretation of the battle would 'sell America to countries threatened with Communist domination . . . [and] put new heart and faith into the world's free people' (cited in Slotkin 1998: 515–16). Wayne was not the only one to find parallels between the Alamo and America's Cold War era conflicts: General Kearie L. Berry stated, 'As the growing menace of Communism seeks to enslave the world, free men everywhere must "Remember the Alamo"' (cited in Linenthal 1988: 515). Just a few years later President Lyndon Johnson stated that he considered Vietnam to be 'just like the Alamo' (cited in Sidey 1968: 32). Thus, the Alamo narrative functions as a uniquely malleable American metaphor whose symbolic value has become much more important than the historical realities of the event itself. Those interpretations that have been more readily embraced – Jose Enrique de la Pena's memoirs *With Santa Anna in Texas: A Personal Narrative of the Revolution* (1975) and Richard Penn Smith's *Colonel Crockett's Exploits and Adventures in Texas* (1836) – are those that emphasise the heroic last stand mythology in which every last man was an unambiguous hero who fought and died for enlightened humanitarian principles. These accounts perform a hagiographic valorisation of the Alamo defenders, in particular the 'Holy Trinity' of Davy Crockett, William Travis and Jim Bowie (see Figure 24). They also inflate both the numbers and the casualties of the Mexican army, portray Santa Anna as a calculating, cruel and strategically incompetent despot, and have become the basis for the legend of the Alamo that endures until today. Those reports that depart from this last stand mythology have been, until recently, largely ignored, purged and forgotten, much as how Iraqi and Afghanistani perspectives on the war on terror have been rejected by the American media. Dan Kilgore even received death threats for challenging one of the Alamo's fundamental events in his book *How Did Davy Die?* (1975), and Philip Thomas Tucker's meticulously researched *Exodus from the Alamo. The Anatomy of the Stand Myth* (2010) was vociferously criticised for its deconstruction of many of the quintessential myths at the heart of the Alamo narrative. Tucker's book opens with the provocative sentence, 'Almost everything Americans have been taught, or think they know, about the Alamo, is not only wrong, it is nearly the antithesis of what really occurred on the morning of March 6, 1836' (2010: vii).

After 9/11 a new version of the story was swiftly given the green light by Touchstone Pictures (a subsidiary of Walt Disney Studios), and one can understand the appeal of this iconic moment in US history at such a turbulent time. The head of Disney, Michael Eisner, was explicit about the political (and perhaps economic motivations) behind the film that he believed would 'capture the post-September 11 surge in patriotism' (cited in McCrisken and Pepper 2005: 207). The new version, directed by John Lee Hancock, self-consciously frames itself as a revisionist text with a shift towards historical accuracy and authenticity that seeks to refute the melodrama of the John Wayne film, which according to Frank Thomas, who acted as a historical advisor to Hancock's *The Alamo*, 'contains not word, character, costume, or event that corresponds to historical reality in any way' (2008: 71). This desire is evident in its remarkably accurate set and period costumes, its removal of many of the defining moments of the battle that have come to be challenged by some historians (for example, cutting Travis's famous 'line in the sand', having the climactic battle not during the day but at night and confining Bowie to bed for much of the siege instead of having him heroically man the battlements) and its wish to humanise the iconic figures of Crockett, Travis and Bowie. Yet, despite this desire, John Lee Hancock's film cannot bring itself to mount a sustained challenge to such a firmly entrenched national myth, and it perpetuates many of the fantasies around the Alamo just as John Wayne's film did several decades before, albeit in a narrative clothed in the veneer of historical accuracy. While it is a richly textured film, keenly aware of the allure of mythology, it is almost paralysed by the desire to simultaneously truthfully recreate *and* valorise an event of such cultural and historical significance. Even though it made these concessions to modern audience sensibilities, *The Alamo* failed to strike a chord with contemporary America as Eisner had hoped it would, and is now recorded as one of the biggest financial disasters of all time, having cost about $150 million to produce and only having generated $25 million at the world-wide box office.

John Lee Hancock's cast of characters are familiar variations on those that have been seen before, but with a more sustained attempt at historical verac-ity than previous accounts. Jim Bowie (Jason Patric) is a charismatic leader of men, but he is shown to have a cruel streak and a tremendous capacity for violence while William Travis (Patrick Wilson) is portrayed as a narcissist, introduced as he is at the start of the film buying his immaculately tailored uniform, before coldly leaving his wife and children for the chance of fame and glory – later redeeming himself in his heroic leadership and death at the Alamo. It is Davy Crockett (Billy Bob Thornton) who emerges as the film's most compelling presence and an encapsulation of its problematic attempt to reconcile history and fantasy. The film shows that Crockett was a legend even before his arrival at the Alamo: something that brings him adulation, but is also a terrible burden that ultimately results in his own death. He is intro-duced attending the stage show 'based' on his own life, *The Lion of the West*, the source of many of the greatest Crockett myths: the romantic fairytales of wrestling bears, jumping rivers, catching cannonballs and a man able to 'whip his weight in wildcats'. However, Crockett is keenly aware of the distinction between the public persona of 'Davy Crockett' and himself, David Crockett, even if those around him are not. He acknowledges that he only wears the famous coonskin cap because, having seen the play, people now expect it of him. His arrival at the Alamo is not portrayed as some grand heroic gesture or idealistic pursuit of liberty, but one of a more practical nature. After being defeated in a bid for re-election to the US House of Representatives, the Texas War for Independence offers him an opportunity for a second chance of a political career and financial security. Thornton's delivery of the line, 'I was given to believe that that the fighting was over ... ain't it?' reveals a man not as eager to sacrifice himself in a battle against tyranny and oppression as many have historically thought. Yet, as well as these humanising touches, Hancock provides him with several overtly mythological scenes that embrace the Davy Crockett lore: a miraculous rifle shot that punctures Santa Anna's shoulder braid from several hundred metres away, a poignant fiddling duel with the Mexican army band on the battlements of the Alamo, ensuring that it is him who first sees the Mexican assault on the thirteenth day of the siege and finally in his defiant reaction to his imminent execution *after* the battle has ended.

Figure 24   The heroic triumvirate: one of the central Master Symbols of American
history is portrayed in *The Alamo* (2004), but some truths prove too
unpalatable for American audiences even almost two hundred years later.

Crockett's characterisation is a personification of the film's struggle to deconstruct the binary divisions in the master narrative of the Alamo that have
become so firmly ingrained in the American understanding of the event.
Hancock presents the cause they are fighting for as a largely unproblematic
pursuit of freedom and liberty from the despotic Santa Anna. The idea that
those defending the Alamo may have been fighting for more material and
pragmatic reasons, like the promise of six hundred and forty acres of prime
farming, or that they refused to adhere to the Mexican constitution and pay
Mexican taxes, becomes erased so as not to detract from their unambiguous
heroism. Similarly the taboo of slave ownership and its inherent connection
to the drive for Texan independence from Mexico is also expunged from the
text. While Hancock's version does concede that both Travis and Bowie own
slaves, it ignores the fact that a large number of the Alamo defenders were
slave owners or aspired to be slave owners themselves.[9] Thus, the freedoms
for which the Alamo defenders are willing to risk their lives included the
freedom to own slaves, as Mexico had abolished slavery in 1824.[10] Rather
than a minor historical footnote as the film portrays it, Philip Thomas Tucker

states, 'The issues and divisions over slavery served as a primary cause of the Texas Revolution, without which there would have been no struggle for the Alamo' (2010: 13). This highly subjective perspective on freedom is a bitterly ironic one and ignores the ramifications of Texan independence that led to the continued enslavement of thousands of African-Americans who remained slaves because of the Texan's great moral victory against oppression. These are inconvenient truths that are unpalatable for Americans who were raised to believe that the Alamo was an idealistic and unambiguous fight for justice and freedom – a romanticised vision disconnected from the muddled realities of statehood and national identity. Similarly the strategic importance of the Alamo is inflated in the film as it has often been in narratives about the conflict. One character remarks, 'This fort is the only thing that stands between Santa Anna and our settlements. As goes the Alamo, so goes Texas.' Yet many, whether they participated in Texan War for independence at the time or wrote about it long after the fact, have challenged this assumption. Historian H. W. Brands suggested, 'San Antonio wasn't essential to the Texan cause. It was too far from the American settlements, too close to the rest of Mexico, too hard to defend. The war would never be won at San Antonio, but it might be lost there' (2004: 288). The Alamo myth requires that the defenders gave their lives for a strategically vital and noble cause; thus, historical and political context finds itself marginalised in favour of the simplified concept of fighting for freedom against tyranny – an act that is decidedly reminiscent not just of George Bush's post-9/11 rhetoric, but of the words of many other leaders taking their country to war regardless of their nationality.

A corollary to this is apparent in the portrayal of the Mexican enemy as an unambiguous Other who are shown to be fighting for no reason except to crush the freedoms of those defending the Alamo. It cannot be contemplated that Santa Anna may have been in any way justified for attempting to prevent the illegal secession from Mexican land. Thus, while the Alamo defenders are plucky 'citizen soldiers' ready to sacrifice themselves for a greater cause, the characterisation of Santa Anna and his army is one-dimensional and certainly mirrors the representation of the faceless insurgents in films about the war in Iraq or the Persian army in *300*. Despite Thomas's claims that 'the motives of the Mexican army are presented with respect and understanding' (2008: 73), Santa Anna is shown to be a pompous egotist and a sexual predator, a man for whom a crystal dinner set is more important than the lives of his men. He is presented as having little understanding of battlefield tactics (where much evidence actually exists to the contrary): he ignores sound tactical advice from his generals, refuses to delay his assault on the Alamo for a single day when the delivery of a large cannon could have a decisive effects on the siege and he asks, 'What are the lives of soldiers . . . but so many chickens?' For the Alamo myth to resonate and function correctly, Santa Anna simply *has to be* the epitome of evil like some figure from a Campbell myth or a Proppian fairytale trope, a bloodthirsty tyrant and a deviant who cruelly offers 'No quarter' to the Alamo defenders.[11] The film presents Santa Anna's racial hatred for the Texans as further justification for the Texan revolution, but given the inherent racism of the received Alamo narrative, to emphasise Santa Anna's racial prejudice shows a remarkable lack of awareness of how the Alamo has played a decisive role in the racial stereotyping of Mexicans ever since. While for America the Battle of Alamo is a site of heroism and honour, for Mexicans it is a site that functions painfully as 'a reminder, a memorial to a stigmatized identity' (Flores 2002: 11), or as Leo Valdez suggested a 'bastion of racism and oppression' (cited in Linenthal 1988: 528).

The Battle of the Alamo (but not the film) concludes with Santa Anna's pre-dawn attack that is portrayed not as evidence of his tactical ingenuity, but rather his perfidy. The film shows a battle in which every one of the defenders dies as a hero, rather than an encounter, which Tucker suggests was more like a 'disastrous chain of miscalculations and erroneous decisions' (2010: 159). The film obfuscates Travis's poor strategic planning and preparation (lack of defensive preparation, not posting sufficient guards, not taking armaments from the city on withdrawal, ignoring reports and fatal overconfidence after the successful campaigns of 1835) in favour of his redemption through violence and his self-sacrifice. The film cannot bring itself to address one of the central elements of the battle that has been growing currency in the last few decades, but that still remains ignored by the public at large, that when the cause was lost, a large number of the defenders may have (understandably) fled for their lives. Alan C. Hufines in *Blood of Noble Men: The Alamo, Siege and Battle* (1999) concedes that 'a large group of Texian defenders' fled the Alamo, but the idea is so contentious that he relegates such an important event to his footnotes (176). Instead the film shows Travis dying a hero (after having earlier picked up a Mexican cannonball and saved Davy Crockett's life), not committing suicide as some historians now speculate (see Tucker 2010: 231). Jim Bowie, while he is confined to his bed, does not die in his sleep, but dies fighting, brandishing two pistols and reaching for his infamous Bowie knife before being killed by several Mexicans. After the battle Crockett is the only one left alive and faces Santa Anna himself as the film exchanges one heroic myth for another. It is at this point that the film jettisons its attempt to reconcile myth and reality and becomes one more example of American cinema choosing to 'print the legend'. Knowing that he is about to die, he finally assumes the role of 'Davy' rather than David by defiantly stating, 'Tell him [Santa Anna] I am prepared to discuss the terms of his surrender.' Santa Anna, in yet another act of cruelty and cowardice, orders Crockett's execution against the pleas from his men for lenience. Crockett's final words are, 'I'm a screamer,' as he directly quotes the play *The Lion of the West* that he had been shown attending at the start of the film.

However, the film cannot end on the loss of the Alamo. Just as how *300, United 93* and *World Trade Center* transmogrify defeat into victory, so does Hancock's film. *The Alamo* shows how the heroic battle against tyranny, injustice and oppression inspired the Texans to unify and fight at the Battle of San Jincento where the Mexican army is crushed and the arrogant Santa Anna is finally disgraced and defeated. The concluding images of the film are not even from the Battle of San Jincento, but of Crockett himself, whose execution was off-screen and who is never actually shown to die, thus allowing the mythology surrounding him to resonate. Hancock returns to the battlements of the Alamo in an elegiac flashback to the duelling fiddle scene from near the start of the siege. The ending is a fitting one for a film that has flirted with historical revisionism but that in the end embraces myth. The battle of the Alamo, while it took place in 1836, continues to be fought in every book or film about it released, or every time it is evoked by a politician, where it has come to function as shorthand for manifest destiny and American exceptionalism (see Poe). Philip French (2004) was right to call Hancock's *The Alamo* 'clearly a post 9/11 movie' in its portrayal of a just war that needed to be fought, one that was not started, but had to be continued. In this way 'Remember the Alamo' and 'Remember 9/11' become symbolically intertwined in the American cultural imaginary. The Alamo narrative is a quasi-spiritual one for Americans, as Edward Tabor Linenthal suggested: 'Like the Exodus story in ancient Israel, the saga of the Alamo has become part of the storehouse of patriotic symbols, just as its heroes and "lessons" have become the measure of each new generation and each new set of crises' (1988: 510). Yet it is a story that is still relevant today, not for these reasons, but others, as Philip Thomas Tucker astutely points out.

> Given the United States' current wars in Afghanistan and Iraq, it all the more behooves us to better understand our past and present military involvements, especially in foreign lands. We must endeavor to strip away as many myths and prejudices as possible in order to more correctly see ourselves, as well as opposing viewpoints of other lands, cultures, ethnic groups, especially those of our enemies. (Tucker 2010: 7)

The taglines used for the marketing of *The Alamo* – 'Ordinary men: extraordinary heroes' and 'You will never Forget' – could easily have been used for Paul Greengrass's *United 93* or Oliver Stone's *World Trade Center*.[12] The Battle of the Alamo is malleable enough to shift its relevance from generation to generation and act as a rally cry for a just war through World War Two, Vietnam or the post-9/11 era. While James E. Crisp was writing about the Battle of the Alamo in 1836, he may just as easily have been writing about September 11th 2001 when he stated, 'Myths offer the false comfort of simplicity, and this simplicity is accomplished by the selective silencing of the past' (2005: 178).

When, in 2003, President George W. Bush was asked by journalist Bob Woodward about his own place in history he infamously answered, 'History ... We don't know. We'll all be dead' (cited in Leung 2007). More than a hundred years before Abraham Lincoln had pondered the very same question and suggested, 'We cannot escape history. We of this Congress and this administration, will be remembered in spite of ourselves. No personal significance, or insignificance, can spare one or another of us. The fiery trial through which we pass, will light us down, in honor or dishonor, to the latest generation' (Lincoln 1862). Many were incredulous at the inanity of Bush's remarks and saw them as a demonstration of his nonchalant attitude towards the Presidency, but in hindsight they seem entirely representative of Bush's awareness and understanding of history. The historical films produced during the post-9/11 years were of varying quality and richness, but their importance should not be underestimated, as films are of central importance as to how historical events are viewed by the public at large, and they often emerge as a contentious battleground for the collective memory of the past. In short, they play 'an exceptionally powerful role in shaping our culture's understanding of the past, an influence that derives not simply from the cinema's unequalled ability to recreate the past in a sensual, mimetic form, but also from its striking tendency to arouse critical and popular controversy that resonates throughout the public sphere' (Burgoyne 2008: 1). In so doing, as Anton Kaes suggested, for good or ill 'history, thus returns forever – as film' (1989: 198).

Notes

1. Susan Aronstein suggested that '*First Knight*, like Bill Clinton, offered Americans a community of hope in which citizens served each other and America fulfilled its humanitarian responsibilities to a global village' (2009: 168).
2. Many suggested that it distorted history in *favour* of the Muslims. Dr. Jonathan Philips, a lecturer in history at London University, suggested, 'It's Osama bin Laden's version of history. It will fuel the Islamic fundamentalists' (cited in Edwardes 2004).
3. As well as these we may have looked to films like *Centurion*, which was co-funded by Pathé, the UK Film Council and Warner Bros., *Agora* (2009) and *The Last Legion* (2007) and the TV series *Rome* (HBO 2005–7) and *Spartacus: Blood and Sand* (Starz 2010).
4. In private conversation with the author Kevin MacDonald commented, 'The primary goal for me as a director was to make a film which had contemporary resonance, to make something like *The Eagle* which is obviously set in the past but certainly relevant to audiences today. It seemed to be that the original book explores the relationship between an empire and the people that it invades and oppresses – and there was a very obvious and definite parallel there between Iraq and more specifically Afghanistan. So one of the decisions we made to highlight that parallel was to cast American actors as the Romans and very deliberately have them speaking in their own accents, I suppose trying to make people see them as Marines' (MacDonald 2012).

5. The subsequent DVD release revealed that McDonald had originally filmed a more challenging ending that was not favoured by test audiences. In it Aquila's rejection of Rome is more pronounced and he does not return the Eagle; instead he melts it down in the burial grounds of those that died fighting over it. He says, 'The Eagle doesn't belong to Rome. It belongs to the men who died fighting in the name of honour: Romans *and* Britons. My father and [to Esca] yours' (emphasis in original).

6. *The 300 Spartans* turns its attention to the Soviet Union with the huge army of mindless and enslaved Persians led by Xerxes, a sexually debauched cruel and despotic leader seeking to take over the free world. The film is widely perceived as a defining anti-Soviet allegory and draws on Domino Theory rhetoric by viewing Sparta as an inspiration to the free world whose fall will precipitate the end of Western civilisation.

7. Here we are able to see echoes between the view of the world promoted by *Act of Valour* and *300*. Interestingly Kurt Waugh was a screenwriter on both films.

8. 'Freedom isn't Free' is carved into a wall at the Korean War veteran memorial in Washington, D. C. In *Team America: World Police* (2009) Trey Parker and Matt Stone featured a heavily satirical song called 'Freedom isn't Free'.

9. The film introduces this angle briefly by having Bowie's slave, Sam, tell Travis's slave, Joe, 'Mexican law says there ain't no slaves.' Joe, who never had a surname, is one of the most compelling figures in the Alamo's history, but is rarely more than an afterthought in depiction of the conflict. After fighting in the defence of the Alamo he was spared by the Mexicans who, because of his slave status, presumed him to be a non-combatant. As their possession he was returned to the Travis family but escaped after the one-year anniversary of the battle never to be heard of again.

10. This is not to say that Mexico was an enlightened country in every way. Santa Anna did go back on his 1824 pledge of no taxes for ten years in 1830 and Mexican society was plagued by a very rigid caste system.

11. Some have suggested that this was a process instigated not by the Mexicans but actually by the Americans (see Tucker 2010: 174).

12. Similarly, the taglines for *United 93* may have been used for *The Alamo*: 'United they stood', 'Every generation has a defining moment. This is ours' and 'a true story of courage and survival' beckoned from posters in 2006.

CONCLUSION

Moreover, although the two towers have disappeared, they have not been annihilated. Even in their pulverised state, they have left behind an intense awareness of their presence. No one who knew them can cease imagining them and the imprint they made on the skyline from all points of the city. Their end in material space has borne them off into a definitive imaginary space.

Jean Baudrillard, *The Spirit of Terrorism*

One way of decoding the traumatic terror at the heart of the codification of '9/11' is in fact to read it as a form of historical amnesia, a collective repression, that corresponds best with the globalised spectacle of its having made the apparently invulnerable evidently vulnerable . . . That vulnerability was too memorable to be allowed to be remembered. Fabricating instantaneous enemies and moving targets, one on the trail of the other, thus became the principal modus operandi of the virtual empire.

Hamid Dabashi, 'Native informers and the making of the American empire'

I think that what people go to the movies for has changed since 9/11. I still think the country is in some form of PTSD about that event, and that we haven't really healed in any sort of complete way, and that people are, as a result, looking more toward escapist entertainment. And look—I get

*it. There's a very good argument to be made that only somebody who has
it really good would want to make a movie that makes you feel really bad.*
Stephen Soderbergh, 'The state of cinema 2013'

In September 2011, exactly ten years after 9/11, Kenneth Lonergan's long
delayed New York-set drama *Margaret* was finally released. The film had actually been shot six years before in 2005 and it is a text imbued with the visceral
intensity of the immediate post-9/11 years: from its heated classroom debates
about American foreign policy to its melodramatic and highly metaphorical
narrative about a privileged American teenager, Lisa (Ann Paquin), whose
momentary flirtation with a bus driver causes a crash that kills a woman who
subsequently dies messily in her arms. Like many films of the era, *Margaret*
provides us with a vivid testimony of the turbulent decade and, as Andrew
O'Hehir (2012) commented, it is like a 'time capsule from George W. Bush's
America'. O'Hehir is entirely correct, but not just about *Margaret*, as a great
many of the films produced in the post-9/11 years are like time capsules from
the past: they are dynamic and highly affective texts almost alive with the fears,
anxieties and the contradictory emotions of the decade.

While President Obama stopped using the phrase the 'war on terror' in
2008, eager to distance his administration from that of his predecessor, preferring instead to suggest that the United States was in 'a battle or war against
some terrorist organisations' (cited in Isikoff 2009), the media and the public
continued to widely use it. Even though Obama insisted it was 'time to turn
the page' (cited in MacAskill 2010: 18), American cinema found it impossible
to do so and the films that emerged from the early years of the Obama administration proved to be not so far removed from those of the Bush era. However,
as the distance between 9/11 grew, some films that may have seemed contentious or difficult to produce in the years immediately after 9/11 were green
lit and released theatrically. It is surely inconceivable that Robert Zemeckis's
Flight (2012), starring Denzel Washington as an alcoholic pilot who makes
a miraculous landing while under the influence of alcohol and drugs, could
have been made and released ten years before in 2003 when the innocuous
romantic-comedy *View from the Top* starring Gwyneth Paltrow as young
woman dreaming of becoming a flight attendant, was pushed back for more
than a year for fear of offending audiences. In 2013 two films with essentially
the same premise were released, both centring on a gratuitously presented terrorist attack on the White House. Antoine Fuqua's *Olympus Has Fallen* and
Roland Emmerich's *White House Down* are both permeated with such graphic
images of the destruction of national monuments and their narratives skirt so
closely to the events of 11 September 2001 that they are suggestive of a fundamental change in attitudes towards how 9/11 will be represented in popular
film in the decades to come (see Figures 25 and 26).

Figures 25   More than ten years after 11 September 2001, Roland Emmerich, who
and 26   had once worried that *Independence Day* (1996) may have inspired the
             terrorist attacks on 9/11, made *White House Down* (2013), an attempt
             to 'move on' from the trauma of 9/11 by returning to imagery and
             situations that would have been unthinkable in the immediate aftermath.

While Justin Chang (2011) asserted, 'Any contemporary film offering up a scenario of mass annihilation is, like it or not, a 9/11 movie', this book has tried to separate modish references to the war on terror from those films that engage with the decade in a sustained and significant fashion, focusing on texts that may reveal to us something about the underlying tensions of the era in which they were made. However, throughout this period even seemingly unconnected narratives became bound to the war on terror, like the search for weapons in the otherwise fantastical *Prince of Persia: The Sands of Time* (2010), where the antagonist Nizam convinces his nephew to attack a rival city with false claims that they are manufacturing weapons. After the city is captured, the search for the weapons continues, but, of course, they are never found. Furthermore, witness the change in emphasis in the *Harry Potter* franchise after 9/11 that becomes reflected in the progressively darker tones of the books and the films as they begin to focus on terror attacks, torture and individuals imprisoned without trial. On this narrative adjustment Judith Rauholfer commented that the books and the films, 'evolved into something more after 9/11 – a social commentary on current events. I think there are certain parallels in the way in which the Ministry of Magic deals with the Voldemort threat and the way the British government deals with the terrorist threat' (cited in Fleming 2007).

The summer of 2013 saw the release of several films that proved that 9/11 and the war on terror remained of significant interest to filmmakers and public alike. While it was the case that films that dealt directly with the wars in Iraq and Afghanistan had, for the most part, stopped being made (Peter Berg's *Lone Survivor* is a notable exception), science-fiction and horror films like *Man of Steel* and *World War Z* continued to find themselves embroiled in debates about the effects of 9/11 and the war on terror on American film:

- While *Iron Man 3* was severely criticised by Manohla Dargis (2013) for the way it 'invokes Sept. 11 and dodges it' leading to it being called 'at once inherently political and empty', it incorporates many of the defining issues of the previous decade into its narrative in a startling fashion for 'just' a comic-book film. By addressing the ethics and efficacy of drone technology, the moral equivalencies between terrorism and big business and even sending one of its heroes (who has his name rebranded from War Machine to the Iron Patriot) to Pakistan in order to locate a suspected terrorist, the film reveals itself to be deeply immersed in the post-9/11 era. The narrative begins shortly after the almost apocalyptic events of *Marvel Avengers Assemble* (discussed in Chapter 5) and features Tony Stark suffering from conspicuous symptoms of PTSD and even flashbacks as a result of the trauma from his near-death experience. His admission, 'Nothing's been the same since New York. You experience things and then they are over. I can't sleep and when I do, I have nightmares,' bleeds out from the screen into the real world. Tony is forced back into action when suicide bombs (detonated by wounded army veterans) are exploded all over America, creating a state of terror and panic across the country. In a series of televised messages a bin Laden-esque villain called the Mandarin takes responsibility for the attacks. He states, 'Some people call me a terrorist. I call myself a teacher. America ready for another lesson?' Tony offers the Mandarin a personal challenge very much in the same vein as Bush's ill-considered 'Bring em on' message to Iraqi insurgents, insisting, 'There's no politics here, just good old-fashioned revenge.' Tony later discovers that the Mandarin is just a fabrication created by those in power behind the scenes/screens, an actor playing a role calculated to resemble how we have come to expect terrorists to look and behave post-9/11– satirising our fears of the Other with his Asian robes, Arabic beard and speeches decrying American Imperialism.

- *Star Trek into Darkness* (2013) provides yet another big-budget science-fiction war on terror narrative, tapping into the franchises' penchant for allegory since the original television series in the 1960s. The crew of the USS *Enterprise* are sent across the galaxy to assassinate a suspected terrorist, the charismatic Khan (Benedict Cumberbatch), responsible for a devastating bomb attack on London and the murder of Captain James T. Kirk's (Chris Pine) mentor and father-figure Christopher Pike. Kirk is desperate for revenge but he is challenged by his crew about the ethics of an extra-judicial assassination rather than apprehending the suspect for trial. It transpires that their commanding officer Admiral Marcus has used Khan to create WMD and engineer a false flag war against the Klingon Empire. The film ends with Kirk's eulogy at Pike's memorial service, which functions as a commentary on the excesses of George W. Bush's ill-advised unilateral foreign policy decisions. He says, 'There will always be those who mean to do us harm. To stop them, we risk awakening the same evil within ourselves. Our first instinct is to seek revenge when those we love are taken from us. But that's not who we are.' One of the stars of the film, Benedict Cumberbatch, said, 'It's no spoiler I think to say that there's a huge backbone in this film that's a comment on recent U.S. interventionist overseas policy from the Bush, Cheney and Rumsfeld era' (cited in Toto 2013). While *Star Trek into Darkness* is a formulaic and largely one-dimensional throwaway summer blockbuster, that it is able to ask more questions about the legitimacy of American foreign policy post-9/11 than a film like *Zero Dark Thirty* is a sad indictment of contemporary American cinema's engagement with real-world politics.

- Guillermo del Toro's *Pacific Rim* (2013) offers a significant departure from the America-centrism of many of the alien-invasion narratives discussed in Chapter 6 in its resolutely global focus on international cooperation. Not coincidentally it takes place twelve years after the catastrophic traumatic attack of a race of aliens known as Kaiju that del Toro commented was like a '9/11 that creates this world' (cited in Lamar 2012). The film warns that unilateralism is a path to destruction and that the only way to fight back is as an international community.

Figure 27   *Pacific Rim* (2013) reveals that 9/11 and the war on terror remained of
significant interest to filmmakers and public alike.

As the hero Raleigh Beckett says, the 'world came together pooling its
resources and throwing aside old rivalries for the sake of the greater
good'. Alongside its huge mech (a robot controlled by a human) versus
alien battles, the film finds time to offer a commentary on the com-
mercialisation of trauma and provides a narrative that teaches that
the need for 'vengeance is like an open wound'. The key to humanity's
victory emerges as not its ability to build giant war machines but for
people to develop empathetic links with one another and even with the
aliens themselves (see Figures 27 and 28).

While these three films each engage with aspects of the tumultuous post-
9/11 decade, they are severely constrained by the demands of the Hollywood
blockbuster that define their construction. Thus, they are able to offer some
criticism of the ideologies of the war on terror, while at the same time revel-
ling in the currency of destruction and devastation that has become par for
their genre. Yet in the absence of American films that explicitly portrayed the
war on terror on the screen from critical perspectives, a counter-narrative as
opposed to the master narrative, they were very often all that were left for
American audiences. These films may appropriate the trauma of 11 September
2001 and the war on terror for entertainment, but they are entirely symptomatic of how America has disavowed and rewritten the events of 9/11. We
can see this process even in the lexicography that surrounds the events of
11 September 2001: phrases we came to know well like 'first responders'

Figure 28   An aerial view of Ground Zero taken in the days after 9/11. Public
domain image. Taken by Andrea Booher ©.

and 'sleeper cells', and even the phrases 'Ground Zero' and '9/11' itself. It is
highly ironic, although has gone largely unobserved, that the phrase Ground
Zero became culturally appropriated to describe the location of the New York
attacks with a characteristic disavowal of its historical use in the American
bombings of Hiroshima and Nagasaki in 1945. What are the implications
of such an unrecognised appropriation? What connections does it establish
between the great trauma of the atomic bombings and the events of 9/11?
Given that America perpetrated that earlier traumatic event, which has subsequently been rewritten as necessary, just and ethical over the ensuing decades
(with a distinct absence of debate or any sense of moral accountability),
despite the considerable evidence to the contrary that now exists (see Dowe
1996; Lifton 2003; Mitchell 2011). However, as Gene Ray observed in *Terror
and the Sublime in Art and Critical Theory: From Auschwitz to Hiroshima to
September 11 and Beyond* (2005), the links between the two acts are unthink-
able to the American public (136–41). Surely this is the pre-eminent example
of cognitive dissonance in the post-9/11 decade? It is a gesture that is symptomatic of the primacy of American experience, victimhood and subjectivity,
which was revivified and reaffirmed by America cinema in the decade after
9/11.[1]

It is tempting to see 9/11 as the great missed opportunity of US history, when the country experienced a colossal rupturing event and had the opportunity to redefine what American responsibility and prerogative may come to mean in the new millennium. However, instead of 'working through' its trauma the Bush administration strove to 'act out' and consolidate its hegemonic status as a global superpower, fighting disastrous wars in the Middle East and alienating many of its allies in the process. Joan Didion in her memorable essay 'Fixed ideas: America since 9/11' rightly discerned the mood in America in the immediate post-9/11 period:

> [W]hat had happened was being processed, obscured, systematically leached of history and so of meaning, finally rendered less readable than it had seemed on the morning it had happened. As if overnight, the irreconcilable event had been made manageable, reduced to the sentimental, to protective talismans, totems, garlands of garlic, repeated pieties that would come to seem in some ways as destructive as the event itself. We now had 'the loved ones,' we had 'the families,' we had 'the heroes'. (Didion 2003: 54)

Not only did the Bush administration estrange itself from those without, but also those within, as citizens looked more critically on their own nation and government than at any time since the Vietnam War. Susan Faludi asserted that the Bush administration's attempt to create safety and security only put America in greater danger:

> By living in a myth, we made the world and ourselves less secure. By refusing to grapple with the actual failures that led to 9/11 and by refusing to listen to the people who tried to call attention to those failures, the nation denied its citizenry any real accounting of the missteps that led to catastrophe and any real assurance that we were any better equipped to prevent or repel another terrorist attack. (Faludi 2007: 293–4)

In many ways American cinema played a central role in perpetuating this myth, as films like *Zero Dark Thirty, Hurt Locker, Act of Valour, Transformers, The Kingdom* and hundreds of others endorsed and reconsolidated ideas about American exceptionalism and pre-eminence around the globe, as it has done for decades. Like the Bush administration sought to simplify and prevent any serious consideration of the reasons for why the attacks on 9/11 were perpetrated, the majority of American films in the post-9/11 era reaffirmed the power and moral authority of the United States in the national imaginary. This is how popular cinema has historically functioned. It is easy to dismiss it as harmless entertainment with the phrase 'It's only a movie', but in doing so it only becomes more resonant. American cinema has rarely created images of itself as it is, but rather, as André Bazin suggested, it 'has been able, in an extraordinarily competent way, to show American society just as it wanted to see itself' (1968: 143–4).

This book has spent much of its time considering allegorical accounts of the era, which I contend were often much more significant than those that attempted to portray 9/11 and the war on terror directly. Yet all of these films, regardless of their political perspective, fulfilled a powerful and necessary psychic function and in years to come they will be regarded as a compelling testimony of the era. In the introduction I quoted Cathy Caruth's statement that 'a traumatic event cannot be "assimilated" or experienced fully at the time, but only *belatedly*, in its repeated possession of the one who experienced it' (1995: 4; emphasis in original). Now, more than ten years after 11 September 2001, it is undoubtedly the time to reflect on the trauma of 9/11, the war on terror and the films that it inspired and continues to inspire. If it is true, as Susannah Radstone has argued, that films 'have the potential to provide a cultural "working through" of traumatic memories' (2010: 334), what has been the effects of post-9/11 American cinema and its steadfast refusal to contemplate the political and historical realities of 9/11? It is a cinema that has largely chosen fantasy over reality, like Piscine 'Pi' Patel did in Ang Lee's *Life of Pi*. Certainly denial and negation are powerful self-defence mechanisms, but they are profoundly unable to reconcile the subject with its trauma in the long term and historically have 'only succeeded in incubating, not obliterating the threat' (Smelser 2004: 51). Accordingly, we may see a reflection of America's relationship with the cinema screen in Van der Kolk's suggestion, 'When the trauma fails to be integrated into the totality of a person's life experiences, the victim remains fixated on the trauma. Despite avoidance of emotional involvement, traumatic memories cannot be avoided; even when pushed out of waking consciousness, they come back in the form of reenactments, nightmares or feelings related to the trauma' (1987: 5).[2] Yet it is imperative to remember that the defining films about the Vietnam War were not made until after the conflict had ended, that is, more than twenty years after it began. The fact that films like *The Hurt Locker*, *In the Valley of Elah* and *Redacted* were made so shortly after the outbreak of the war is indication of a shift in the way that the American film industry is prepared to address modern conflicts, even if they do so in only a limited fashion. Certainly America has yet to produce a new millennial equivalent to those epoch-defining texts like *The Deer Hunter*, *Apocalypse Now* or *Platoon*, which embody the era regardless of their political perspective. This may be seen as an indication that the defining films of the war on terror era have yet to be made – and whether they ever will be remains to be seen.

Figures 29   *Adam & Steve* (2005): before and after 9/11. Just as a bright image
and 30   continues to appear on one's retina long after the original has
              disappeared, 9/11 is the quintessential after-image of the new millennium
              and has continued to linger on the frames of American film ever since.

NOTES

1. We can see another example of this in the appropriation of '9/11', which is now only
   used to describe the events of 11 September 2001 rather than Chile's own traumatic
   9/11 that occurred on 11 September 1973. The Chilean, coup d'état, supported
   by the CIA, saw the democratically elected Salvador Allende replaced by Augusto

Pinochet who ushered in an age of terror and repression that continues to resound as a cultural trauma more than thirty years later. The film *11'09"01 – September 11* (2002), which features eleven short films by a variety of international filmmakers from all over the globe, has a section directed by Ken Loach that explores the Chilean 9/11. At the Venice Film Festival in 2002 it received the UNESCO Award and Ken Loach's segment was the winner of the 2002 FIPRESCI prize for Best Short Film. Even so the film was released on one cinema screen in July 2003 and it was on the same weekend that the bombastic Michael Bay film *Bad Boys 2*, which name-checks 9/11, was released at 3,186 cinemas and earned nearly $50 million.

2. Originally quoted in Smelser (2004: 41).

BIBLIOGRAPHY

Anonymous, 'Palmares 2000', *Cahiers Du Cinema*, (n.d.s.), www.cahiersducinema. com/PALMARES-2000.html, accessed: 6 April 2014

Anonymous, 'Torture on TV rising and copied in the field', *Human Rights First*, (n.d.s.), accessed: 13 March 2014, secure.humanrightsfirst.org/us_law/etn/primetime/index. asp

Anonymous, 'French jokes', *About.com*, http://politicalhumor.about.com/library/ blfrenchjokes.htm

Anonymous, 'Bush urges anti-terror allies to act', *BBC*, 6 November 2001, accessed: 9 January 2014, news.bbc.co.uk/1/hi/world/europe/1642130.stm

Anonymous, 'President George Bush discussed Iraq in national press conference', *The White House*, 6 March 2003a, accessed: 28 February 2012, georgewbush-whitehouse.archives.gov/news/releases/2003/03/20030306-8.html

Anonymous, 'Bush declares war', *CNN*, 19 March 2003b, accessed: 24 May 2012, articles.cnn.com/2003-03-19/us/sprj.irq.int.bush.transcript_1_coalition-forces-equip ment-in-civilian-areas-iraqi-troops-and-equipment/2?_s=PM:US

Anonymous, 'Kerry says U.S. now has "backdoor draft"', *Associated Press*, 3 June 2004a, accessed: 7 June 2010, www.msnbc.msn.com/id/5129079

Anonymous, 'Bin Laden speaks to American people', *Reuters*, 30 October 2004b, p. A16. Anonymous (translator), 'United Airlines flight no. 93 cockpit voice recorder tran-script', *CNN*, 12 April 2006, accessed: 26 March 2014, http://i.a.cnn.net/cnn/2006/ images/04/12/flight93.transcript.pdf [Translated from Arabic.]

Anonymous, 'Filmmakers take a closer look', *Associated Press*, 12 December 2007, accessed: 15 September 2010, www.msnbc.msn.com/id/20711050

Anonymous, 'Bush: I regret saying "bring em on"', *The Huffington Post*, 11 November 2008a, accessed: 29 February 2012, www.huffingtonpost.com/2008/11/11/bush-i-regret-saying-brin_n_143109.html

Anonymous, 'Obama on Economic Crisis, Transition,' *60 Minutes*, CBS, 16 November 2008b.

Anonymous, 'CIA "often lied to congressmen", *BBC News*, 9 July 2009, accessed: 13 March 2012, news.bbc.co.uk/1/hi/world/americas/8143081.stm

Anonymous, 'How did David slay Goliath at Oscars?', *Today Movies*, 3 August 2010a, accessed: 8 September 2010, today.msnbc.msn.com/id/35770342/ns/today-entertainment

Anonymous, 'Out of action: *The Expendables* has thrown cinema back to the bad old days of muscle-bound 1980s bombast', *The Independent*, 22 August 2010b, accessed: 29 May 2012, www.independent.co.uk/arts-entertainment/films/features/out-of-action-the-expendables--has-thrown-cinema-back-to-the-bad-old-days-of-musclebound-1980s-bombast-2055954.html

Anonymous, 'Preparedness 101: Zombie apocalypse', *CDC website*, 7 May 2011, accessed: 11 June 2012, blogs.cdc.gov/publichealthmatters/2011/05/preparedness-101-zombie-apocalypse

Anonymous, 'Marvel's *The Avengers* to close 2012 Tribeca Film Festival on April 28', 28 March 2012a, accessed: 7 November 2012a, www.tribecafilm.com/festival/media/MARVELS_THE_AVENGERS_TO_CLOSE_2012_TRIBECA_FILM_FESTIVAL__ON_APRIL_28.html

Anonymous, 'Who's the Daddy?', *Cineworld Magazine*, September 2012b, p. 17.

Anonymous, 'Intelligence and Security Committee of parliament', 7 November 2013, accessed: 9 January 2014, isc.independent.gov.uk/news-archive/7november 2013-1

Abramowitz, Rachel, 'Scared silly', *Los Angeles Times*, 8 May 2005a, p. E26.

—, 'Stone assesses Sept. 11 project', *Los Angeles Times*, 13 July 2005b, p. E1.

Acuna, Kirsten, 'John Wayne movie *The Searchers* inspired the ending to *Breaking Bad*', *Business Insider*, 1 October 2013, accessed: 2 November 2013, www.businessinsider.com/searchers-inspired-breaking-bad-ending-2013-10#ixzz2jPgdPmQ0

Adorno, Theodor, 'Cultural criticism and society', in *Prisms*, trans. Samuel and Shierry Weber (Cambridge, MA: MIT Press, 1967), pp. 17–34.

Alabassi, Mamoon, 'Two "Iraq war" movies compete for awards', *Scoop*, 24 February 2010, accessed: 21 June 2012, www.scoop.co.nz/stories/HL1002/S00202.htm

Alexander, Jeffrey C., 'Toward a theory of cultural trauma', in Jeffrey C. Alexander *et al.*, *Cultural Trauma and Collective Identity* (Berkeley and London: University of California Press, 2004), pp. 1–30.

Alford, Matthew, *Reel Power: Hollywood Cinema and American Supremacy* (London: Pluto Press, 2010).

Alvarez, Alex, 'On *60 Minutes*, ex-CIA clandestine service head defends group against "torture" allegations', *Mediaite.com*, 29 April 2012, accessed: 3 August 2013, www.mediaite.com/tv/on-60-minutes-ex-cia-clandestine-service-head-defends-group-again st-torture-allegations

Anderton, Terry, *Bush's Wars* (Oxford: Oxford University Press, 2011).

Aronstein, Susan, 'Revisiting the Round Table: Arthur's American Dream', in Marnie Hughes-Warrington (ed.), *History on Film Reader* (London and New York: Routledge, 2009), pp. 161–76.

Arrendt, Hannah, *Eichmann in Jerusalem. A Report on the Banality of Evil* (New York: Viking Press, 1965).

Au, Laurie, 'Obama notes "tragic" past', *The Star Bulletin*, 28 July 2008, accessed: 15 May 2012, archives.starbulletin.com/2008/07/28/news/story05.html

Azeb, Sophia, '*Zero Dark Thirty* and the problem of Pakistan', *The Feminist Wire*, 24 February 2003, accessed: 3 August 2013, thefeministwire.com/2013/02/zero-dark-thirty-and-the-problem-of-pakistan

Baer, Robert, *See No Evil: The True Story of a Ground Soldier in the CIA's War against Terrorism* (London, Arrow Books, 2002).

Baker, Brent, 'Letterman denounces Iraq War, Sheehan critics', *News Busters*, 3 January 2006, accessed: 3 April 2014, newsbusters.org/node/3454.

Balswick, Jack and Charles Peek, 'The inexpressive male: A tragedy of American society', in D. S. David and R. Brannon (eds), *The Forty-nine Percent Majority: The Male Sex Role* (Boston: Addison-Wesley, 1976), pp. 55–7.

Barker, Jason, *The 9/11 Wars* (London: Allen Lane, 2011).

Baron, Cynthia, '*Doctor No*: Bonding Britishness to racial sovereignty', in Christoph Linder (ed.), *The James Bond Phenomenon: A Critical Reader* (Manchester and New York: Manchester University Press, 2009), pp. 153–68.

Barthes, Roland, *Mythologies*, trans. Annette Lavers (London: Vintage, 2009).

Baudrillard, Jean, *The Spirit of Terrorism*, trans. Chris Turner. (New York: Verso Books, 2003).

Bazin, André, '*La Politique Des Auteurs*', in Peter Graham (ed.), *The New Wave* (London: Secker and Warburg, 1968), pp. 143–4.

Bell, Michael Mayerfield, 'The ghosts of place', *Theory and Society*, 26: 6 (December 1997), 813–36.

Benjamin, Walter, *The Origin of German Tragic Drama* (New York: Verso, 1977).

Bennett, Tony and Janet Woollacott, *Bond and Beyond: The Political Career of a Popular Hero* (London: Macmillan, 1987).

Bergen, Peter, '*Zero Dark Thirty*: Did torture really net bin Laden?', *CNN*, 11 December 2012, accessed: 3 August 2013, edition.cnn.com/2012/12/10/opinion/bergen-zero-dark-thirty

Berriman, Ian, 'R is for Romero', *The A–Z of Zombies*, 62 (special edition) (September 2013), 78–81.

Bhabha, Homi, 'The other question . . . Homi K. Bhabha reconsiders the stereotype and colonial discourse', *Screen*, 24: 6 (1983), 18–36.

Bigelow, Kathryn, 'Kathryn Bigelow addresses *Zero Dark Thirty* torture criticism', *Los Angeles Times*, 15 January 2013, accessed: 3 August 2013, articles.latimes.com/2013/jan/15/entertainment/la-et-mn-0116-bigelow-zero-dark-thirty-20130116

Bishop, Kyle, 'Dead man still walking: Explaining the zombie renaissance', *Journal of Popular Film and TV*, 37: 1 (2009), 16–25.

Biskind, Peter, 'Free Willis', *Vanity Fair*, June 2007, accessed: 2 May 2012, www.accessmylibrary.com/coms2/summary_0286-31284713_ITM

Boal, Mark, *Zero Dark Thirty: The Shooting Script* (New York: Newmarket Press, 2013).

Bolter, Jay David, 'Preface', in Geoff King (ed.), *The Spectacle of the Real* (Bristol: Intellect Books, 2005), pp. 9–12.

Bone, James, 'Flight 93 families weep again as their heroes die on screen', *The Sunday Times*, 27 April 2006, accessed: 21 September 2010, entertainment.timesonline.co.uk/tol/arts_and_entertainment/article709953.ece

Booker, M. Keith, *Encyclopaedia of Comic Books and Graphic Novels. Volume 1* (Westport: Greenwood, 2010).

Bowcott, Owen, 'Osama bin Laden death: Pakistan says US may have breached sovereignty', *The Guardian*, 5 May 2011, accessed: 3 August 2013, www.theguardian.com/world/2011/may/05/osama-bin-laden-pakistan-us-sovereignty

Bowden, Mark, '*Zero Dark Thirty* is not pro-torture', *The Atlantic*, 3 January 2013 accessed: 3 August 2013, www.theatlantic.com/entertainment/archive/2013/01/zero-dark-thirty-is-not-pro-torture/266759

Boyle, Kirk, '*Children of Men* and *I Am Legend*: The disaster-capitalism complex hits Hollywood', *Jump Cut*, 51 (Spring 2009), accessed: 28 December 2013, www.ejumpcut.org/archive/jc51.2009/ChildrenMenLegend/text.html

Bradshaw, Peter, 'Review', *The Guardian*, 2 June 2006, p. 11.

Brands, H. W., *Lone Star Nation: How a Ragged Army of Volunteers Won the Battle for Texan Independence – and Changed America* (New York: Doubleday, 2004).

Braudy, Leo, *The World in a Frame: What We See in Films* (Chicago: University of Chicago Press, 2002).

Brayton, Sean, 'The racial politics of disaster and dystopia in *I Am Legend*', *The Velvet Light Trap*, 67 (spring 2011), 66–76.

Brigham, Robert, K., *Iraq, Vietnam, and the Limits of American Power* (New York: Public Affairs, 2006).

Brody, Richard, '*The Avengers*: Not unlike an F-16 stunt run', *The New Yorker*, 4 May 2013, accessed: 28 January 2013, www.newyorker.com/online/blogs/movies/2012/05/the-avengers-review.html

Broeske, Pat, 'Coming to grips with Sly Stallone', *Los Angeles Times*, 14 September 1986, p. 35.

Brooks, Brian, 'Kathryn Bigelow and Mark Boal defend *Zero Dark Thirty* at NY Film Critics circle', *Movieline*, 8 January 2013, accessed: 21 November 2013, movieline.com/2013/01/08/kathryn-bigelow-mark-boal-zero-dark-thirty-new-york-film-critics-circle

Brown, Peter Falkenberg, 'A call to eliminate horror films', *Significato*, 29 December 2001, accessed: 11 July 2012, http://significatojournal.com/columns/culture-of-heart/call-to-eliminate-horror-films

Buchanan, Kyle, 'Is it possible to make a Hollywood blockbuster without evoking 9/11?', *The Vulture*, 13 June 2013, accessed: 9 November 2013, www.vulture.com/2013/06/hollywood-blockbusters-cant-stop-evoking-911.html

Burdeau, Emmaneul, 'Critique. In the shadow of 9/11', trans. Sally Shafto, *Cahiers du Cinema*, 603 (July–August 2005), accessed: 11 November 2013, www.cahiersducinema.com/Critique-In-the-Shadow-of.html

Burgoyne, Robert, *The Hollywood Historical Film* (Oxford: Blackwell Publishing, 2008).

Burr, Ty, 'The Sum of All Fears', *The Boston Globe*, 29 June 2005, p. E1.

Buscombe, Edward, *The Searchers (BFI Film Classics)* (London: BFI, 2008).

Bush, George W., '9/11 address to the nation', Washington, DC, 11 September 2001(a).

—, 'Address to a joint session of congress and the American people', Washington, DC, 20 September 2001(b).

—, 'State of the union address', Washington, DC, 29 January 2002(b).

—, 'West point address', New York, 1 June 2002(a).

—, 'Ellis Island speech', New York, 12 September 2002(c).

—, 'George Bush's address on the start of war', Washington, DC, 20 March 2003(a).

—, 'Loyalty day proclamation', Washington, DC, 30 April 2003(b).

—, 'President Bush's acceptance speech to the Republican National Convention', New York, 2 September 2004(a).

—, 'Remarks in a discussion in Clive, Iowa', Clive, Iowa, 4 October 2004(b).

Butler, Judith, *Precarious Life: The Powers of Mourning and Violence* (London: Verso, 2004).

Butterfield, Herbert, *The Whig Interpretation of History* (London: G. Bell and Sons, [1931] 1950).

Byron, Stuart, '*The Searchers*: Cult movie of the new Hollywood', *New York Magazine*, 5 March 1979, pp. 45–8.

Cameron, Irin, '*Zero Dark Thirty* goes feminist', *The Salon*, 1 February 2013, accessed: 10 August 2013, www.salon.com/2013/02/01/zero_dark_thirty_goes_feminist

Campbell, Joseph, *The Hero with a Thousand Faces* (New York: Pantheon Books, 1949).

Carnevale, Rob, '*Cloverfield* Matt Reeves interview', *indielondon*, (n.d.s.), accessed: 19 November 2012, www.indielondon.co.uk/Film-Review/cloverfield-matt-reeves-interview

Caruth, Cathy, *Trauma: Explorations in Memory* (London: Johns Hopkins University Press, 1995).

Chambliss, Julian, 'A terrible privilege: The invincible Iron Man and the burden of hegemonic power', a paper delivered at The Popular Culture Association/American Culture Association in the South Annual Conference, Nashville, Tennessee, 27 September 2012.

Chang, Justin, '9/11 lessons: A time for restraint', *Variety*, 20 August 2011, accessed: 13 December 2013, variety.com/2011/film/news/9-11-lessons-a-time-for-restraint-1118041552

Cheney, Dick, appearance on NBC's *Meet the Press*, 16 September 2001, accessed: 12 September 2010, afpakwar.com/blog/archives/576

Child, Ben, 'CIA requested *Zero Dark Thirty* rewrites, memo reveals', *The Guardian*, 7 May 2013, accessed: 3 August 2013, www.guardian.co.uk/film/2013/may/07/zero-dark-thirty-cia-memo

Chomsky, Noam, *9-11* (New York: Seven Stories Press, 2001).

Christensen, Terry, *Reel Politics: American Political Movies from Birth of a Nation to Platoon* (New York: Basil Blackwell, 1987).

Chute, Hillary, 'Temporality and seriality in Spiegelman's *In the Shadow of No Towers*', *American Periodicals: A Journal of History, Criticism and Bibliography*, 17: 2 (2007), 228–44.

Cieply, Michael, 'Families of victims complained. A 9/11 victim's family raises new objections to *Zero Dark Thirty*', *The New York Times*, 22 February 2013, accessed: 3 August 2013, www.nytimes.com/2013/02/23/movies/9-11-victims-family-raises-objection-to-zero-dark-thirty.html?_r=0

Clarke, Richard A., *Against All Enemies* (London: Free Press, 2004).

Cloud, David S., 'U.N. report faults prolific use of drone strikes by U.S.', *Los Angeles Times*, 3 June 2010, accessed: 3 August 2013, articles.latimes.com/2010/jun/03/world/la-fg-cia-drones-20100603

Cohen, Kfir, 'Narrating the global: pedagogy and disorientation in Syriana', *Jump Cut: A Review of Contemporary Media*, 54 (fall 2012), accessed: 28 February 2013, www.ejumpcut.org/currentissue/KCohenSyriana/text.html

Cohen, Tom, 'Obama tells families of 9/11 victims that "justice has been done"', *CNN*. 2 May 2011, accessed: 3 August 2013, edition.cnn.com/2011/POLITICS/05/02/bin.laden.white.house/index.html

Coll, Steve, *Ghost Wars: The Secret History of the CIA, Afghanistan and Bin Laden* (London: Penguin, 2004).

Comer, Todd A. and Lloyd Isaac Vayo (eds), *Terror and the Cinematic Sublime: Essays on Violence and the Unpresentable in Post-9/11 Films* (London: McFarland and Company, 2013).

Comolli, Jean-Louis and Jean Narboni, 'Cinema/Ideology/Criticism', in Bill Nichols (ed.), *Movies and Methods*, vol. 1 (Berkeley: University of California Press, 1976), pp. 22–30.

Cooper, M., 'Lights! Camera! Attack! Hollywood enlists', *The Nation*, 21 November 2001, accessed: 29 May 2012, ics.leeds.ac.uk/papers/vp01.cfm?outfit=pmt&folder=34&paper=121

Corliss, Richard, '*2012* end of the world disaster porn', *Time*, 12 November 2009, accessed: 27 May 2010, www.time.com/time/arts/article/0,8599,1938799,00.html

Cousins, Mark, 'Widescreen', *Prospect*, 130 (January 2007), 63.

—, 'America seeks comfort in westerns', *The London Evening Standard*, 16 October 2003, accessed: 29 May 2012, www.thisislondon.co.uk/film/article-7212796-america-seeks-comfort-in-westerns.do

Cox, David, 'Attempting the impossible: Why does western cinema whitewash Asian stories?', *The Guardian*, 2 January 2013, accessed: 1 December 2013, www.the-guardian.com/film/filmblog/2013/jan/02/attempting-the-impossible-asian-roles#start-of-comments

Crisp, James E., *Sleuthing the Alamo, Davy Crockett's Last Stand and Other Mysteries of the Texas Revolution* (Oxford: Oxford University Press, 2005).

Crozier, Dayna, 'Gareth Edwards and the war on monsters', *Flux*, 26 October 2010, accessed: 11 December 2010, flux.net/gareth-edwards-and-the-war-on-monsters

Dabashi, Hamid, 'Warriors of faith', *Sight and Sound* (May 2005), 24–7.

—, 'Native informers and the making of the American empire', *Al-Ahram Weekly Online*, 797 (1–7 June 2006), accessed: 11 October 2013, weekly.ahram.org.eg/2006/797/special.htm

Daly, Steve, 'Double-edged sword', *Entertainment Weekly*, 11 March 2007, accessed: 26 June 2012, www.ew.com/ew/article/0,,20014479,00.html

Dargis, Manohla, 'A rejected superhero ends up at Ground Zero', *The New York Times*, 18 July 2012, accessed: 30 July 2012, movies.nytimes.com/2012/07/20/movies/the-dark-knight-rises-with-christian-bale.html?pagewanted=all

—, 'Bang, boom: Terrorism as a game', *The New York Times*, 2 May 2013, accessed: 9 November 2013, movies.nytimes.com/2013/05/03/movies/iron-man-3-with-robert-downey-jr.html?pagewanted=all&_r=0

de la Pena, Jose Enrique, *With Santa Anna in Texas: A Personal Narrative of the Revolution* (College Station: Texas A & M Press, 1975).

de Man, Paul, *Allegories of Reading: Figural Language in Rousseau, Nietzsche, Rilke, and Proust* (New Haven: Yale University Press, 1979).

Denby, David, 'Anxiety tests', *The New Yorker*, 29 June 2009, accessed: 30 January 2010, www.newyorker.com/arts/critics/cinema/2009/06/29/090629crci_cinema_denby?currentPage=all

Department of Justice, Office of the Inspector General, *A Review of the FBI's Involvement and Observations of Detainee Interrogations in Guantanamo Bay, Afghanistan, and Iraq*, May 2008.

Dershowitz, Alan, *Why Terrorism Works: Understanding the Threat, Responding to the Challenge* (New Haven: Yale University Press, 2008).

Didion, Joan, *Fixed Ideas: America since 9/11* (New York: New York Review of Books, 2003).

Dijck, José van, *Mediated Memories in the Digital Age* (Stanford: Stanford University Press, 2008).

Dipaolo, Marc, *War, Politics and Superheroes: Ethics and Propaganda in Comics and Film* (Jefferson: McFarland and Company, 2011).

Doss, Erika, *Memorial Mania: Public Feeling in America* (Chicago: University of Chicago Press, 2012).

Dowe, John, 'The bombed: Hiroshima and Nagasaki in Japanese Memory', in Michael Hogan (ed.), *Hiroshima in Memory and History* (Cambridge: Cambridge University Press, 1996), pp. 116–42.

Drezner, Daniel W., *Theories of International Politics and Zombies* (Princeton: Princeton University Press, 2011).

Ducat, Stephen, *The Wimp Factor: Gender Gaps, Holy Wars, and the Politics of Anxious Masculinity* (Boston: Beacon Press, 2004).

Du Toit, Kim, 'The pussification of the Western male' (n.d.s.), accessed: 22 June 2013, talltown.us/guns/nancyboys.htm

Ebert, Roger, *Roger Ebert's Movie Year Book 2007* (Kansas City: Andrews McMeel Publishing, 2007).

Eco, Umberto, 'Narrative Structures in Fleming', in Christopher Lindner (ed.), *The James Bond Phenomenon: A Critical Reader* (Manchester: Manchester University Press, 2003), pp. 34–55.

Edelstein, David, 'Flight sequence', *New York Magazine*, 23 April 2006, accessed: 21 June 2010, nymag.com/movies/reviews/16756/

Edwardes, Charlotte, 'Ridley Scott's new crusades film "panders to Osama Bin Laden"', *The Daily Telegraph*, 18 January 2004, accessed: 4 December 2010, www.telegraph. co.uk/news/worldnews/northamerica/usa/1452000/Ridley-Scotts-new-Crusades-film-panders-to-Osama-bin-Laden.html

Ehrenhaus, Peter, 'Why we fought: Holocaust memory in Spielberg's *Saving Private Ryan*', *Critical Studies in Media Communication*, 18: 3 (September 2001), 321–37.

Eller, Claudia, 'Hollywood executives rethink what is off-limits', *The Los Angeles Times*, 14 September 2001, p. A36.

Epstein, Daniel Robert, 'Roland Emmerich of *The Day After Tomorrow* (20th Century Fox)', *UGO Entertainment* (n.d.s.), accessed: 29 September 2010, www.ugo.com/ channels/filmTv/features/thedayaftertomorrow/rolandemmerich.asp

Esch, Deborah, 'No time like the present', *Surfaces*, 3 (1999), accessed: 11 May 2012, www.pum.umontreal.ca/revues/surfaces/vol3/esch.html#fn9

Escobedo, Tricia, 'Controversy surrounds new Tom Hanks movie, "Captain Phillips"' *CNN*, 8 October 2013, accessed: 10 January 2014, edition.cnn.com/2013/10/08/ showbiz/captain-phillips-movie-controversy/

Esposito, Joey, 'Iron Man versus the war on terror: The way it should be', *C22K*, (n.d.s.), accessed: 22 July 2010, www.cc2k.us/index.php?option=com_content&tas k=view&id=985&Itemid=2

Everhart, Bill, 'Summer comes earlier to movie season', *The Berkshire Eagle*, 1 May 2009.

Ezra, Elizabeth and Terry Rowden, 'General introduction: What is transnational cinema?' in Elizabeth Ezra and Terry Rowden (eds), *Transnational Cinema: The Film Reader* (London: Routledge, 2005), pp. 1–11.

Fairclough, Paul, 'Review', *Littlewhitelies*, 22 March 2012, accessed: 29 May 2012, www.littlewhitelies.co.uk/theatrical-reviews/act-of-valor-18318

Faller, Stephen, 'Iron Man's transcendent challenges', in Mark D. White (ed.), *Iron Man and Philosophy* (Hoboken: John Wiley & Sons, Inc., 2010), pp. 256–64.

Faludi, Susan, *The Terror Dream: Fear and Fantasy in Post 9/11 America* (Melbourne: Scribe, 2007).

Fanon, Franz, *Black Skin, White Mask* (London and Sydney: Pluto Press, 1967).

Faraci, Devin, 'The Badass interview: Kevin Macdonald, director of *The Eagle* talks Rome, Vietnam and Afghanistan', 9 February 2011, accessed: 13 March 2012, badassdigest.com/2011/02/09/the-badass-interview-kevin-macdonald-director-of-the-eagle-talks-rome-vietn

Farhi, Paul, 'When Hollywood makes history', *Washington Post*, 28 April 2006, p. A1.

Feinstein, Nancy, Dianne Feinstein, Carl Levin and John McCain, 'Feinstein releases statement on *Zero Dark Thirty*', 19 December 2012, accessed: 7 August 2013, www. feinstein.senate.gov/public/index.cfm/press-releases?ID=b5946751-2054-404a-89b7 -b81e1271efc9

Feingold, Russ, *While America Sleeps* (New York: Crown Publishing Group, 2012).

Fellerath, David, 'Why are the Iraq movies tanking?', *Indy Week.com*, 28 October 2007, accessed 10 September 2010, www.indyweek.com/indyweek/why-are-the-iraq-war-movies-tanking/Content?oid=1205360

Ferguson, Niall, *The War of the World: History's Age of Hatred* (London: Penguin, 2007).

Festinger, Leon, Henry Riecken and Stanley Schachter, *When Prophecy Fails: A Social and Psychological Study of a Modern Group that Predicted the Destruction of the World* (Minnesota: University of Minnesota Press, 1956).

Filkins, Dexter, 'bin Laden, the movie', *The New Yorker*, 17 December 2012, accessed: 3 August 2013, www.newyorker.com/talk/2012/12/17/121217ta_talk_filkins

Fingeroth, Danny, *Superman on the Couch* (New York and London: Continuum, 2004).

Fiske, John, *Television Culture*, 2nd edn (Abingdon: Routledge, 2011).

Fleming Jnr, Mike, 'A glimpse into pure artistic passion, courtesy of Paul Greengrass and "United 93"', *Deadline*, 11 October 2013, accessed: 12 October 2013, www.dead line.com/2013/10/a-glimpse-into-pure-artistic-passion-courtesy-of-paul-greengrass-and-united-93/#more-609643

Fleming, Nic, 'Harry Potter and the war on terror', *The Telegraph*, 17 July 2007, accessed: 27 March 2012, www.telegraph.co.uk/news/worldnews/1557723/Harry-Potter-and-the-war-on-terror.html

Flores, Richard R., *Remembering the Alamo: Memory, Modernity, and the Master Symbol* (Austin: University of Texas Press, 2002).

Ford, Peter, 'Europe cringes at Bush "crusade" against terrorists', *Christian Science Monitor*, 19 September 2001, accessed: 3 December 2010, www.csmonitor.com/2001/0919/p12s2-woeu.html

Foster, John and Robert McChesney, 'The American Empire: Pax Americana or Pox Americana?', *Monthly Review*, 56: 4 (September 2004), accessed: 29 May 2012, monthlyreview.org/2004/09/01/the-american-empire-pax-americana-or-pox-americana

Foster, Thomas, 'Cynical nationalism', in Dana Heller (ed.), *The Selling of 9/11: How a National Tragedy became a Commodity* (New York: Palgrave Macmillan, 2005), pp. 254–87.

Foucault, Michel, *The Order of Things* (London: Vintage Books, 1970).

Foucault, Michel, 'Society must be defended', in Imre Szeman and Timothy Kaposy (eds), *Cultural Theory an Anthology* (Oxford: Blackwell, 2011), pp. 124–33.

French, Phillip, 'Field of screams', *The Guardian*, 15 September 2002, accessed: 23 July 2010, www.guardian.co.uk/film/2002/sep/15/philipfrench

—, 'Review', *The Observer*, 5 September 2004, accessed: 22 December 2012, film.guardian.co.uk/News_Story/Critic_Review/Observer_review/0,4267,1297391,00.html

—, 'Review', *The Observer*, 29 April 2012, p. 22.

Frederick, Jim, *Black Hearts: One Platoon's Descent into Madness in Iraq's Triangle of Death* (New York: Random House, 2010).

Friedman, Josh and David Koepp, *War of the Worlds. The Shooting Script* (New York: Newmarket Press, 2005).

Gaine, Vincent M., 'Remember everything, absolve nothing: Working through the trauma in the *Bourne* trilogy', *Cinema Journal*, 51: 1 (fall 2011), 159–63.

Gallup, Presidential Approval Ratings, 2001, www.gallup.com/poll/116500/Presidential-Approval-Ratings-George-Bush.aspx

Galupo, Scott, 'Crusade of controversy; Ridley Scott's *Kingdom* flawed history', *The Washington Times*, 6 May 2005, accessed: 29 May 2012, www.washingtontimes.com/news/2005/may/5/20050505-105340-5484r/?page=all

Gans, Herbert, *Popular Culture and High Culture: An Analysis and Evaluation of Taste* (New York: Basic Books, 1999).

Giuliani, Rudolph, 'Getting it right at Ground Zero', *Time*, 1 September 2002, accessed: 22 June 2010, http://content.time.com/time/magazine/article/0,9171,1003231-1,00.html

Goff, Stan, *Full Spectrum Disorder: The Military in the New American Century* (Brooklyn: Soft Skull Press, 2004).

Goldberg, Danny, *It's a Free Country: Personal Freedom in America after September 11* (New York: RDV Books, 2002).

Gray, Richard J. and Betty Kaklamanidou (eds), *The 21st Century Superhero: Essays on Gender, Genre and Globalization in Film* (Jefferson: McFarland and Company, 2011).

Groen, Rick, '*The Hunger Games*: A modern allegory and a rare treat', *The Globe and Mail*, 20 March 2012, accessed: 27 March 2012, www.theglobeandmail.com/news/arts/movies/the-hunger-games-a-modern-allegory-and-a-rare-treat/article2374635/page2

Groneman, Bill, *Defense of a Legend, Crockett and the de la Pena Diary* (Plano: Wordware Publishing, 1994).

Grossberg, Josh, 'Movie studios react to attack', *E! News*, 12 September 2001, accessed: 16 December 2013, http://uk.eonline.com/news/42154/movie-studios-react-to-attack

Gunn, Joshua, 'Father trouble: Staging sovereignty in Spielberg's *War of the Worlds*', *Critical Studies in Media Communication*, 25: 1 (March 2008), 1–27.

Gupta, Prachi, '*Zero Dark Thirty* writer says "it's misreading the film" to say torture led to bin Laden capture', *Salon*, 11 December 2012, accessed: 3 August 2013, www.salon.com/2012/12/11/zero_dark_thirty_writer_says_its_misreading_the_film_to_say_torture_led_to_bin_laden_capture

Hansen, Miriam, '*Schindler's List* is not *Shoah*: Second commandment, popular modernism, and public memory', in Yosefa Loshitzky (ed.), *Spielberg's Holocaust: Critical Perspectives on Schindler's List* (Bloomington: Indiana University Press, 1997), pp. 77–103.

Hantke, Steffen, 'The return of the giant creature: *Cloverfield* and the political opposition to the war on terror', *Extrapolation*, 51: 2 (summer 2010), 235–57.

Hard, Andrew, '*ET* turns invader in *War of the Worlds*', *Fox News*, 29 June 2005, accessed: 25 June 2010, www.foxnews.com/story/0,2933,160952,00.html

Harkaway, Nick, 'America's heroes', *Prospect*, 26 January 2011, accessed: 29 May 2012, www.prospectmagazine.co.uk/2011/01/captain-america-insecurities-anxieties-comic-book-metaphor

Harnden, Toby, 'Bin Laden is wanted: Dead or alive, says Bush', *The Telegraph*, 18 September 2001, accessed: 9 January 2014, www.telegraph.co.uk/news/worldnews/asia/afghanistan/1340895/Bin-Laden-is-wanted-dead-or-alive-says-Bush.html

Harrickton, Patrick, 'Patrick Harrington interviews, Jacks Shaheen, author of *Reel Bad Arabs*', *Thirdway*, 30 January 2008, accessed: 2 December 2013, thirdway.eu/2008/01/30/reel-bad-arabs

Harris, John, 'Skating on thin ice', *The Guardian*, 25 May 2010, accessed: 21 September 2010, www.guardian.co.uk/commentisfree/2006/may/25/anothersurrendermonkey

Headrick, Daniel R., *Power over Peoples: Technology, Environments, and Western Imperialism, 1400 to the Present* (Princeton: Princeton University Press, 2012).

Hearts, David, 'Through a lens darkly', *The Guardian*, 25 January 2008, p. 6.

Hedegaard, Erik, 'Mark Wahlberg handles his business', *Men's Journal*, 30 January 2012, accessed: 7 March 2012, www.mensjournal.com/mark-wahlberg-handles-his-business/3

Hedges, Chris, *War Is a Force that Gives us Meaning* (Cambridge, MA: Perseus Books, 2002).

Heller, Dana, 'Introduction: Selling 9/11', in Dana Heller (ed.), *The Selling of 9/11: How a National Tragedy Became a Commodity* (New York: Palgrave Macmillan, 2005), pp. 1–26.

Herodotus, *The Histories*, trans. Tom Holland (London: Penguin, 2013).

Herscher, Elaine and Psyche Pascual, 'Special report: Coping with the trauma of 9/11', *Consumer Health Interactive*, 26 February 2008, accessed: 29 May 2012, drugtools. caremark.com/topic/trauma

Hignett, Charles, *Xerxes' Invasion of Greece* (Oxford: Clarendon Press, 1963).

Himmelfarb, Gertrude, *The New History and the Old: Critical Essays and Reappraisals* (Cambridge, MA: Harvard University Press, 2004).

Hirsch, Joshua, *Afterimage: Film, Trauma, and the Holocaust* (Philadelphia: Temple University Press, 2004).

Hitchens, Christopher, 'Of sin, the left & Islamic fascism', *The Nation*, 8 October 2001, accessed: 29 February 2012 www.thenation.com/article/sin-left-islamic-fascism

Hobbes, Thomas, *Leviathan or the Matter, Form, and Power of a Common-wealth, Ecclesiastical and Civil* (Menston: Scolar Press, [1651] 1969). 1651.

Hoberman, J., 'Unquiet Americans', *Sight and Sound* (October 2006), 20–3.

—, 'Laugh, cry, believe: Spielbergization and its discontents', *The Virginia Quarterly Review* (winter 2007), accessed: 23 November 2010, www.vqronline.org/arti cles/2007/winter/hoberman-spielbergization

—, '*The Avengers*: Why Hollywood is no longer afraid to tackle 9/11', *The Guardian*, 11 May 2012, accessed: 14 March 2013, www.guardian.co.uk/film/2012/may/11/ avengers-hollywood-afraid-tackle-9-11

Holmlund, Chris, 'Masculinity as multiple masquerade. The "mature" Stallone and the Stallone Clone', in Steve Cohen and Ina Rae Hark (eds), *Screening the Male. Exploring Masculinities in Hollywood Cinema* (New York: Routledge, 1993), pp. 213–29.

Holloway, David, *9/11 and the War on Terror* (Edinburgh: Edinburgh University Press, 2008).

Hornaday, Ann, 'Raw courage', *Washington Post*, 28 April 2006, p. C1.

Hoskins, Andrew, *Televising War: From Vietnam to Iraq* (New York: Continuum Publishing Group, 2004).

Hubbard, Glenn and Tim Kane, *Balance: The Economics of Great Powers from Ancient Rome to Modern America* (New York: Simon Schuster, 2013).

Hufines, Alan C., *Blood of Noble Men: The Alamo, Siege and Battle* (Austin: Easkin, 1999).

Hughes-Warrington, Marnie (ed.), *History on Film Reader* (London and New York: Routledge, 2009).

Hurwitz, Macy, 'Bush regrets "mission accomplished" banner', *The Telegraph*, 12 November 2008, accessed: 20 February 2012, www.telegraph.co.uk/news/world news/middleeast/iraq/3447776/Bush-Regrets-Mission-Accomplished-Banner.html

Inuhiko, Yomota, 'The menace from the south seas: Hondo Ishirõ's *Godzilla*', in Alastair Phillips and Julian Stringer (eds), *Japanese Cinema: Texts and Contexts* (New York: Routledge, 2007), pp. 102–11.

Isikoff, Michael, 'War on words', *Daily Beast*, 3 February 2009, accessed: 29 May 2012, www.thedailybeast.com/newsweek/2009/02/03/war-on-words.html

Jaafar, Ali, 'Confessions of a dangerous mind', *Sight and Sound* (March 2006), 17.

—, 'Casualties of war', *Sight and Sound*, 18: 2 (February 2008), 16–22.

James, Nick, 'Films of 2008', *Sight and Sound*, 19: 1 (January 2009), 16–29.

Jameson, Frederic, *The Political Unconscious: Narrative as a Socially Symbolic Act* (Ithaca: Cornell University Press, 1981).

Al Jazeera, 'Hollywood and the War Machine', *Empire*, 16 December 2010, accessed: 8 May 2012, www.aljazeera.com/programmes/empire/2010/12/2010121681345363 793.html

Jeffords, Susan, *Hard Bodies: Hollywood Masculinity in the Reagan Era* (New Brunswick, NJ: Rutgers University Press, 1994).

Jenkins, Tricia, *The CIA in Hollywood. How the Agency Shapes Film and Television* (Austin: University of Texas Press, 2012).

Jensen, Jeff, '"The Dark Knight rises": Bring on the camera', *Entertainment Weekly*, 18 July 2012, accessed: 30 July 2012, www.ew.com/ew/article/0,,20610393_20612774,00.html

Jewers, Caroline, '"Mission historical, or [t]here were a hell of a lot of knights": Ethnicity and alterity in Jerry Bruckheimer's *King Arthur*', in Lynn Ramey and Tison Pugh (eds), *Filming the Other Middle Ages: Race, Class and Gender in Medieval Cinema* (New York: Palgrave Macmillan, 2007), pp. 91–107.

Jewett, Robert and John Shelton Lawrence, *Captain America and the Crusade against Evil. The Dilemma of Zealous Nationalism* (Grand Rapids: W. B. Eerdmans, 2003).

Johnson, Chalmers, *Blowback: The Costs and Consequences of American Empire* (London: Time Warner, 2000).

Johnston, Robert K., *Useless Beauty: Ecclesiastes through the Lens of Contemporary Film* (Ada: Baker Academic, 2004).

Jolin, Dan, 'Monsters: Dark Continent', *Empire Magazine*, July 2014, pp. 16–18.

Joneidi, Majid, 'Iranian anger at Hollywood "assault"', *BBC News*, 16 March 2007, accessed: 10 December 2010, news.bbc.co.uk/1/hi/6455969.stm

Jones, George, 'We will help hunt down evil culprits, says Blair', *The Telegraph*, 12 September 2001, accessed: 13 March 2013, www.telegraph.co.uk/news/uknews/1340258/We-will-help-hunt-down-evil-culprits-says-Blair.html

Jordan, Gregor, Personal communication, email, 2 July 2012.

Kaes, Anton, *From Hitler to Heimat: The Return of History as Film* (Cambridge, MA: Harvard University Press, 1989).

—, *Shell Shock Cinema: Weimar Culture and the Wounds of War.* (Princeton: Princeton University Press, 2009).

Kant, Immanuel, *Religion within the Boundaries of Mere Reason: And Other Writings*, trans. Werner S. Pluhar. (Indianapolis: Hackett Publishing Company, 2009).

Kaplan, E. Ann, *Trauma Culture: The Politics of Terror and Loss in Media and Literature* (New York and London: Rutgers University Press, 2005).

Kaplan, E. Ann and Ban Wang (eds), *Trauma and Cinema, Cross-cultural Explorations* (Aberdeen and Hong Kong: Hong Kong University Press, 2009).

Keegan, Rebecca Winters, '*Cloverfield*: Godzilla goes 9/11', 16 January 2008, accessed: 28 February 2012, www.time.com/time/arts/article/0,8599,1704356,00.html

Kellner, Douglas, *Cinema Wars: Hollywood Film and Politics in the Bush-Cheney Era* (Chichester: Wiley Blackwell Press, 2010).

Kelly, Kevin, 'Io9 talks to *Cloverfield* director Matt Reeves', *io9*, 18 January 2009, accessed: 9 November 2012, io9.com/346501/io9-talks-to-cloverfield-director-matt-reeves

Kilgore, Dan, *How Did Davy Die?* (College Station: Texas A & M Press, 1975).

King, Claire Sisco, *Washed in Blood: Male Sacrifice, Trauma, and the Cinema* (New Brunswick, NJ: Rutgers University Press, 2012).

King, Geoff, '"Just like a movie"?: 9/11 and Hollywood spectacle"', in Geoff King (ed.), *The Spectacle of the Real: From Hollywood to 'Reality' TV and Beyond* (Bristol: Intellect Books, 2005), pp. 47–58.

Klein, Naomi, *The Shock Doctrine: The Rise of Disaster Capitalism* (London: Penguin, 2007).

Kleinfield, N. R., 'A creeping horror. Buildings burn and fall as onlookers look for elusive safety', *The New York Times*, 12 September 2001, accessed: 9 May 2011, www.nytimes.com/2001/09/12/nyregion/12SCEN.html?pagewanted=all

Klerck, Kevin, 'Rename *The Two Towers* to something less offensive petition', *Petition*

Online, (n.d.s.), accessed: 28 December 2013, archive.org/web/20021113001352/ www.petitiononline.com/twotower/petition.html

Knowles, Harry, 'Whoa whoa whoa . . . Who says it aint gonna be called John Rambo?', *Aint it Cool News*, 12 October 2007, accessed: 17 August 2010, www.aintitcool. com/node/34423

Knowlton, Brian, 'Terror in America/"We're going to smoke them out": President airs his anger', *The New York Times*, 19 September 2001, accessed: 9 January 2014, www.nytimes.com/2001/09/19/news/19iht-t4_30.html

Kolker, Robert, *A Cinema of Loneliness* (Oxford: Oxford University Press, 2011).

Kracauer, Siegfried, *From Caligari to Hitler: A Psychological History of the German Film* (Princeton: Princeton University Press, 1947).

Krauthammer, Charles, 'Oscars for Osama', *The Washington Post*, 3 March 2006, accessed: 2 September 2012, www.washingtonpost.com/wp-dyn/content/article/20 06/03/02/AR2006030201209.html

Kurtz, Michael L., 'Oliver Stone, *JFK*, and history', in Robert Brent Toplin (ed.), *Oliver Stone's USA: Film, History and Controversy* (Lawrence: University of Kansas Press, 2000), pp. 166–77.

LaCapra, Dominick, *Writing History, Writing Trauma* (Baltimore: Johns Hopkins University Press, 2000).

—, *History in Transit: Experience, Identity, Critical Theory* (New York: Cornell University Press, 2004).

Lacey, Mark, 'War, cinema and moral anxiety', *Alternatives*, 28 (2003), 611–36.

Lamar, Cyriaque, 'Guillermo Del Toro tells us why baby Godzilla will not appear in *Pacific Rim*', io9, 12 October 2012, accessed: 13 December 2013, io9.com/5951196/ guillermo-del-toro-tells-us-why-baby-godzilla-will-not-appear-in-pacific-rim

Landesman, Cosmo, 'A terrifying flight back in time', *The Sunday Times*, 4 June 2010, accessed: 21 September 2001, entertainment.timesonline.co.uk/tol/arts_and_enter tainment/article670048.ece

—, 'Review', *The Sunday Times*, 19 August 2007, accessed: 17 September 2010, entertainment.timesonline.co.uk/tol/arts_and_entertainment/film/film_reviews/article 2265209.ece

Landsberg, Alison, 'Prosthetic memory: *Total Recall* and *Blade Runner*', in Mike Featherstone and Roger Burrows (eds), *Cyberspace/Cyberbodies/Cyberpunk: Cultures of Technological Embodiment* (London: Sage, 1995), pp. 175–90.

—, 'Prosthetic memory: The ethics and politics of memory in an age of mass culture', in Paul Grainger (ed.), *Memory and Popular Film* (Manchester: Manchester University Press, 2003), pp. 144–61.

—, *Prosthetic Memory. The Transformation of American Remembrance in the Age of Mass Culture* (New York: Columbia University Press, 2004).

La Salle, Mick, 'Agony, heroism of *United 93* shown with nearly unbeara-ble realism', *San Francisco Chronicle*, 28 April 2006, accessed: 21 September 2010, www.sfgate.com/cgi-bin/article.cgi?f=/chronicle/reviews/movies/UNITED93. DTL#ixzz109WWmS3I

—, '*Zero Dark Thirty* review: On target', 3 January 2013, accessed: 3 August 2013, www.sfgate.com/movies/article/Zero-Dark-Thirty-review-On-target-4164885. php

Laub, Dori, 'September 11th 2001 – An event without a voice', in Judith Greenburg (ed.), *Trauma at Home: After 9/11* (Lincoln: University of Nebraska Press, 2003), pp. 204–15.

Lawrence, John Shelton and Robert Jewett, *The American Monomyth* (Lanham: University Press of America, 1988).

—, *The Myth of the American Superhero* (Grand Rapids: W. B. Erdmans, 2002).

Laxer, James, *The Perils of Empire: America and Its Imperial Predecessors* (London and New York: Penguin, 2008).

Lee, Nathan, '*Cloverfield* is one giant, incredibly entertaining "screw you!" to yuppie New York', *The Village Voice*, 15 January 2008, accessed: 9 September 2010, www.villagevoice.com/2008-01-15/film/cloverfield-is-one-giant-incredibly-entertaining-scr ew-you-to-yuppie-new-york

Leung, Rebecca, 'Woodward shares war secrets', *CBS News*, 5 Decemeber 2007, accessed: 30 July 2012, www.cbsnews.com/2100-18560_162-612067.html

Lev, Peter, *American Films of the 1970s: Conflicting Visions* (Austin: University of Texas Press, 2000).

Lévinas, Emmanel, *Face to Face with Lévinas*, ed. Richard A. Cohen (Albany: State University of New York Press, 1986).

Lifton, Robert Jay, *Superpower Syndrome: America's Apocalyptic Confrontation with the World* (New York: Nation Books, 2003).

Lifton, Robert Jay, and Greg Mitchell, *Hiroshima in America: A Half Century of Denial* (New York: Avon, 1995).

Lim, Dennis, 'Dante's inferno', *The Village Voice*, 22 November 2005, accessed: 16 May 2012, www.villagevoice.com/2005-11-22/film/dante-s-inferno

Liminick, Lou, 'London crawling', *New York Post*, 11 May 2007, accessed: 22 June 2010, www.nypost.com/p/entertainment/movies/item_IwtodzvYF50jbAIUdquMXJ

Lincoln, Abraham, 'Annual message to congress – concluding remarks', *Abraham Lincoln Online*, Washington, DC, 1 December 1862, accessed: 30 July 2012, http:// showcase.netins.net/web/creative/lincoln/speeches/congress.htm

Lindley, Arthur, 'Once, present and future kings: *Kingdom of Heaven* and the multitemporality of medieval film', in Lynn Ramey and Tison Pugh (eds), *Filming the Other Middle Ages: Race, Class and Gender in Medieval Cinema* (New York: Palgrave Macmillan, 2007), pp. 15–30.

Linenthal, Edward Tabor, '"A reservoir of spiritual power": Patriotic faith at the Alamo in the twentieth century', *The Southwestern Historical Quarterly* 1: 4 (April 1988), 509–31.

Linklater, Magnus, 'Kevin Macdonald will bring to film pre-Celtic clash of the cultures', *The Times*, 3 August 2009, accessed: 25 August 2009, https://login.thetimes. co.uk/?gotoUrl=http%3A%2F%2Fwww.thetimes.co.uk%2Ftto%2Fnews%2Fuk% 2Fscotland%2F

LoCicero, Don, *Superheroes and Gods: A Comparative Study from Babylonia to Batman* (Jefferson: McFarland and Company, 2007).

Longstreth, Andrew, 'Analysis: Legal questions remain over bin Laden killing', *Reuters*, 5 May 2011, accessed: 26 March 2011, www.reuters.com/article/2011/05/05/us-binladen-usa-legal-idUSTRE7442NA20110505

Lovece, Frank, 'Soldier showdown: Joe and Anthony Russo take the helm of "Captain America" franchise', *Film Journal International*, 25 March 2014, accessed: 9 June 2014, http://www.filmjournal.com/filmjournal/content_display/news-and-features/ features/movies/e3ie3493397f4a48111966630c800986a35

Lowenstein, Adam, *Shocking Representations: Historical Trauma, National Cinema and the Modern Horror Film* (New York: Columbia University Press, 2005).

Lowry, Brian, 'Review', *Los Angeles Times*, 1 January 2008, accessed: 17 August 2010, www.variety.com/review/VE1117935910.html?categoryid=31&cs=1

Maas, Peter, 'Don't trust *Zero Dark Thirty*', *The Atlantic*, 13 December 2012, accessed: 4 August 2013, www.theatlantic.com/entertainment/archive/2012/12/dont-trust-zero-dark-thirty/266253

MacAskill, Ewen, 'Barrack Obama ends war in Iraq "now it's time to turn the page"', *The Guardian*, 1 September 2010, p. 18.

Maalouf, Amin, *The Crusades through Arab Eyes* (New York: Schocken Books, 1984).

MacDonald, Kevin, Personal communication. telephone. 10 October 2012.

Malcolm, Noel, 'Is America the new Rome?', *The Telegraph*, 9 March 2008, accessed: 29 December 2013, www.telegraph.co.uk/culture/books/non_fictionreviews/3671722/ Is-America-the-new-Rome.html

Markert, John, *Post-9/11 Cinema: Through a Lens Darkly* (Lanham: The Scarecrow Press, Inc., 2011).

Maslin, Jared, '*Syriana* highlights complexities of war', *Yale Daily News*, 12 January 2006, accessed: 10 June 2013, http://yaledailynews.com/blog/2006/01/12/syriana-highlights-complexities-of-war

Matheson, Richard, *I am Legend* (London: Orion Books, 1999).

Matthews, John, 'An interview with David Franzoni', *Arthuriana*, 14: 3 (2004), pp. 115–20.

Matthews, Melvin E., *Hostile Aliens, Hollywood and Today's News 1950s Science Fiction Films and 9/11* (New York: Algora Publishing, 2007).

Matthews, Peter, 'Aftermath', *Sight and Sound*, 11: 11 (November 2001), 20–2.

Mayer, Jane, *The Dark Side: The Inside Story of How the War on Terror Turned into a War on American Ideals* (New York: Doubleday, 2008).

—, 'Zero conscience in *Zero Dark Thirty*', *The New Yorker*, 14 December 2012, accessed: 3 August 2013, www.newyorker.com/online/blogs/newsdesk/2012/12/ torture-in-kathryn-bigelows-zero-dark-thirty.html

McCrisken, Trevor and Andrew Pepper, *American History and Contemporary Hollywood Film: From 1492 to Three Kings* (Edinburgh: Edinburgh University Press, 2005).

McSweeney, Terence, 'The *Land of the Dead* and the home of the brave: Romero's vision of a Post 9/11 America', in Jeff Birkenstein, Anna Froula and Karen Randell (eds), *Reframing 9/11 Film, Popular Culture and the 'War on Terror* (London: Continuum, 2010), pp. 107–17.

Medved, Michael, *Hollywood against America* (New York: Harper Collins, 1992).

Melnick, Jeffrey P., *9/11 Culture: America under Construction* (Oxford: Wiley-Blackwell, 2009).

Millar, Greg, 'Many held at Guantanamo not likely terrorists', *The Los Angeles Times*, 22 December 2002, accessed: 3 August 2013, articles.latimes.com/2002/dec/22/ nation/la-na-gitmo22dec22

Mitchell, Alison and Richard L. Berke, 'After the attacks: The congress; differences are put aside as lawmakers reconvene', 13 Septmber 2001, accessed: 10 January 2014, www.nytimes.com/2001/09/13/us/after-the-attacks-the-congress-differences-are-put-aside-as-lawmakers-reconvene.html

Mitchell, W. L. T., *Cloning Terror. The War of Images, 9/11 to the Present* (London: University of Chicago Press, 2011).

Monahan, B. A. *The Shock of the News: Media Coverage and the Making of 9/11* (New York: New York University Press, 2010).

Moreman, Christopher M., 'Let this hell be our heaven: Richard Matheson's spirituality and its Hollywood distortions', *Journal of Religion and Popular Culture*, 24: 1 (2012), 130–47.

Morgenstern, Joel, 'Old English goes new Hollywood in Epic 'Beowulf', *Wall Street Journal*, 16 November 2007, accessed: 12 January 2007, online.wsj.com/article/ SB119517337319395051.html

Morrison, Grant, *SuperGods: Our World in the Age of the Superhero* (London: Random House, 2011).

Morro, John H., *Taken by Force: Rape and American GIs in Europe during World War II* (Basingstoke: Palgrave Macmillan, 2007).

Morrow, Lance, 'The case for rage and retribution', *Time*, 14 Septembr 2001, accessed: 9 July 2012, www.time.com/time/nation/article/0,8599,174641,00.html

Moss, Mark, *The Media and the Models of Masculinity* (Lanham: Lexington Books, 2007).

Muller, Christine, 'Power, choice, and September 11 in *The Dark Knight*', in Richard j Gray and Betty Kaklamanidou (eds), *The 21st Century Superhero Essays on Gender, Genre and Globalization in Film* (Jefferson: McFarland and Company, 2011), pp. 46–59.

Muntean, Nick, 'It was just like a movie': Trauma, memory, and the mediation of 9/11', *Journal of Popular Film and Television*, 37: 2 (summer 2009), 50–8.

Muntean, Nick and Matthew Thomas Payne, 'Attack of the livid dead: Recalibrating terror in the Post 9/11 zombie film', in Andrew Schopp and Matthew Hill (eds), *The War on Terror and American Popular Culture* (Madison: Fairleigh Dickinson University Press, 2009), pp. 239–58.

Murphy, Cullen, *Are We Rome? The Fall of an Empire and the Fate of America* (New York: Houghton Mifflin, 2007).

Murphy, Jarrett, 'Bring "em on" fetches trouble', *CBS News*, 3 July 2003, accessed: 9 January 2014, www.cbsnews.com/news/bring-em-on-fetches-trouble/

National Commission on Terrorist Attacks Upon the United States, *9/11 Commission Report* (New York: W. W. Norton & Company, 2004).

Newitz, Annalee, *Pretend We're Dead: Capitalist Monsters in American Pop Culture* (Durham, NC: Duke University Press, 2006).

Nicholson, Amy, '*Lone Survivor* is a jingoistic snuff film about a navy SEAL', *The Village Voice*, 24 December 2013, accessed: 2 February 2014, www.villagevoice.com/2013-12-25/film/lone-survivor-movie-review

Nilges, Mathias, 'The aesthetics of destruction: contemporary US Cinema and TV culture', in Jeff Birkenstein, Anna Froula and Karen Randell (eds), *Reframing 9/11 Film, Popular Culture and the 'War on Terror'* (London: Continuum, 2010), pp. 23–33.

Nolan, Christopher, Jonathan Nolan and David S. Goyer, *The Complete Screenplays. The Dark Knight Trilogy* (London: Faber & Faber, 2012).

Noonan, Peggy, 'Welcome back, Duke: From the ashes of Sept. 11 arise the manly virtues', *Wall Street Journal*, 12 October 2001, accessed: 12 May 2012, online.wsj.com/article/SB122451174798650085.html

—, 'The Right Man', *The Washington Post*, 30 January 2003, accessed: 29 May 2012, online.wsj.com/article/SB10438958769267100064.html

NPR, 'Hunt for bin Laden more than just one woman's fight', 16 December 2012, accessed: 10 August 2013, www.npr.org/2012/12/16/167366573/hunt-for-bin-laden-more-than-just-one-womans-fight

O'Hehir, Andrew, '*'Margaret*': The great NYC movie that crashed and burned', *Salon*, 29 September 2011, accessed: 10 July 2012, www.salon.com/2011/09/29/margaret

—, '*The Dark Knight Rises*: Christopher Nolan's evil masterpiece', *Salon.com*, 18 July 2012, accessed: 30 July 2012, www.salon.com/2012/07/18/the_dark_knight_rises_christopher_nolans_evil_masterpiece

Okwu, Michael and Katie Couric (narrators), 'Controversy over movie *United 93*', *Today Show*, NBC. 18 April 2006. [Transcript: 15 August 2006]

O'Reilly, Bill, 'The Bourne buffoonery', 9 August 2007, accessed: 13 March 2012, www.billoreilly.com/newslettercolumn?pid=21662

Parry, Robert, 'Bush's My Lai', *Consortium News*, 30 May 2006, accessed: 20 June 2012, www.consortiumnews.com/2006/052906.html

Paul, Joanna, *Film and the Classical Epic Tradition* (Oxford: Oxford University Press, 2013).

Peebles, Stacey Lyn, *Welcome to the Suck: Narrating the American Soldier's Experience in Iraq* (Ithaca and London: Cornell University Press, 2011).

Perkis, Edward, 'Mahmoud Ahmadinejad, hates *300*', *Cinema Blend*, 23 March 2007, accessed: 10 December 2010, www.cinemablend.com/new/Mahmoud-Ahmadinejad-Hates-300-4747.html

Peyser, Andrea, 'Extremely, incredibly exploitive', *New York Post*, 19 January 2012, accessed: 16 December 2013, nypost.com/2012/01/19/extremely-incredibly-exploitive

Phillips, Joshua E. S., *None of Us Were Like This Before: American Soldiers and Torture* (London: Verso, 2012).

Phillips, Kate, 'Kennedy: "George Bush's Vietnam"', *The New York Times*, 9 January 2007, accessed: 28 December 2013, thecaucus.blogs.nytimes.com/2007/01/09/kennedy-george-bushs-vietnam/?_r=0

Pilger, John, 'The real invasion of Africa is not news and a licence to lie is Hollywood's gift', *JohnPilger.com*, 31 January 2012, accessed: 3 August 2013 johnpilger.com/articles/the-real-invasion-of-africa-is-not-news-and-a-licence-to-lie-is-hollywoods-gift

Poe, Ted, 'The Alamo: The thermopylae of Texas', *Poe.House.Gov*, (n.d.s.), accessed 10 January 2014, poe.house.gov/poe-notes/the-alamo-the-thermopylae-of-texas

Pollard, Tom, *Hollywood 9/11: Superheroes, Supervillains, and Super Disasters* (Boulder: Paradigm Publishers, 2011).

Prince, Stephen, *Firestorm: American Film in the Age of Terrorism* (New York: Columbia University Press, 2009).

Pulliam, Jane, 'Our zombies, ourselves: exiting the Foucauldian universe in George A. Romero's *Land of the Dead*', *Journal of the Fantastic in the Arts*, 21: 1 (2009), 42–57.

Pye, Douglas, '*Ulzana's Raid*', *Movie*, 27/28 (winter/spring 1981), 79.

Quart, Alissa, 'Networked', *Film Comment*, 41: 4 (July/August 2005), 48–51.

Radstone, Susannah, 'Cinema and memory', in Susannah Radstone and Bill Schwarz (eds), *Memory: Histories, Theories, Debates*. (New York: Fordham University Press, 2010), pp. 325–342.

Rae, Graham, 'Dead reckoning', *Cinefantastique*, 37: 3 (July 2005), 44–51.

Ray, Gene, *Terror and the Sublime in Art and Critical Theory: From Auschwitz to Hiroshima to September 11 and Beyond* (New York: Palgrave Macmillan, 2005).

Redman, Erich, Personal communication, email. 17 October 2012.

Redmond, Sean, 'When planes fall out of the sky: the war body on-screen', in Sean Redmond and Karen Randall (eds), *The War Body On Screen* (London: Continuum, 2008), pp. 22–35.

Refrag, 'Political correctness gone amok on Tolkien?', *Kuro5hin*, 9 May 2002, accessed: 15 September 2010, www.kuro5hin.org/story/2002/5/9/10155/29581

Rich, B. Ruby, 'Out of the rubble: 9/11 special', *Sight and Sound* (October 2006), 14–18.

Ricks, Thomas E., *The Gamble: General Petraus and the American Military Adventure in Iraq, 2006–2008* (New York: Penguin Press, 2009).

Ridge, Tom, 'Remarks by Secretary of Homeland Security Tom Ridge at the American Legion National Conference', 1 September 2004, accessed: 21 September 2010, www.dhs.gov/xnews/speeches/speech_0202.shtm

Robb, David L., *Operation Hollywood: How the Pentagon Shapes and Censors the Movies* (New York: Prometheus Books, 2004).

Roberts, Garyn, 'Understanding the sequential art of comic strips and comic books and their descendants in the early years of the new millennium', *The Journal of American Culture*, 27: 2 (2004): 210–17.

Roberts, Randy and James S. Olson, *A Line in the Sand: The Alamo in Blood and Memory* (New York: The Free Press, 2001).

Rogers, Simon, 'Iraq body count report: How many died and who was responsible?',

The Guardian, 3 January 2012, accessed: 2 April 2014, www.theguardian.com/news/datablog/2012/jan/03/iraq-body-count-report-data

Rommel-Ruiz, W. Bryan, *American History Goes to the Movies. Hollywood and the American Experience* (New York: Routledge, 2011).

Rosenbaum, Ron, 'Hijacking the hijack', *Slate*, 27 April 27 2006, accessed: 29 May 2012, www.slate.com/id/2140676

Rosenstone, Robert, *Visions of the Past: The Challenge of Film to Our Idea of History* (Cambridge, MA: Harvard University Press, 1995).

Rothman, Lily, '*Zero Dark Thirty*, declassified: Bigelow dishes on deeper meaning of closing scene', 28 January 2013, accessed: 3 August 2013, entertainment.time.com/2013/01/28/zero-dark-thirty-declassified-bigelow-dishes-on-the-deeper-meaning-of-the-closing-scene/#ixzz2ggfXpH4Q

Rushkoff, Douglas, *Present Shock: When Everything Happens Now* (New York: Penguin, 2012).

Russo, Audrey, 'An *Act of Valour* would help our foreign policy', 28 February 2012, accessed: 8 May 2012, www.examiner.com/article/an-act-of-valor-would-help-our-foreign-policy?cid=PROD-redesign-right-next

Ryan, Michael and Kellner, Douglas, *Camera Politica: The Politics and Ideology of Contemporary Hollywood Film* (Bloomington: Indiana University Press, 1990).

Ryan, Tom, 'In defence of big, expensive films', *The Age*, 14 July 2005, accessed: 6 September 2013, www.theage.com.au/news/film/defending-the-blockbuster/2005/07/14/1120934352863.html

Sanchez, Robert, 'Exclusive interview: Avi Arad and the IESB Go 1:1!', *IESB*, 24 April 2007, accessed: 29 May 2012, iesb.net/index.php?option=com_content&task=view&id=2344&Itemid=99

Schlesinger Jr, Arthur, 'The crisis of American masculinity', in *The Politics of Hope: And, The Bitter Heritage: American Liberalism in the 1960s* (Princeton: Princeton University Press, 2008), pp. 292–303.

Schivelbusch, Wolfgang, *The Culture of Defeat: On National Trauma, Mourning, and Recovery*, trans. Jefferson Chase (New York: Metropolitan Books, 2001).

Schlegel, Johannes and Frank Habermann, '"You took my advice about theatricality a bit . . . literally": Theatricality and cybernetics of good and evil in *Batman Begins*, *The Dark Knight*, and *X-Men*', in Richard J. Gray and Betty Kaklamanidou (eds), *The 21st Century Superhero Essays on Gender, Genre and Globalization in Film* (Jefferson: McFarland and Company, 2011), pp. 29–45.

Schnall, Peter, 'George W. Bush: The 9/11 interview', *National Geographic*, 2011.

Schopp, Andrew and Matthew B. Hill, 'Introduction: The curious knot', in Andrew Schopp and Matthew B. Hill (eds), *The War on Terror and American Popular Culture: September 11 and Beyond* (Madison: Fairleigh Dickinson University Press, 2009), pp. 11–42.

Schreffler, Laura, 'Sorry, Mark, real-life's not like the movies: Wahlberg apologises for "ridiculous" claim that he could have fought 9/11 terrorists and landed plane', *The Daily Mail*, 19 January 2012, accessed: 7 March 2012, www.dailymail.co.uk/news/article-2088506/Mark-Wahlberg-9-11-comment-Actor-apologises-ridiculous-claim.html#ixzz1uNpc537a

Scott, A. O., 'Soldiers on a live wire between peril and protocol', *The New York Times*, 26 June 2009, accessed: 30 January 2010, movies.nytimes.com/2009/06/26/movies/26hurt.html

Sealy, Shirley, 'Review', *Film Journal International*, 14 April 2011, accessed: 5 December 2013, www.filmjournal.com/filmjournal/content_display/reviews/major-releases/e3ifcd1fe204284481b2d467d8e40305bcf

Serle, Jack and Chris Woods, 'Six-month update: US covert actions in Pakistan,

Yemen and Somalia', 1 July 2001, accessed: 3 August 2013, www.thebureauinvesti gates.com/2013/07/01/six-month-update-us-covert-actions-in-pakistan-yemen-and-somalia

Seymour, Gene, 'Scenes of mayhem are too close to home', *The Los Angeles Times*, 21 September 2001, p. F10.

Shaheen, Jack, *Reel Bad Arabs: How Hollywood Vilifies a People* (New York: Olive Branch Press, 2009).

Shane, Scott, 'Cheney is linked to concealment of C.I.A. project', *The New York Times*, 11 July 2009, accessed: 15 May 2012. www.nytimes.com/2009/07/12/us/politics/12intel.html

Shaviro, Steven, *The Cinematic Body* (Minneapolis: University of Minnesota Press, 1993).

Shippey, Tom, 'Fuqua's *King Arthur*: More myth-making in America', *Exemplaria*, 19: 2 (Summer 2007), 310–26.

Sidey, Hugh, 'Deep grow the roots of the Alamo', *Life*, 31 May 1968, p. 32.

Simon, Richard Keller, *Trash Culture: Popular Culture and the Great Tradition* (Berkeley: University of California Press, 1999).

Simpson, David, *9/11: The Culture of Commemoration* (Chicago: University of Chicago Press, 2006).

Slotkin, Richard, *Regeneration through Violence* (Norman: University of Oklahoma Press, 1973).

—, *Gunfighter Nation: The Myth of the Frontier in Twentieth-Century America* (Norman: University of Oklahoma Press, 1998).

Slouka, Mark, 'A year later. Notes of America's intimations of mortality', *Harper's Magazine*, September 2002, pp. 35–44.

Smelser, Neil J., 'Psychological trauma and cultural trauma', in Jeffrey C. Alexander et al. (eds), *Cultural Trauma and Collective Identity* (Berkeley and London: University of California Press, 2004), pp. 31–59.

Smith, Kyle, 'One-sided battle', *New York Post*, 7 May 2008, accessed: 10 June 2010, www.nypost.com/p/entertainment/movies/item_ySm9YTznFM7S7v6SGjYu4M;jsess ionid=A26BF23D93894D6499A77C0185365B99

Smith, Richard Penn, *Colonel Crockett's Exploits and Adventures in Texas* (New York: Penguin Group, 2003).

Smith, Terry, 'The dialectics of disappearance: Architectural iconotypes between clashing cultures', *Critical Quarterly*, 45: 1–2 (2003), 33–51.

Soderbergh, Steven, 'The state of cinema 2013', The San Francisco International Film Festival, 27 April 2013.

Solomon, Jon, '"Everybody Loves a Muscle Boi": Homos, heroes, and foes in post-9/11 spoofs of *The 300 Spartans*', in Almut-Barbara Renger and Jon Solomon (eds), *Ancient Worlds in Film and Television: Gender and Politics* (Leiden: Koninkklijke Brill NV, 2013), pp. 95–121.

Sontag, Susan, *On Photography* (New York: Farrar, Strauss & Giroux, 1977).

—, 'The talk of the town', *The New Yorker*, 24 September 2001, accessed: 25 September 2011, www.newyorker.com/archive/2001/09/24/010924ta_talk_wtc

Sorlin, Pierre, *Film in History: Restaging the Past* (Totowa: Barnes & Noble Books, 1980).

Soufan, Ali, *The Black Banners: The Inside Story of 9/11 and the War against al-Qaeda* (New York: W.W. Norton & Company, 2011).

Spanakos, Antony Peter, 'Exception Recognition. The US global dilemma in *The Incredible Hulk, Iron Man*, and *Avatar*', in Richard J. Gray and Betty Kaklamanidou (eds), *The 21st Century Superhero Essays on Gender, Genre and Globalization in Film* (Jefferson: McFarland and Company, 2011), pp. 15–28.

Sterrit, David, 'Playing on our fears', *Beliefnet,* 27 June 2010, accessed: 29 November 2013, www.beliefnet.com/Entertainment/2005/07/Playing-On-Our-Fears.aspx

Stevens, Dana, 'Queen bees. Sofia Coppola and Marie Antoinette have a lot in common', *Slate,* 19 October 2006, accessed: 19 March 2010, www.slate.com/id/2151855

—, 'No joke', *The Slate,* 17 July 2008, accessed: 20 June 2010, www.slate.com/id/2195523

Stewart, Garett, 'Digital fatigue: imaging war in recent American film', *Film Quarterly,* 62: 4, 45–55.

Storey, John, 'The articulation of memory and desire: from Vietnam to the war in the Persian Gulf', in Paul Grainge (ed.), *Memory and Popular Film* (Manchester: Manchester University Press, 2003), pp. 99–119.

Stossel, John, 'Will America too fall, just as Rome did?', *Fox News,* 31 July 2013, accessed: 29 December 2013, www.foxnews.com/opinion/2013/07/31/will-america-will-soon-fall-as-just-like-rome-did

Summers, Anthony and Robbyn Swann, *The Eleventh Day* (London: Corgi, 2012).

Sturken, Marita, *Tangled Memories: The Vietnam War, the AIDS Epidemic, and the Politics of Remembering* (Los Angeles and London: University of California Press, 1997).

Suskind, Ron, 'Faith, certainty and the presidency of George W. Bush', *New York Times Magazine,* 17 October 2004, accessed: 20 June 2013, www.nytimes.com/2004/10/17/magazine/17BUSH.html?_r=1&ex=1255665600&en=890a96189e162076&ei=5090&partner=rssuserland

Svetkey, Benjamin, 'Q+A director's chair', *Entertainment Weekly,* 25 July 2008, accessed: 9 March 2012, www.ew.com/ew/article/0,,20215252,00.html

Tasker, Yvonne, *Spectacular Bodies Gender, Genre and the Action Cinema* (London and New York: Routledge, 1993).

—, *Action and Adventure Cinema* (London and New York: Routledge, 2004).

Taylor, Matthew, 'Q&A: The report into CIA prisoner interrogation', *The Guardian,* 24 August 2009, accessed: 3 August 2013, www.theguardian.com/world/2009/aug/24/cia-prisoner-interrogation-report

Thomas, Frank, 'Reprinting the legend: The Alamo on film' in Peter C. Rollins and John E. O'Connor (eds), *Why We Fought: America's Wars in Film and History* (Lexington: University Press of Kentucky, 2008), pp. 63–76.

Thompson, A., 'Films with war themes are victims of bad timing', *The New York Times,* 17 October 2001, p. E1.

Thompson, Ann, 'Big directors turn to foreign investors', *Variety,* 11 September 2008.

Thompson, Mark D., 'Luther on despair', in Brian Rosner (ed.), *The Consolations of Theology* (Grand Rapids: W. B. Eerdmans, 2008), pp. 51–74.

Tirman, John, *The Deaths of Others: The Fate of Civilians in America's Wars* (Oxford: Oxford University Press, 2011).

Tobias, Scott, 'Review', *AV Club,* 18 July 2012, accessed: 30 July 2012, www.avclub.com/articles/the-dark-knight-rises-review-batman,82624

Toh, Justine, 'The tools and toys of (the) war (on terror): Consumer desire, military fetish, and regime change in *Batman Begins*', in Jeff Birkenstein, Anna Froula and Karen Randell (eds), *Reframing 9/11: Film, Popular Culture and the 'War on Terror'* (London: Continuum, 2010), pp. 127–39.

Toto, Christian, '*Star Trek* actor: sequel critiques Bush/Cheney foreign policy', 14 May 2013, accessed: 11 June 2013, www.breitbart.com/Big-Hollywood/2013/05/14/star-trek-darkness-bush-cheney

Tucker, Philip Thomas, *Exodus from the Alamo. The Anatomy of the Stand Myth* (Philadelphia: Casemate Publishers, 2010).

Uhlich, Keith, 'Lone survivor (review)', *Time Out New York*, 14 December 2013, accessed: 2 February 2014, www.timeout.com/us/film/lone-survivor-movie-review

Ulaby, Neda, 'NPR's Neda Ulaby talked with the creators of *I Am Legend*', 14 December 2007, accessed: 7 September 2007, www.npr.org/templates/story/story.php?storyId=17260869. NPR

United States Congress, Civil Liberties Act of 1988, Pub. L. 100-383, title I, 10 August 1988, 102 Stat. 904, 50a.

Van der Kolk, Bessel A., *Psychological Trauma* (Arlington: American Psychiatric Publishing, 1987).

Vergano, Dan, 'Half-million Iraqis died in the war, new study says', *National Geographic*, 15 October 2013, accessed: 2 April 2014, http://news.nationalgeographic.com/news/2013/10/131015-iraq-war-deaths-survey-2013

Vicini, James and James Pelofsky, 'U.S. attorney general: bin Laden operation lawful', *Reuters*, 3 May 2011, accessed: 22 November 2013, www.reuters.com/article/2011/05/03/us-binladen-holder-idUSTRE7424JR20110503

Vidal, Gore, *Imperial America: Reflections on the United States of Amnesia* (Forest Row: Clairview Books Ltd., 2004).

Waid, Mark, 'The real truth about Superman: and the rest of us, too' in Tom Morris and Matt Morris (eds), *Superheroes and Philosophy: Truth, Justice, and the Socratic* (Chicago: Open Court Press, 2006), pp. 3–10.

Walsh, Declan, 'Fallout of bin Laden raid: aid groups in Pakistan are suspect', *New York Times*, 2 May 2012, accessed: 3 August 2013, www.nytimes.com/2012/05/03/world/asia/bin-laden-raid-fallout-aid-groups-in-pakistan-are-suspect.html?pagewanted=all&_r=0

Walsh, Jeffrey and Alf Louvre, 'Introduction', in Jeffrey Walsh and Alf Louvre (eds), *Tell Me Lies about Vietnam* (Milton Keynes and Philadelphia: Open University Press, 1988), pp. 1–29.

War of the Worlds, DVD special features, 'Revisiting the invasion' (2005).

Warmington, Joe. 'New York smells like death; Foul odour is unmistakable, say city residents', *The Toronto Sun*, 13 September 2001, p. S14.

Washburn, Jason, 'Rules of engagement', in Aaron Glantz (ed.), *Winter Soldier. Iraq and Afghanistan. Eyewitness Accounts of the Occupation* (Chicago: Haymarket Books, 2008), pp. 20–2.

Weiner, Robert G. (eds) *Captain America and the Struggle of the Superhero* (Jefferson: McFarland and Company, 2005).

Wiesel, Elie, 'Foreword', in Annette Insdorf, *Indelible Shadows: Film and the Holocaust*, 3rd edn (New York: CU, 2003), pp. xi–xii.

Westwell, Guy, *War Cinema: Hollywood on the Front Line* (London: Wallflower Press, 2006).

Wetmore, Kevin J., *Back from the Dead: Remakes of the Romero Zombie Films as Markers of their Times* (Jefferson: McFarland and Company, 2011).

—, *Post 9/11 Horror in American Cinema* (New York: The Continuum International Publishing Group, 2012).

Will, George, 'The end of our holiday from history', *Jewish World Review*, 12 September 2001, accessed 11 January 2013, www.jewishworldreview.com/cols/will091201.asp

Williams, Joe, '*Dark Knight Rises* to spectacular heights', *St. Louis Dispatcher*, 19 July 2012, accessed: 30 July 2012, www.stltoday.com/entertainment/movies/reviews/dark-knight-rises-is-a-spectacular-high-dive-into-chaos/article_e36ec612-d0fd-11e1-8dc5-001a4bcf6878.html

Williams, Rudi, 'War will continue until Americans live without fear', US Department of Defense, 29 October 2001, accessed: 28 December 2013, www.defense.gov/News/NewsArticle.aspx?ID=44599

Wills, Gary, *John Wayne's America: The Politics of Celebrity* (London: Faber & Faber, 1997).

Wilson, Rob, 'Ridley Scott's *Gladiator* and the spectacle of empire: Global/Local rumblings inside the Pax Americana', *European Journal of American Culture*, 21: 2 (2002), 62–73.

Winter, Jessica, 'Kathryn Bigelow: The art of darkness', *Time*,181: 4 (4 February 2013), 30–7.

Wolf, Joerg, 'German 9/11 victim defamed in *United 93* movie', *Atlantic Review*, 10 September 2006, accessed: 26 June 2010, atlanticreview.org/archives/396-German-911-Victim-Defamed-in-United-93-Movie.html

Wolf, Naomi, 'A letter to Kathryn Bigelow on Zero Dark Thirty's apology for torture', *The Guardian*, 4 January 2013, accessed: 3 August 2013, www.guardian.co.uk/commentisfree/2013/jan/04/letter-kathryn-bigelow-zero-dark-thirty

Wood, Robin, *Hollywood from Vietnam to Reagan* (New York: Columbia University Press, 1986).

—, 'Fresh Meat: *Diary of the Dead*', *Film Comment* (January/February 2008), accessed: 21 July 2013, www.filmcomment.com/article/fresh-meat-diary-of-the-dead

Woodward, Bob, *State of Denial: Bush at War* (London: Simon and Schuster, 2002).

Wyke, Maria, *Projecting the Past: Ancient Rome, Cinema, and History* (London and New York: Routledge, 1997).

Yuran, Noam, 'Disaster movies as the last remnants of utopia', 14 January 2003, accessed: 26 June 2010, www.haaretz.com/culture/arts-leisure/disaster-movies-as-the-last-remnants-of-utopia-1.22290

Zacharek, Stephanie, 'Review', *Salon*, 18 January 2008, accessed: 9 September 2010, www.salon.com/ent/movies/review/2008/01/18/cloverfield/index.html

Zakarin, Jordan, 'Avengers' damage to Manhattan would cost $160 billion, disaster expert estimates (exclusive)', *The Hollywood Reporter*, 9 May 2012, accessed: 22 December 2013, www.hollywoodreporter.com/news/avengers-damage-manhattan-would-cost-160-billion-322486

Žižek, Slavoj, 'What Rumsfeld doesn't know that he knows about Abu Ghraib', *In These Times*, 21 May 2004, accessed: 22 June 2010, www.inthesetimes.com/article/747

—, 'On 9/11, New Yorkers faced the fire in the minds of men', *The Guardian*, 11 September 2006, p. 30.

—, 'Green berets with a human face', *New Statesman*, 23 March 2010, accessed: 22 July 2011, www.egs.edu/faculty/slavoj-zizek/articles/green-berets-with-a-human-face

—, *Welcome to the Desert of the Real* (London: Verso, 2012).

SELECT FILMOGRAPHY

9/11 (Jules Naudet and Gédéon Naudet, 2002)
11'09"01 – September 11 (numerous, 2002)
21 Grams (Alejandro González Iñárritu, 2003)
28 Days Later (Danny Boyle, 2002)
28 Weeks Later (Juan Carlos Fresnadillo, 2007)
300 (Zack Snyder, 2006)
The 300 Spartans (Rudolph Maté, 1962)
2012 (Roland Emmerich, 2009)
Act of Valour (Mike McCoy and Scott Waugh, 2012)
Adam & Steve (Craig Chester, 2005)
Agora (Alejandro Amenábar, 2009)
A.I. Artificial Intelligence (Steven Spielberg, 2001)
The Alamo (John Wayne, 1960)
The Alamo (John Lee Hancock, 2004)
American Beauty (Sam Mendes, 1999)
American Soldiers: A Day in Iraq (Sidney J. Furie, 2005)
Amistad (Steven Spielberg, 1997)
Apocalypse Now (Francis Ford Coppola, 1979)
Argo (Ben Affleck, 2012)
Armageddon (Michael Bay, 1998)
Avatar (James Cameron, 2009)
Babel (Alejandro González Iñárritu, 2006)
Bad Boys 2 (Michael Bay, 2003)
Bad Company (Joel Schumacher, 2002)
Batman & Robin (Joel Schumacher, 1997)
Batman Begins (Christopher Nolan, 2005)
Battle for Haditha (Nick Broomfield, 2007)
Battle: Los Angeles (Jonathan Liebesman, 2007)

Battleship (Peter Berg, 2012)
Bee Movie (Simon J. Smith and Steve Hickner, 2007)
Behind Enemy Lines (John Moore, 2001)
Ben-Hur (William Wyler, 1959)
Beowulf (Robert Zemeckis, 2007)
Big Tits Zombie (Takao Nakano, 2010)
Big Trouble (Barry Sonnenfeld, 2002)
The Birds (Alfred Hitchcock, 1963)
The Birth of a Nation (D. W. Griffith, 1915)
Black Hawk Down (Ridley Scott, 2001)
Body of Lies (Ridley Scott, 2008)
Body Snatchers (Abel Ferrara, 1993)
The Boondock Saints II: All Saints Day (Troy Duffy, 2009)
Born on the Fourth of the July (Oliver Stone, 1989)
The Bourne Identity (Doug Liman, 2002)
The Bourne Supremacy (Paul Greengrass, 2004)
The Bourne Ultimatum (Paul Greengrass, 2007)
The Bridge on the River Kwai (David Lean, 1957)
Bright Lights, Big City (James Bridges, 1988)
Brothers (Jim Sheridan, 2009)
Bruce Almighty (Tom Shadyac, 2003)
Buffalo Soldiers (Gregor Jordan, 2003)
The Cabin in the Woods (Drew Goddard, 2012)
The Cabinet of Dr. Caligari (Robert Wiene, 1920)
Cannibal Holocaust (Ruggero Deodato, 1980)
Captain America: The First Avenger (Joe Johnston, 2011)
Captain Phillips (Paul Greengrass, 2013)
Casablanca (Michael Curtiz, 1942)
Casino Royale (Martin Campbell, 2006)
Casualties of War (Brian De Palma,1989)
Catwoman (Pitof Comar, 2004)
Centurion (Neil Marshall, 2010)
Chernobyl Diaries (Bradley Parker, 2012)
Children of Men (Alfonso Cuarón, 2006)
Chinatown (Roman Polanski, 1974)
Close Encounters of the Third Kind (Steven Spielberg, 1977)
Cloverfield (Matt Reeves, 2008)
Collateral Damage (Andrew Davis, 2002)
Coming to America (John Landis, 1988)
Conan the Barbarian (John Milius, 1982)
Conspiracy (Adam Marcus, 2008)
The Conspirator (Robert Redford, 2010)
Contraband (Baltasar Kormákur, 2012)
The Crazies (George Romero, 1973)
The Dark Knight (Christopher Nolan, 2009)
The Dark Knight Rises (Christopher Nolan, 2012)
Dawn of the Dead (George Romero, 1978)
Dawn of the Dead (Zack Snyder, 2004)
The Day After Tomorrow (Roland Emmerich, 2004)
Day of the Dead (George Romero, 1986)
The Day the Earth Stood Still (Robert Wise, 1951)
The Dead (Howard J. Ford and Jonathon Ford, 2010)

Dear John (Lasse Hallström, 2010)
Death Wish (Michael Winner, 1974)
Deep Impact (Mimi Leder, 1998)
The Deer Hunter (Michael Cimino, 1978)
Diamonds are Forever (Guy Hamilton, 1971)
Diary of the Dead (George Romero, 2007)
Die Another Day (Lee Tamahori, 2002)
Die Hard (John McTiernan, 1988)
Dirty Harry (Don Siegel, 1971)
Dr. No (Terence Young, 1962)
The Eagle (Kevin Macdonald, 2011)
Edge of Tomorrow (Doug Liman, 2014)
Eternal Sunshine of the Spotless Mind (Michel Gondry, 2004)
E.T. the Extra-Terrestrial (Steven Spielberg, 1982)
Evan Almighty (Tom Shadyac, 2007)
Executive Decision (Stuart Baird, 1996)
The Exorcist (William Friedkin, 1973)
The Expendables (Sylvester Stallone, 2010)
The Expendables 2 (Simon West, 2012)
Extremely Loud and Incredibly Close (Stephen Daldry, 2011)
Fahrenheit 9/11 (Michael Moore, 2004)
Fantastic Four (Tim Story, 2005)
Fido (Andrew Currie, 2006)
First Knight (Jerry Zucker, 1995)
Flight (Robert Zemeckis, 2012)
The Forgotten (Joseph Ruben, 2004)
Fred Claus (David Dobkin, 2007)
The French Connection (William Friedkin, 1971)
Full Metal Jacket (Stanley Kubrick, 1987)
Gangs of New York (Martin Scorsese, 2002)
Ghost Rider (Mark Steven Johnson, 2007)
G.I. Joe: Retaliation (John M. Chu, 2013)
G.I. Joe: The Rise of Cobra (Stephen Sommers, 2009)
Gladiator (Ridley Scott, 2000)
Godzilla (Ishirō Honda, 1954)
Godzilla (Roland Emmerich, 1998)
Godzilla (Gareth Edwards, 2014)
Goldeneye (Martin Campbell, 1995)
Goldfinger (Guy Hamilton, 1964)
Gone Baby Gone (Ben Affleck, 2007)
Good Will Hunting (Gus Van Sant, 1997)
The Green Berets (Ray Kellog, 1968)
Green Lantern (Martin Campbell, 2011)
Green Zone (Paul Greengrass, 2010)
Halloween (John Carpenter, 1978)
The Happening (M. Night Shyamalan, 2008)
Hearts and Minds (Peter Davis, 1974)
Hereafter (Clint Eastwood, 2010)
Home Alone (John Hughes, 1990)
Homecoming (Joe Dante, 2005)
Hostel (Eli Roth, 2005),
House of the Dead (Uwe Boll, 2004)

How I Spent My Summer Vacation (Adrian Grunberg, 2012); US title: *Get the Gringo*
The Hulk (Ang Lee, 2003)
The Hurt Locker (Kathryn Bigelow, 2008)
I am Legend (Francis Lawrence, 2007)
The Impossible (Antonio Bayona, 2013)
The Incredible Hulk (Louis Leterrier, 2008)
Independence Day (Roland Emmerich, 1996)
Inside Man (Spike Lee, 2006)
In the Valley of Elah (Paul Haggis, 2008)
Invasion of the Body Snatchers (Don Siegel, 1956)
Invasion of the Body Snatchers (Philip Kaufman, 1978)
Iron Man (Jon Favreau, 2008)
Iron Man 2 (Jon Favreau, 2010)
Iron Man 3 (Shane Black, 2013)
I Walked with a Zombie (Jacques Tourneur, 1943)
Jack Ryan: Shadow Recruit (Kenneth Branagh, 2014)
Jarhead (Sam Mendes, 2005)
Jerry Maguire (Cameron Crowe, 1996)
JFK (Oliver Stone, 1991)
Julie & Julia (Nora Ephron, 2009)
Kindergarten Cop (Ivan Reitman, 1990)
King Arthur (Antoine Fuqua, 2004)
The Kingdom (Peter Berg, 2007)
Kingdom of Heaven (Ridley Scott, 2005)
King Kong (John Guillermin, 1976)
Klute (Alan J. Pakula, 1971)
Knowing (Alex Proyas, 2009)
Land of the Dead (George Romero, 2005)
The Last Detail (Hal Ashby, 1973)
The Last House on the Left (Wes Craven, 1972)
The Last Legion (Doug Lefler, 2007)
The Last Man on Earth (Ubaldo Ragona and Sidney Salkow, 1964)
Life of Pi (Ang Lee, 2012)
Little Big Man (Arthur Penn, 1970)
Live Free or Die Hard (Len Wiseman, 2007)
Lone Survivor (Peter Berg, 2013)
The Lord of the Rings: The Fellowship of the Rings (Peter Jackson, 2000)
The Lord of the Rings: The Two Towers (Peter Jackson, 2002)
Lost in Translation (Sofia Coppola, 2003)
The Lucky Ones (Neil Burger, 2008)
The Manchurian Candidate (Jonathan Demme, 2004)
Manhattan (Woody Allen, 1979)
Man of Steel (Zack Snyder, 2013)
Man on Fire (Tony Scott, 2004)
The Man Who Shot Liberty Valence (John Ford, 1962)
Margaret (Kenneth Lonergan, 2011)
Marie Antoinette (Sofia Coppola, 2006)
Marvel Avengers Assemble (Joss Whedon, 2012); US title: *The Avengers*
Martyrs of the Alamo (Christy Cabanne, 1915)
Memento (Christopher Nolan, 2000)
The Messenger (Oren Moverman, 2009)
Metropolis (Fritz Lang, 1927)

Michael Clayton (Tony Gilroy, 2007)
A Mighty Heart (Michael Winterbottom, 2007)
Minority Report (Steven Spielberg, 2002)
Miracle (Gavin O'Connor, 2004)
The Missing (Ron Howard, 2003)
Mission: Impossible (Brian de Palma, 1996)
Mission: Impossible III (J. J. Abrams, 2006)
Monsters (Gareth Edwards, 2010)
Monsters: Dark Continent (Tom Green, 2014)
Munich (Steven Spielberg, 2005)
Mystic River (Clint Eastwood, 2003)
The New World (Terrence Malick, 2005)
New York Stories (Martin Scorsese, Woody Allen and Francis Ford Coppola, 1989)
Night of the Giving Head (Rodney Moore, 2008)
Night of the Living Dead (George Romero, 1969)
A Nightmare on Elm Street (Wes Craven, 1984)
Nosferatu (F. W. Murnau, 1922)
Olympus has Fallen (Antoine Fuqua, 2013)
The Omega Man (Boris Sagal, 1971)
Oscar (John Landis, 1991)
Pacific Rim (Guillermo del Toro, 2013)
Pearl Harbor (Michael Bay, 2001)
People I Know (Daniel Algrant, 2002)
Platoon (Oliver Stone, 1986)
The Poseidon Adventure (Ronald Neame, 1972)
Prince of Persia: The Sands of Time (Mike Newell, 2010)
Prisoners (Denis Villeneuve, 2013)
Quantum of Solace (Marc Forster, 2008)
The Quiet American (Joseph L. Mankiewicz, 1958)
The Quiet American (Philip Noyce, 2002)
Rain Man (Barry Levinson, 1988)
Rambo (Sylvester Stallone, 2008)
Rambo: First Blood Part II (George P. Cosmatos, 1985)
The Reaping (Stephen Hopkins, 2007)
REC (Jaume Balagueró and Paco Plaza, 2007)
The Recruit (Roger Donaldson, 2003)
Redacted (Brian De Palma, 2007)
Reign Over Me (Mike Binder, 2007)
Remember Me (Allen Coulter, 2010)
Rendition (Gavin Hood, 2007)
Rent (Chris Columbus, 2005)
Resident Evil (Paul W. S. Anderson, 2002)
Resident Evil: Retribution (Paul W. S. Anderson, 2012)
The Road (John Hillcoat, 2009)
Road to Perdition (Sam Mendes, 2002)
Rosemary's Baby (Roman Polanski, 1968)
Rules of Engagement (William Friedkin, 2000)
The Sands of Iwo Jima (Allan Dwan, 1949)
Saving Private Ryan (Steven Spielberg, 1998)
Scary Movie (Keenan Ivory Wayans, 2000)
Schindler's List (Steven Spielberg, 1993)
Scream (Wes Craven, 1996)

The Searchers (John Ford, 1956)
The Secret Life of Walter Mitty (Ben Stiller, 2013)
Serendipity (Peter Chelsom, 2001)
Shaun of the Dead (Edgar Wright, 2004)
Shortbus (John Cameron Mitchell, 2006)
Sidewalks of New York (Edward Burns, 2001)
Signs (M. Night Shyamalan, 2002)
Sisters (Brian De Palma, 1973)
Skyfall (Sam Mendes, 2012)
Soldier Blue (Ralph Nelson, 1970)
Somewhere (Sofia Coppola, 2010)
Spartacus (Stanley Kubrick, 1960)
Spartan (David Mamet, 2004)
Spider-Man (Sam Raimi, 2002)
Sophie's Choice (Alan J. Pakula, 1982)
Source Code (Duncan Jones, 2011)
Star Trek into Darkness (J. J. Abrams, 2013)
Star Wars (George Lucas, 1977)
Stop-Loss (Kimberly Peirce, 2008)
Stop! Or My Mom Will Shoot (Roger Spottiswoode, 1992)
Straw Dogs (Sam Peckinpah, 1971)
The Sum of All Fears (Phil Alden Robinson, 2002)
Superman (Richard Donner, 1978)
Superman Returns (Bryan Singer, 2006)
Survival of the Dead (George Romero, 2009)
Syriana (Stephen Gaghan, 2005)
Taken (Pierre Morrel, 2008)
Taken 2 (Oliver Megaton, 2012)
Tango & Cash (Andrei Konchalovsky, 1989)
Taxi Driver (Martin Scorsese, 1976)
Team America: World Police (Trey Parker, 2004)
Tears of the Sun (Antoine Fuqua, 2003)
Terminator (James Cameron, 1984)
Terminator 2: Judgment Day (James Cameron, 1991)
The Texas Chainsaw Massacre (Tobe Hooper, 1974)
There Will Be Blood (Paul Anderson, 2007)
The Thing from Another World (Howard Hawks, 1951)
Thirteen Days (Roger Donaldson, 2000)
Thor (Kenneth Branagh, 2011)
Thor: The Dark World (Alan Taylor, 2013)
The Three Burials of Melquiades Estrada (Tommy Lee Jones, 2005)
The Time Machine (Simon Wells, 2002)
Titanic (James Cameron, 1997)
Tomorrow Never Dies (Roger Spottiswoode, 1997)
Top Gun (Tony Scott, 1986)
Traitor (Jeffrey Nachmanoff, 2008)
Transformers (Michael Bay, 2007)
Transformers: Age of Extinction (Michael Bay, 2014)
Transformers: Dark Side of the Moon (Michael Bay, 2011)
Transformers: Revenge of the Fallen (Michael Bay, 2009)
Transsiberian (Brad Anderson, 2008)
Tremors (Ron Underwood, 1990)

Tropic Thunder (Ben Stiller, 2008)
True Lies (James Cameron, 1994)
Ulzana's Raid (Robert Aldrich, 1972)
United 93 (Paul Greengrass, 2006)
Vanilla Sky (Cameron Crowe, 2001)
Vanishing on 7th Street (Brad Anderson, 2010)
View from the Top (Bruno Barreto, 2003)
The Village (M. Night Shyamalan, 2004)
The Virgin Suicides (Sofia Coppola, 1999)
Walking Tall (Phil Karlson, 1973)
War of the Worlds (Steven Spielberg, 2006)
Warm Bodies (Jonathan Levine, 2013)
White House Down (Roland Emmerich, 2013)
The Wild Bunch (Sam Peckinpah, 1969)
World Trade Center (Oliver Stone, 2006)
World War Z (Marc Forster, 2013)
X-Men (Bryan Singer, 2000)
X-Men 2 (Bryan Singer, 2003); US title: *X2*
XXX (Rob Cohen, 2002)
Zero Dark Thirty (Kathryn Bigelow, 2012)
ZMD: Zombies of Mass Destruction (Kevin Hamedini, 2009)
Zombieland (Ruben Fleischer, 2009)
Zombie Strippers! (Jay Lee, 2008)
Zoolander (Ben Stiller, 2001)

INDEX

Page numbers in **bold** denote a figure